CROWN and SHAMROCK

April 2014, Windsor
For Stuart
How great to meet up
again & recall our
days together in
the Evening Standard
with warm wishes

Mary K

CROWN

and

SHAMROCK

Love and Hate

Between Ireland

and the

British Monarchy

MARY KENNY

**NEW
ISLAND**

First published 2009
by New Island
2 Brookside
Dundrum Road
Dublin 14

www.newisland.ie

ISBN 978-1-905494-98-9

British Library Cataloguing Data. A CIP catalogue record for this book is
available from the British Library.

Printed by

New Island received financial assistance from
The Arts Council (An Comhairle Ealaíon), Dublin, Ireland

10 9 8 7 6 5 4 3 2 1

For Patrick, Marie-Louise, Edward and Emma

And in memory of Sarah

May the union of hearts ever endure in the family

CONTENTS

ACKNOWLEDGEMENTS

I owe many debts of gratitude and acknowledgement in the research and writing of this book.

I thank Her Majesty Queen Elizabeth II for permission to research in and quote from the Royal Archives at Windsor. I thank the Registrar, Pamela Clark, and especially the archivist, Jill Kelsey, for so conscientiously making available to me material from the diaries of Queen Victoria and King George V, and much other material relating to the reigns of King Edward VII, King Edward VIII and King George VI.

I thank Gregory O'Connor of the National Archives of Ireland for his courtesy, help and assistance in steering me towards the historical material relating to Anglo-Irish relations. I would also like to thank Jenny Moran for making available to me archives only recently uncovered; thanks also to our former Ambassador in London, Daithí Ó Ceallaigh (and his wife Antoinette), who spoke to me about these archives. In November 2008 these papers were published in volume four of *Documents on Irish Foreign Policy*, an extraordinary work of scholarship produced by the Royal Irish Academy and edited by Catriona Crowe, Ronan Fanning, Michael Kennedy, Dermot Keogh and Eunan

O'Halpin. I would also like to thank our recent Ambassador in London, David Cooney, and his wife, Geraldine, for their hospitality, advice and co-operation.

I am extremely grateful to Margaret MacCurtain for reading my chapter on Victoria and Ireland, for making such helpful suggestions, and in such an encouraging way. If the Order of St Patrick should ever be revived, strictly on merit, Margaret MacCurtain – a scholar-nun of such distinction, previously known as Sister Benvenuta – should surely be the first recipient. I also thank Father Fergus O'Donoghue SJ, the editor of *Studies* for his reading of Victoria and Ireland; and I would specially like to thank Sister Íde ní Riain who provided me with such an interesting insight into Victoria's visit to Mount Anville school in Dublin. I would like to thank my friend Tony Duff for reading the chapter on Edward VII and gently indicating my infelicities.

I thank Professor John Murphy, University College Cork, and Professor Alvin Jackson, Edinburgh University, and Geoffrey Wheatcroft for their generous reading of my chapter on George V and Home Rule, their good counsel, and for providing such insights into this dramatic period of Anglo-Irish history.

I thank Professor Ronan Fanning for reading my chapter on the Free State and the development of independent Ireland, and, again, for making many helpful suggestions. And I thank Professor R. B. McDowell for cheerful conversation directing me towards much useful reading. Special thanks to Professor Roy Foster for his reading suggestions and general encouragement.

I thank Noel Dorr, previously Irish Ambassador in London and a highly experienced diplomat in the sphere of Anglo-Irish relations, for reading my chapter on modern times from 1953, and for his valuable suggestions and insights.

I am most grateful to the Librarian and staff at the National Library of Ireland in Kildare Street, Dublin, one of the most peaceful and humane places in which to work. In an era of impersonal institutions, the welcome from the staff on the door is always so friendly. Special thanks there to Francis Carroll, James O'Shea, Gerard Kavanagh, Lucy de Courcy, John O'Sullivan, Sophia O'Brien and John L. O'Sullivan.

I would also like to thank the Librarian, Inez Lynn, and staff at the London Library, where there is now a terrific supply of Irish books. Our local library in Deal in Kent not only ordered any books I requested, but also allowed me to access the on-line edition of the *Oxford Dictionary of National Biography*, a most superb source (to which I am honoured to have also contributed). Thanks to Lynn Steward and her team for the excellent Kent library services.

I am also grateful to the British Library in London, and the obliging staff at the BL newspaper library in Colindale.

I thank my friend Michael O'Sullivan for his matchless expertise on protocols and the Irish constitution. I thank William Shawcross for his encouragement and advice about archives, and Gyles Brandreth for useful general directions. Thanks to Robert Hardman for his expertise on monarchy.

I am grateful to Lord Snowdon for his recollections of life in Ireland with Princess Margaret, and to the Earl and Countess of Rosse for their kindness in showing me their archive at Birr Castle for that period.

Thanks to Lord Hurd for responding to my questions about the role of the Secretary of State for Northern Ireland in relation to royal visits. Thanks to Anne Griffiths at Buckingham Palace for information about royal visits to Northern Ireland; to Paddy Harverson, the Communications Secretary to the Prince of Wales and the Duchess of Cornwall; to the late Hugh Montgomery-Massingberd; to Desmond Guinness; Mavis and Bruce Arnold; Archdeacon Gordon Linney; Dr Raymond Refausse at the Church of Ireland archives; to Monsignor Alan Malone – and others – who explained to me such terms as 'Vicar Forane' (Curate); to Dr Robert MacCarthy, dean of St Patrick's; to Lord St John of Fawsley at the House of Lords; to Mark Mulqueen at the Dáil and Kate O'Toole at the Taoiseach's office.

My thanks to Dr David O'Donoghue who unfailingly made helpful suggestions, and to Maura Meaney in London whose fund of knowledge about royalty and Ireland is superb. Thanks to my cousin Professor Colum Kenny who provided some fascinating material about his grandfather and my uncle, Kevin Kenny, a man

who (in a seamless example of inclusiveness) served simultaneously as an advertising agent for both Patrick Pearse and His
Majesty's forces in 1912–14, later going on to provide an occa-
sional safe house for Michael Collins on the run, as well as being
the power behind the Knights of St Columbanus. Thanks to Joe
and Julie Steeples for their kindly work on Lord Granard at
Granard Public Library – a most useful background illumination
to the Southern Unionists; and to Michael Harlick for lending
me some of his fabulous books on Prince Albert. Thanks for suggestions and introductions to Noeleen Dowling, Marjorie
Wallace, Alan Wilkes, and to Edward Kelly in Budapest. Gratitude
also to our national treasure, Dr Garret FitzGerald, who
responded to e-mails with his customary grace. Thanks to Bill
Horgan who went to some trouble to access folio copies of *The
Irish Catholic* for Edward VII's reign, and to Michael Kelly who
instantly answered every query I put to him about religious ceremonials. And thanks to Tommy Graham of *History Ireland*.

Thanks to Tim West for theatrical background on *Richard II*
and its (alleged) Irish connections, and to Katie Harrington in
Limerick for helping me with King John. Thanks to my
neighbour in Dublin John Patrick Colclough for his enthusiastic
knowledge of Edward VII's cars, and for directing me to Don
Montgomery, archivist at the Royal Irish Automobile Club.
Thanks to Colin Whittington for his work on my website, and to
Karen Oliver of Zebedee Creations for implementing it.

Special thanks to Sebastian Barry for allowing me an extensive
quote from his unforgettable play *The Steward of Christendom*.

Thanks are due to Margaret McSharry, Martina Devlin, Kim
Bielenberg, Mary Lodge, Damian Thompson, and, very especially,
my dear brother Carlos Kenny, for his wonderful memories of
the Abdication of Edward VIII.

I solicited letters and e-mails via the *Irish Independent*, *The Irish
Times*, the *Irish Examiner*, the *Belfast Telegraph*, the *Irish News*, the
Catholic Herald, the *Irish Catholic* and the *Church of Ireland Gazette*
about attitudes in Ireland to the monarchy and the royals. I thank
the publications mentioned, all of whom were most helpful. I had
so many fascinating replies, almost all interested and friendly,

ACKNOWLEDGEMENTS

reflecting in such a lively way the manner in which the British royal family has played a role in the imaginative life of Ireland: the effect on love, marriage, family values, and health issues. Many of these correspondents are mentioned throughout the book or the references, and although I was not able to use all the material, everything contributed to expanding my understanding. I would especially like to thank Keith Haines of Campbell College, Belfast, for going to some trouble over the visit of the Queen Mother and Princess Margaret to the school in June 1951; Dr F. D. O'Reilly for a fascinating memory of being Irish in England during the 1950s; and Tim Horgan for his memories of 1953 – centred not on Elizabeth's coronation, but on Christy Ring's glorious game at Casement Park in Belfast! Thanks, too, to Bernard Leddy of Lismore, who provided an excellent account of Prince Charles's private visits to Co Waterford, and to many other correspondents, including Brian Fitzelle, Vincent Jennings, Brendan Ó Cathaoir, Vincent Nordell, Tom Morley, Arthur Kerrigan, Rose Lavelle, Maud Keery (who knows a lady in Co Louth who has slept all her life with a Union Jack under her pillow in tribute to the Crown), Nan Dwyer, June Stapleton, Maureen Twomey, Samuel Rowden, Pat Fleming, Sylvia Bools, Senator Mary Henry, Rosaline Matthews, Dr R. A. Somerville (Trinity College, Dublin), Peadar Cassidy, Brendan Cardiff (who helpfully suggested further reading about Ireland and the intro-duction of TV at the time of the 1953 Coronation), James Carroll, John Colgan (and his excellent book about Leixlip), Bill McCormack, Maurice Bryan, Tom and Eithne Kavanagh, Elizabeth O'Callaghan, Finnbar Lyons, Áine Ní Chonaill, Sister Marie Merriman, Bob Rockett, Anna Mackey, Donie O'Sullivan, Maurice Twomey, Monica Little, and Patrick Howard, who directed me so brilliantly to various points of the National Archives of Ireland.

Thanks to the anonymous correspondents too, many of whom were from Northern Ireland. One lady wrote: 'I am a nationalist from Belfast and would be open to a visit from the Queen to Northern and Southern Ireland. I have a problem with the Monarchy when they do not allow a Catholic on the throne.

Many of her subjects are Catholics and I think their feelings should be respected. Other than that I respect the Monarchy.' And the other anonymous person from Northern Ireland who wrote: 'I have a lot of respect for the Queen, who is a good Christian woman. But you would not be encouraged to express that opinion openly in Nationalist Belfast.' All comments helped me to understand more. Special thanks to Nick Nolan, a Corkman who, as Mayor of Coventry, received Elizabeth and Philip on a visit there, and gave a kindly account of how pleasant the royal couple were (and how his wife found Philip 'great craic'). Thanks especially too to Christy Gillespie for a riveting account of how his father, Dan, scooped the world (inadvertently) by announcing Philip and Elizabeth's engagement – in Irish – on Radio Éireann on 9 July 1947. The report had been embargoed and the announcement caused a furore. (After Dan Gillespie died in 2001, his widow received a letter on behalf of Queen Elizabeth offering her condolences and recalling how amused she had been at Mr Gillespie's role in her wedding plans.)

Very special thanks to my agent, Louise Greenberg, who is unfailingly encouraging, sensibly critical and always reliable. At New Island, I would like to thank my editor Deirdre O'Neill, who, as midwife to this book, has shown patience and humour, as well as knowledge and wisdom, and thanks too to her predecessor Deirdre Nolan who was most responsive and helpful. Cathy Thompson has been a meticulously conscientious copy-editor whose hard work I greatly appreciated. Thanks to Inka Hagen for designing the beguiling cover, and to Gráinne Killeen and Mariel Deegan for their professionalism in marketing and publicity. And above all, my gratitude to Edwin Higel, the publisher, who has an unfailing zest for books, and has always been so kind to me personally.

I greatly appreciate the picture research done by Joanne King in London and Neil Ryan in Dublin. Both have been absolutely superb at finding exactly what I was looking for in this narrative.

My daughter-in-law-to-be, Emma Grove, did a hugely helpful job of reading some of the chapters at an early stage, and made extremely good suggestions about shaping the text; it pleased me greatly when she said that the story brought out the human aspect of the history, which is what I aim at.

My niece Marie-Louise Kenny helped me out with some research in Dublin, and Valerie and Trevor Grove very hospitably put me up when I had to journey to the newspaper library in Colindale.

My sons, Patrick and Edward West, have both been enormously supportive and helpful in many practical ways; I am so pleased that both love history so much, and I am impressed by how much they both know. Patrick has written two academic theses on Irish themes, one on Northern Ireland in modern times, and one on the Irish working class in 19th century Manchester, and I felt very informed by reading these again.

My husband, Richard West, has been terrifically encouraging at all times, and if he sometimes feels, with Dr Johnson, that 'a man is better pleased to have his dinner on the table than when his wife speaks Greek', he never shows it. Our conversations over the past 35 years have been a rich stimulus in historical discourse, including the predictable differences about the history of our two islands.

I have tried to write this story accurately, but it is human to err, and if there are any errors, they are my responsibility, and I apologise for any that occur: and hope to correct any such mistakes in future editions.

Mary Kenny
Deal and Dublin
2009

A ROYAL EVENT
IN A REPUBLICAN CHILDHOOD

I t was the summer of 1953 and I was nine. I was living with my uncle and aunt in Sandymount, that pleasing Dublin suburb which seemed to feature as many Protestants as Catholics, genially neighbourly. On this particular evening in mid-summer my uncle and aunt were preparing to go out to some special event.

My aunt Dorothy was one of those sensible women who didn't primp much before a mirror: she preferred horses and dogs to haute couture. But now she was applying lipstick and arranging her hair neatly.

'Where are you going?' I asked.

'Curiosity killed the cat!' was her reply. There was an air of mystery and excitement. I persisted.

'Oh please tell …'

'It's a secret. You'll only blab to everyone.'

'I won't … I promise!'

But I wasn't informed of the purpose of their soirée: instead, I was taken off to a neighbour's house to spend the evening under

1

child-minding arrangements. My uncle and aunt were careful organisers.

Some time later, my aunt took me aside and confided the secret: it was a little like a discreet lesson in sex education. Well! They had gone to a private gathering at the Methodist Hall in Sandymount village, where, behind closed doors, they had watched the film of the coronation of the Queen of England, Elizabeth II. It had been shown to a select band of Sandymount Protestants, who had brought along a handful of trusted Catholic friends. I think Aunty Dorothy was pleased that her Protestant neighbours had thought to include her.

'You're not to tell anyone!' she warned. 'You know it's not approved of in this country.'

I understood perfectly well, because children soak up the values around them by a process of osmosis. What my uncle and aunt did was not illegal – but it was certainly not politically correct in an Ireland that had recently been declared a republic. Moreover, my uncle was a senior civil servant with Customs & Excise. He was respected, in his job, for his command of the Irish language, and could deal with complex trade documents in Irish.

In such a milieu, in de Valera's Ireland, Republicanism was a virtue to be aspired to: fawning on royalty was the mark of the lickspittle with the 'slave mind' – rather well described by that weaselly Irish word, *shoneen*.[1] There was also the occasionally disparaging reference to 'Castle Catholics' – those well-to-do Catholics who accepted British rule, as symbolised by Dublin Castle – but by the 1950s that concept was already archaic.

Protestants were, of course, given something of a dispensation. Their historical attachment to the Crown was to some extent allowed for. But the rules were broadly those of Westerners in dry Arab states imbibing liquor: the practice was to be kept private and discreet, and not paraded in the public realm.

My uncle and aunt greatly enjoyed their evening in the Sandymount Methodist Hall. Aunty Dorothy's brown eyes sparkled as she described the dazzling performance: the splendour, the pageantry, the ceremony, the frocks, the tiaras, the orb and sceptre, the exquisite Irish State Coach, the beautiful horses in livery, the fabulous Household Cavalry, and then the radiant young woman on whose head the crown was so magnificently placed. It was like being present at a great event in history, she said, for the ceremony dated back to before William the Conqueror in 1066.

I kept my word and did not allude to my aunt and uncle's secret tryst for many years: not, indeed, in their lifetime.

*

Although viewing a film of Elizabeth's coronation was not illegal, it might have been thought risky. Because, while the coronation film* was not technically banned, Dublin cinemas had withdrawn plans to show it after bomb threats from the Irish Anti-Partition League, which campaigned against the existence of the border between the Six Counties of Northern Ireland and the Twenty-Six Counties of the Republic.[2]

While the *Irish Independent* called the Anti-Partition League's stance 'an attack on liberty' (but added that the anti-partitionists' 'motives were sincere'), as far as I know the Gardaí were not asked to protect the public from violent threats and to uphold the rule of law. However fawning and *shoneen*-ish (and, from this distance, the 1953 coronation movies I have since seen were certainly adoring, and the Anna Neagle documentary decidedly awe-struck) the production did not come under any legal prohibition and could therefore have been shown publicly.

Thus a working compromise somehow emerged: certain Anglican and Nonconformist Protestant church halls around the country were offered a film of the coronation and agreed to a

---

*There were two documentary films being shown in cinemas in Britain, *A Queen is Crowned* and *The Coronation* – the standard documentary drawing on the televised event. The first was written by Christopher Fry and narrated by Sir Laurence Olivier. The second was put together by Pathé Newsreels and narrated by Anna Neagle. Both were shown privately in the Republic of Ireland – most usually, I believe, the second. In Britain the ceremony was of course televised, enormously boosting TV's popularity. But TV sets in Ireland were rare, and in Dublin reception from the BBC consisted of a blizzard of moving shadows.

screening, on a basis of private, rather than commercial, contract (although sums of money were voluntarily collected at said church halls to pay the distributors' fees). And under this dispensation of private viewing, the documentary was duly seen, not just by Irish Protestants, but also by their many Catholic friends and neighbours.

I have since heard many accounts, from all over Ireland, of the excitement and secrecy of queuing up outside Protestant halls to be shown a screening of the coronation of Elizabeth II. Correspondents remember screenings – always discreetly carried out – at Zion Parish Hall in Rathgar, at Leopardstown Military Hospital (thanks to the British Legion), at Knox Hall in Monkstown, at a Protestant school hall in Clyde Road, Ballsbridge, and at the Methodist Hall in Lower Abbey Street, among others. Maeve O'Connor, who was on the clerical staff of *The Irish Times*, remembers the Abbey Street showing: 'The [coronation] made little or no news here on radio or newspapers, but the film was shown in the Protestant Hall in Lower Abbey Street and many people attended. It seemed to be hush-hush – there were no public notices … it was a splendid display such as only English Royalty can show. I loved it all.'

Father Jim Duffy, now parish priest in a London suburb, remembers seeing the coronation documentary 'at a private showing in the Garda Depot in the Phoenix Park. It was billed as a showing of the film in connection with "crowd control" for Gardaí, but every mother and child that wanted to go, got in.' Subsequently, he recalls, there was a letter of protest in the Dublin *Evening Mail* that the Garda depot should be used in such a manner. There were also letters in *The Irish Times* protesting that it could not be screened in public commercial cinema, which would be the normal procedure: the protests were led by a scion of the old Anglo-Irish gentry, Major E. A. S. Cosby of Stradbally House, 'Co Leix' (in the correct Irish appellation, 'Co Laois').[3]

In Raphoe, Co Donegal – a village that was half-Protestant and half-Catholic – a comical 'Little-World-of-Don-Camillo' episode occurred. The local cinema had plans to show a 60-

minute documentary of the coronation compiled by Pathé. Noel
Gault, who grew up in Raphoe, recalls:

> We naturally assumed that it would be shown, as
> newsreels were an integral part of the [cinema]
> entertainment. It then emerged that the owners had
> been 'advised' that the feelings of some people in the
> town would be offended if the feature was screened,
> and that it, and indeed future films, might be
> boycotted … It was never clear who proffered this
> advice or latent threat, but as Raphoe had its share
> of armchair Republicans, there were a number of
> candidates. This caused a lot of resentment, but, in
> common with other Southern Irish Protestants at
> the time, most of us kept our heads down and said
> nothing in public.

However, a redoubtable Yorkshirewoman in the nearby
village of Convoy was not so easily cowed. She hired a bus and
organised a trip to Strabane, over the border in Northern
Ireland, 'where it was being shown to packed houses … She
filled the bus in record time, and men, women and children
went off to Strabane, including a number of non-Protestants
from both Convoy and Raphoe.' The expedition was a great
success and Noel Gault estimates that '75 per cent of the
audience' were from the Nationalist community. Some intense
Loyalists in the cinema audience insisted on standing up each
time a band was heard to play a strain from 'God Save the
Queen': about 20 bands in all did so during the screen event.
The result was hilarious.

For a few months after that, Noel Gault recalls, there was
'some coolness' between the communities in Raphoe because of
the coronation film episode. This, however, was unusual. A more
usual outcome of the coronation experience was an increased
sense of cordiality between Irish Catholics and their Protestant
neighbours. Catholics recall being invited into the homes of
Protestant neighbours they had never previously visited and new
friendships emerged.

A few people did have television, and nearer to the border with the North, where booster aerials within the Six Counties were erected, reception was reasonable. Some groups from Dublin and Cork also travelled to Belfast for a viewing – the British Legion organised at least one such charabanc.

Others heard it on the radio, broadcast by the BBC. Some schools allowed senior pupils to listen to the wireless broadcast (nuns were particularly ecstatic about the event). Marie Sheridan of Dublin, born in 1937, was allowed to hear it on the radio and 'one student in our class proposed that we all pray hard for the lovely young Queen, that she would have a long & successful reign. The nuns & lay-teachers applauded this proposal.' Radios were even switched on in certain hospitals. Eileen Moloney of Monaghan, whose husband was a surgeon, says that he was 'quite republican in his views … [and] was greatly annoyed when in an operating theatre in a Dublin Hospital, to hear the radio blaring a report on the coronation from a ward nearby.' At school, future Senator Mary Henry and her class listened ardently and speculated on the Queen's dress, which was said to contain some Irish lace.

Despite the involvement of the British Legion and the Protestant churches in the screening of coronation films and the organising of TV trips, for most people the coronation event was not political. One man recalls his mother abandoning him, aged six, to the care of relations because she was so determined to take the boat to England to experience the coronation, 'and she was a lifelong Fianna Fáil and de Valera supporter!'

Eileen Moloney recalls how much her aunt in Limerick, with whom she stayed during term-time at Laurel Hill Convent, loved 'the Royals and their doings and on the rare occasion that she bought a book it was invariably to do with the Queen and her family. This book was in due course passed on to my mother. Both of them were ardent admirers of Michael Collins, but they saw no contradiction.' Indeed, what did Michael Collins and the Queen have in common? Eileen Moloney says 'glamour', and also suggests that:

> … because the 1950s were so lacking in excitement
> …that a Royal Coronation with all the jewels,

beautiful gowns, etc, were irresistible. Remember the war with all the scarcity of food, clothes and all kinds of luxuries wasn't long over. The only other colour/spectacle in people's lives in this country was in Church with all the beautiful vestments the priests wore & the incense, gold chalices and ciboriums, etc, and the elaborate Eucharistic processions.

The following year, 1954, was declared a 'Marian Year' by the Vatican, focusing on special devotion to the Blessed Virgin, and 'it was a high point'. Eileen Moloney's aunt 'gave her engagement ring for inclusion in the Crown on the statue of the Virgin Mary at Mount St Alphonsus Church as a result of an appeal from the Redemptorists! Could you see that happening now?' Many devout Catholic ladies, apparently, voluntarily sacrificed their jewels to enhance the beauty of church ceremonials.

*

Elizabeth II's coronation on 2 June 1953 elicited worldwide interest. In Britain 24 million people took part in local or family celebrations, and two million watched the procession live in a cold and wet London.[4] In Melbourne there was dancing in the streets. 'In the Canadian Arctic', reported one witness, 'Eskimos had gathered in the grey, cold dawn to hear the Abbey service. In Cape Town, immense crowds, flocking into the centre of the city to see the decorations and illuminations, brought all the traffic to a halt.' In Hong Kong, Santiago in Chile, in Colombo in Sri Lanka, among the UN troops in Korea, in Paris and Copenhagen, British flags were flown and there were fireworks and public celebrations.

In Berlin, at the height of the bitter Cold War, the Soviet Premier Malenkov, with Foreign Minister Molotov, toasted the new Queen. In Dublin the Anti-Partition League picketed the British Embassy, carrying a black flag with a banner that read, 'England: we want our country, not your Queen.' A Union Jack was publicly burned in Earlsfort Terrace, near to the site of University College Dublin.

The *Irish Press* was the voice of the 'official culture' on the theme of Elizabeth's coronation. It was an 'affront', said the editorial on 3 June, that Queen Elizabeth's royal titles should be 'used to re-assert Britain's claim to dominion over part of this island.' That, indeed, was the specific grudge of the Anti-Partition League: the division of the island of Ireland by the nefarious British into the Six Counties of Northern Ireland and the 26 Counties of the Irish State. 'The British people may hold the Crown dear,' wrote the newspaper we always associated with Mr de Valera, but the Irish people viewed the British Crown as 'the symbol and instrument of a tyranny that we have struggled against for seven centuries.'

The coronation was certainly reported, since it could hardly be ignored, but the reportage was restrained. The *Irish Press* had it on the front page with the headline, 'Tumult and Pageantry in Rain-Soaked London – Elizabeth II Crowned At Westminster', but it was in secondary place to the news that President Seán T. O'Kelly and His Excellency John Cardinal D'Alton had been made 'Freemen of the City of Dublin' (reported by the Omagh writer Ben Kiely).

The paper assured its readers that 'two-thirds of the population gave the British coronation a cold reception',[5] although some anxiety was expressed about the influence of British TV 'via the Six Counties'. An editorial warned, 'Television is too powerful an instrument, especially because of its influence on the minds of the young, to be left solely in the possession of people to whom the traditional Ireland is an alien country.'

The *Irish Press* readers were also informed that the Irish Ambassador in London, Mr F. H. Boland, had been present at the coronation service – but were then quickly reassured that 'he did not take part in any other social engagement connected with the event'. Even so, there were protests to the Minister for External Affairs. Some satisfaction was derived by the *Irish Press* from the claim that 'Nationalist Derry Flew No Flags', and 'two-thirds of the [Derry] population gave the British Coronation a cold reception'.

The *Irish Independent* was never as Anglophobe as the *Press*, and put a priority on news rather than a political agenda. But both newspapers (as Eileen Moloney senses) highlighted the ceremonials of the Catholic Church as a kind of parallel monarchy, often, I would say, quite unconsciously. Whenever a news story (or picture) involved British royalty, there would usually be an accompanying story about the Catholic clergy, or the devotional rituals of the people. The *Irish Press* reported, in the wake of the Westminster coronation, 'Corpus Christi Procession in Meath Street – Banners and Bunting.' In the *Independent*, pictures of various princes of the church in full canonicals were much favoured ('Nuncio Apostolic, Most Revd Dr O'Hara, and Secretary to the Nunciature, Right Revd Mons Benelli', receiving a military salute by President O'Kelly).

The Irish Times, whose Protestant traditions also permitted a certain dispensation from the official culture, sent a special reporter to London to cover the coronation: Cathal O'Shannon.[6] His most vivid memory of the event tells us more about the *unofficial* culture. On the Aer Lingus plane returning home the air hostesses tore the coronation pictures and souvenirs from his hands, desperate for royal memorabilia.

My purpose here is to describe the relationship between the British Monarchy and Ireland since the time of Queen Victoria, drawing on the evidence as I have found it. I do not seek to advocate or disparage either a monarchy or a republic as an ideal constitutional framework. I think people should have the kind of governance and constitutions that they choose to have: and I am certain that the people in the Republic of Ireland wish to keep the Republic broadly as it is, with its graceful President and humane and adaptable written Constitution. Many Irish people aspire to an Ireland united, north and south, but the focus has shifted substantially from brooding about a Partition allegedly imposed by 'British Imperialism' to a dialogue about democracy and consent.

But building a state takes a long time: those new nations who imagine that an independent charter and a new flag and presidential palace construct a nation soon learn otherwise. A new state has to be built, brick by brick: and it can all too easily become a failed state. Had it not been for the austerity and dedication of those who constructed the Irish state over the decades since 1923, the Irish project of sovereignty could have failed. This project sometimes took the form of a bitter anti-Englishness (one of my correspondents points out 'we always said English, not British') deriving both from history and geography. Yet the majority of the people were not of that ilk: the majority of the Irish people were practical, had decent experiences of encounters with those from the neighbouring nation, worked with and intermarried with the neighbours, and were imaginative enough to allow for feelings of ambivalence and paradox.

'The Crown' may have symbolised many oppressive aspects of English rule: the much-hated 'Black and Tans' were always referred to as 'the Crown forces', for example. However, the institution of 'the Crown' and the actual royals (who constituted, above all, a *family*) were two quite different things in the minds of most people.

Moreover, the disappearance of a monarchy from the 26 counties of Ireland after independence left a certain gap in the country's public life of ceremony, pageantry and ritual. For 50 or 60 years after the foundation of the Irish state, the Catholic Church filled that ceremonial gap: indeed, it already played a role as a 'parallel monarchy' even before Irish independence.

It is especially evident from the photographic records of the Irish state from the 1920s onwards: wherever there is a national ritual to be performed, a prince of the Church is wheeled on to perform it, adorned with the full ecclesiastical regalia. Until well into the 1960s, politicians – including Éamon de Valera, a proud and lofty man – are pictured sinking to their knees to kiss the ring of 'His Grace the Archbishop', or 'His Lordship the Cardinal', while 'His Grace' or 'His Lordship' displays the bearing of a Florentine nobleman. (Seldom was an Irish bishop or archbishop referred to without the ducal prefix 'His Grace', and, where an Archbishop was also a Cardinal, 'His Lordship'.) The representative of the Pope, the papal legate, took precedence over all the diplomatic corps in Ireland and was lavishly and lovingly and respectfully photographed, should he attend so much as a budgerigar auction.

This deference for ecclesiastics is now as despised and disparaged in contemporary Ireland as monarchical trappings are despised and disparaged by progressive thinkers and *Guardian* readers in Britain. (Besides which, the Irish Catholic Church itself has become as plain as Presbyterianism in its procedures.) But it seems that human psychology is such that there has to be *somebody* who is the cynosure of rituals and ceremonies, for where these have been abolished they are somehow reinvented in new livery. The ceremonial and pageantry once represented by throne and altar are increasingly now carried out by the celebrity culture and by mass-marketed sporting events. Perhaps this is neither better nor worse, only different: but ceremony and ritual there must be.

We are a world away from 1953 now. Attitudes have changed all round. Irish culture today is more confident and successful than it has ever been, and British attitudes to Ireland are nothing like they used to be. When I saw the most patriotically British of the British political parties – the United Kingdom Independence Party – visibly dressed in green and holding up great banners saying, 'Respect the Irish Vote' (after Ireland voted against the Lisbon Treaty in June 2008), I thought how the shades of Lord Salisbury and Lord John Russell (not to mention Lord Carson) must have nodded ruefully. As astonished, perhaps, as the ghosts of Carson and the old Home Rulers would have been at the sight of the Revd Ian Paisley placing flowers on the grave of John Redmond.

There has been so much change over the past half-century in so many spheres, and most emphatically, in British-Irish relations. The only aspect of life that hasn't changed since 1953 is that Elizabeth II still reigns. And in the very continuity of that reign lies one of the most reassuring aspects of monarchy: an enduring fixture in an ever-shifting universe.

BEFORE VICTORIA –
A VERY BRIEF HISTORY OF
MONARCHY AND IRELAND,
1014–1837

After 1169, Irish and English politics were inextricably linked.
(Christine Kinealy, *A New History of Ireland*, 2008)

Ireland lost her own monarchy with the death of Brian Boru, High King of Ireland, who famously died in 1014 at the Battle of Clontarf, while inflicting a glorious defeat upon the marauding Danish Vikings. As James Loughlin of the University of Ulster points out, there is a mythic and genealogical link between the British monarchy and the Irish high kings. According to some Irish legends, Scotland's 'Stone of Scone' (the Scottish, and then British, coronation stone that resided at Westminster Abbey until 1997) had originally been the coronation stone for the high kings of Ireland at Tara, from which it was transported to Scotland in the 6th century, before being removed to England by Edward I in 1297.[1] The present British royal family can also claim descent from the historic kings of Ireland.

By the early twentieth century the monarchs of England had reigned over the island of Ireland, wholly or in part, since at least the time of Henry II. He invaded in October 1171, bringing with him 400 ships, 5,000 knights and archers, and the full approval of the Pope, who considered the Irish church disordered and in unhealthy thrall to the monasteries. As I was taught in my schooldays, Henry came at the shameful invitation of the King of Leinster, Dermot MacMurrough, who sought Anglo-Norman assistance in his rivalry with Rory O'Connor, King of Connacht. Subsequently the kings of England – who were Normans and spoke French until the fifteenth century – were termed 'Lords of Ireland'. From the period of Henry II's governance in Ireland (1171–1189) the Anglo-Normans, often admixed with Gaelic chieftains, more or less ruled Ireland, generally in a state of conflict and dispute, but also bringing such benefits as sheriffs, juries and the county boundaries which the Irish cherish to this day.

Henry's son, John 'Lackland' (1167–1216), was to become perhaps the most despised king of England for his weakness and treachery, but Henry awarded him lordship of Ireland while he was still a prince. Yet in his favour, he founded two hospitals in Limerick and established Dublin Castle as the focus of English government in Ireland. He also gave Dublin an exchequer. Like many of his successors up until King George V (1865–1936), John had plans for a residence in Ireland that never came to pass.

Richard II (1367–1399), born in Bordeaux and crowned at the age of ten, was the first English king to visit Ireland after John: he led an expedition in 1394 and again in 1399 in a bid to assert his authority. During his absence from home base, Richard was overthrown by his first cousin Henry Bolingbroke, son of John of Gaunt, and on his return to England, Bolingbroke had Richard murdered and was crowned Henry IV. Shakespeare's *Richard II* has sometimes been called 'the Irish play'.

It can be said, however, that Ireland first truly became an English kingdom in 1541, when 'the status of the country was elevated from lordship to kingdom' and the energetic and turbulent Henry VIII was formally declared king of Ireland.

Thereafter, as English monarchs succeeded to the throne – good, bad, and merely indifferent – many felt it their mission to make Ireland Protestant. Henry's teenage son by Jane Seymour, Edward VI (1537–1553), started the plantations of Ireland. His half-sister, Mary Tudor (1516–1558) – known in England as Bloody Mary – sought to reverse these policies, but her methods were so brutal that she gave Catholic monarchs rather a bad name.

Elizabeth I (1533–1603) was a mighty sovereign for England, but as merciless and unforgiving of Irish Catholics as Mary had been of English Protestants, driving from their country the Gaelic chieftains and crushing native Irish culture. She sought to Anglicise Ireland through brute military force.

The Stuart cause was embraced by the Irish with the coming of James I (1566–1625), son of Mary Queen of Scots and the first monarch to be king of England, Scotland and Ireland. However it was James I who enforced the Ulster Plantations, from which derive the long divisions in Irish politics and religion. Charles I (1600–1649) was a Catholic sympathiser, finally executed by the Lord Protector Cromwell (1599–1658), whose infamy lives in ballad and story.

The restoration of the Stuart Charles II (1630–1685), the 'Merry Monarch', was much welcomed in Ireland, and he reconvened the Dublin parliament, but the Elizabethan and Cromwellite penalties against Catholics were left untouched. After his father's decapitation, Charles was the first king to understand fully that power lay with parliament, and that he had to do parliament's bidding. At least Irish playwrights in the London theatre flourished under his reign.

Then came his brother James II (1633–1701), who lost for Catholic Ireland the Battle of the Boyne – and native Ireland's royalist sympathies thereafter. The victor was William of Orange (1650–1702), the iconic and original Orangeman who ever rules in the hearts – and on the gable ends – of Ulster Loyalists. He reigned jointly as William III with his wife Mary II. After the reign of the Stuart Queen Anne (1665–1714) came the Hanoverian Georges, German Protestants with scant interest in, or sympathy for, Ireland. Most notably there was mad George III (1727–1820), calamitously preventing the enactment of Catholic Emancipation in tandem with the Act of Union in 1800; George IV (1762–1830), fat and drunk, who dubbed Dublin's loveliest harbour (Dunleary) 'Kingstown', and was popularly acclaimed in Ireland because, according to an English historian, the Irish knew so little about him; and William IV (1765–1837), the 'sailor king', father of ten illegitimate children but no legitimate heir, scarcely any more sober than his dissolute brother. And so we finally come to Victoria.

To the scholars of long history I leave the subject of the infinitely complex military and political relationship between the monarchs of England and the land of Ireland. Some commentators have suggested that English monarchs only ever came to Ireland to fight out their conflicting claims to the crown of England – because 'who controlled Ireland was important to England'.

I choose to begin with Victoria because, to me, the Victorian era is the start of modern times. My father was born in the Victorian age, and my mother only a year after it ended. I seem to hear the heartbeat of Victorian values transmitted through my aunts and uncles, and their recollections of an Ireland that was, in so many ways, a Victorian society, both in the positive and the negative sense: from Sinn Féin's own original slogan, 'Ireland Sober is Ireland Free!' (echoing the great temperance campaigns and social reforms of the Victorian era), to the profound cult of respectability, and of dislike of the 'low' (a favourite word of the monarch's, and of my aunts'). Some English historians have claimed that, far from conquering Ireland, Victoria lost it to Irish nationalism. And yet it can plausibly be suggested that her long reign had a profound cultural impact on Ireland, and even on the Irish Catholicism which characterised Irish culture for so long after her departure.

Chapter One

VICTORIA:

GREAT EMPRESS

OR FAMINE QUEEN?

Poor Ireland. It holds but a small place in her heart.
(Gladstone on Queen Victoria, 1886[1])

A totally unexpected development followed: the Queen
and the Irish people fell in love with each other.
(Cecil Woodham-Smith, *The Great Hunger: Ireland 1845–49*, 1962)

I n the years when I was growing up in Dublin, Queen
Victoria had a bad press. My family had somehow acquired
a painting of Victoria as a young woman: the presentation
was pleasing and the young girl's face was cherry-pink and
bright-eyed. But Irish Nationalists would refer to this monarch as
'the Famine Queen', for she had reigned over the United
Kingdom of Great Britain and Ireland at a time of the greatest
calamity that had ever befallen 'the most distressful country that
ever yet was seen', as a famous popular ballad described Ireland.[2]

The last public statue of Queen Victoria in Dublin, which had
resided in front of Leinster House (now the seat of the Dáil and

Seanad in Kildare Street), was finally removed in 1948, to some rejoicing. And particularly the rejoicing of aesthetes, for it was notably ugly. Dubliners had informally referred to the statue as 'the Auld Bitch'.[3]

Victoria's reign was an exceptionally long one, and it was not all bad, even for Ireland. The years between 1837 and 1901 brought as much social and technological change as those between 1937 and 2001. Victoria herself changed, too, from the slight and pink-cheeked young girl in the portrait to a gnarled old grandmother of 82. Over the course of her reign, Ireland went through many different moods about the Queen, and Victoria, in her turn, showed many changeable feelings about Ireland. First she pitied it; then she warmed to it; then she yearned to improve it; then she loathed it; and finally, she was touched by it once again, on the eve of her death.

Victoria visited Ireland four times during her 63 years on the throne of Britain and Ireland. But the four occasions only added up to five weeks in all. By contrast, she spent a total of seven years in Scotland. (Wales, strangely, she only visited once and then only for seven days.)[4] She adored Scotland for a number of reasons: firstly, the 'Scotch' people, as they were then called, were unanimously 'loyal' to her and to the Crown. Secondly, there was religion – a matter of great importance to her. Victoria was, in all but name, a Scottish Presbyterian. She was much more at home listening to improving sermons in plain 'Scotch' churches than she was in her very own rather more formalised Church of England.[5]

Victoria was half-German on her mother's side and mostly of German descent on her father's (he was one of the scallywag sons of George III). Her husband, Prince Albert, was a serious-minded German Lutheran. Neither Victoria nor Albert felt quite at ease in the Church of England, with its divisions between 'High Church' (sometimes called 'Ritualism', referring to its emphasis on more elaborate ceremony) and 'Low Church', with its stress on Bible-based simplicity and strong reverence for the Sabbath.

Victoria abhorred 'Ritualism' and strove to discourage any 'Romish tendencies' apparent in the higher end of Anglicanism, while she thought the Low Church 'so very narrow-minded'.

She did not believe Sunday should be *too* gloomy. But 'Scotch Presbyterianism' was just right, for her. She liked a simple but sincere approach to faith, and she relished a good sermon. Her favourite preacher was a Scot, the Revd Norman Macleod.

There were other reasons for liking Scotland, too. 'The moors and glens about Balmoral were … to thrill her with their rugged beauty,' wrote her biographer Algernon Cecil. 'The Highlanders, as exemplified by John Brown [the Scots gillie who became especially close to her after the death of Prince Albert], were to fascinate her with their rough forthrightness of speech in a way that the lakes and mountains, the bogs and blarney of the Emerald Isle had no power to do.'[6] Thus Scotland was a source of pleasure, of romance, and of artistry – for she painted and drew in Scotland. By contrast, Ireland was always a problem.

'Really, they are a terrible people,' she once wrote, in contemplation of the Irish in general. More particularly, she had in mind the pattern of attacking, and sometimes assassinating, landlords. There was also a total of seven attempts on her own life, of which three were by Irishmen, admittedly in some cases owing to mental disturbance rather than to political motives. Victoria referred to a category she called the 'worst type of Irish', sometimes to be bracketed with that other low category, socialists.[7]

And yet Victoria was not consistent in her loves and hates and feelings. She was passionate, volatile, given to strong rushes of affection and equally strong feelings of hostility. Hers was a personality of contradictions. She could be reactionary at one moment and progressive at another.

She – in common with the age she personified – had a reputation for prudishness. But there is evidence that Victoria herself was a woman of strong sexual responses, who found the deepest fulfilment in the conjugal side of marriage. But she didn't like overt or indecorous sexuality: she castigated Lord Palmerston as a rake and a near-rapist (which he was), and she certainly did not hold with loose conduct.

She was against women's emancipation, but progressive about women's health – particularly in the relief of pain in childbirth. She could be judgemental about foreigners, and yet she was also anti-racist and disapproved of South Africa's regulations for separating soldiers according to race.

She didn't think the lower orders should be over-educated – and yet she opposed class distinctions. She upbraided Gladstone for taxing the beer of the poor man, rather than the brandy of the rich. She preferred the poor to the rich and was more at ease with servants than with courtiers. She was not an intellectual, but she was intelligent and alert: she wrote copious letters and journals, and it is claimed that she spoke, or at least had some mastery over, eleven languages, including some Hindi.

She disapproved of her son Bertie, Prince of Wales, having so many Jewish friends, whom she thought raffish and too fond of the turf and the baccarat table, and yet she was a vehement pro-Dreyfusard, deploring the false charges against the French officer Alfred Dreyfus, which had been prompted by anti-Semitism.

Her attitudes to Ireland – now disparaging, now affectionate, now furious, now warm – were of a piece with her ardent and reactive personality.[8]

As a young girl, Victoria had been idealistic and tender-hearted. In that phase of her life she had been inclined to express sympathetic and compassionate feelings for her 'poor Irish subjects', and to worry about the misfortunes that befell Ireland. But her first Prime Minister and political mentor, Lord Melbourne, a languid and worldly cynic who exercised enormous influence over her, had a regrettable impact on her judgement. Victoria was only 18 when they first met and she had been brought up in an enclosed, feminine world. Melbourne was 56, and a political figure of wide experience.

Melbourne told the young Victoria that she should not fret about the Irish poor. Why, they brought their troubles on themselves! 'When the Queen asked Melbourne what happened to the "poor Irish" who were evicted by their landlords,' writes Elizabeth Longford, 'Melbourne replied, "They become *absorbed* somehow or other" – which made them all laugh amazingly."[9] The Irish dispossessed, as it were, just faded into the background. Under Melbourne's callous tuition, Lady Longford concludes, the Queen gradually came to believe that every rebellious Irishman was a so-called 'low Irishman'.

Melbourne was an upper-class Whig so typical of the Regency period, who believed that no good could come of meddling with the poor, English or Irish, and that most change was for the worse. He thought the wisest policy, in regard to the human condition, was to leave well enough alone. Furthermore, he felt that most problems have no solution, and that the prevailing human characteristic is the general folly of mankind: none of us ever learns anything from experience, instead we go on making the same mistakes over and over again.

Melbourne had an Irish title, had lived in Ireland, and he supported Catholic Emancipation – which, coming in 1829, was one of the most significant liberalising causes of the age.[10] His support for emancipation derived from his belief in tolerance towards private faith and yet he noted drily that giving the Irish what they wanted in this sphere had failed to 'pacify' Ireland. If anything, Catholic Emancipation had emboldened Ireland, through Daniel O'Connell, to ask for more. He did not think that Ireland's miseries arose from unfavourable circumstances, but from 'the natural disposition of the people and the natural state of society'.[11]

In time, Victoria would come to differ from her first mentor and yet, in those early years, the master–pupil relationship was so intense that London joked about a romantic affair, and referred to the young Queen as 'Mrs Melbourne'. While there is no hint of such an intimacy, from Victoria's accession to the throne in 1837 until her marriage to Albert in 1841, she spent more time with Melbourne than any other person – often four to five hours a day.

She did clash with him over the virtues of religion, and held her ground. He thought that religion 'shouldn't interfere with private life' – that is to say, mere parsons should not lecture aristocrats on matters such as adultery. He disliked prejudice against

Catholics, but he thought Catholicism itself 'tyrannical and super-stitious': Roman ritual was not 'gentlemanly' and 'too theatrical', although – power being power, in the eyes of all politicians – he had a certain respect for the Vatican as an historical institution.[12]

Melbourne regretted that by the 1830s people in general were becoming too religious – there was indeed a religious revival under way. And because of that they were not so 'gay'. With the revival of religion, he said, there would be more 'meddling' in private life – people 'interfering with one another about going to church and so on.'[13]

The young Queen disagreed vehemently: it was quite *right* that society should be increasingly religious, she affirmed! It was good. It would have an improving effect on the populace. If Melbourne had merry memories of the Regency period, the Queen, who was born in 1819 towards its last days, had a tem-peramental dislike of the hard-drinking, hard-gambling and dissipated reputation of that swashbuckling era.

Victoria was a moralising, upright and committed Christian, although by no means joyless – she loved dancing and parties when young. In her coronation oath the Queen had sworn to 'inviolably maintain and preserve the settlement of the true Protestant Religion, with the Government, Worship, Discipline, Rights and Privileges of the Church of Scotland.'[14] And she meant every word of it.

She had, moreover, read with a firm voice the 'Royal Declaration against Transubstantiation, the Sacrifice of the Mass and the Invocation and Adoration of Saints', all of which she had declared to be 'superstitious and idolatrous' and affirmed confi-dently that:

> it is contrary to the laws of England that any Roman Catholic Prince shall sit on the Throne of England. Even if a Protestant Prince should, after his accession, marry a Roman Catholic, he would thereby forfeit the Crown and be excluded from and for ever be incapable to inherit, possess or enjoy the Imperial Crown of Great Britain and the dominions thereunto belonging.[15]

These religious matters were central to the relationship with Ireland. The connection between Britain and Ireland was historically always difficult. Since the Reformation it had been complicated by the fact that, in the majority, the two islands were of different strands of Christianity, with quite different attitudes to worship and tradition.

Can a Protestant monarch reign serenely over a Catholic people in a religious age? Possibly, yes, but it has never been easy: and such a reign is unlikely to be serene if those Catholic subjects are disfavoured by law, as they were for so long, and feel dispossessed of their land by the Crown's aristocratic supporters. As the mainly Catholic and moderately Nationalist newspaper the *Freeman's Journal* reminded its readers in 1849, while the Queen's forthcoming visit was welcome, the majority of Catholics in the Irish nation remained in 'subjugation to a Protestant Queen, to a Protestant Prime Minister and to an almost entirely Protestant Parliament.'[16]

To the Victorian establishment, the Catholicism of the Irish was another problem with the Irish, who were widely believed to be under the sway of 'priestcraft'. To the Irish, the rule of an Ascendancy caste that was overwhelmingly Protestant added to the alienation from the Crown.

Victoria fell ardently in love with her cousin, Albert of Saxe-Coburg, and married him in 1840. Albert was an earnest-minded German prince who had himself grown up in a somewhat rackety household. His parents had had many extra-marital affairs and took a liberal eighteenth-century attitude towards sexuality, which was in accordance with their inclinations, but had a somewhat confusing impact, it seems, on their offspring. Albert, anyway, had reacted by embracing a high-minded Lutheranism.

He was deeply opposed to the Church of Rome, and was keen to boast that 'not a single Catholic Princess had been introduced into the Coburg family since the appearance of Luther in 1521'.[17]

It had to be specifically underlined, at the time of the betrothal, that Prince Albert was a Protestant. (Actually, there was a Catholic branch of his family, albeit a collateral one.) Albert had been to Rome and had visited the Pope, Pius VIII. He recoiled from the sight of the pontiff blessing the crowd assembled before the Vatican – to him a repulsive act of idolatry. He also challenged the Pope over some doctrinal matters.

Anti-Catholicism was a constant element in British culture in the mid-nineteenth century (Daniel O'Connell was the only Roman Catholic present at Queen Victoria's coronation[18]) and it reached an apogee in the 1850s. There was a bitter wave of anti-Papist feeling following the re-introduction to England and Wales of the Catholic diocesan structure, with its attendant hierarchy of archbishops and bishops.

All the bishops and archbishops of the Church of England, with the exception of the Bishops of Exeter and St David's, protested to the Queen against this measure, which they called 'the papal aggression'. Journals such as *The Times* and *Punch* magazine made much sport, with lurid anti-Papist cartoons showing sinister agents of Romish stratagems suborning honest Protestant John Bull, and wily, robed cardinals secretly preparing to re-enact Guy Fawkes 'preparing to blow up all England!' There were many sermons against 'priestcraft', angry 'No Popery' demonstrations, and attacks on Catholic churches.[19]

When the Irish Catholic hierarchy gathered for the first time since the Reformation at Thurles in Co Tipperary under the formidable leadership of Archbishop Paul Cullen, this ecclesiastical meeting of bishops was seen as a deeply suspicious conspiracy of alien prelates, underlining the questionable 'loyalty' of the Irish to the Crown.[20]

In language that the English would deplore in Ulster Protestant extremists a century later, the Catholic Church was denounced by respectable English preachers as 'Babylon the Great, the mother of harlots, and the abomination of the earth.'

One of the most influential offenders in stirring up these heated feelings was Lord John Russell, the Famine-period Prime Minister, who had written of his 'alarm' at the reintroduction of

Roman Catholicism to England, describing it as 'a pretension to supremacy over the realm of England, and a claim to sole and individual sway, which is inconsistent with the Queen's supremacy, with the rights of our bishops and clergy and with the spiritual independence of the nation …'[21] He proceeded to introduce legislation which forbade Catholic clerics to assume ecclesiastical titles and prohibited the wearing of religious habits.

To her credit, Victoria deplored this adversarial attitude, and sought to reduce what she saw as bigotry. She declared:

> Sincerely Protestant as I always have been and always shall be … I much regret the unchristian and intolerant spirit exhibited by many people at the public meetings. I cannot bear to hear the violent abuse of the Catholic religion, which is so painful and so cruel towards many good and innocent Roman Catholics.[22]

She had reacted similarly when there had been opposition to the establishment of Maynooth for the training of Roman Catholic priests (there was a Protestant view that 'error should not be subsidised').[23] In spite of this she did not admire the *products* of Maynooth, and did not hold in high regard the Irish priesthood: 'the low standard of the Priests & their insufficient education, are one of the real misfortunes of Ireland', she observed in her diary.[24] Nevertheless, she abhorred seeing the institution besmirched by Protestants: 'It is not honourable to Protestantism to see the bad, and violent, and bigoted passions displayed [against Maynooth].'[25]

In her visits to Ireland, Victoria showed the same – perhaps feminine – tendency to react according to her feelings and her experience rather than by a set formula. In theory, she often complained about the Irish: but when she encountered Ireland and the Irish personally, she enthused and even grew quite sentimental.

The Irish reaction to Victoria echoed the contradiction: in theory, disliked; in person, often shown much warmth.

*

Victoria was only 18 when she came to the throne in 1837, a slip of a girl, as it seemed, after a series of monarchs who had done Ireland few favours, and who were not always greatly esteemed in Britain either.

There was mad George III, who successfully – and lamentably – opposed Catholic Emancipation, which should have accompanied the Anglo-Irish Act of Union in 1800. Then there was George IV, in his youth the handsome Prince Regent and friend of the dandy Beau Brummell, but in later years profligate, bad-mannered and drunk. And finally William IV, an 'inveterate womaniser' who had 'a girl in every port' and fathered ten children with the actress Dorothea Jordan before dumping her unceremoniously when he became king in 1830.[26]

William IV did not favour Catholic emancipation, though he was associated with other admirable measures such as the Reform Act of 1832 (of which Daniel O'Connell was a leading advocate); the Factory Act 1833, which reduced child labour; and the Slavery Abolition Act 1833, which emancipated slaves held in British colonies. Yet William was a dullard and he died of cirrhosis after seven years on the throne, without a legitimate heir. The Duke of Wellington described him as 'an old fool'.[27]

Small wonder, after this *galère*, that the young Victoria – fresh, spirited, and virtuous, seemed to presage a new dawn for Great Britain and Ireland. Her first ringing affirmation was 'I *will* be good.'

Alas, for Ireland: within ten years of the new Victorian reign, the worst catastrophe that had ever befallen the nation – the Great Famine – had struck.

Later on in the century Victoria would be dubbed 'the Famine Queen' – a soubriquet devised in 1876 by Anna Parnell, fiery and reckless sister of Charles Stewart Parnell, but most successfully promulgated by the iconic Maud Gonne, who had something of a genius for catchy slogans and inventive agitprop stunts.[28]

A legend was launched that Victoria had cared so little for the starving Irish that she contributed a mere £5 to famine relief – and, so as not to be accused of sympathy with Popish rebels, sent an equal fiver to the Battersea Dogs Home. This was not the case:

the Queen was rather more concerned about the Famine in Ireland than some in her own government, led by the aforementioned Lord John Russell.

She made the largest single donation to famine relief. The first three names on a famine relief fund launched by Lionel de Rothschild and Abel Smith were 'Her Majesty The Queen, £2,000. Rothschild, £1000. The Duke of Devonshire £1000.'[29] Victoria even rationed the bread supply at Buckingham Palace to focus attention on 'the poor Irish'.[30] She was initially more responsive than certain Irish Catholic bishops: Archbishop MacHale of Connaught returned money sent from Rome for the starving people, saying that there was no need for charity in his province. And Bishop Cantwell of Meath was criticised by the Bishop of Derry for choosing to give £10,000 for a university project rather than to the starving.[31]

She also deplored the attitude manifest by some English ecclesiastics – notably Samuel Wilberforce, Bishop of Oxford and Winchester – who preached that the Irish Famine was a punishment from God for Ireland's sins, misdemeanours, and Popishness.[32] Indeed Victoria sent a petition around to be read in Church of England parishes urging people to be charitable to Ireland, at a time when it seems many Anglicans took the Melbourneish view that the Irish had brought their troubles on themselves by their general lack of the Protestant virtues of thrift, prudence and sobriety.

Prime Minister Russell – grandfather of the philosopher Bertrand Russell – did not at all grasp the magnitude of the Famine problem, nor the long-lasting potential for repercussions, which would include an abiding hatred of Britain, particularly in America, to endure another century and a half.

John Russell had previously shown himself to have certain sympathies towards the betterment of life in Ireland: the Irish poet Thomas Moore was one of his dearest friends, about whom he wrote an affectionate biography. Yet on the very cusp of the first Famine wave, in the autumn of 1845, Russell publicly declared himself a convert to free trade.[33]

For well over a century after the Great Famine, the Irish blamed free trade for their miseries. In my own schooldays I was repeatedly taught the legend that the harsh English insistence on total liberty of the free market resulted in ships laden with food leaving the port of Dublin daily, while the afflicted Irish starved from hunger, plague and cholera. It was all a little more complex than that, but it is probable that the interests of the industrialised English consumer were not the same as the agricultural Irish producer. Free trade meant cheap food for Britain, and was held afterwards to mean cheap prices for the Irish agriculturalist.

The Famine remains the subject of voluminous historical research: and the analysis of events is rather more nuanced now than it was in my schooldays of the 1950s and 1960s. The historian Professor J. J. Lee has even suggested that the Famine eventually benefited Irish farmers by enlarging their holdings – since not only the insecure tenancies of the many landless peasants, but also the small 15-acre farms were reduced in number and land was consolidated into more viable holdings.[34] That does not, however, alter the fact that it was a calamitous event, as well as a tragedy, and involved pitiful suffering that left a deep imprint on the Irish psyche.

Victoria herself had felt, by 1844, that she *ought* to go to Ireland: that, seven years after the beginning of her reign, it was time to do so. But in the end she had been dissuaded from making the trip by her Prime Minister of the time, Robert Peel (after whom the 'Peelers', and the 'Bobbies' were nicknamed). Sir Robert regarded Ireland 'with a mixture of scepticism and, paradoxically, a sense of duty'. But the Irish thought him patronising and hostile to Daniel O'Connell.

For it was during this period that Daniel O'Connell – known as 'The Liberator' – began to organise his popularly named 'monster meetings'. These public meetings were organised to demand the Repeal of the 1800 Union between Britain and Ireland, and were notable not only for the immense crowds of hundreds of thousands they attracted, but also for their order and pacifism. During his lifetime, O'Connell was often unfairly assessed by the British establishment, who expected his organised gatherings – carefully regulated and supported by the Catholic clergy – to burst into unruly violence at any moment.

Thus was Victoria warned that anywhere in Ireland she might be met by political demonstrations and violent agitators. British Monarchs have frequently lacked advisors who properly understood Ireland. Many British authorities were themselves woefully ignorant of the realities of Irish life — it took a leading British agricultural official 20 years to discover that land acres in Ireland were of a different dimension to the traditional English acre.[35] There was no one to explain to Victoria that O'Connell's vast political meetings were models of order and peaceful congregation (indeed, they were *criticised* by more advanced Nationalists for shrinking from confrontation and agitation.)

In the early years of her reign, Victoria had been responsive enough to O'Connell, and he had been positively gallant about 'the dear little Queen' (to whom he had dedicated a book).[36] But by the 1840s, Victoria had taken against the Great Dan, regarding him as a dangerous man who stirred up 'disloyalty'. This was a serious misjudgement. Daniel O'Connell was a man of upright Christian conscience, at least in politics; he stood against slavery, and supported the emancipation of the Jewish community, which did not yet have full legal rights in the United Kingdom.

He had, for his time, certain progressive ideas, but he was a bourgeois Irishman from a Catholic gentry background — and a lawyer. He believed in constitutional reform and in pursuing political change through parliamentary methods and, above all, the rule of law. He loathed revolution and bloodshed. He was a traditional Catholic — though also a friend and admirer of the utilitarian Jeremy Bentham. But his reformist ideas did not make O'Connell an anti-royalist radical. His campaign for repeal of the 1800 Act of Union between Britain and Ireland did not include breaking with the monarchy — indeed, to him the Monarchy was to be the 'golden link' between the sister islands.

Victoria could agree with Catholic Emancipation — O'Connell's first cause. But she could not agree with repeal of the Union — his next campaign — or admit of the blatant evidence that for the majority of the Irish it had brought few benefits. But perhaps, like some other members of the British political class who distrusted O'Connell, she also feared the growth of democracy – of the 'people power' that he so obviously commanded. Victoria could also harbour feelings of jealousy towards popular public men – she was jealous of Gladstone's popular appeal, for example – and this, too, may have played some part in her dislike of O'Connell.

A man like Daniel O'Connell who could summon a gathering of three-quarters of a million people certainly was in moral possession of a weighty democratic force. By 1880 – long after his death – *The Times* proclaimed what Victoria could not admit – that 'O'Connell was a leviathan among Irish leaders'.[37]

*

Two years later, in 1846, there were new plans afoot for a royal visit to Ireland, but again the Prime Minister, Lord John Russell, decided that with the onset of the appalling potato famine it too must be postponed. Had he had any talent for what we now call 'public relations' – that Princess Diana instinct for high public visibility while walking through minefields or cuddling AIDS orphans – he might have understood that this was the exact moment a royal visit might have been most appreciated. But he felt that no good would come of such a visit, and so it did not take place.[38]

At this point, the Queen had no very strong personal desire to visit Ireland. Moreover she was a bad sailor and was always desperately sick on sea-voyages; she never cared for the Navy on that account, besides which she thought sailors 'low'. Yet to visit Ireland was, she thought, her *duty* – and she thought it wrong to shirk duty.

She also didn't like the implication that she *dare* not go, for fear of hostility. Daring she had in abundance: it went with her natural self-confidence about her right to reign.

The Irish themselves, reciprocating the Queen's mixed feelings, both complained at her absence and resented her presence. When at last she did arrive in Dublin, in August 1849, the Nationalist newspaper, the *Freeman's Journal*, expressed 'mingled and conflicting feelings' about her visit. And the paper was critical that she had been slow to visit Ireland in the first place:

> Eleven years had she sat upon the throne, and never had she been advised that Ireland was worthy of those affectionate regards which a Sovereign [sic] gracefully manifests when she pays a personal visit to a portion of her subjects remote – if in these times any portion of the British Isles can be called remote – from the seat of central government and the circle of self-indulgent fashion.[39]

The degree of interest in the royal visit could be best gauged by the copious number of adverts in the *Freeman's Journal* for platforms and other elevated locations which commanded an 'Excellent View' of the royal line of procession to arrive in Dublin, which would be the high point of the visit. Such platforms were sometimes erected outside Catholic churches, with tickets selling at five shillings and half a crown – five times the price of a decent dinner at a time, when it cost about one shilling to dine. Nevertheless, it was a devastated Ireland that she alighted upon in 1849, just as the worst of the Famine was over; it is now reckoned to have lasted, on and off, from 1845 until 1850 and a million people perished as a consequence.

But even in the midst of devastation ordinary life goes on, and people go about their lives as best they can. Victoria's first sight of Ireland was at Cove, in Cork, which she liked so much she proceeded to re-name it 'Queenstown'. It became a famous harbour for the great liners embarking for North America, and was the last port of call for the *Titanic*. (After independence, the name was restored to its original, spelt in the Irish language version, 'Cobh'.)

But she noted, not for the last time, the strange foreignness of Ireland – in temperament and in appearance, it was so unlike England. 'Cork is not like an English town and has rather a foreign look to it,' she wrote. 'The crowds are very noisy and excitable, but very good-humoured, running and pushing about, and laughing, talking & shrieking.'[40] This was a theme she would return to over the course of her life: the *foreignness*, to English eyes, of Ireland. She got the point, perhaps better than many of her political decision-makers, that Ireland was *not* England and was *not* Britain. It was different.

Victoria loved beauty, both in men and women, and quite often judged individuals according to their looks. (She fell for the Catholic Archbishop of Dublin, Dr Daniel Murray, just because he was such a good-looking old gentleman.) 'The beauty of the women is very remarkable & struck us very much. Such beautiful dark eyes & hair & such fine teeth, nearly every 3rd woman was pretty, some remarkably so, also among the higher classes, there were pretty women to be seen.' [41]

She also noted that the women were bare-headed and wore long blue cloaks, while 'the men are often poorly & even raggedly clad, many wearing blue coats & short breeches with blue stockings.' She was certainly pleased by the welcome accorded to her arrival. 'I never heard more saluting, guns and even artillery … the town was very prettily illuminated & all the ships lit up and fired "feux de joie" [an artillery salute].'[42]

The Queen was accompanied by her husband, Albert, and their two eldest children: Victoria, aged eight, and Albert Edward (known as Bertie), aged seven – Albert Edward would become Edward VII. The royal party proceeded eastwards from Cork around the Irish coast. They called at Passage in Waterford, and arrived on August 7 in Kingstown, Co Dublin. Kingstown had been named in honour of her uncle, George IV, who had received a tumultuous welcome in Dublin in 1821. (It was said that the King had scarcely drawn a sober breath on Irish soil.) Subsequently Kingstown also reverted to its Irish name, Dún Laoghaire.[43]

After a rough night at sea, the Queen beheld the Wicklow hills, which she described as 'very fine', and was enraptured by the welcome that awaited her in Kingstown Harbour:

> which was covered with thousands and thousands of spectators, cheering most enthusiastically. It is a beautiful harbour … the whole scene glowing with

> lights was truly beautiful, and heart stirring. We were
> soon surrounded by boats of all kinds & the enthu-
> siasm and excitement shown by the Irish people was
> extreme.[44]

Cecil Woodham-Smith, author of the sympathetic popular
account of the Famine, *The Great Hunger*, wrote that Victoria's
'simplicity, lack of stiffness and touchiness and her admiration of
Dublin were having their effect'. The Queen was just 30 years of
age, and at this time was still 'pretty, eager and with a great deal
of vitality'.

Thus was a pattern established which was to repeat itself
throughout Victoria's reign. She was often disparaging about the
Irish in theory: she criticised their 'disloyalty', felt that their
'Romish' priests were 'uneducated', and generally regarded
Ireland as a dangerously unlawful place. And yet, when she experienced Ireland personally, she was overwhelmed by feelings of
affection for the place, and touched by the 'wonderful, striking
scene', as she made her way into Dublin:

> such masses of human beings so enthusiastic, so
> excited and yet such perfect order maintained there
> ... the bursts of welcome that rent the air, all of
> which made it a never to be forgotten scene, partic-
> ularly when one reflects on what state the country
> was in, quite lately: in open revolt & under martial
> law.[This, after a brief and unsuccessful uprising in
> 1848.][45]

Dublin, she called 'a very fine town', many of whose streets
were 'handsome and wide': although she also noted 'wretched
cottages & wretchedly raggy, dirty people & children, the latter
very handsome.' Yet 'everywhere the same enthusiasm &
laughing, shrieking, calling out, jumping and making every
kind of gesture. Jaunting cars followed us, full of people, who
made such a noise – very amusing and quite unlike anything
anywhere else.'

She observed the extreme poverty of some of those greeting
her, though ascribing some of their appearance to the reputation

of the Irish for heedlessness. 'The raggedness of the people is beyond belief, men & boys having really hardly any proper covering, for they never mend anything.' How different, one can almost hear her thinking, from the provident and thrifty Scotch!

And yet, she repeatedly admired the beauty of so many of the Irish people. 'One sees such beautiful women & children, the latter, ever so ragged & always barefooted. They have such fine dark eyes & hair. Equally remarkable are the beggars or very poor people, all in the most dreadful tatters, also the boys who run along by the carriages.'[46]

Some of those who turned out to greet Victoria would have been Irish Loyalists – the Anglo-Irish gentry and big landlords, (she mentions many of these by name, such as the Duke and Duchess of Leinster and Lord Lansdowne) and those employed, indirectly, by the Crown – '6,160 men including the constabulary – a remarkably fine body of men'.[47]

Yet there can be little doubt that even in the direct aftermath of the terrible Famine that had scorched the land, large numbers of ordinary Irish people also warmly welcomed Queen Victoria. The *Freeman's Journal* – the newspaper of Nationalist Ireland – published page after page giving the names of those who attended levees, drawing-room receptions, and many other occasions. Just as royals sell celebrity magazines in our time, royal visits sold newspapers in the Victorian century. 'Never had Queen such a Levee as was seen yesterday', the newspaper enthused on August 9. '… never was there, since the Coronation, a Levee more gratifying to a Sovereign than that held at Queen Victoria's Castle of Dublin yesterday.'

Apart from the grandeurs of Dublin Castle – although the royal party actually stayed at the Viceregal Lodge, now Áras an Uachtaráin, the Presidential residence – there was a valiant attempt to entertain Victoria with music and dancing. In Co Kildare she watched the local people dancing jigs:

> which was very amusing. It is different to the Scotch Reel, not so animated & the steps different, but very droll. The people were very poorly dressed in thick coats and the women in shawls. There was one, who

was a typical specimen of an Irishman with his hat
on one ear & a great deal of swagger ...[48]

The welcome that Victoria received puzzled strong
Nationalists such as John Mitchel, the author of *Jail Journal,* a
textbook of great reverence for subsequent Irish Republicans.
(He also founded the *United Irishman.)* Mitchel did not personally witness Victoria's visit – having been convicted of treason by
a packed jury and transported to Van Diemen's Land (Tasmania),
from which he subsequently escaped to the US. But he sought
some explanation for the enthusiasm shown to Victoria. Initially
he seems to have felt that she was welcomed principally by those
directly or indirectly in the employ of the British Crown and 'the
great army of persons who are paid to be loyal.'[49]

Those who opposed her visit must, he reckoned, have been
officially shut up. He cited the case of a Mr O'Reilly who had
fashioned a banner proclaiming 'Famine and Pestilence', which
was suppressed by the police as soon as unfurled. A man who
called out 'Mighty Monarch – Pardon Smith O'Brien' was
similarly whisked away, reports Mitchel, although the supplication
itself is poignantly phrased to pay honour to the exalted status of
the monarch. [50]

And yet John Mitchel had to concede that these utilitarian
explanations of suppression or paid loyalty did not fully explain
the 'crowds in the street'. Finally, he came to the conclusion that
it was 'the natural courtesy of the people', which carried them
away. Hospitality to the stranger – the *céad mile fáilte* of 'a
hundred thousand welcomes' was an ingrained Irish tradition.
Thackeray observed this well in his travels around Ireland in the
1840s, just before the Famine: however poor or even destitute
people might be, they would always extend a warm welcome to
a stranger.

And however melancholy their circumstances, the Irish would
always get up some kind of merriment. Victoria was a visitor, after
all, to whom hospitality was due, just by the *fáilte* tradition.
Moreover, a royal visit was an occasion, with a bit of ceremony
and an air of jamboree thrown in – when life is short and includes
much suffering, why not enjoy whatever party is going?

Perhaps there was another factor too, which has always had a strong appeal in Irish culture, so deeply rooted in clan and kin. Queen Victoria was a young wife and mother, with a husband and – at this point – four young children. This was not a party of stove-hatted rulers or parliamentarians. This was a *family*, and that touched a chord.

As the royal party embarked from Kingstown on August 10, the Queen noted in her diary:

> Arrived very speedily at Kingstown, where there were just as many people, and as enthusiastic, as on the occasion of our disembarkation, but it made one feel quite sad to hear these parting shouts & cheers. We feel so deeply touched at the affectionate loyalty of the poor Irish, who called out 'come every year', 'when will you come back' & one man gave '3 cheers for next summer'.[51]

The party proceeded by sea to Belfast where the Queen noted that 'the reception was as hearty, though I thought not quite as enthusiastic as in Dublin, I mean not quite so typically Irish.' Indeed, for all her concerns about 'loyalty', Victoria always preferred Dublin to Belfast.

As their boat made its way back to Britain, the Queen made a resolution concerning her young son, the Prince of Wales. 'I intend creating Bertie <u>Earl of Dublin</u> as a compliment to the town & country.' The title would always hereafter be borne by the Heir Apparent to the Crown, reported *The Times*.[52] This never came to pass: the on-off relationship between Queen Victoria and Ireland intervened.

*

The 1850s (rather like the 1950s) were the most culturally quiescent of the century. Women's clothes were at their most constricting and restricting – always a sign of cultural conservatism – and the Victorian project of respectability and self-improvement, and of the decline in crime (no mean achievement) had properly begun.

Ireland was recovering from the miseries of the Famine, and retreating from the clamour of the O'Connell years – the Great Dan had died in 1847 – without achieving repeal of the Union. The revolutionary (and romantic) Young Ireland movement which flourished in this decade, inspired by Thomas Davis, John Blake Dillon, and Gavin Duffy's newspaper *The Nation*, produced a brief and (in the words of F. S. L. Lyons) 'futile' rebellion in 1848, the European 'year of revolutions'. No revolution occurred in Ireland, but the Young Ireland movement did sow the seeds of an 'ideological revolution' which would bear fruit in subsequent generations. But not in the 1850s, that most sober of eras.

At this time and in this mood, Prince Albert believed that Ireland could be coaxed out of her 'irrational' religious faith by progress and technology. He was most optimistic about the potential for Ireland's advance, planning the Dublin Exhibition of 1853 to promote crafts and technology, and imagining (as did many inspired by the Enlightenment) that locomotive trains and the spread of education would wean the Irish away from their rosaries and devotions: and that 'rational' religion could replace the 'irrational' kind.

Victoria's husband believed that the experience of the Famine would destroy the 'power of the priests' in Ireland. Albert regarded Irish Catholics as 'superstitious' (true, although paradoxically the Catholic Church tried to abolish the more malign folklore about bad fairies swapping babies for changelings, or 'little people' casting 'unlucky' spells). Albert consequently supposed that, after the Famine, the Irish would cease to adhere to their supernatural faith, and turn, instead, to science and medicine.[53]

Contrary to the Prince Consort's predictions, after the Famine the institutional Catholic Church strengthened and grew apace. The ratio of priests to people doubled between 1840 and 1871: in 1840 there was one priest for every 3,000 persons; 30 years later there was one priest for every 1,500. Likewise, convents prospered and Irishwomen flocked into the religious orders, at home and abroad. The ratio of nuns to lay people changed from one nun for every 6,500 lay people to one nun for every 1,100 lay people.[54]

The revolution that took place was a 'devotional revolution'. Catholic church-going trebled, particularly since so many more churches were built under the organising energy of Paul Cullen, the first Irishman ever to be made a Cardinal. Cullen was arguably the true ruler of Ireland between the death of O'Connell in 1847 and the rise of Parnell in the later 1870s – certainly he was its most effective administrator.[55]

Catholic devotions of every kind increased: rosaries, benedictions, litanies, novenas, devotions to the Sacred Heart, and the Miraculous Medal (the latter after an 1830 Marian apparition at the rue du Bac in Paris – a particular devotion of my late mother's, it being so pleasingly convenient to the Bon Marché department store), pilgrimages, shrines, processions and retreats.

The second royal visit made by Victoria and Albert in 1853 came in the full flush of the mid-Victorian fervour for industrialisation and the progressive aspect of the railway. Although this was a private visit and not an official occasion, again the Queen was greeted warmly. 'We … stepped onshore, in the midst of salutes & tremendous & regular <u>Irish</u> cheerings … the streets were immensely full … & the reception most enthusiastic.' She felt 'quite at home' in the Phoenix Park – as before, she and Albert stayed in the Viceregal Lodge [56]

Victoria believed that Ireland was now settling down to a more diligent and industrious pattern of general self-improvement. 'The State of the country *generally* has *wonderfully* improved since we were here 4 years ago,' she remarks. 'There is an entire absence of all political excitement & religious dissension even, is not apparent.' The reason the country was so quiet was more to do with post-Famine exhaustion and the fact that the population had dropped by approximately two millions – about one million dead and one million emigrated.

She was again taken aback by the ragged attire of the very poor, yet she certainly was entertained by the Irish. 'The population, as usual, amused me much, & the little ragged boys, whose attire can no where be surpassed for tatters, made us laugh much. The Irish are most amusing – so lively and excitable.'[57] She is repeatedly struck by how different in character Ireland is to England, a lesson sometimes lost on the politicians of the period. 'The country itself has a totally different character to England.' (Victoria would never have made the mistake of saying that *any* part of Ireland was as 'British as Finchley', as did Mrs Thatcher when discussing Northern Ireland.) Sometimes her observations, although well-intended and honest, do seem patronising, as when she comments, 'The people are too amusing but the rags one sees, & the apparent satisfaction of their wearers, is marvellous & I should think unequalled in any country. Albert said he had never seen anything like it excepting perhaps amongst the Italian beggars'.[58]

Much influenced by Albert's interest in mechanisation, the Queen developed a positive crush on William Dargan, the Irish railway engineer and contractor. Dargan was born in 1799 and worked on the construction of the Holyhead road in Wales in the 1820s. He then returned to Ireland and started his own construction business – foreshadowing generations of Irish builders who would do likewise – and in 1831 he constructed the first Irish railway, from Dublin to Kingstown. By 1853 Dargan had built over 600 miles of railway, as well as the Ulster Canal. (His statue, a little stained and neglected, still stands on the lawn of the National Gallery at Merrion Square in Dublin: he was a most generous donor to its foundation, endowing this beautiful gallery with £40,000.)[59]

Victoria was convinced that Ireland was proving responsive to Albert's support for such enterprises as the Dublin Exhibition of 1853, promoting industrial innovation and artisanal progress, and that William Dargan, the Exhibition's main sponsor, would prove to be Ireland's saviour:

> There is a great inclination amongst the people to apply themselves to industry & to foster this, the Exhibition will be of great use. It has raised the feeling of enterprise amongst the people, showing them that if they try, they <u>can</u> succeed. Mr Dargan's own life story they are likewise inclined to study & reflect upon. This is very satisfactory.[60]

Victoria loved the story of Dargan's accomplishments, and the fact that he had built himself up from modest beginnings through that quintessentially Victorian method of self-improvement. 'Mr Dargan has risen from being a labouring man, originally a road maker, & has accumulated an immense fortune,' she wrote admiringly. She thought it would be so much better for the Irish if they could emulate such characters as William Dargan, rather than Daniel O'Connell. Dargan gives to the people, she hears someone say: O'Connell took (referring to his penny collections).

She is told by the Duke of Leinster that 'O'Connell is quite forgotten'.[61] She is ready to believe this: later, she would have been disabused when O'Connell's centenary, in 1875, brought the whole of Nationalist Ireland out in salutation of the Liberator. He had certainly not been forgotten, although regrettably, Dargan the railway pioneer, rates few mentions in the Irish story now.

However, the Queen still notices people in 'tatters and rags' while visiting Bray and Arklow in Co Wicklow. Again what strikes her is not just the extremity of the rags, but the fact that the destitute Irish feel no self-consciousness about their condition, or any shame about their bodies:

> The country is wild & there were such wretched looking people all in rags standing in the cornfields, along the roads & indeed everywhere – belonging to the lower orders, more or less, but *not* by any means beggars. They were dirty & did not seem the least ashamed of their tatters, which in some cases showed naked limbs. The women & girls are generally very pretty, dark with brilliant complexions & *all* so lively, shrieking & screaming. Everything is untidy & unfinished about the dwellings. But the people are so warm-hearted & friendly, full of talent & certainly prospering.[62]

Although always taken aback by the ragged attire of the very poor in Ireland, she frequently expressed her feeling of being entertained. 'The population, as usual, amused me much, & the little ragged boys, whose attire can nowhere be surpassed for tatters, made us laugh so much. The Irish are most amusing – so lively and excitable.' Once again she repeats: 'The country itself has a totally different character to England.'

Once more, she felt sorrow at leaving, as they drove away from Phoenix Park, through Dublin's 'immensely crowded' streets, and once again, there was a rousing farewell scene at Kingstown. 'The evening was beautiful & the sight was a very fine one – all the ships saluting & they as well as yachts, decked out & thousands assembled near the quay, cheering.' Again, Victoria reflected on the exotic element in the Irish soul: as the coast of Ireland receded, along with the singing and the cheering of the crowds, 'the people made one quite imagine one was in a foreign part, in the south.' It is calculated that a million people turned out in the Dublin area to see the Queen.[63]

*

There was to be one more visit in mid-century, shortly before Prince Albert's death, and then she would not come to Ireland again for almost 40 years. The last visit of the royal couple, in August 1861, elicited, once again, the enthusiastic response of the people. Her eldest son Bertie, now aged 20 – later Edward VII – was billeted at the Curragh, an army garrison then (as now). 'Many people out and cheering loudly,' the Queen noted in her journal, as she drove from the Viceregal Lodge to Dublin. 'Great numbers of people out,' she noted again, 'cheering very enthusiastically.' The Irish people were, as ever, 'very demonstrative & enthusiastic'.[64]

She visited Killarney's lakes and dells and admired it all. It is not too much to claim that Victoria put Killarney on the tourist map, and the websites advertising this legendarily beautiful Irish town in Co Kerry are now pleased to note their link with the Queen: she came, she stayed, she was smitten – after all, Killarney's lakes and mountains did resemble, in gentler contour, her beloved Scotland!

Yet in truth, the Queen was somewhat out of sorts on this 1861 trip. Her mother, the German-born Duchess of Kent (from whom she derived her own name of Victoria), had died that summer. Although the Queen had had reason to disagree with her mother – she distanced herself from the Duchess upon becoming queen, rightly affirming her entitlement to reign without the interference of a clinging parent – nonetheless she felt the loss sorely.

And perhaps she had some kind of a presentiment that her beloved Albert would not live much longer. She was concerned about his failing health as they made their way to the Curragh. 'God bless & ever preserve my adored Husband!' she wrote anxiously. Queen Victoria remained ardently in love with Albert: they had nine children and still enjoyed a deeply satisfying conjugal life. When a doctor, at one point, suggested that the royal pair should curtail their love-making so as to reduce the Queen's pregnancies, she was quite offended, retorting, 'Can't I have no more fun in bed?'[65] Victoria's fertility proceeded not just from their active married life, but from the regrettable practice of employing wet-nurses. Disdaining breast-feeding herself, the Queen would hand each baby over to a wet-nurse, and immediately recommence ovulating, 'exposing' her – as obstetrics now put it – to pregnancy.[66]

The loss of her husband and the onset of an enclosed and lonely widowhood was partly, for the Queen, an experience of woefully felt sexual frustration. She desperately missed Albert's physical love. Her premonition, in Ireland, about Albert's health was well-founded. As well as worrying about Albert, she was also concerned about her son Bertie, who had launched himself, in Ireland, on a style of life that his parents regarded as licentious and debauched – they believed in *married* love, not consorting with floozies. Bertie, it seems, had been relieved of his virginity by a young Irish actress, Nellie Clifden, and this had become common knowledge.[67] This escapade much distressed his parents, particularly Prince Albert.

Despite the charms of Killarney, the landscape of Ireland in 1861 seemed to reflect the Queen's low mood. Passing through the midlands, she observed that the countryside seemed so mournfully lacking in people – the effects of the Famine were to deprive Ireland of a sustainable population level for more than another hundred years.

And although the Queen still encountered kindness, the Irish character had somehow altered after the Famine: the gaiety that visitors had remarked upon was replaced by a sober prudence, a cautious approach to courtship, marriage and the founding of families, and many more young Irish people pledged to celibacy within the priesthood or the convent. Melbourne would have been confirmed in his view that more religion made people 'less gay'.

Victoria certainly thought the midlands sad. 'How utterly denuded of population the whole of the country is … A good deal cultivated with here & there a small house and awful cabins but no villagers & hardly any towns.'[68]

Albert was to die that autumn, in November 1861, ostensibly of typhus, though it is possible that he had cancer, as he had visibly declined.[69] She vented some of her desolation and anger on her son Bertie; he had been in another scrape at Cambridge, causing his father to embark on the journey to East Anglia that brought on his final fever. After 1861 Victoria went into a howl of misery and widowhood: she would not think of Ireland – which must also have reminded her of Albert – for some time. Indeed, for a whole decade, she could barely even think about England – only her inconsolable loss of Albert.

Until the 1860s, most Irish people were monarchists, according to James H. Murphy, the historian and scholar.[70] And Tom Garvin writes that, prior to the nineteenth century, 'most Irish Catholics were probably monarchist in their political thinking, such as it was. Many harkened back wistfully to the lost Jacobite cause and sang ballads in both the country's languages in praise of the white-headed boy, Bonny Prince Charlie' (the Stuart hope against the Hanoverian monarchy).[71] Monarchy had been a Catholic cause historically, and the first parliamentary Republican had been the regicide Oliver Cromwell, tormenter of Ireland.

But the 1860s saw the real beginnings of the modern Irish Republican movement. The Irish Revolutionary Brotherhood (later known as the Irish Republican Brotherhood) had been founded in Dublin on St Patrick's Day 1858, and they were known after that as 'Fenians'. Similarly a radical movement expressing a form of British Republicanism was evident across the water. As Victoria retreated ever deeper into her widowhood, so she became ever more unpopular: as did, by the same token, the whole royal family.

When the Prince and Princess of Wales' (Bertie and Alexandra's) third child died on the day it was born in 1871, a London radical newspaper printed a comment that even the most committed Irish Republican might have baulked at: 'We have much satisfaction in announcing that the newly-born child of the Prince and Princess of Wales died shortly after its birth, thus relieving the working classes of England from having to support hereafter another addition to the long roll of State beggars they at present maintain.'[72]

Republicanism was not confined to the disgruntled classes in Britain: the idea was fashionable among the intellectuals. The hero of the age was Giuseppe Garibaldi, the Italian Republican, given a tumultuous welcome in England (partly because he was an enemy of the 'Papists'). The French, too, had just launched into their own radical Third Republic in 1870. Although there were only two republics in Europe – Switzerland and France – Republicanism was seen by some as the progressive future.

Not only did the Queen seem absent from the national scene: she seemed greedy and spendthrift too. A popular tract was published about her finances in the 1870s entitled *What Does She Do With It?* This claimed that she had only retreated to seclusion so as to hoard her Civil List revenue. The Liberal MP Sir Charles Dilke called on Parliament to depose the Queen and declare Britain a republic. As it turned out, the Queen endured, but Sir Charles rather lost his reputation after a three-in-a-bed sexual scandal.

The Fenian Brotherhood in Ireland did not enjoy widespread support: but it had a huge impact, over the years, in the United

States, where its ideology, arguably, shaped Irish-American politics for the next 150 years. Irish nationalism, in Ireland, has generally taken a wider and more nuanced form than Irish nationalism in America: besides that, the Catholic Church in Ireland was sternly opposed to secret societies and to violent revolution (the 1789 French Revolution was anathematised until the 1960s). The Bishop of Kerry, David Moriarty, thundered that 'eternity is not long enough nor hell hot enough to punish such miscreants.'[73] The Church almost certainly helped to keep such revolutionary movements contained. But, again, if Fenianism did not have a mass following, it had an influence from the late 1860s onwards.

Fenianism appealed to a long romantic Irish tradition of rebellion going back to Emmet, Wolfe Tone and Patrick Sarsfield (who died upon a French battlefield, valiantly crying 'oh that this were for Ireland!'). Yet Irish Republicanism, as Garvin points out, was more a matter of 'anti-British insurrectionist nationalism' and 'hatred of the British monarchy as a symbol' than a coherent political philosophy.[74] Defining the essence of Irish Republicanism is the subject of many fine minds: in my experience it is a broad church and may range from tender feelings about home and hearth, ballad and folklore, to Wolfe Tone's ideology abhorring altar and throne; or from a natural sense of patriotism aligned with a drive for Irish sovereignty, across the spectrum to an obsessive Anglophobia and racist ideas of excluding people not 'properly' Irish.

But the Victorian fashion for British Republicanism faded. Pressed by her family – and by Prime Minister Disraeli – the Queen made an effort to emerge from mourning. And then in November 1871, Bertie, Prince of Wales, was taken seriously ill with typhoid. A dramatic illness – from which there is eventually a dramatic recovery – can evoke sympathy. And, as Bertie lingered between life and death, the nation rallied around in concern for the heir.

His eventual recovery helped to restore the monarchy as a binding force. As did an attempt on the Queen's life by one Arthur O'Connor, described as 'a madman': he had made five previous attempts on the Queen's life. He was a nephew of the

Chartist leader Fergus O'Connor. It seems that Arthur O'Connor was attempting to get Victoria to sign a Fenian amnesty petition, although he had no known links with the Fenians.[75] Victoria was saved by her devoted Highland servant, John Brown (so memorably played by Billy Connolly in the film about their friendship, *Mrs Brown*). As she had done previously, the Queen showed sang-froid in the face of physical danger, although she was cross that O'Connor's punishment was merely a year's hard labour and 20 strokes of the birch.[76]

But Ireland and the British monarchy were marching to different drumbeats from the late 1860s. Some of the indications that this was the case caused the deepest personal hurt to the Queen. There was a proposal in Dublin to erect a statue of the late, beloved Albert, initially in St Stephens Green in Dublin – along with a plan to re-name the park itself 'Albert Green'. This was – fortunately, for the sake of history – not acceptable to the residents surrounding the Green, who, as ratepayers, mustered some clout. Then the nearby site of College Green, just outside Trinity College Dublin and opposite what had been the original Irish Parliament (now the Bank of Ireland), was proposed. But before the statue was even completed it was attacked by a member of the public.[77]

A sculpted bust of Albert that Victoria had sent to Dublin was also returned unwanted: nothing could have upset the Queen more than the rebuff of her adored late husband, whom she worshipped almost to the point of mania. She wanted every male descendant in her family to be called Albert (and desired that her son should reign as King Albert).

Victoria's long-term private secretary, Lord Ponsonby, wrote of the froideur between the Queen and Ireland:

> when the Prince Consort died the Queen presented a statue of him to the city of Dublin, but the Mayor and Corporation refused to accept it and sent it back to her. This occurred when she was in such deep grief that it completely overshadowed her whole life, and she is reported to have said that she would never forgive Ireland.[78]

Indeed, she had considered revisiting Ireland in the late 1860s, but after the insult to Albert's memory, abruptly rejected the idea.

Lord Ponsonby did not get this story right, however – although the fact that he believed it is itself revealing. What actually occurred was that Dublin Corporation – by a narrow vote of 29 to 24 – rejected placing Albert's statue in the prominent location of College Green. Different factions of Nationalists were jostling for power and control of the munici-pality at this time, and Albert's statue took on something of the role of scapegoat. (Some Irish Nationalists called him 'a foreign Prince', because he was *German*. They also criticised his dis-paraging attitude to Catholic Poland.)[79]

However, the Albert statue (by the renowned sculptor John Foley) was eventually completed, and erected in the grounds of Leinster House in 1871. Leinster House was the location of the Royal Dublin Society, where the 1853 Industrial Exhibition had been held, so it was really quite appropriate.

Subsequently, as everyone knows, Leinster House became the Dáil (and Senate), first of the Free State and then the Republic of Ireland; and to this day Prince Albert's statue still graces the grounds of the Parliament building on the Merrion Square side, half-hidden by a discreet hedge, and, strangely, without any name or details on the plinth. But he has stood undisturbed, the last royal statue in Dublin, surrounded by his four allegorical figurines representing agriculture, the arts, engineering, and scientific exploration, through all the turbulent changes of the twentieth century (including the destruction or removal of many statues associated with the Imperial regime). So Victoria – though hyper-sensitive to any insult to Albert in the 1860s – may have been to some degree mollified that the statue did finally appear, and her shade might be comforted by its survival.[80]

*

When the Queen began to resume her public life in the 1870s, she found herself at the head of an expanding Empire, rising to its zenith: an Empire on which 'the sun never set', since it stretched through all quarters of the globe. She was also the head of an ever-increasing family, now marrying and reproducing copiously.

In matters both political and familial, Victoria was again a contradiction. She was pleased and proud to be declared Empress of India and was fascinated by India, adoring her Indian servant (known as the Munshi) and bridling fiercely at any racist prejudice directed against him. And yet she did not favour the more triumphalist element of imperialism. 'We do *not* annexe territories,' she wrote icily to Gladstone, on learning that Fiji had been 'annexed' to Great Britain.[81]

When it came to the family, she doted on her grandchildren and showed tender concern for their well-being: but she could snap impatiently that there was such a thing as having too many children. She enjoyed matchmaking through the various branches of European royals, and yet wrote that the single life in contentment was far superior to 'getting married for marriage's sake'.

As the Empire expanded, Ireland's importance to London diminished. Many in Queen Victoria's circle regarded Ireland as a despairing place most vividly associated with crime and 'outrages'. To read through popular publications such as the *Illustrated London News* – or indeed, to read through despatches sent to Queen Victoria herself – is to get the impression of a wild, brutal, lawless country, in which landlords are routinely assassinated and animals horribly and gratuitously maimed. Indeed, another gripe that Victoria had against the Irish was that she thought them cruel to animals. She was fond of animals and led the opposition to vivisection.

John Morley's description of Ireland sums up a whole attitude: 'There lay Ireland – squalid, dismal, sullen, dull, despondent, sunk deep in hostile intent.'[82] As a Liberal statesman, sometime Chief Secretary for Ireland and biographer of Gladstone, one might expect him to have a sympathetic view, but even he sometimes saw the country as benighted.

In truth, it was 'a most distressful country' with many justified grievances over land tenure and unfair rents. The years after the Famine saw a new type of hard-faced landlord develop in Ireland

– business managers driven by revenue and profit. And then, by the 1870s, a new agricultural depression had set in, and waves of mini-famines threatened the western and north-western coast. There were dreadful scenes of eviction and heart-breaking melo-dramas of exile. It was a world away from Windsor Castle and Westminster.

With economic depression on the rise, organised nationalism was gathering pace in Ireland from the 1870s. The effective part of that organised nationalism starts with the rise of Charles Stewart Parnell in the mid-1870s. And with the appearance of Parnell – perhaps significantly, popularly known as 'the uncrowned King of Ireland' – connections between the evicted tenants of Donegal and the politicians of Westminster began to correlate a little more meaningfully.

Democracy was expanding throughout Victoria's reign: at the beginning of the Victorian era only one man in 20 could vote: by 1900, one man in 3 had the franchise.[83] And by 1900 the agitation for women's votes was well into its stride.

The Home Rule for Ireland movement was founded (as the Home Rule League) by Isaac Butt in 1873, establishing a consti-tutional and parliamentary outlet for Nationalist aspirations. The following year, the Home Rulers won 59 seats in the House of Commons, and would soon exercise their democratic power in Westminster.

Nationalism had not been an organised parliamentary force until the appearance of Parnell. Daniel O'Connell had been a formidable political leader, but his most successful campaign had been for Catholic emancipation, which liberated Irish Catholics from many – though not all – of their disadvantages. The Young Ireland movement provided an aspiration to real Irish nation-hood. But Ireland was too poor and too underdeveloped to form a coherent political party with the declared object of self-gov-ernment.

It was Parnell's leadership that finally provided that necessary party. The politically influential Land League was formed in 1879 by Parnell and Michael Davitt, initially to redress the grievances of poor tenants subjected to unfair rents, uncertain tenure and absentee landlords. Almost at the same time – and almost in the same place in Co Mayo – came reports of an apparition of the Blessed Virgin at Knock, just at a time when the western seaboard was experiencing another wave of famine.

These things may or may not be related – some sceptics ascribe the appearance of Our Lady to the hallucinations brought on by eating fermented potato peelings – but for many Irish people, to this day, Knock is a centre of Marian devotion deeply intertwined with notions of suffering, endurance and at the same time divine consolation. If Parnell was the political 'uncrowned King of Ireland', the Blessed Virgin Mary was a vision of the 'Queen of Heaven' appearing in a poor and neglected spot to bring solace to her people.[84]

Such religious devotion tended to inhibit political revolt, as the prevailing religious teaching was that endurance under suffering was a virtue: but the religious emphasis on patience might also have benefited parliamentary constitutionalism rather than lawless and unfocused anger.

William Gladstone, four times Liberal Prime Minister, announced his conversion to Irish Home Rule in 1885: the insight that Ireland must have a form of self-government came to him during a visit to Rome and the Vatican.

Once committed to this cause, Gladstone worked tirelessly for it. Queen Victoria thought he 'self-sacrificed' his life to this cause she deplored. (When a peer was said to have 'converted' to Home Rule, Victoria's interpretation was 'perverted'.[85]) Gladstone had steered through the Irish Church Disestablishment Act 1869: this uncoupled the Church of Ireland from the Crown, and for this, he was loathed as a traitor by some Irish Anglicans.

Victoria reacted to this in a somewhat detached way, and accepted the will of parliament on the Irish Church (the Established status of the Church of Ireland had meant that Roman Catholics were obliged to pay tithes to the Protestant Establishment). The Queen might not have reacted quite so coolly if the measure had involved the Scottish Church. 'I would never give away *the Scottish Church*,' she declared to Lord Rosebery, 'which is the real and true stronghold of Protestantism.'[86]

Unfortunately for Ireland, the chemistry between Gladstone and Victoria was disastrous. He did not understand that she wanted to be treated like a woman, not a public institution. She infinitely preferred Gladstone's Tory rival, Disraeli, who had not only an inclination for flattery, but also an instinctive feeling for the feminine disposition, with an added dandified charm and what we now call 'emotional intelligence'. Disraeli was not interested in Ireland – he described the Irish way of life as 'coarse idolatry interspersed with clannish brawls'. As between Gladstone and Disraeli – the Queen was infinitely more at ease with the intuitive 'Dizzy'.

Victoria disliked Gladstone for a number of reasons, but his Home Rule cause (and the way he went about it) was central. Gladstone's increasing obsession with Ireland (his memos to the Queen on Ireland might run to 40 pages) certainly did nothing to warm her to the cause. It is thought that Victoria confided some very bilious material about Gladstone to her diary, later censored and destroyed by her daughter Beatrice, who copied and edited the whole journal.

Quite unethically, she even showed some of Gladstone's letters about Ireland to his later opponent Lord Salisbury. The Queen was utterly opposed to what she saw as the break-up of the United Kingdom: 'giving up what one has is always a bad thing', she said.[87] This is a common view among those who rule and reign: *what we have, we hold.*

Neither did the Queen like Parnell. He was a member of the landlord class and of a Protestant background, and thus, in a caste sense, more presentable than O'Connell. He was also an animal-lover, who, like the Queen, thought the Irish were callous to animals. But she still disliked him. She must have resented his soubriquet of 'uncrowned King of Ireland': her nickname for him was 'the Pretender'.[88] Moreover, once his adultery was revealed, that was a singularly black mark in her eyes.

*

As the nineteenth century progressed, the *froideur* between Ireland and Victoria continued. She refused to contemplate suggestions, put forward over a number of years, that there should be a permanent royal residence in Ireland.

There were reports that the secret Republican society of the Fenians were planning to assassinate the Queen; although it is doubtful that this was ever seriously contemplated. She certainly deeply deplored the Fenian recourse to dynamiting, as in the Clerkenwell explosions of 1867, when two Fenians carried out an abortive attempt to effect a prison rescue, causing the death of 12 and injuries to 50. Yet towards these men, the 'Manchester Martyrs' (the Fenians William Allen, Michael Larkin and Michael O'Brien who were executed for the murder of Sergeant Charles Brett in Manchester in September 1867) Victoria displayed her characteristic contradictions. She deplored them; but she prayed for them just the same.[89]

She was appalled by the Phoenix Park murders in 1882, as was all her family. 'I cannot sufficiently express my horror and indignation,' wrote Bertie, as Prince of Wales, 'at the last terrible tragedy enacted in Ireland.' The whole of England, and indeed most of Ireland, felt similarly about the event.[90]

Lord Frederick Cavendish and Mr Thomas Burke were assassinated in a particularly gruesome way: they were hacked to death with surgical knives. Cavendish and Burke were not cruel or absentee landlords. Burke came from a Galway family and his sister was a nun, and Lord Frederick was married to Gladstone's niece, Catherine, herself a supporter of Home Rule with a great fondness for Ireland.

Like Gladstone himself, Catherine was also a committed Christian and despite the loss of her beloved young husband, 'she forgave Ireland and sent her husband's two days salary' – he had only been *en poste* for a couple of days – 'to the fishermen in the West [of Ireland] and she sent a silver cross to the murderer.'

She continued to support her uncle's efforts to bring peace and Home Rule to Ireland.[91] She made a point of telling A. M. Sullivan, the Nationalist MP, who sent his condolences, that she 'didn't blame the Irish'. Much to the disgust of Unionists she remained on kindly terms with Irish Nationalists and was seen dining with John Redmond at the House of Commons some years later.[92]

Lord Frederick was described by the London-Irish journalist and Parnellite T. P. O'Connor as a 'gentle, straight, courageous' man, who tried to come to the rescue of Burke when the latter seemed the more seriously wounded.

There was a poignant sequel, almost worthy of a Victorian melodrama: one of the Invincibles condemned to death for the assassinations, Joe Brady, was 'prepared for Eternity' by a particularly gentle and caring nun. Just before he mounted the gallows, the religious sister revealed that T. H. Burke – Brady's victim – had been her brother.[93]

Not everyone reacted with Catherine Cavendish's Christian forgiveness, and some of the repercussions of the famous Phoenix Park murders were politically disastrous. Lord Frederick's elder brother, the Duke of Devonshire, made it his particular business to obstruct the progress of Gladstone's Home Rule Bills in the House of Lords thereafter and brought all his influence to bear on the matter. As Gladstone struggled to carry his Home Rule Bills through Parliament, the Phoenix Park murders were frequently held up as an example of a lawless people unfit to govern themselves.

Thus, in the last three decades of her reign, Victoria reverted to the opinions she had held about Ireland before her well-received visits of 1849, 1853, and 1861. The Irish were 'a terrible people'. And so 'low'. Forgotten now were her former feelings for her 'warm-hearted' Irish subjects.

She pressed her ministers, repeatedly, to pursue a policy of coercion in Ireland. No repression was too harsh for this 'terrible people'. Even before the Phoenix Park murders, her letters, insistently underlined – sometimes doubly underlined – had urged her government to take action. 'The danger [is] … *hourly increas-*

ing, of allowing a state of affairs like the present in Ireland to *go on*. The law is *openly defied, disobeyed &* such an example may spread to England, if it prove successful in Ireland.

Victoria 'wore down' her ministers by the energy with which she expressed her feelings. 'It *must* [double underline] be put down & nothing but *boldness* and firmness will succeed ... declare that you will not be parties to a *weak* and vacillating policy, which is ruining the country & bringing great discredit on the Government. ... it is *most painful* to [the Queen] and she *has a right* to her Ministers to uphold her authority & to expect them to do so.' If radical parliamentarians such as John Bright and Joseph Chamberlain were threatening to resign as a protest against over-harsh methods towards Ireland, '... *let* them *go* ...', she said. She did not want politicians with emollient ideas towards the Irish.[94]

Victoria's letters and diaries in the 1880s are full of condem-nations of Irish lawlessness. She was appalled by the murder of a magistrate, Thomas Boyd, at New Ross on September 1 1880, and even more appalled at the murder of Lord Montmorres in the Neale area of Co Mayo later in September of that year: it was a shocking killing of a harmless minor landlord, whose body was found by the roadside riddled with bullets, all the more distress-ing when no one would rescue his corpse.

She was enraged by the murder of Lord Leitrim, who had been shot two years previously. Nobody was ever apprehended for the murder. The shooting of the Earl of Leitrim did not quite elicit the same response among his peers. One member of the Irish gentry wrote that 'it was certain to happen sooner or later'. Leitrim was incorrigibly quarrelsome and was suspected of prac-tising droit de seigneur with the young maidens on his estates.[95] Most people were more saddened – as was the Queen – that his driver and a young clerk were killed alongside the Earl. There were other murders too, regularly reported to the Queen, sometimes of defenceless female members of the gentry just out for a carriage drive.

These events have been seen differently by Irish and British historians – the Irish perspective is often that such 'outrages' were the actions of a desperate people, ground down by injustice and despair. General Gordon felt driven to express his dismay at the dreadful conditions that prevailed in the poorest parts of Ireland, which he thought more impoverished than the worst hovels of India.[96] But, to Victoria's cast of mind, there was no excuse for lawlessness, and it especially infuriated her when no culprits were brought to trial. She permitted herself sometimes to outbursts of near-anarchy over Ireland. 'They should be lynch-lawed and on the spot', she once wrote of the perpetrators of an Irish act of violence.[97]

During this tempestuous decade of the 1880s, Victoria disliked members of the royal family visiting Ireland (and the Prince and Princess of Wales got some rough treatment in Mallow, Co Cork). She even tried to stop the popular Empress Elisabeth of Austria-Hungary – known as 'Sissi' – from hunting in Ireland. Sissi was so obsessed with hunting – she might go hunting 28 days in a month – that nothing would dissuade her. She thought Ireland great hunting country and rebuffed the Queen's counsel.

The Austro-Hungarian Empress was adored by the Irish peasantry – who did not connect her with their bad landlord regime, and regarded her as 'one of their own' for being a Catholic. They would pick up as treasured mementoes objects such as the little linen handkerchiefs she sometimes dropped while vaulting over the stone walls of the Irish countryside, seated side-saddle on her hunter.[98] Indeed, the 1880s were witnessing the rise of modern terrorist tactics for political ends. Sissi herself was to die by the assassin's knife, wielded in the cause of anarchism.

The hostile feelings that Victoria felt towards Ireland were increasingly returned by the Irish. In July 1883, a trade exhibition opening in Cork was boycotted because it was accompanied by 'God Save the Queen'. Even the 'moderate' Irish Nationalists were now more nationalistic – and more confident. Official bodies in Dublin gradually ceased toasting the Queen on formal occasions, and 'God save the Queen' was gradually replaced by 'God save Ireland'. Occasionally, toasts to 'the Queen' were also accompanied by 'parity of esteem' toasts to 'the Pope'.[99]

The founding of the Gaelic Athletic Association in 1884, to promote 'Gaelic Games', was an important milestone in the cultivation of national self-confidence. Two years after Parnell's death, in 1893, the scholar Douglas Hyde made his ground-breaking speech on the 'De-Anglicisation of Ireland', and from then on, the culture of a 'Gaelic Ireland', in opposition to Anglicising influences, took root – and took hold of the imagi-nation of Irish intellectuals, artists, teachers, and the young.

This was also the period when the Irish Parliamentary Party was making such a sensational impact on Westminster with their lively oratory, brilliant delaying tactics, and dazzling ability to hold the House to political ransom.

Paradoxically, or perhaps logically, it was Queen Victoria's Golden Jubilee in June 1887 that stimulated more Irish cultural nationalism – and more opposition to the monarchy.

Victoria's sixty years on the throne were to be marked in a blaze of glory at the very summit of the British Empire's brilliance; but the occasion was muted in Dublin. 'In the Queen's Jubilee of 1887', recalled her private secretary Sir Frederick Ponsonby, 'addresses and telegrams of congratulation came not only from the Dominions and Colonies, but from most of the countries in the world, but nothing from Dublin or the South of Ireland.'[100]

Dublin Corporation was more absorbed by the debate to re-name Sackville Street 'O'Connell Street'. At Westminster, the Irish Parliamentary Party, along with British radicals, opposed the motion to vote funds for the Jubilee: T. P. O'Connor told the House of Commons that during Victoria's reign three-and-a-half million people had been evicted in Ireland and a quarter of a million starved to death – this was scant cause for celebration. A couple of days later, the Queen visited the East End of London and was booed: this was ascribed to 'Socialists and the worst Irish'.

But while the Irish Parliamentarians abstained from jollities, Victoria was supported in a joyous Jubilee by the mass of the British people. They had cause to celebrate – great progress had been made in the lives of ordinary people during Victoria's reign: thousands of miles of railway lines laid; an unsurpassed postal service costing a penny a letter installed; drainage systems advanced; the telegraph and telephone invented; medical progress unprecedented, while Florence Nightingale's leadership made nursing a respectable career for women; elementary education was made available to all; and the franchise expanded. Moreover, from 1850, crime had fallen year on year – including in Ireland – and this, coupled with decent drains and working lavatories, immeasurably improved the everyday lives of millions.[101]

Ireland shared in many of the advances of the Victorian era: the cheap and reliable Royal Mail was particularly appreciated because emigrants could now safely send money back to Ireland via postal orders (the novelist Anthony Trollope, who invented the public letter-box, had effectively brought the Victorian postal system to Ireland). And individual Irish people did send the Queen personal gifts for her jubilee – gifts of lace, shawls, even fresh eggs.[102] But among the politically aware resentment against the British political system seethed: Gladstone's monumental Home Rule Bill of 1886 had so recently been defeated – only just – by combined Unionist forces.

Increasingly, British celebrations of the monarchy were met by counter-celebrations in Ireland, either of Irish patriotism or Catholicism. So it was that, as Britain prepared for the Queen's 1887 Golden Jubilee, Ireland very ostensibly celebrated the 50th anniversary of Pope Leo XIII's ordination.

Ten years later, for the Diamond Jubilee, Gladstone's struggle had drawn to a close: he died in 1898, having valiantly and vainly battled for so long to bring Home Rule to Ireland. Parnell died in 1891, after his fall from public grace over Katharine O'Shea's divorce scandal – and the maladroit way, too, in which it was handled by virtually all concerned.

Queen Victoria had disliked Parnell even more than O'Connell (although, just like O'Connell, Parnell had never been an anti-monarchist) and yielded to malicious feelings of *schadenfreude* on his downfall: 'it is satisfactory to see wickedness punished even in this world.'

On hearing of his death, she declared: 'He was a really bad & worthless man who had to answer for many lives lost in Ireland [103].' Parnell's supporters were making rather similar claims about Her Majesty.

By the 1890s, the repeated reports of 'Irish outrages' sent back to Windsor began to dwindle, and the constabulary despatches reflected a greater tranquillity in the countryside. The era of the terrible evictions too – with the battering ram at the door – was largely over. Crime in general was much reduced.[104]

The Conservatives were returned to power in 1895, led by the resolutely Tory Lord Salisbury. Although anti-Catholic and anti-Irish, his administration set about developing an Irish policy they called 'constructive unionism', which others dubbed 'killing Home Rule with kindness'. This would mean local government reform, and a series of Land Acts that eventually radically reformed the entire system of land ownership. Men, women and families in possession of land are less liable to be revolutionaries, and if the cultural nationalism of the Celtic Revival was growing, so was the *embourgeoisement* of the farming classes.

Gladstone died without achieving his long-fought goal of Home Rule for Ireland, yet he had achieved something which may have been, in the long run, of greater value: he had 'raised consciousness' about Ireland's wrongs, and her democratic claim to nationhood.

For the 1897 Diamond Jubilee, there was a new element in the equation: politically motivated women. Fiery female activists had shown even more hostility to Queen Victoria than men. Anna and Fanny Parnell (Charles Stewart Parnell's sisters) and their Ladies' Land League, founded in 1881, had been implacable opponents of any form of British dominion, with a special dislike of Queen Victoria. Anna Parnell had coined the soundbite 'the Famine Queen', which damaged Victoria's reputation for the next century: where reputation is concerned, a snappy slogan is worth a hundred scholarly textbooks.

VICTORIA: GREAT EMPRESS OR FAMINE QUEEN?

The Ladies' Land League involved women in political activity, and probably imparted to many women a sense of empowerment. But although it had been launched to support the campaign while male members were in jail, Parnell and the male Land Leaguers abhorred its 'recklessness', and Parnell himself closed it down.[105]

But following the example of the Parnell sisters, another woman would emerge to lead the most dramatic opposition to Queen Victoria: the tall and beautiful Maud Gonne, Yeats' muse, ardent Irish Nationalist by persuasion although – not unusually – an upper-class Englishwoman by birth. Maud Gonne was a committed revolutionary socialist (later, after the Great War, and an experience of nursing in the trenches, she would become a pacifist, though she always remained an uncompromising Irish Nationalist).[106]

Keir Hardie, the Scottish socialist and Labour Party founder, had asked Maud to lead an anti-Monarchist opposition to the previous 1887 Jubilee celebrations, but Miss Gonne had little faith in the English capacity for rebellion. The English, she had concluded from earlier experiences, would never take to rioting in the streets – and they would always settle for a compromise. Many foreigners admired the English inclination for compromise: Maud despised it. As with many an English-born revolutionary, Maud saw the potential for revolution to be much greater – and more exciting – in Ireland.

Maud Gonne's political commitments were sincere. She had witnessed heart-breaking evictions in the 1880s in Donegal and was passionately moved to activity by the injustice of it. Appearing on horseback and in her beautiful, though careless, Parisian costumes, she was hailed by the Donegal peasantry as a redeeming fairy queen herself – and certainly, with her tall stature, striking beauty, and rich, flowing locks, she made a much more suitable queen than small, dumpy, 12-stone, podgy-fingered Victoria. (James Joyce unkindly described Queen Victoria as a 'dwarf' – she was under five feet high.)

Maud hated Victoria with particular venom. Her invective against the Queen was vehement and personal, describing the ageing monarch as every kind of vile and odious harridan. Subconsciously there may have been a feeling that Maud herself was the competing – and superior – queen. When Yeats, who adored the divine Miss Gonne, wished to cast a queen in his play, *Cathleen ni Houlihan*, he modelled that ideal on Maud.

And when she took on the role, what an impact she made! As *Cathleen ni Houlihan*, the personification of the risen Ireland, men swore then and there to sacrifice themselves for Maud and the cause she embodied. Arthur Griffith called her 'Queenie': and, indeed, in this period of the 1890s and 1900s, this extraordinary woman was queen of any enterprise she undertook.

Maud Gonne recounts in her autobiography – provocatively called *A Servant of the Queen* (this 'queen' being Ireland) – the zest and ingenuity with which she set about sabotaging Victoria's 1897 Diamond Jubilee. She coaxed Dublin Corporation workmen to help her cut the electric wires 'to prevent the display by the Unionist shops' (in all probability, ordinary Dublin small traders who had displayed Jubilee decorations). Along with James Connolly, the Marxist leader, Maud arranged an anti-Jubilee display and, on a huge screen in Parnell Square, projected harrowing eviction scenes, and photographs of Irishmen executed during the Queen's reign – a stunningly innovative use of technology. She also cut out and sewed – with her own hands – black flags displaying in white lettering the numbers who had died during the Famine.

Finally, in an especially striking example of street theatre, Maud enlisted Connolly's assistance to construct a large coffin, which would be marched through Dublin city and plunged into the river Liffey, the marchers chanting all the while: 'Here goes the coffin of the British Empire! To hell with the British Empire!'

It was an innovative example of gesture politics – the concept has been copied many times since, not least by the Suffragettes, but it was then original – and it thrilled Irish Nationalists. And in all this, she had W. B. Yeats in tow, whose emotional response to these events was to produce some of the best lyrical poetry of the twentieth century, and arouse some of the most impassioned Nationalist feelings. Maud also had the support of Anna Parnell and the Belfast-born authoress Alice Milligan in her street activities.

Afterwards, Miss Gonne was so exhausted by her part in the 'anti-Jubilee' that she repaired to the spa of Aix-les-Bains, a respite unavailable to small shopkeepers deprived of trade by revolutionary activities. [107]

Joyful celebrations took place throughout the British Empire for the Queen's Jubilee, but in Ireland the main Catholic nationalist newspaper said that there was a 'cold indifference of the Irish people to-day towards the Sovereign'.[108] And, as usual, Irish Nationalists were working up to rival celebrations: the 20th anniversary of Pope Leo XIII's accession to the papacy (though His Holiness had supported London against rebellious Irish Catholics) in 1898, and the centenary of the famed 1798 Rebellion led by Wolfe Tone. There would also be a 50th anniversary of the 1848 phase of the Famine. There is always an anniversary in Ireland.

Queen Victoria was past 80 when the twentieth century dawned. It was her habit to visit continental Europe in the spring of the year – generally the south of France. But in 1900 she suddenly took it into her head to go to Ireland. According to her private secretary, Sir Frederick Ponsonby, it was all her own idea. She had felt a surge of gratitude to the Irishmen who had fought bravely for her in the Boer War and, reports Sir Frederick, it was the exceptional valour of the Irish fighting men which reconciled Victoria to Ireland at the end of her life.

Irishmen had fought on both sides in the Boer War: Irish Nationalists had fought for the Boers (who, inconveniently, were the white South Africans who subsequently imposed racial apartheid). But many working-class Irishmen, particularly Dubliners, had fought bravely for the Crown. The Queen, indeed, was most especially touched by the courage of the Dublin Fusiliers.

She thus inaugurated the Irish Guards for the occasion of her 1900 visit and endorsed the wearing of the shamrock. Until 1900, the old song about Napper Tandy and the shamrock had it that: 'the shamrock is by law forbid / to grow on Irish ground'. It had not exactly been forbidden to grow it, but it had been against regulations to wear it.

Again, there were many objections to Victoria's visit from active Nationalists. Arthur Griffith, the Sinn Féin writer, and even George Moore, the Anglo-Irish writer, bohemian and landlord, claimed that Victoria's only interest in Ireland was to recruit more men to die in South Africa.

Maud Gonne reprised her vituperative hostility against the elderly Queen. She called the monarch 'vile and selfish', and held her responsible for '60 years of organised famine'. She described Victoria as 'Queen of the famines, of the pestilences, of the emigrant ships, of the levelled homesteads, of the dungeons and the gallows.'[109] She claimed that 'poor Irish emigrant girls' were exploited and destroyed in the name of this reigning harridan whose only interest in visiting Ireland was exploitation:

> For Victoria, in the decrepitude of her 81 years, to have decided after an absence of half a century to revisit the country she hates and whose inhabitants are the victims of her criminal policy ... the survivors of 60 years of organised famine, the political necessity must have been strong ... Queen, return to your own land; you will find no more Irishmen ready to wear the red shame of your livery![110]

Yeats, utterly in thrall to Maud's mesmerising allure, did his muse's bidding and wrote letters full of bile to the press, claiming that Victoria had a 'hatred of our individual National life', and reiterating the Sinn Féin claim that the Queen only sought to recruit soldiers from the Irish. He announced that, 'Whoever stands by the roadway cheering for Queen Victoria cheers for [her] Empire, dishonours Ireland and condones a crime ... her crime in South Africa.' As about a third of those serving in the

British Empire at this time were Irish, this was a considerable constituency to condemn.[111]

Reprising the demonstrations against the Queen's Jubilees, more demonstrations were planned during the course of Victoria's Dublin visit of April 1900. However, there was a crucial difference between the occasions of the Queen's Jubilee celebrations and the 1900 visit: in 1887 and 1897 the Queen was ensconced in London and it all seemed quite remote and irrelevant. In 1900 the Queen was actually setting foot in Ireland again, and a royal visit generally softened – at least temporarily – the edges of public ire.

The collective *céad mile fáilte* gene in the Irish people is always stronger than the sum of political resentments. And for all the flair and combined talent of the Dublin anti-royalist Nationalists – Maud Gonne, James Connolly, Arthur Griffith, and W. B. Yeats were no mean combination – the plain people of Ireland turned out in their hundreds of thousands to give Queen Victoria the warmest welcome she had ever had in Ireland. Even as she approached the end of her long life she was moved to 'unforgettable' tears by the sight of this 'warm-hearted people'.

On her final visit to Ireland, so soon before her death, the Queen arrived again at Kingstown, as she relates, at 'half past 2' on April 3. The following day, she rode in her carriage from what is now Dún Laoghaire to the Viceregal Lodge (now Áras an Uachtaráin) in the Phoenix Park. 'The whole route from Kingstown to Dublin was much crowded,' she recorded, 'all the people cheering loudly & the decorations were beautiful.'

She noticed that there were hardly any police on the route, so unthreatening was the crowd. 'There were many loyal inscriptions put up suspended across the road, the following [being] 2 of them: "Blest for ever is she who relied on Erin's hour & Erin's pride" & "In her a thousand virtues closed as mother, wife & queen".' At Ballsbridge (then called Ball's Bridge) the travelling escort was replaced by a sovereign's escort of Life Guards. At Leeson Street Bridge a temporary archway had been erected inscribed with the words: 'Her Most Gracious Majesty the Queen.'[112]

It was hot, her secretary Sir Frederick Ponsonby recorded, and the carriages – there were three in all, escorted by Life Guards – went at a slow trot. It was, he remembered, a long journey into Dublin (about eight miles), and they all felt the heat, and yet:

> there were crowds of people practically all the way, but when we got into Dublin the mass of people wedged together in the street and in every window, even on the roofs, was quite remarkable. Although I had seen many visits of this kind, nothing had ever approached the enthusiasm and even frenzy displayed by the people of Dublin.[113]

True, there was some dissent: in two locations, he heard sounds like booing, one 'outside the offices of a Nationalist newspaper', and then, from a house along the Quay. But it did not diminish the overwhelming enthusiasm with which the frail old monarch was generally met.

Victoria had always had a kind of Christian feeling for the poor – perhaps more especially the 'deserving poor' – and now she especially noted the Dublin poor coming out to greet her. 'We went all along the quays in the poorer parts of the town where thousands had gathered together & gave me a wildly enthusiastic greeting.' Trinity College Dublin, then a hotbed of Unionism, was more predictably excited.

> At Trinity College the students sang 'God Save the Queen' & shouted themselves hoarse. The cheers & often almost screams were quite deafening. Even the Nationalists from the City Hall seemed to forget their politics & cheered & waved their hats. It really was a wonderful reception I got & most gratifying.[114]

Victoria and her party reached their destination at Viceregal Lodge. She was familiar with the lovely neoclassical mansion from previous visits many decades earlier, except that now, because of her age and infirmity, Victoria had to be carried upstairs. Over the next days the royal party toured around Dublin, almost always meeting, personally, with kindness and hospitality.

Between hosting a party for children at the Phoenix Park – 'it was a wonderful sight & the noise of the children cheering quite overpowering', the Queen wrote – and going about the principal streets of Dublin where the 'crowds were just as large [as on her arrival] & the enthusiasm immense' – she received telegrams of congratulations on 8 April about the recent relief of Ladysmith in South Africa. This was a military endeavour in which the Dublin regiments had played an active part. She dealt daily with 'telegrams of congratulations … from every part of Ireland & from Irish everywhere', congratulations for Ladysmith, and for the Irish visit.[115]

Even when preoccupied by the Boer War, Victoria so enjoyed 'driving along the banks of the Liffey', which she thought so pretty, and almost Parisian. She visited Kilmainham and Clondalkin, again to an immensely warm reception. At Clondalkin, she noted, 'the little town had been so prettily decorated. Wherever I go the people come out & cheer … call out "God Bless You".'[116] She also noted the 'lace and embroidery done by the very poorest people & quite beautiful.'

This last visit marked a rapprochement between Victoria and Catholic Ireland. She was careful to visit both Protestant and Catholic institutions, and to invite clergy from both denominations to dine: Victoria was Protestant and Unionist, but not sectarian – she had once refused to contribute to a charity that only ministered to Protestants.[117] Cardinal Logue and the Queen liked one another: 'they both seemed surprised to find how well they got on together' wrote Sir Frederick. 'The Queen went out of her way to make herself agreeable, while the Cardinal was quite captivated by her charm.'[118]

But it was the convents that most impressed Victoria. She visited three of them: the Deaf and Dumb Institute in Cabra run by the Dominican nuns; Loreto Abbey at Rathfarnham; and, on April 17, the Convent of the Sacred Heart at Mount Anville.

The Mount Anville trip was especially meaningful to her, because the convent house itself had once been William Dargan's home, which she had visited and loved, nearly 50 years previously in the company of her beloved Albert. Dargan, alas, had died in poverty after losing his fortune in a stroke of ill-luck.[119] And now, perhaps symbolically, the splendid house and demesne was taken over by a convent school: it was the highly organised and structured Catholic church, not the railway magnates, who were gaining in power and status in 1900.

What met Victoria's old eyes was the sight of a group of well-ordered, well-educated, neat, young convent girls. Fifty nuns and 500 schoolgirls, all dressed in white and bearing lilies and daffodils, awaited the Queen as she arrived. The nuns noticed that she was 'a very old lady and had to be awakened from a dozing sleep by her daughter Beatrice on their arrival by carriage', writes Sister Íde ní Riain of Mount Anville, drawing on convent memories.[120] 'Not to tire her, the visit took place on the beautiful carriage sweep in front of the grand house.'

The congregation and girls lined up, and 'tea was offered, a beautiful china tea set having been acquired for the occasion.' The Reverend Mother Provincial, Janet Erskine Stewart (a remarkable Englishwoman of scholarship and piety who had converted from Anglicanism) was present for the occasion, and kissed the Queen's hand in greeting. Victoria was deeply touched.

Victoria had once disparaged convent life as pointless, but now she saw how ladylike, how respectable, how presentable – indeed, how *Victorian* in its self-improving ethos convent education was – and she greatly endorsed it.

Altogether, the Queen was well pleased with her afternoon and, she noted, when she drove away there were 'great outbursts of cheering'.

Victoria met many Catholic dignitaries on this visit – reverend mothers and monsignori and canons. As well as Mount Anville, she also visited the Mater Misericordiae Hospital, the Protestant Adelaide Hospital, and an orphanage run by the Vincent de Paul nuns. The edge of hostility that she had once had towards Catholic Ireland was quite gone: in the evening of her life, Victoria had mellowed. By the same token, Catholic Ireland had by now become a markedly Victorian culture – even 50 years later, my generation felt that aura of Victorian respectability and self-improvement that penetrated Irish, Catholic, and even Nationalist institutions. The Irish Catholic hierarchy praised Tennyson as the most admirable of poets and he was Victoria's very own favourite.[121] Sinn Féin itself took on improving Victorian virtues, such as temperance and 'manliness'.

As she departed from the shores of Ireland for the last time, Victoria recorded that:

> this eventful visit, which created so much interest & excitement had, like everything in this world, come to an end. Though I own I am very tired & long for rest & quiet, I can never forget the really wild enthusiasm & affectionate loyalty displayed by all in Ireland & shall ever retain a most grateful remembrance of this warm hearted & sympathetic people. Even when I used to go round the grounds [of the Viceregal lodge] in my pony chair & the people outside caught sight of me they would at once cheer & sing 'God Save the Queen'.[122]

Queen Victoria had made her peace with Ireland, and Ireland said goodbye with grace to the Queen who had presided over a turbulent and often sorrowful century. But, for all the warmth of the welcome, Ireland was well on a path to detach itself from the Crown. In the archives of Mount Anville, the details of Queen Victoria's afternoon there were subsequently, and mysteriously, torn from the convent record, presumably by a nun-archivist who sympathised with Maud Gonne's view of the British monarchy.

Victoria's last visit to Ireland took a toll on her health, and she never really recovered from the exertions of the voyage. She died the following January. At her death, there were some acerbic criticisms of the Queen's long reign. The *Irish Independent* wrote:

> Viewed as Sovereign of Ireland, it can only be recorded of her late Majesty that she was eminently forgetful of her obligation towards this Kingdom. As a wife, as a mother, and as the head of a great Court, the late Queen was beyond reproach. ... She never

tolerated the presence at her Council Board or in her audience chamber [of] either man or woman against whose moral worth any charge had ever been publicly laid ... Nevertheless – so far as Ireland was concerned – no reign ... more destructive for our people or more ruinous for their national prosperity has ever been witnessed since the time of the Tudor Queen [Elizabeth I], than was hers. [123]

Yet there would have been many veteran Irish soldiers who must have cherished the memory of Queen Victoria, as did the old man, Thomas Dunne, in Sebastian Barry's acclaimed play *The Steward of Christendom*:

I loved her for as long as she lived ... When I was a young recruit it used to frighten me how much I loved her. Because she had built everything up and made it strong, and made it shipshape. ... All the harbours of the earth were trim with their granite piers, the ships were shining and strong. The trains went sleekly through the fields and her mark was everywhere, Ireland, Africa, the Canadas, every blessed place. ...Among her emblems was the gold harp, the same harp we wore on our helmets. We were secure ... Ireland was hers for eternity ... she was the very flower and perfecter of Christendom. Even as the simple man I was I could love her fiercely. *Victoria*.[124]

Chapter Two

KING EDWARD:
'FRIEND OF OUR POPE',
1901–1910

The Earl of Aberdeen presents his humble duty to the King and has the
honour to report that the condition of things in Ireland as a whole has
[for] some time past been quiet and satisfactory.
(Official report from Aberdeen, the Lord Lieutenant of Ireland,
to King Edward VII, June 9 1906.[1])

Let bygones be bygones ... I admire the man personally. He's just an
ordinary knockabout like you and me. He's fond of his glass of grog and
he's a bit of a rake perhaps, but he's a good sportsman.
(James Joyce on Edward VII, *Dubliners*, 1914)

When Albert Edward – known in his family as 'Bertie' – became King Edward VII in January 1901, the new monarch was warmly welcomed in Ireland. He represented such a change from Queen Victoria whose long tenure had carried many mournful memories. The 'high noon' of the Victorian empire had seemed to coincide, in Ireland, with famine, wretchedness, land wars and evictions.

'The Catholics of this country owe no debt of gratitude to Queen Victoria,' wrote the *Irish Catholic* newspaper (Dublin's leading Catholic voice, founded by T. D. Sullivan) upon the Queen's death. 'She never spoke one kindly word or displayed the least perception of the cruelty of the injustice under which they labour.' This was emphasising the negative in the Victorian century, but it was a view shared by many.[2]

Bertie was more popular, and always had been. He was thought of as a 'lad' – or, in the tactful expression employed by the *Irish Independent* 'a manly man' (meaning a ladies' man) – and that laddishness gave him a certain appeal to the Irish. The well-known London-Irish journalist and Nationalist parliamentarian T. P. O'Connor wrote, on Bertie's accession: 'The King has more friends in Ireland than perhaps he knows, for he is regarded as full of good feeling for Ireland.'[3]

It was widely believed that the new king was especially sympathetic to Ireland and that he favoured Irish Home Rule. It was also supposed that his pretty Danish wife, Queen Alexandra, who felt strongly about the Schleswig-Holstein question (in which Imperial Germany bullied a smaller and weaker Denmark), also identified with Ireland. Forgotten now was an ungallant remark, made decades previously in a Dublin Corporation debate, that the Danes had slain Brian Boru (in 1014!), and that Alexandra, as a Dane, must bear the stigma.[4]

It was especially believed that Bertie was pro-Catholic: so pro-Catholic, some imagined, that he was on the point of becoming a Roman Catholic, or might even have done so secretly. This was not so, but he was to show – notably just before his death – a veneration for Lourdes which was striking.

Albert Edward's popularity with the Irish was in part justified. He always meant well. He was given credit for bringing the Boer War to a close: just as monarchs are disproportionately blamed in disasters, so they are disproportionately praised in triumphs.[5] He wrote to several Prime Ministers of his 'deep interest' in Irish affairs. 'I would like to assist in making friends with the Irish,' he once wrote, 'who are excellent fellows at heart and the best soldiers in the world.'[6] His mother, alas, did not trust him with Irish affairs, or with any affairs of state.

Bertie was open to the suggestion – long favoured by Gladstone and always vetoed by Victoria – that he might take up a permanent royal residence in Ireland. And although it was a playful point, Bertie especially liked the Irish racecourses, particularly Punchestown, and never failed to spend a day at the races when in Dublin. The horse is a great unifier and, in Ireland, a great leveller: 'the Catholic, the Protestant, the Jew, the Presbyterian' are all described as mingling happily on the turf in a popular ballad called 'Galway Races'. More macabrely, it was said that 'all are equal on the turf – and under it'.

Bertie was so enamoured of Punchestown races in Co Kildare that Queen Victoria had tried, on at least one occasion, to halt an Irish visit for fear he would spend all his time at the racetrack. (Even one of Bertie's own lord lieutenants had thought his attachment to Punchestown 'infra dig'.)

Albert Edward's horses had won the Derby three times: with his beautiful bay, Persimmon, in 1896; with Persimmon's brother, Diamond Jubilee, in 1900; and once again in 1909 with Minoru – a famously exciting day at the races that saw the crowd in an ecstasy of joy. More ordinary men and women shared that pleasure with the monarch than, perhaps, anything else, and especially in Ireland. The King also endeared himself to the racing community by bestowing very large tips – sometimes as much as £500 – on jockeys and grooms.[7]

When the King visited the heart of Catholic Ireland – the ecclesiastical seminary at Maynooth – the clerical students adorned the college with Bertie's racing colours of purple, scarlet, and gold, cheering the sporting king all the while. This was an enormously jolly occasion, although it has been suggested that it was also a canny strategy by the then President of the college, Dr Daniel Mannix, to avoid flying the Union Jack. Proof once again that where national flags separate, the horse is ever a unifier.[8]

*

Bertie was of a genial temperament in most matters, with one single and significant exception – the subject of dress codes and regalia. On such he was a stickler, to an almost obsessive degree. He noticed every medal and decoration; he had three personal tailors and was known to change clothes up to 12 times a day.[9] On any other matter he was usually pleasantness itself.

He had the graceful gift of never turning a political issue into a personal dislike. He did not at all approve of Gladstone's politics for example, but, unlike his mother, he never displayed antipathy towards him. He never allowed politics to interfere with his kindly and courteous feelings for Prime Minister Gladstone. Gladstone's son had been Bertie's childhood playmate (one of the few non-royal or non-aristocratic children his over-protective parents would allow at Windsor) and that personal link seemed more significant to him than differences over Home Rule.

However, while his liking for Ireland was undoubtedly sincere, Bertie was not (as the Irish imagined) favourable towards Home Rule. This touches on a frequent misunderstanding in Anglo-Irish relations over the centuries: the English often mistook friendly feelings for 'loyalty' to the Crown, and the Irish repeatedly confused sympathy for the country and a liking for the people with support for Irish independence.

While a monarch may have no public politics – it is considered unconstitutional for the sovereign, or heir, to vote – all must have private preferences: and Albert Edward was privately Conservative. He thoroughly approved each time the House of Lords frustrated the will of the Commons in rejecting Irish Home Rule. And he fully supported his friend, the 8th Duke of Devonshire, who led the movement against Home Rule in the House of Lords.[10]

Devonshire, owner of the beautiful Lismore Castle in Co Waterford, was one of those English landlords who owned vast tracts of land in Ireland. Thanks to his ancestor, the ultra-Protestant Richard Boyle, Earl of Cork and Elizabethan settler, Devonshire was the possessor of 60,000 acres in Cork and Waterford at a time when many Irish farms consisted of less than 20 acres.[11] And Devonshire also had a personal reason for not ceding any ground to the notion of Irish independence: his brother, Lord Frederick Cavendish, had been one of the victims of the notorious 'Phoenix Park murders' in 1882, sliced to death with a surgeon's knife by political assailants.

The Duke was a strange, diffident man, detached in society, careless and aloof in appearance, but in his personal attachments a romantic, devoted to the turf, and esteemed as a trustworthy political administrator. He was a decent landlord, and generous to his Irish tenants, but always implacably opposed to anything that would damage the Union. He also believed that Irish Catholics were incapable of running an economy, and had no capacity for financial management – a common viewpoint amongst those of his ilk, and well disproved a century later.

In the Ireland of this Edwardian heyday there were 34 English landlords who owned over 100,000 Irish acres and they sat in, or were represented in, the House of Lords.[12]

The British union with Ireland was, to this class, sacrosanct. Bertie shared his class's values, while always maintaining his genial demeanour. He once debated monarchy versus Republicanism with the French arch-Republican – and arch-anti-clerical – Léon Gambetta. Although Gambetta had the upper hand in the debate – 'it is logical, Monsignor, that you should be a monarchist!' – the French Republican was charmed by Bertie's manners and they remained friends until death.[13]

On religious matters Bertie's reputation for tolerance was well-founded. For a man of his time and class, he was unusually liberal on questions of religion: so tolerant of Roman Catholics that he was dubbed 'Popish Ned' in Belfast. When visiting Connemara in 1903, the King was greeted with a banner proclaiming: 'King Edward – Friend of Our Pope.'[14]

It was reported in the *Irish Catholic* that, during his regular visits to Biarritz, the King had been seen visiting nearby Lourdes, and that he had raised his hat when a Catholic procession honouring the Blessed Virgin had passed by – a respect unknown in any previous English Protestant monarch.[15] In the early 1900s,

Catholic Maytime processions were still regarded as 'provocative' in parts of London, and until the 1890s had usually been banned.[16]

As a teenage Prince of Wales, Albert Edward had visited the Pope (the first heir to the British Throne to do so since the Reformation) and spent time in friendly discussion with Pius IX, both speaking in French. (Bertie was trilingual from an early age, speaking English, German and French: he always retained a very slight German nuance in pronouncing some English words.) As Prince, he met Pius four times over the years. Such visits were often courtesies rather than signals of special affinity. Conversations with the Pontiff were limited – by the Prince of Wales' nervous British minders – to pleasantries, and possibly to conversations about liturgical regalia and the protocol of ceremonial dress.

By personal religious inclination, Bertie was, according to his official biographer, Sir Sydney Lee, 'a cheerful Protestant'. He was also an enthusiastic Freemason – which again included a thrilling element of ritual, ceremony and dressing up. But Bertie just did not see why belonging to one religion should make you hate another. He had established his dislike of religious 'sectarianism' as a young man on a Canadian visit, when he had been embarrassed by the over-enthusiastic reception from members of the Orange Order calling out various insults against the Pope and Roman Catholics.[17]

In maturity, two of his closest friends were Roman Catholics. These were the Marques de Soveral, the aristocratic Portuguese envoy at the Court of St James, and the German-born Ernest Cassel, who had been born Jewish, but converted to Catholicism for the love of his wife. He still remained Catholic after she died.

Cassel was a fabulously rich financier and philanthropist whose railroads and banks stretched from America and Mexico to the Nile. He had a splendid art collection, and gave away vast sums to charity, health, and welfare. But his adored wife died young, as did his beloved only daughter, from tuberculosis.

He thereafter lavished his affection and fortune on his granddaughter, Edwina Ashley, who married Lord Mountbatten. In a bitter twist of fate Mountbatten was assassinated by the IRA in

1979, as a continuing gesture of Republican hostility against the symbol of England's Crown.

In the company of his cronies Cassel and Soveral, Albert Edward would spend time every year, from the middle of August to about 10 September, at the Bohemian spa of Marienbad. As the name implies ('Mary's Spring') Marienbad was originally a holy place of healing dedicated to the Virgin Mary, and it was run by the Catholic monks of nearby Tepl.

On one occasion, in 1903, Bertie told the Abbot that he would like to attend a special Mass for the Emperor Franz Joseph of Austria, celebrated on August 18.[18] He did so, and continued to do so each year, wearing the Order of the Garter and an Austrian order; or sometimes dressed in the uniform of an Austrian hussar regiment of which he was honorary colonel. He afterwards made friends with Abbot Helmer, dined with him, and invited him to London.

As king, Edward was the first British monarch since the Reformation to attend a Catholic Mass in London. He had no sense of taboo about entering a Catholic church, and did so publicly for a Requiem Mass – at St James's, Spanish Place – for the murdered King Carlos of Portugal in 1908; this was despite the Cabinet specifically advising against the gesture.[19]

He also repaired each April to the ravishing Atlantic resort of Biarritz on the Basque coast of France. It was during his Biarritz sojourns, reportedly, that he was wont to visit nearby Lourdes, the place of pilgrimage where St Bernadette had had an apparition of the Blessed Virgin in 1859.

So it was unsurprising – and a welcome signal to the Irish – that the first and immediate controversy that occurred in the new King Edward's reign was over the knotty matter of the coronation oath.

*

Albert Edward, aged 59, became King Edward VII upon his mother's death in January 1901. He had served a long apprenticeship as an increasingly stout Prince of Wales – as king he weighed 16 stone. Although he was no intellectual (the politician Sir Charles Dilke thought him a blockhead), and neither he, nor his wife Alexandra, was ever seen to read a book, he had accumulated a certain wisdom, sometimes as a consequence of youthful scrapes and follies.

He was shrewd about people and, within certain political arenas (such as foreign affairs), was quite skilled at creating a positive climate for negotiation. As king and emperor he also found himself at the apex of the greatest empire ever – the Union flag prevailed over a quarter of the globe – and a very great diversity of peoples. For his coronation, Claridges and the Savoy were said to be 'stuffed with Maharajahs' gathered for the occasion.

One of Albert Edward's first concerns, upon his accession, was the wording of the Protestant affirmation that he was due to recite for the opening of Parliament. He strongly objected to this avowal and sought to have it altered.

Following the Bill of Rights of 1689, a new sovereign was expected to make a declaration from the throne: to affirm that the Bishop of Rome had no jurisdiction in the realm of England, and to repudiate, specifically, the Catholic doctrine of transubstantiation (that the bread and wine becomes the body and blood of Jesus Christ during the consecration of the Mass). The sovereign was then to state that 'the invocation or adoration of the Virgin Mary or any other saint, and the Sacrifice of the Mass as they are now used in the Church of Rome are superstitious and idolatrous'.

This was to be followed by the formal statement that the denunciation of the practices of the Church of Rome was made 'without any evasion, equivocation, or mental reservation whatever, and without any dispensation past or future or possibility of it from the Pope or any other authority.'[20]

The new king thought the wording of this formula offensive to his many Roman Catholic subjects throughout the Empire. Possibly because of his friendship with the monks at Marienbad, he particularly disliked the insult to the Marian cult, of which his experience had been benign. Surely, he argued, it would be quite sufficient for him to state that he was a sincere Protestant, that he would defend the Protestant faith and succession, and leave it at that? It was not necessary to go into doctrinal detail in rebuffing others' creeds.

He took up the matter with the Tory Prime Minister, Lord Salisbury, than whom there could scarcely have been a less sympathetic listener. Salisbury was a man of many contradictions: a devoted family man who practised permissive child-rearing long before Doctor Spock; but, for all that, a scion of the Cecil family, which had, since the reign of Elizabeth I, kept England Protestant. The Elizabethan Cecils had been priest-hunters on a savage scale and no friends to Ireland. Salisbury had compared the Irish to 'Hottentots' (by which he meant unmanageably primitive), and spoke contemptuously of the 'ignorant peasantry of Ireland.'[21]

Salisbury took a firm line against Bertie's pleas for change. Constitutionally, he emphasised, the King must enunciate the full formula, repudiating the superstitions and idolatry of the Church of Rome. It was, said the arch-Tory Prime Minister, an 'obligation'. Not to do so would create no end of trouble. It would arouse 'the Protestant party' in the country.[22] Laxity over Protestant principles of monarchy might even open the door to a Stuart claimant.

The King countered that not only was it offensive to his Catholic subjects all over the globe, but it was outdated: 'not in accordance with public thinking at the present day'.

Salisbury then rather disingenuously said that he agreed with the *spirit* of the King's thinking (doubtful). And yet it was clear that he was simultaneously conspiring in cabinet against the King's wishes, arguing that Parliament would not accept the change, and that it would require legislation that would generally provoke trouble around the country.

Any number of obstructions were put in the way of altering the formula of the Protestant affirmation – and when a king of England clashes with his political masters, the constitutional monarch will always cede the argument.

A British monarch forever has before him the example of Charles I, decapitated by Parliament to make that very point. In the end, Bertie agreed to go through with the established declaration, since he saw no way around it, constitutionally. But it was observed that he said the words, on 14 February 1901, with such an unhappy countenance and in such a low voice that he could scarcely be heard.

The Catholic weekly *The Tablet* thanked the King for the 'rare delicacy and considerateness with which he discharged a hateful duty.'[23]

The controversy was not lost on Ireland. 'It is generally recognised', editorialised the *Irish Catholic*, 'that the King would gladly have been spared the horrible profanity which an antique bigotry imposed on him ...' There was recognition throughout the Catholic world of 'his evident desire to discharge his task with as little offence as possible.'

This was not just a point of principle, but a very pertinent practical issue in Ireland in the early 1900s. The *Irish Catholic* was particularly exercised about the way in which Catholics still found it difficult to advance in the field of employment in Ireland, let alone in Britain. In the wider British Empire, where there were fewer obstacles to their careers, opportunities for Catholics were improving, but in Ireland itself there was resentment among a rising Catholic middle class that its advance was barred in many areas of work.

In January 1901 more than 20 major insurance companies in Dublin apparently had no Catholic employees at all, including the Norwich Union, the Sun, the Guardian, the Commerical Union, the Royal Exchange, the Manchester and the Alliance. The Stock Exchange had hardly any Catholics, even as clerks; and Catholics were 'scandalously under-represented' in employment directed by the Crown.

Long lists were published in the *Irish Catholic* – now owned by William Martin Murphy and the Irish Independent Group – of senior posts governing Ireland held exclusively by Protestants, including Lord Lieutenant of Ireland, Chief Secretary, Under-Secretary, and Assistant Under-Secretary. Of the 56 members of the Irish Privy Council, there were only 7 Catholics. Of the 28 members of the Lord Lieutenant's households, there were 26 Protestants and 2 Catholics. And so on, down a detailed naming of official positions in which Catholics were under-represented, in what the newspaper called 'the land that God gave them'. The English government in Ireland, concluded the paper, had a persistent record of not engaging Catholics.[24]

It was not the intention to 'strike a sectarian note of personal acrimony': the newspaper believed that 'the majority of the Protestant gentlemen are quite friendly to the Catholic cause and are desirous of rendering full justice to the majority of their fellow-countrymen'. But the facts spoke for themselves: there was widespread discrimination against Catholics in jobs and Crown appointments.[25]

Indeed, either beknownst or unbeknownst to the journalists making this point, senior civil servants in the Irish administration were urging the government to promote only 'sound Unionists' (which usually meant loyal Protestants) to significant jobs. As Chief Secretary to Ireland in 1905, the ultra-Unionist Walter Long was emphatic about the preferment of loyalist Unionists, and the exclusion of Nationalists.[26]

All this was flowing into the growing cultural nationalism that would increase during Edward's short, historically rich, and often glittering reign. The Darwinian struggle for dominion was, to a considerable extent, about *jobs*.

Soon after his accession to the throne, the question arose as to when the new king might pay a state visit to Ireland. Bertie had first visited Ireland as a 7-year-old with his parents in 1849, looking very engaging in a child's sailor suit. In 1860, just before his father's death, he had been billeted at the Curragh, where he had almost certainly lost his virginity to Nellie Clifden, an actress, described as 'a vivacious, cheerfully promiscuous and amusing girl who was also unfortunately most indiscreet'. (She later migrated to London, had some luck on the London stage, and then disappeared into the mists of history.)[27]

This adventure persuaded his parents that Albert Edward needed to be married off (pronto!) to a suitable Protestant princess, marriage being St Paul's 'remedy against fornication'. After several candidates were considered, Alexandra of Denmark was selected: an uncomplicated, sweet-looking, and family-minded girl who had been brought up with Scandinavian simplicity. A very fine girls' school in Dublin, Alexandra College, would be founded in her honour.

Bertie had had two successful visits to Dublin in the 1860s: the first in 1865 for the Second Dublin Exhibition, to promote Irish industry. The moderate Nationalist newspaper, the *Freeman's Journal*, wrote on that occasion: 'Throughout the city for the past week the topic of general conversation was the expected visit of the Prince of Wales.'[28]

As Prince of Wales and Earl of Dublin he had an escort of the 10th Hussars as he drove in open carriage from Westland Row (now Pearse Station) along D'Olier Street and Abbey Street, hearing the cheers of the crowds and seeing banners entwining shamrocks and Prince of Wales plumes, bearing such messages as 'Our Future King, God Bless Him'.

On the subsequent visit, in 1868, this time accompanied by the charming Princess Alexandra (she had been pregnant previously, and unable to travel), his welcome was rapturous, and this time the *Freeman's Journal* said that 'every street has put on an aspect of gaiety – every citizen has assumed the air of cheerfulness and good will … to-day [because of] the illustrious visitors.' The newspaper described the Irish people as 'Instinctively monarchical, hereditarily loyal, lovers of order and good judgement', as they enthused over Bertie and Alix 'in the spring tide of their youth'.[29]

Again, there was much pageantry on their arrival at Kingstown, with the thunder of guns and the band of the Grenadier Guards, which had been his regiment in his days at the Curragh.

Bertie was, on this visit, to be installed as a Knight of St Patrick: this was thought a good thing, although it was noted by the *Freeman's Journal* that very few Catholics were ever given this award. As he loved decorations, he was delighted about the Patrick, and the ceremony duly took place at St Patrick's Church of Ireland Cathedral in Dublin. The spectacle was reported to be especially magnificent as dean, clergy, members of the official

CELL 87 FOR MISS ERIN

50 YEARS OF PROSPERITY AND GENTLE RULE

JUBILEE COERCION BILL

EVICTIONS

CLOSURE

POVERTY

"REJOICE, OH! GREATLY."

Erin having deposited her Decoration at the Shrine of "LOYALTY" retires (on invitation) to an Imperial Institu... to celebrate the Queen's Jubilee.

Erin with Victoria: Victoria's reign from 1837 to 1901 included many sorrowful and distressful times for Ireland: the Queen alternatively loved and loathed the Irish, and feelings were fully reciprocated. © National Library of Ireland

Victoria in Ireland 1901: After a long reign, and a turbulent love-hate
relationship with the Irish, Victoria's last visit, just before her death, was met
with great warmth and she was deeply touched. © The Picture Desk

Edward VII (1902–1910) was popular with the majority of the Irish: he was believed to be pro-Catholic – taunted as 'Popish Ned' in Belfast – and his passion for the turf was much appreciated. He brought one of the first Daimlers to Ireland.

DUBLIN METROPOLITAN POLICE.

DETECTIVE DEPARTMENT,
EXCHANGE COURT,
DUBLIN, 8th July, 1907.

STOLEN

From a Safe in the Office of Arms, Dublin Castle, during the past month, supposed by means of a false key.

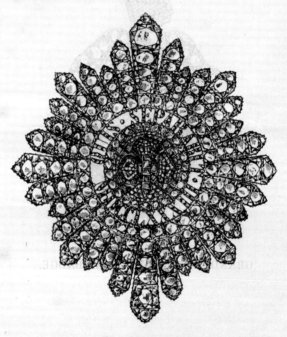

GRAND MASTER'S DIAMOND STAR.

A Diamond Star of the Grand Master of the Order of St. Patrick composed of brilliants (Brazilian stones) of the purest water, 4⅝ by 4¼ inches, consisting of eight points, four greater and four lesser, issuing from a centre enclosing a cross of rubies and a trefoil of emeralds surrounding a sky blue enamel circle with words, "Quis Separabit MDCCLXXXIII." in rose diamonds engraved on back. Value about £14,000.

Taken from a Dublin Metropolitan Police Poster

Edward's cheerful relationship with Ireland – in an age of optimism and growing prosperity – was soured by the famous theft of the Irish Crown Jewels in 1907, now thought to have been linked to a gay scandal (the jewels were never recovered). Courtesy of the Director of the National Archives of Ireland, Ref NAI, csorp 1913/18 119.

George V (1910–1935) was the last King of the United Kingdom
of Britain and Ireland. His fabulously ceremonial State visit to
Dublin in 1911, with his wife Mary, was the last time a British
monarch set foot in the Irish capital. © Getty Images

Queen Mary at Maynooth: It was considered wise for British monarchs to
visit Maynooth, then the powerhouse of Catholic Ireland. Cardinal Mannix
– seen here with Mary in one of her signature hats – was anti-British, but
had diplomatically flown the King's racing colours for Edward VII, and
courteously received George and Mary. © National Library of Ireland

Stamp: George V was a dedicated stamp-collector; and as the British
Empire covered a quarter of the globe, his image appeared on the stamps
of many lands. In 1922, his image on Irish stamps was superimposed
with 'Irish Free State' (Saorstát Éireann). © Courtesy of An Post

1932: The Eucharistic Congress of 1932 was a huge event in Dublin, and for the Irish nation. The
sumptuous ceremonial of Mother Church was now replacing that of the Crown and politicians duly
showed deference to the power of the Holy See, which they regarded as somehow Irish. © Corbis

1932: The arrival of the Papal Legate at Dun Laoghaire followed the pattern set by previous royal visits. Here Irish state aircraft escort the Legate's arrival by flying in cruciform formation (shaping a Christian cross aerially). © National Library of Ireland

1932: A special cavalry regiment, the Mounted Escort (also known as the Blue Hussars), decked out in blue tunic with gold frogging, and blue and gold breeches, was devised for the Eucharistic Congress: alas, the regiment was subsequently disbanded and considered too extravagant for the Irish state which now underlined the virtues of plain living and folk traditions. © John Conway

households, and Knights of the Order entered St Patrick's to a flourish of trumpets.[30]

Bertie tactfully insisted on visiting the Mater Misericordiae Hospital, a Catholic foundation that had just been established in Dublin by the tireless Cardinal Cullen. Albert Edward had met Cullen in Rome in 1859, where he had insisted on visiting the Irish College, again despite warnings from official sources that this would arouse anti-Papist reaction in Britain. That Rome visit occurred on St Patrick's Day and Cardinal Cullen had cheerfully stuck a bunch of shamrock into the Prince of Wales' hat.

As the Prince of Wales entered the Mater hospital lobby, he was pleased to behold a portrait of himself, and the Empress Eugenie of France. The French empress was much liked by Bertie, who had known her since he was 14. For Cardinal Cullen, she had the added benefit of being a Catholic sovereign (if not for long – another French Republic would shortly replace Napoleon III and Eugenie). Cullen was not a monarchist, as such, though he did believe in 'constitutional authority' – an acceptance of the correct authority as laid down by St Paul.[31]

As Albert Edward departed from Dublin on 27 April 1868, there was an assassination attempt on his brother, Alfred, Duke of Edinburgh, in Clontarf, near Sydney, Australia. The would-be assailant was the Fenian Henry James O'Farrell who cried, 'I'm a Fenian. God save Ireland!' as he was captured.[32] Alfred received a severe wound to the back. O'Farrell was seeking to avenge the Manchester Martyrs, but he was tried (in Australia) and executed for the attempted assassination. Daniel O'Sullivan, as Mayor of Cork, praised Henry James O'Farrell as a man 'imbued with as noble and patriotic feelings as Larkin, Allen and O'Brien'. Queen Victoria was incensed: as would any would-be victim's mother, no doubt.

But, as has already been noted, this was the flavour of times to come. Royal relations with Ireland were ever more strained as the Victorian era wore on.

Bertie and Alix visited Ireland again in 1871 and in 1875, and on these two later occasions the welcome was marked by more dissent. At Curraghmore, near the Marquis of Waterford's residence, 'ugly feelings' were shown to the royals. (Lord Waterford was the possessor of 100,000 acres of fine land in a land-starved country.) At Mallow railway station in north Cork, three Nationalist politicians, John Redmond, William O'Brien and John O'Connor, led a crowd seeking to insult the Prince and Princess of Wales. At Cork, Limerick and Tralee the royal pair were met with demonstrations that included flags bearing skulls and crossbones, and black flags fluttering, all to indicate hostility to the Crown.[33]

Bertie showed composure in the face of an unusual wave of unpopularity, and said, before his departure, that he looked forward to another visit to Ireland in the near future. But he chose not to return for the rest of the century, and was heard to speak disparagingly against Irish Home Rule Members of Parliament, calling them 'abominable agitators'[34]

Thus, soon after Bertie inherited the crown, the Lord Lieutenant of Ireland, the Earl of Cadogan (who was considered responsive to Irish sensibilities) urged the King to come back to Ireland. As king, Bertie was willing: he wanted to make a fresh start, and besides, Ireland in the 1900s was a much calmer land than it had been in the mid-1880s. Poor Parnell was dead (in 1891) and lamented in James Joyce's *Portrait of the Artist* as 'my dead king!' The reports sent to Windsor Castle from the authorities in Dublin repeatedly underlined the satisfactory condition of Ireland in the early 1900s. Thus Cadogan pressed for King Edward to come to Ireland on a rising tide – although still worrying about the lure of Punchestown races.

But then there was the matter of the Boer War. King Edward was accustomed to protests against the conduct of the Boer War each time he went to Paris, and he was aware how unpopular it was on the Continent. But he was nevertheless furious at reports that Irish MPs in the House of Commons had cheered a British defeat. There was a difference between dissent and bad form.

(Later it was claimed that this was a misunderstanding: the Irish members were not gloating over casualties among the British – and Irish – troops. [35])

The Boer War, which had begun in 1899, had created deep divisions among the Irish, who fought on both sides. Nationalist Ireland, led by Arthur Griffith (who would become the Sinn Féin founder in 1905), was wholly with the 'gallant little Boers' (although neither Catholics nor Jews – let alone blacks – could vote in the Boer territories of South Africa). By contrast, much of mainstream (and particularly working-class) Dublin fought for the Crown.

But the Boer War was brought to an end. The British Empire triumphed, but lost face and credit, and it had been demonstrated that small nations could take on great empires in a challenging manner. Yet Bertie was often credited with assisting the peace process, as a 'peacekeeping' king.

As it happened, Bertie's first visit to Ireland as king did not take place until 1903, since ill health intervened. It turned out to be rather nice timing, for the King and Queen's official arrival in Dublin (in July 1903) coincided with the third reading in the House of Commons of George Wyndham's Land Purchase Bill.

This was (along with Lloyd George's introduction of the old age pension in 1908–9) the most beneficial piece of legislation ever brought to Ireland during the long centuries of British rule.

George Wyndham, who was Chief Secretary for Ireland* from 1900 to 1905, [36] was a Conservative romantic, yet a descendant of the Irish rebel leader Lord Edward Fitzgerald, and a cousin of Lord Alfred Douglas, Oscar Wilde's lover. He also admired Patrick Pearse.

The King felt somewhat patronised by Wyndham, who was undoubtedly his intellectual superior; but, as ever, Bertie always showed perfect geniality towards his Chief Secretary. And Wyndham ensured that the royal visit in 1903 went swimmingly.

Wyndham, following his mentor A. J. Balfour, carried through a mission that meant a good deal to the Irish peasant, for he

---

*The Chief Secretary was the political head of the British administration in Dublin (also a member of the Cabinet); the Lord Lieutenant or Viceroy was the ceremonial representative of the Crown.

devised a Land Act that (not unlike Margaret Thatcher's wheeze to sell council houses to their occupiers) made it possible for the land tenant to purchase a farm for which he had been resentfully paying rent for years.

The radically improving Wyndham Land Acts were to achieve a legendary status, following, as they did, various local government and land reforms commenced earlier. John Redmond, the Irish Parliamentary Party leader (at this time often critical of British proposals) paid a generous tribute to George Wyndham, saying that the Wyndham measures had brought about a 'condition of the public mind ... more at peace and more filled with hope than ever before'.[37]

The drafting of legislation is an art in itself, and this legislation was cleverly crafted; Wyndham had worked very hard on it. Landlords were to be compensated when they chose to sell their smallholdings, so that not only was there reduced resistance among the landlord class, but some were grateful for the bonus that allowed them to repair their estates.

In the six years following the Act 287,000 purchases were made by former tenants. The social impact was tremendous: people started to invest in their homes, and take a pride in them. Agricultural husbandry flourished. Women felt a new self-esteem as chatelaines of their farmhouses, now deemed worthy of devolopment from their previous condition as 'tumbledown cabins'. The Catholic Church was warmly approving: such measures, they believed, would improve home and family life and decrease habits of public drinking.

Edward VII, preparing to append his signature to such an enlightened piece of legislation, could hardly have chosen a better or more optimistic moment to come to Ireland as king.[38] And then, as luck would have it, Edward and Alexandra sailed to Ireland on the very day that Pope Leo XIII died, on 20 July 1903, aged 93, from tuberculosis he had contracted while tending pilgrims to Rome.

*

The death of Leo XIII also turned out to be an opportunity for Bertie to show courtesy and magnanimity. Leo was a reforming Pope in one sense: he had issued the celebrated *Rerum Novarum* encyclical in 1891 to support workers' rights, a just wage, trade unions and social justice. He had also much enhanced the prestige of the Catholic church universally, and, not very ecumenically, had declared Anglican orders null and void.

Bertie did not seem to hold this against him: as a king must defend monarchy, so a Pope must defend the papacy. He and the Pope had met several times and they had conversed in a friendly manner.

As soon as Leo's death was announced, the King immediately sent a thoughtful text of condolence, through the Irish Cardinal Logue, for the College of Cardinals in Rome.

This action was warmly applauded in Ireland. George Wyndham heard a little Irish girl saying, 'I am so glad that we may love the King now because he spoke so nicely about the Pope.'[39]

'With his usual tact and sympathy', wrote the *Freeman's Journal*, 'his Majesty divined the national mood of mixed feelings: hope from his influence in an exalted station, and sorrow in a bereavement that in a Catholic land, unsurpassed in its long loyalty to the Chair of St Peter, goes to every heart.'[40]

The Irish newspapers were a study in semiotics. Sharing splash headlines were welcoming greetings for the King, and black-rimmed mourning for the Pope: in the Nationalist papers, the Pope's attention just a mite greater. Admittedly, a deathbed scene is often dramatic.

As Bertie and Alix arrived in Dublin the crowds thronged the streets in their hundreds of thousands. George Wyndham, accompanying the royal party, could scarcely believe the joyous scenes he witnessed:

> we drove, mostly at a walk, through 11 miles of bunting and cheering crowds, growing denser and more vociferous. It culminated in the triangular space bounded by Trinity College and the Old Parliament House [now the Bank of Ireland]. ... Every window and housetop was packed. The Bands took up 'God Save the King' for mile after mile.

Dublin women held up their babies to see Bertie and Alix, shouting 'God *bless* the King'. The greatest welcome for the royals came from the poor people living in the inner city. In Sackville-O'Connell Street, Queen Alexandra turned to the Chief Secretary and said, moved with emotion, 'the poorer they are, Mr Wyndham, the louder they cheer'.[41] Wyndham noted that the intense, even hysterical, reception given to their Majesties by the poor of the North Circular Road brought tears to the Queen's eyes: and a lump to his own throat.

It was in that true tradition of the *céad mile fáilte* of Irish lore. And, in an age before cinema or television, there was the excitement of pageantry and spectacle – vividly evoked in James Plunkett's novel of the period, *Strumpet City.*

Nationalist feelings certainly existed and were displayed: the Nationalist Lord Mayor of Dublin, Tim Harrington, said it was time to stamp out 'flunkeyism and toadyism'. He gave his word to Maud Gonne that he would not meet the King – Maud claimed that Edward had *supported* the anti-Catholic oath – which, in truth, had made him so unhappy.[42] But among the general populace, and the more moderate Nationalists, there was a friendly spirit of welcome.

Bertie held a levee at Dublin Castle, which was attended by the Catholic Archbishop of Dublin, Dr Walsh, known to be an Irish Nationalist. Dr Walsh approved of the King's interest in housing for the poor – as illustrated by Edward and Alexandra's visit to the working-class dwellings in Dublin, recently built by the Guinness Trust. (The King had sat on a Royal Commission of Inquiry on public housing, along with Cardinal Manning, the English Cardinal who had once been a married Anglican priest).

It was also on this royal trip to Ireland, while visiting the Maynooth seminary for the training of Catholic priests, that the clerical students charmingly displayed a picture of the King's great Derby winner Persimmon, and adorned the college with the King's racing colours of purple, scarlet, and gold, giving him a rousing welcome. Three archbishops were present – indeed, never since the reign of James II were so many Irish Catholic senior ecclesiastics gathered together to welcome a British monarch.[43]

And then, in a final winning act of respect for the late Pope, Bertie cancelled the jollities that were due to be held at the Theatre Royal in Dublin. But he still attended the Phoenix Park races – as did everyone else.

The sovereigns sailed on to Belfast on 25 July, thence to Derry and Buncrana, and after that to Connemara where they proceeded with their tour of the west. 'The Royal Yacht arrived at Killary Harbour, where a nine-car motorcade, comprising two Daimlers and seven Panhards, were waiting to carry the Royal party through Connemara,' writes Kathleen Villiers-Tuthill, the Connemara historian.[44] It was the first time a British monarch had set foot in Connemara, and was a source of wonder and excitement. The King and Queen were accompanied by the Earl and Countess of Dudley (Dudley had succeeded Cadogan in 1903), and by Sir Henry Robinson, the very Unionist civil servant who recorded it all in his memoir. Sir Horace Plunkett and Princess Victoria (Bertie and Alix's spinster daughter) were also among the cortege.

The motor cars in which the party travelled were an object of great fascination – the first motor car had only appeared in Ireland in 1898, and Lord Dudley had brought the first motor car to the west of Ireland in 1901. (The Dudleys were the proud possessors of a fine Panhard et Levassor, and Sir Henry, an enthusiastic car buff, had a Cadillac.) The King himself favoured Daimlers.

The royal party visited Bundorragha, a village near Killary, going on to Delphi, and then to Leenane; in the last village some trouble with the King's car provided another side-show for the locals.

At Recess, a hundred horsemen on Connemara ponies made their appearance for the King and Queen, calling themselves the 'Connemara Cavalry'; a 'good woman' petitioned the Queen for clemency for her imprisoned husband and apparently obtained it.[45] At the village of Tully, the party met with the welcoming banner to Edward VII – 'Friend of Our Pope'. At Killary, a priest had kissed the King's ring, 'no doubt feeling that he could not show him less deference than he paid to a bishop'. Following the priest's example, a 'burly peasant' came forward and did likewise.

A very old man, somewhat confused by all this, cried, 'Three cheers for King Henry the Sixth'. Robinson's memoir is full of would-be comical 'Oirish' episodes, and yet the Connemara visit clearly was a very merry jaunt.[46] The royal party then proceeded to Kerry and Cork and departed from Ireland on August 3.

The royal visit had passed off 'without a single unpleasant incident', reported the *Freeman's Journal*, 'just shorn of its gaiety by the death of the Pope.'[47] The newspaper thought the King had also grasped the fact that the Irish aspired to improve their country through self-reliance and opportunity, rather than through English benevolence.

The King himself said that he was 'deeply touched by the kindness and goodwill' shown by the people. 'Our experience on previous visits had, indeed, prepared us for the traditional welcome of a warm-hearted race. But our expectations have been exceeded.' Wherever they went in the country, he said, they were greeted with 'loyalty and affection'.

There had been dissenters, to be sure. Maud Gonne – now Maud Gonne MacBride, after her (ill-fated) marriage to the pro-Boer War veteran John MacBride – had arranged another protest, as she had during Victoria's visits. She denounced Bertie as 'the English king', although in truth she was rather more English than he was. W. B. Yeats, under Maud's influence, had also objected to the presence of the British royals, although in a somewhat two-faced way, saying one thing to one group and another to another.[48] And the corporation of Dublin had voted not to give the King a 'loyal address' of welcome – not until Ireland had Home Rule. (James Joyce's short story 'Ivy Day in the Committee Room', in *Dubliners*, is about the political canvassing around this matter.)[49]

Other Nationalists were more nuanced. The influential founder of *The Leader*, D. P. Moran, an energetic campaigner for an 'Irish-Ireland', thought there was no harm in acknowledging the King, especially if it would enhance prosperity – he recognised the brand value of a monarch in promoting trade.[50]

And there were 82 'loyal addresses' – from a range of organisations – presented to the King during his visit. The most impressive, Wyndham thought, was the address signed by 1,200 Dublin jarveys, and presented by two car-men (taxi-drivers, in effect) of their number. They presented their good wishes with a charm that delighted the royal party: 'they had not put on their Sunday best, but their best ordinary clothes, scrupulously brushed. They never faltered and invented something between a bow and a curtsey that seemed exactly appropriate.'[51]

As Bertie and Alix sailed away, from Queenstown–Cobh, an old woman on the quay cried, 'Come back, Ah! Ye will come back', and the cry was echoed down the little streets around the harbour.

*

Many observers believed that this successful royal visit in 1903 would set the seal upon a better relationship between Britain and Ireland. The country had quietened down a great deal – only Co Clare still experienced the continuing 'agrarian outrages' that had been such a common feature of the 1880s. Moreover, an early proto-type of the 'Celtic Tiger' economy was starting up in the 1900s: the pursuit of prosperity and investment.

Horace Plunkett, sometime Member of Parliament and crusading agricultural reformer (a man of diligent devotion to the country, but often flawed judgement), wrote to the King to say how much he had spread good Anglo-Irish relations through-out the land. The King had shown himself 'not only the people's leader, but that he is in real sympathy with them: that he felt for them in their sorrow when they lost the head of their church and that he went to extraordinary exertions in order to see for himself the darker side of their poverty.'

There was, said Sir Horace, a 'general belief' that His Majesty had exercised his personal influence in getting the Land Bill through Parliament: 'I have gained the impression that no king has been as popular among the majority of the Irish as is His Majesty since the days of James II [the hapless loser at the Boyne].'[52]

No doubt Bertie left a benign feeling behind him in the Ireland of 1903, but Sir Horace might have been wiser to heed de Tocqueville's warning that optimistic times become revolutionary times: in other words, revolutions happen when people are feeling confident, not when they are dejected.

The brief Edwardian age was a time of rapid change and, indeed, constant excitements: strikes, revolutions, assassinations, aggressive feminism, radicalism, cultural change. And Ireland was very much affected by the radical movements that were so much part of this period.

The King next visited Dublin in July 1904 to inaugurate the laying of the foundations for the imposing Royal College of Science in Merrion Street (now the very splendid Department of the Taoiseach). Increasingly the press was affected by Irish cultural nationalism. More material in the Irish language was appearing in the newspapers and, although no real discourtesy was shown to the King, there was a cooling.

Moreover the Nationalist movements, which had been a minority element, were moving into the mainstream, rather in the way that, little by little, the radicals of the 1960s gradually infiltrated and came to dominate mainstream values in later decades.

When the King appeared at the fabulous old Theatre Royal in Dublin (lamentably knocked down by brutal property developers in 1963) for a performance of Shakespeare's *Richard II*, it was observed that only a 'very small proportion of the audience' joined in when 'God Save the King' struck up.

Queen Alexandra was much admired for her beauty – she remained remarkably youthful-looking even into her sixties, wearing make-up at a time when only actresses and fast women usually did so. It was also observed that, in truth, the King was rather 'commonplace' in his appearance.[53]

His welcome by the general populace was, as ever, hospitable, but it was significant that prominent Catholic priests and even bishops were now more likely to be openly critical of the Crown. At a meeting of the United Irish League (a Nationalist organisation gaining ground at this time) a member called Mr Thomas Barry put forward a resolution that 'we condemn as foolish and unpatriotic the policy of presenting addresses to the King. Royalty did not confer any advantage to this country.'

The priest who was chairing the meeting, the Revd M. B. Kennedy of Fermoy, was in full agreement: while he 'did not want to be discourteous to the King, yet the resolution commended itself.' People should respect the King personally, said Father Kennedy, but abhor English rule, which was 'a record of despair and beggary to this suffering nation.'[54]

The Church had generally been prudent in its endorsement of Nationalism (and always wary of *revolutionary* Nationalism), but it too was feeling the undercurrent of a rising cultural Nationalism, with increasing numbers of priests joining the Gaelic League for the promotion of the Irish language and culture. The Bishop of Kilmore, Dr Boylan, concurred with Father Kennedy, and urged continued Nationalist pressure on the Crown. 'No reform was ever granted except as the effect of vigorous and constant agitation,' he stated.[55]

There was also some general grumbling that the promises of London, both in the progress of the Land Purchase Act and in the development of education, had not yielded enough. This was not quite fair, since steady social progress was indeed being made, and some of the problems with setting up a Catholic university could be ascribed to the Catholic Church's determination to control education, and to obstruct any form of religiously integrated university.

The 1904 visit by King Edward is now better remembered in literature than in history,[56] since the Lord Lieutenant of the time, the popular Lord Dudley, occupies three pages of James Joyce's *Ulysses*, set in June 1904. 'William Humble, earl of Dudley, and Lady Dudley, accompanied by lieutenant colonel Hesseltine, drove out after luncheon from the viceregal lodge...' begins a passage in the 'Odyssey' section, about a third of the way through the great saga.

Lord and Lady Dudley's progress through the various parts of central Dublin are described, as some onlookers salute and some do not. Lady Dudley also appears in an earlier section of the book. She was born into a Quaker family and concerned herself with many good works, notably launching the 'Lady Dudley nurses' who were much esteemed, especially in the west of Ireland. The

Dudleys were to part in 1912 and the Countess would die in her beloved Connemara, in 1920, in a swimming accident.

Lord Dudley was tall, lame (from an accident at Eton as a schoolboy) and entertained lavishly, especially when royalty visited. Eunan O'Halpin, the Irish historian, describes him as 'woolly', but he was well-liked in Ireland and was regarded as privately having 'irrepressible Home Rule sentiments', which partly pleased Nationalists while much irking Unionists.[57]

Dudley was on excellent terms with King Edward. His mother, Georgiana, a noted beauty in her time (painted by Millais) had been a favourite of Bertie's as a young Prince of Wales: she had almost certainly been his mistress. Small world!

Dudley arranged a very grand dinner for the King and Queen with the Iveaghs at St Stephen's Green (the house is now the Department of Foreign Affairs, and a great ornament to the Irish state, by the gift of Lord Iveagh); and then a rather picaresque trip to Kilkenny, where the royal party stayed with the Ormondes at Kilkenny Castle, although not without mishaps.

*

In 1905 the trends that would dominate Irish political and cultural life over the twentieth century were well-established. In the North of Ireland, the Ulster Unionist Council held its first meeting, and successfully drove from office the Hibernophile George Wyndham. (He later had a nervous breakdown – largely, it was said, brought on by trying to reconcile Nationalist and Unionist Ireland – and died unexpectedly in a Paris hotel in 1913.) In Dublin the Gaelic League was ever expanding, and the Nationalist organisation founded by Arthur Griffith was named 'Sinn Féin' by Máire Butler, who was (rather surprisingly) a cousin of Sir Edward Carson.[58]

The first resolution passed by Sinn Féin was 'that the people of Ireland are a free people, and that no law made without their authority or consent is, or can ever be, binding on their conscience.' Sinn Féin claimed that the patronage of the Crown, centred on Dublin Castle, encouraged snobbery and title-hunting, which was undoubtedly true; although no social change has as yet managed to delete the snobbery gene from the human condition. At the start, Sinn Féin was a non-violent, cultural movement as well as a political one: my own grandmother, a schoolteacher from Connemara, joined Sinn Féin because of an interest in the Irish language, and because of its campaigning reputation ('Ireland Sober is Ireland Free!').

King Edward would return one more time to Ireland before his death in 1910 – but, sadly, it would all end on a mournful note, and not for reasons of serious politics, but for reasons affecting ceremonial regalia. This last visit took place in 1907 – and a sensational episode it turned out to be.

Bertie was visibly older, fatter, and unhealthier by 1907. He ate prodigiously (an Edwardian dinner might consist of as many as 11 courses), drank with gusto, though in the continental style (regularly, rather than excessively), and smoked cigars continuously. During the course of his life he had also exerted himself sexually with a string of beauties, among whom were (most notoriously) Lily Langtry, 'Daisy' Greville, the Countess of Warwick, and (at the end) Mrs Keppel (great-grandmother of Camilla Parker-Bowles, now the Duchess of Cornwall).

Queen Alexandra turned the customary blind eye, but it is possible that she did not greatly object to being relieved of her husband's attentions. By 1907 she was in her sixties, profoundly deaf and wholly absorbed in her family life. Alexandra had borne five children who survived infancy, but her eldest son, Albert, Duke of Clarence, had died suddenly in 1892, which made her ever more attached to her second son, George. She was so possessive of her youngest daughter, Victoria, that she stopped the girl from marrying, and the spinster princess carried a torch all her life for Lord Rosebery, briefly Prime Minister in the 1890s.

Interestingly the Catholic Church (in Ireland or elsewhere) never spoke a word of disapprobation against Albert Edward's sexual conduct. The Victorian and Edwardian code of hypocritical discretion held to one abiding rule: so long as behaviour did not become a matter of public scandal, it was regarded as a man's own business.

Oscar Wilde had broken that code when he brought his relationships under scrutiny with an unwise lawsuit that placed his private life in the public realm. Parnell had been felled by the same social view only when Katharine O'Shea's husband sued for divorce, thus making their private arrangement public and a matter for the courts. In stark contrast to our own time, which regards 'cover-up' as worse than the offence, Victorian-Edwardian rules insisted that private dirty linen was *never* washed in public.

T. P. O'Connor, the Irish Home Rule MP and virtual leader of the Irish community in Britain in the Edwardian age, was himself separated from his American wife and kept a Greek mistress. He never attracted condemnation because it never became a public issue (though his estranged wife used the situation to extract more alimony).[59]

In 1906 the new Liberal Prime Minister was Henry Campbell-Bannerman, a businesslike Scot to whom Bertie recommended a trip to Biarritz and a glass of champagne as a remedy for failing health. Campbell-Bannerman appointed to Ireland, as Lord Lieutenant, the Marquess of Aberdeen, John Campbell Gordon.

Aberdeen and his remarkable wife, Ishbel, were ardent Home Rulers and plain-living Scots: they had been *en poste* in Ireland for a brief period under Gladstone in 1886, and had come to love the country. They were strong promoters of Irish industry, and Ishbel was an enterprising campaigner against the scourge of tuberculosis and the founder of an admirable system for baby and child welfare.

Like many busy and intelligent wives, Ishbel Aberdeen is often described (notably by male historians) as 'domineering'. Her pioneering crusades for health and welfare were not always appreciated by the separatist Nationalists, and unkindly interpreted as imperialist meddling. Some Irish separatists, including Arthur Griffith, had reactionary attitudes to certain areas of medicine and welfare, particularly if advanced by British sources. Griffith called Lady Aberdeen's sanatoria 'concentration camps for consumptives', and the patriotic versifier Brian O'Higgins paranoically believed that Britain was 'planning a new famine' in Ireland by 'inventing' the idea of microbes.[60]

The King, by contrast, much approved of Ishbel Aberdeen's anti-tuberculosis campaigns: he was supportive of medical initiatives, enthusiastic about founding hospitals, and somewhat over-optimistically claimed that cancer could be conquered in his lifetime.

The Aberdeens were keen to bring Edward and Alexandra to Ireland for the Irish International Exhibition at Ballsbridge (to promote crafts and industry). From 1906 onwards, the Lord Lieutenant pressed Windsor Castle for another Irish date, with regular missives as to the very satisfactory condition of the country. 'The Earl of Aberdeen presents his humble duty to the King and has the honour to report that the condition of things in Ireland as a whole has for some time past been quiet and satisfactory.'[61]

Incidents of anti-Crown hostility Aberdeen anxiously smoothed over. The private secretary, Lord Knollys, made reference in October 1906 to an 'obnoxious incident' involving an alderman called Kelly, which had only just come to Windsor Castle's notice.

It seemed that Alderman Kelly 'removed the [Union] flag from the stern of a steamboat …let it fall into a river, [and] Mrs Kelly declined to join in drinking the King's health.' Lord Aberdeen hastened to assure the King that 'the Episode should in no sense be regarded as indicative of any check or alteration' in the steady development of good relations.

Most people in Ireland were of more moderate views. It was best that all parties should draw together 'rather than say anything which would accentuate differences'.[62]

It was broadly true that most people in Ireland were moderates, but Alderman Tom Kelly was a significant indication of the way the wind was blowing: the Dublin shopkeeper had been elected as a Home Ruler to Dublin Corporation, but defected to Sinn Féin when it was founded in 1905. (He would become Lord Mayor of Dublin during the War of Independence, and ended up as a Fianna Fáil TD.)

There were other odd more significant episodes, such as the shooting of a constable in Athenry (non-fatal), or the Marquess of Clanricarde's agent having been told to quit his premises. With regard to the latter, it was Aberdeen's view that Lord Clanricarde (a notorious absentee landlord) should be persuaded to take advantage of the Wyndham Act and 'allow his Irish Estates to be thus acquired by the tenants'. Still, through it all, Aberdeen continued to insist that the country was peaceable and all would go well with a royal visit.[63]

And so the visit was duly scheduled for 10 July 1907. The King and Queen were to be accompanied by their unmarried daughter, Victoria, who had now become her mother's companion.

But alas for poor Lord Aberdeen, as he went to greet the King from the royal yacht *Victoria and Albert* at Kingstown-Dún Laoghaire, he had to impart to the monarch some quite appalling news: so much worse than Alderman Kelly doing away with the Union flag or the shooting at a member of the constabulary – the Irish Crown Jewels had been stolen![64]

If Lord Aberdeen had been obliged to report a revolution, a plague or the collapse of civil life throughout the land, he might have expected more sympathy from King Edward than the theft of precious regalia – for it was said that Edward VII was never a tyrant in *anything* except dress and ceremonial regalia. And he was *incandescent* with anger to be told by Aberdeen that the Irish Crown Jewels had disappeared.

These Irish 'Crown Jewels' consisted of the official regalia and jewellery connected with Viceregal state occasions, and they were brought out when someone was to be invested with the Order of St Patrick.[65]

They consisted of a 'diamond star of the Order of St Patrick made of brilliant Brazilian stones, enclosing a cross of rubies with a trefoil of emeralds and sky-blue enamel'. 'Quis separabit ['Who Shall Separate Us?'] MDCCLXXXIII' was written across this confection in rose diamonds, surmounted by a harp in diamonds and a loop.

There were also, as an accompaniment, 'Five Collars of Knights Companions of the Order of St Patrick composed of gold, with roses and harps alternately tied together with knots of gold leave, enamelled, and an imperial jewelled crown sur-mounting a harp of gold.' The swag was worth in excess of £40,000, a considerable sum in 1907 – but the symbolism was more significant than the price.

The King was the head of the Order of St Patrick and Lord Aberdeen was the Grand Master. Not only was Bertie particularly exercised about ceremonial, medals and regalia of any kind, but the jewels were also the property of the Crown.

Moreover they were specifically required on this visit because Lord Castletown of Granston Manor, Offaly (then called King's County) – a man generally known as 'Barnie' –was due to be invested with the Order of St Patrick. Though a member of the Ascendancy, Barnie Castletown saw himself as an Irishman, sometimes called himself 'MacGiolla Padraig', spoke Irish, and had been honoured in Wales as a druid after he had founded a pan-Celtic association. But without the regalia, there would be no investiture for Barnie.[66]

It was a sensation in the newspapers – both the robbery and the disclosure about the jewels' existence. The Irish revolutionary Bulmer Hobson, who greatly interested himself in the case, commented that the Irish public had never heard of the 'Irish Crown Jewels' until they were reported stolen. The Dublin con-stabulary were put on the case, although without any results, despite a government offer of a reward of £1,000. Scotland Yard was called in, but this, too, was to no avail.

Although the King and Queen did their best to keep up appearances for this visit, privately Bertie brooded unhappily over the theft and kept pressing the unfortunate Aberdeen for some answers. 'I have a theory,' Aberdeen began at one point. 'I don't want theories!' snapped the King, uncharacteristically bad-tempered. 'I want my jewels!'[67]

Somebody had to be held responsible for the theft, and so the herald in charge of their safe keeping, Sir Arthur Vicars (whose title was Ulster King of Arms), was fingered. Poor Sir Arthur was driven to such desperation in his frantic search for the regalia that he consulted a medium. (This may have been at the prompting of Sir Arthur Conan Doyle, who was a cousin of Vicars). The medium, in the course of a seance, informed Sir Arthur that the jewels were buried in a disused graveyard near Clonsilla, north Dublin. The graveyard was duly searched, in a mixture of despair and farce, without yielding anything. Sir Arthur's despair grew ever more frantic and, as a consequence, the rest of his life was to be a misery, and would end in a tragedy.

A hundred years on, there can be little doubt that Sir Arthur Vicars was the scapegoat in a many-layered mystery that has been the subject of speculation – and some well-researched books – ever since.

Although there were several suspects in the frame, from the start the King demanded that Sir Arthur be dismissed for his apparent carelessness. He insisted. He wanted revenge. Somebody had to pay. Aberdeen stalled for a little while, which annoyed the King even more, but eventually Vicars had to go.

Sir Arthur refused to resign in the gentlemanly way, and called for an enquiry. He was supported in this by his half-brother, Pierce O'Mahony, a former Home Rule MP. Their mother had been Jane Gun-Cunninghame, who had married Pierce O'Mahony of Kilmorna in Co Kerry, and subsequently Colonel William Henry Vicars of Leamington in Warwickshire. Arthur was the youngest of his mother's children through both marriages and, orphaned at ten, had more or less been brought up by his siblings.[68] He had fallen out with his half-brother O'Mahony, but when the Crown Jewels story emerged differences were forgotten, and Pierce O'Mahony rushed back from Bulgaria (where he had generously endowed an orphanage) to support Sir Arthur.

O'Mahony got up a petition for an enquiry, with the backing of various Knights of St Patrick, including the Marquesses of Ormonde and Waterford, the Earls of Carysfort, Dunraven, Rosse, Bandon, Mayo, Listowel, Lucan, Longford, Enniskillen and Meath, as well as Lord Monteagle of Bandon and Field Marshal Earl Roberts (who later withdrew).[69]

Vicars wrote pitiful letters to Lord Knollys, to Lord Iveagh ('a fellow Mason'), and to anyone who would hearken to him. He pleaded with the King, over and over again, to accept his innocence. The royal archives at Windsor have much correspondence over this matter; it is a key issue in relation to Ireland during the Edwardian reign.

Back and forth the letters went between Windsor and Dublin, the police, Lord Lieutenant Aberdeen, Private Secretary Knollys (speaking for the King), and Chief Secretary Birrell. Birrell was inclined to be sympathetic to Vicars, since the man's reputation as a heraldic specialist had been excellent, and his work was regarded as scrupulous.

The King constantly complained of dawdling over apprehending the culprit: 'the King knows that you personally are anxious that the mystery of this audacious robbery should be cleared up and the blame fastened on the proper shoulders,' Aberdeen was informed, 'but it does not appear to His Majesty that feeling is universal and the enquiry ... seems to be dawdling in a somewhat leisurely fashion, while every day's delay obscures and lessens the chances of discovery.'[70]

On and on the King harried, but from the start he had clearly felt sure that the 'Ulster King at Arms' (the hapless Sir Arthur) was responsible, since it was he who had had charge of the regalia. Sir Arthur again pleaded and protested: he had done everything to keep the regalia secure. Indeed – and this was true – he had asked the authorities to provide a special safe for the regalia.

There was, however, another implication in the correspondence. Aberdeen had suspicions, and indeed 'more than suspicion about scandalous conduct'. The scandalous conduct 'of that particular sort about which every teacher [is aware that] some painful reference is made & which has at times been such a source of anxiety in some of our public schools'. Sir Antony MacDonnell, Under-Secretary for Ireland (her most senior civil servant), and a Catholic who was liked by the King, also put forward his view that the episode involved a homosexual conspiracy: that Sir Arthur Vicars, and certain young men of doubtful character befriended by Sir Arthur, had had access to Dublin Castle and thus purloined the regalia.

Sir Arthur heard of this and was outraged: he repudiated 'many of the suggestions that have been made concerning high members of society as wicked concoctions'. He begged for an audience with the King. He lamented that he had been made a scapegoat. He protested what a loyal subject and loyal civil servant he had been. He pointed out that his brother had supplemented the government reward offered for the jewels with an extra £500. He underlined that the Lord Lieutenant was the true custodian of the jewels ... and then he wailed in a letter to Windsor Castle, 'How could I be responsible for the jewels in *'out of office' hours?'*

But nothing would convince the King that Sir Arthur Vicars was innocent: since there was no break in, it had to be an 'inside job', and Sir Arthur had been in charge.

A Commission of Enquiry was set up, and found that Sir Arthur had not exercised due care and vigilance. He was therefore dismissed from his position, though his brother valiantly went on campaigning to clear his name, even seeking – without success – the support of both John Redmond of the Irish Parliamentary Party, and the leader of Sinn Féin, Arthur Griffith.

From that day to this, the regalia have never been traced; and from that day to this, speculation has remained constant about the mystery of the Irish Crown Jewels. It is astounding to note that the saga is still being discussed and puzzled over on the internet.

In 2008 the historical researcher Sean J. Murphy claimed in the *Sunday Independent* that the probable thief had been Francis Shackleton, the 'disreputable' brother of Ernest Shackleton, the Anglo-Irish polar explorer.[71] In fact, Sir Arthur Vicars had himself named Shackleton as the likely culprit, although he exposed his personal life in doing so. For Francis Shackleton – who was, it seems, a homosexual – had shared a house with Sir Arthur Vicars in Clonskeagh, Co Dublin, and they had entered into joint financial dealings.

Sir Arthur claimed that Shackleton stole the key to the safe while he, Sir Arthur, was sleeping (others suggested that drink was involved), and had it copied. And that Shackleton, possibly with an accomplice, thereby subsequently removed the jewels.

It is puzzling that even though Shackleton was asked to resign from his Dublin Castle post (along with two other assistants,

Goldney and Mahony), he was never interviewed by the Dublin police, nor by the Scotland Yard detective Chief Inspector John Kane.[72]

Francis Shackleton had a checkered career, and was later declared bankrupt. He subsequently fetched up in Portuguese West Africa, and was imprisoned for fraud. He was described as 'a young man of extravagant tastes and doubtful character'. Francis Goldney, one of the other heralds at the heraldic office, was also an individual of dubious reputation: he was found to have stolen artefacts and documents from a number of institutions. Pierce Mahony, the third herald with access to the regalia, was a nephew of Sir Arthur (and of his half-brother Pierce O'Mahony). But both Goldney and Mahony have been discounted as possible culprits.[73]

The question remains unanswered: why, despite Shackleton's profile as a prime suspect, was he never interviewed? Was he protected from investigation by a blackmailer's power?

Francis Shackleton had frequented a known homosexual circle, which included gentlemen in high places, including those who had connections with the royal family. He was a friend of Lord Ronald Gower, described as a 'promiscuous homosexual', and apparently the original model for the character of Lord Henry Wootten in Wilde's *The Picture of Dorian Gray*. Gower's nephew was the 9th Duke of Argyll, previously the Marquess of Lorne, and married to the King's sister, Louise. Argyll was also reputed to be gay.[74]

If Shackleton had inside information about the Duke of Argyll, it could have caused a public scandal of sensational proportions, touching the very Crown itself.

The rumour that he may have had such knowledge could conceivably have halted any further investigation during King Edward's lifetime. It was said that the King was 'terrified' that any homosexual connections might emerge publicly. 'I will have no scandal!' he was reported as saying, adding, 'I will never come to Dublin again!'[75]

Bertie was liberal on sexual matters – in view of his own *train de vie* he had to be! – and that extended to gay friends and relations. In 1889, he had privately intervened on behalf of a young artist and son of the Duke of Beaufort, Lord Arthur Somerset, who was apprehended in a notorious homosexual brothel at 19 Cleveland Street, London, in what was an eerie prequel to the Oscar Wilde affair. Somerset obligingly took the traditional route out of the difficulty for Englishmen of the period – the boat to France, where he resided in peace. But Bertie later privately prevailed upon Prime Minister Salisbury to allow Somerset's discreet return to England in order to visit his parents, without fear of police arrest.[76]

However, that was playing by the rules of the Victorian and Edwardian game: discretion meant *no public scandal*. The King did not judge anyone's conduct in private, but private conduct must not be made public. There had been a homosexual scandal involving the King's nephew, the Kaiser, when a certain Prince Philip Eulenberg, during a cross-dressing Prussian officers' party, suffered a heart attack and died.[77] It emerged that Eulenberg, described as 'effeminate', had been very close to the Kaiser, addressing him as 'Liebehan' or 'little darling'; there had also been another gay Prussian aristocrat, Count Kuno von Moltke, an aide-de-camp of the Kaiser's, involved.

So, although Bertie had the urge to press Lord Aberdeen for more news on 'this disagreeable business', in the end he let it drop. Finally, for fear of prompting a public scandal, the matter of the Irish Crown Jewels faded from further enquiry during King Edward's lifetime. It does all seem rather unjust from Sir Arthur Vicars' viewpoint: he had simply been unlucky and possibly unwise in sharing a house with the unreliable Francis Shackleton. However, it is also probable that he was highly naïve when it came to judging trustworthiness in colleagues.

It is very strange, too, that many files pertaining to the case were later 'lost' or somehow destroyed.[78] Under the circumstances, it would be reasonable to suggest a conspiracy – and such theories do abound. The researchers Hannafin and Cafferky claim that the theft of the regalia was organised by ultra-Unionists in an effort to discredit the Irish administration – and that such ultra-Unionists wished to destroy 'the gay court' associated with the heraldry tradition. Hannafin and Cafferky also claim that the jewels were secretly returned to the Crown in 1908, although other experts conclude they were sent to the Netherlands and broken up.

There was to be a sad personal ending for Sir Arthur Vicars. Still maintaining his innocence, he went off to live on his brother's (Pierce O'Mahony's) estate at Kilmorna, near Listowel in Co Kerry. In 1917 at the age of 53 he married a Miss Gertrude Wright, a sister-in-law of his nephew Pierce Mahony (who had worked with Sir Arthur in the herald's office).

When the Troubles came in 1921 and the IRA went about the countryside burning down 'Big Houses' belonging to the gentry, Kilmorna was raided and set alight. Sir Arthur was unwell, but eventually emerged from the house. He was shot dead by armed men, and a notice was left on his body with the words, 'Spy. Informers Beware'. The house was indeed burned – and most of Sir Arthur's papers with it. IRA sources formally disclaimed having killed Sir Arthur Vicars, and so it was rumoured that his strange death was somehow connected with the theft of the Irish Crown Jewels in 1907.[79]

It seems that nobody ever knew the full truth – if Francis Shackleton did, the secret died with him in 1941. However in his will, disclosed only in 1976, Sir Arthur Vicars formally named Shackleton as the Crown Jewels thief.

King Edward never returned to Ireland again. He was expected to make an appearance in Dublin in February 1908, when a statue of Queen Victoria was unveiled on Leinster Lawn. But he sent his apologies saying that he could not be present, and Lord Aberdeen did the honours in his stead.[80]

It was also, surely, significant that the regalia bore the legend, 'Who shall separate us?' In mocking tones, history answered back – many were preparing just such a separation.

Indeed the cultural separation of Ireland and Britain was continuing apace. In February 1908, Sinn Féin contested its first by-election in Leitrim North; Patrick Pearse opened his school for boys, St Enda's (Scoil Éanna) in Rathfarnham – a seedbed for the rising strain of 'Irish-Ireland' revolutionaries; and the Irish Women's Franchise League was founded by Hanna Sheehy-Skeffington and Margaret Cousins.

The Abbey Theatre was greatly animated by the Irish cultural renaissance, and the Gaelic League had become a power in the land (having successfully established St Patrick's Day as a national holiday in 1903, they subsequently successfully campaigned to have all public houses shut for the celebrations).

The scheme to 'kill Home Rule with kindness' was not quite working to plan: the Wyndham Land Acts were enthusiastically embraced, but the more that devolution was delayed, the more the appetite for separation grew.

The King, meanwhile, was ever more concerned – as well he might be – with European and overseas affairs. He could not, of course, act directly, but he believed he could bring goodwill through his many family connections in royal houses all over Europe, and he tried to restrain his nephew the Kaiser, although without much success. Paradoxically, Edward VII was best loved in a Republic to which he had no family connection – France.

His daughter Maud had married his Danish brother-in-law, Christian, who became the King of Norway as Haakon I. This development was applauded by Arthur Griffith and some Irish Nationalists, because the Norwegians had democratically voted for their monarchy in order to move away from the imperial relationship with Sweden. A voluntary monarchy, said Griffith, was acceptable – a coerced one was not. This surely was a fair point, but it also tells us that Arthur Griffith's Sinn Féin was not at this point anti-monarchist in principle.

In 1908 and 1909, the King undertook travels to France, Russia, Germany, Austria, Denmark, Sweden, Norway, Spain and Malta. He helped the Nordic countries to form a North Sea alliance; he tried to build relations with Russia, though he was castigated by the rising Labour leader, Keir Hardie, for having any truck with Tsar Nicholas, described as 'a murderer' for his autocratic regime.

Bertie foresaw trouble brewing in the Balkans when Austria annexed Bosnia-Herzegovenia and, indeed, this turned out to be the embryonic cause of the First World War. He also deplored the forays by King Leopold of the Belgians into Africa, and his involvement in the cruel rubber trade (so honourably revealed – and denounced – by Sir Roger Casement).

Some of the concerns which featured in the King's in-tray would have resonance a century later: there was much worry over instability in Persia (Iran) and Afghanistan; arguments about a proposed Channel Tunnel (the King was against it); and trouble with the House of Lords that directly concerned Ireland, since the Lords (three times) sought to frustrate Irish Home Rule acts democratically passed in the Commons.

The King's last direct communication about Ireland was a mournful little note regretting reports of atrocities committed against cattle: 'cattle-driving' had been a common anti-landlord gesture during the Land War of the 1880s, and there was another outbreak in February 1909. 'Their Majesties look upon these cruelties as horrible & it is hardly to be credited that they could take place in a so-called civilised country,' the Lord Lieutenant was told by the King's private secretary. 'They deeply regret that the Irish Executive appears to be totally unable to take the necessary measures to put an end to these savage acts.'[81]

The King and Queen were told, by a Dublin Castle anxious to assuage feelings, that 'in the vast majority of cases "cattle driving" is not accompanied by cruelty'. It was also pointed out that certain atrocities against animals also took place in England – such as attacks on horses in Staffordshire. 'Mr Birrell will do all he can,' the King was assured. Augustine Birrell did all he could: but seven years later, when the Easter 1916 Rising occurred in Dublin, Mr Birrell was thoroughly blamed by the Unionist establishment for never having taken a firm enough line in Ireland.

*

From 1909 the King's health was obviously deteriorating. He was growing so heavy that he was breathless when climbing stairs and he had constant attacks of coughing and bronchitis, occasionally marked by shows of blood. It depressed him, and he would occasionally consider abdicating. And, a century before the paparazzi became such an insistent feature on the royal scene, he also felt oppressed by the 'incessant searchlight of publicity' surrounding him.

He repaired ever more frequently to his favourite places of restoration: Marienbad and Biarritz, which he had grown to love perhaps more than anywhere else. He was so concerned about the drains of Biarritz (which he feared might be unhealthy) that he got Prime Minister Clemenceau, an old pal from Marienbad, to intervene. With proper sewerage, Biarritz, with its southern, warm climate and bracing Atlantic air, came to represent the perfect restorative and the King's last days were spent at his beloved Hotel du Palais on the Basque coast.

Despite Bertie's prescriptions of champagne and Biarritz, the Liberal Prime Minister, Henry Campbell-Bannerman, died and was succeeded by Herbert Asquith, a Liberal and an intellectual committed to seeing through Irish Home Rule – but cautiously.

Since Asquith only had a majority of two over the Tories in the House of Commons after the general election of January 1910, he depended upon the support of the 82 Irish Parliamentary Party members led by John Redmond. Thus the closing months of Edward VII's life, in the spring of 1910, were politically dominated by Ireland (and by a crucial financial bill, for which Asquith also depended on Irish support). Never before – and perhaps never again – would Irish interests wield so much power at Westminster as the Irish Parliamentary Party did in that last Edwardian springtime.

There was also a threatened constitutional crisis in late 1909 and early 1910, which was not at all to the King's liking for he disliked quarrels in domestic politics, especially when these were linked to the monarch's position. The House of Lords had rejected the Liberal party's recent Finance Bill (which was challenging aristocratic interests). Asquith was threatening to nullify the established power of the Lords by requiring the King to create

500 new Liberal peers, flooding the Upper House with government supporters. For the Unionists, this would turn the King into a party-political pawn. Moreover, as the House of Lords had repeatedly obstructed Irish Home Rule, its disempowerment was very much in the Irish Parliamentary Party's interest.

Bertie's personal instinct was to side with the Lords, now led by Lord Lansdowne, another fabulously wealthy Anglo-Irish landowner (Lansdowne Road rugby and football grounds derive their name from his ownership of a fine slice of Dublin 4). However, much as the King sensed that demoting the Lords might be dangerous for the monarchy, he also knew that he must take the advice of his Prime Minister (he sometimes complained he did not get enough advice from his Prime Ministers). So he was bound to proceed with caution.

Shrewdly, he counselled an election, and an election duly took place in December 1910. The results were very similar to what had gone before. Asquith, returned to office, said he did not wish to press the King into action, and stalled on the matter of politically castrating the House of Lords in King Edward's lifetime.

From early 1910, Bertie was wracked by apoplectic onsets of a bronchial cough. The King went back and forth to Biarritz in an effort to restore his health – always feeling a little better there than in the pollution of London.

It was during his last visit to Biarritz (and just 15 days before his death) that King Edward paid an apparently respectful visit to the grotto of Lourdes. He visited the Bernardine nuns there, and spent some time with the Reverend Mother Isabelle in the Chapel of St Bernard. He also visited La Roque church, which he had apparently been to see several times previously. It was reported in a Catholic newspaper that 'His Majesty always finds time during his brief annual spring holidays to visit this ancient and beautiful sanctuary of Our Lady.' He was, it seems, especially thoughtful on this particular occasion, and 'the respectful attitude of King

Edward throughout his visit made a very favourable impression upon the pilgrims who were assembled there at the time.'[82]

Did King Edward have a premonition that his life was drawing to a close? Was he just being cordial and polite in a part of France that was familiar to him? Did he think that places of pilgrimage are akin to spas – Lourdes is very near the ancient spa waters of Gavarnie – and that there are healing powers in such locations? Did he find – as many have done – a sense of comfort in the Lourdes grotto? Or was his 'respectful attitude' to the Marian shrine a political gesture? The Catholic Church was under pressure (some called it a 'persecution') from strongly secularising forces at this time.

Or is there any truth in the rumour that Edward VII died a secret Roman Catholic? In Nora Robertson's account of the life of the Anglo-Irish during the early years of the twentieth century, she claims that it was widely believed that the King was a 'secret RC'.[83] I have seen no evidence of this, but it is clear that Edward was more tolerant of Catholicism than many of his caste, and that he was drawn to places of Marian healing. And that certainly endeared him to many in Ireland.

Bertie arrived in London in cheerful enough spirits, but within three days he was seriously unwell. He seemed, at one point, almost to court trouble by walking in the garden and subjecting himself to a chill. The Queen was called back from a Mediterranean cruise, and when he did not meet her at Victoria Station, as was the usual practice, the press was alerted to the seriousness of his condition.

King Edward died gracefully, working on his papers up to the end. On the last day of his life, May 6, he insisted on seeing his friend, Sir Ernest Cassel, and they spoke briefly about the King's horse, Witch in the Air, having won its race at Kempton Park. On the evening of that day Bertie slipped into a coma, and soon after peacefully departed this life.

Bertie's friendly visits to Ireland were well-remembered when he died, and particularly, perhaps, his exceptional lack of religious sectarianism. The *Nationalist and Leinster Times* warmly commended Bertie as a peacemaker whose death had caused 'a general heart-throb' throughout Ireland. It commented that he was 'the first British sovereign to begin the work of reconciling the races which centuries of oppression, misgovernment and misunderstanding had well-nigh made impossible.' Former sovereigns of England and Great Britain passed away, and as far as Ireland was concerned they died '"unwept, unhonoured, and unsung". History will therefore record that in the year 1910 Ireland was sorrow-swept at the news of the death of England's king.'[84]

The *Freeman's Journal* recorded messages of sympathy from all over Ireland – Limerick, Cork, Kildare, and many public bodies, including Dublin Corporation. Many local authorities had indeed passed motions of sincere regret: the Cahirciveen (Co Kerry) Board of Guardians had issued a statement that 'the late King was a sincere friend to Ireland and a sincere friend to the Catholic Church'. More than thirty local authorities and public bodies all over Ireland passed resolutions of regret and sympathy at the passing of the King. Among the many who expressed condolence on the King's death was William O'Brien of the United Irish League.

The *Irish Independent,* the pages bordered in mourning black, wrote of Edward VII, 'The death of King Edward VII inflicts irreparable loss on Ireland, on the Empire and on Christendom. The late Sovereign was not only one of the most manly of men, but also one of the most sagacious of rulers and far-seeing of statesmen.'[85]

In Dublin Archbishop Walsh immediately ordered a Solemn Votive Mass to be said at Dublin's major Catholic church, known as the Pro-Cathedral. Dr Walsh praised the King as a great peacemaker and a sovereign better loved in Ireland than any before. 'His death has evoked a feeling of respectful sympathy which, to an extent wholly without precedent in any other such case in this country, has found expression in the resolutions of our representative bodies throughout the length and breadth of this land.' 'Veni Creator Spiritus' was also to be sung for the widowed Queen and the new King.[86] The church was crammed with Catholic dignatories, all carefully recorded in the newspapers of the day.

Sinn Féin distanced itself from any words that might imply approval of the link with the British monarchy: they would not commiserate, they announced, on the passing of the 'ruler of Britain' (although a monarch reigns, rather than rules). The theatres in Dublin generally went dark as a mark of mourning for the King, but Yeats and Lady Gregory chose to keep the Abbey Theatre, uniquely, open.[87] The decision cost them the financial support of Annie Hornimann, the Manchester philanthropist who had done so much to launch the Abbey as Ireland's national theatre. She severed her links with the theatre after that. Madame Maud Gonne MacBride, however, was jubilant that the 'English King' would not be mourned in the forum of Ireland's National Theatre.

The fare being offered at the Abbey was not, by all accounts, particularly distinguished. The main play was a morose work about life in a poorhouse by the poet Padraic Colum called *Thos Muskerry*, preceded by a somewhat forgotten comedy by W. B. Yeats called *A Pot of Bother*. Of the Colum play, the *Irish Independent* critic 'Jacques' wrote: 'It gave me two hours of the gloomiest entertainment like to which I thankfully record I have rarely experienced.' The Yeats playlet went unreviewed.[88]

The funeral certainly was a splendid spectacle of ceremonial and rite. A firmament of international royalty marched behind the coffin to the muffled drums of an array of regiments: the new King of England, George V, and his cousin the Kaiser of Imperial Germany; the kings of Norway, of the Hellenes, of Spain, of Bulgaria, of Denmark, and of Portugal; the hereditary Prince of the Ottoman Empire; the King of the Belgians; the Archduke Franz Ferdinand; and the princes of Japan, Bavaria, Serbia, Egypt, and China. Twelve thousand people lined the route, and the *Irish Independent* was proud to report that the Lord Mayor of Dublin was among the assembled crowd.

The King's wire-haired fox terrier, Caesar, led the funeral procession, alone at the head of the cortege, taking precedence over the pomp of the various crowns and coronets.

*

Edward VII himself was in some respects a moderniser: he was internationalist, and he believed that a monarch should encourage people to 'be happy'. He was of his class and his milieu: he was a conservative politically and socially and, for example, could not stand the female suffragists. But he was an instinctive communicator, in that he could 'signal' his views to people without upsetting the constitutional apple cart. He was not a policy-maker, but he could create a 'climate' in which policy was made: his efforts for European peace might have had more success if his politicians had taken more advantage of the 'climate' he sought to create.

Irish intellectuals – like English intellectuals – thought his artistic taste undistinguished. Bertie would have been an unlikely patron of the Abbey Theatre: he much preferred the variety hall (though he also loved the plays of Oscar Wilde, and saw them repeatedly). In Paris, he was so at home at the boulevard variety shows that when he appeared in a Parisian *boîte*, the ugly, but fascinating, performer known as 'La Goulue' (famously painted by Degas), greeted him throatily with, 'Ullo, Wales!' And he delighted in the boulevardier cockiness of the greeting.[89]

The Edwardian character that Edward VII stamped on his age became part of Irish culture and society too. There were many Irish people who could see themselves as Irish patriots – even Nationalists – who nonetheless contentedly shared British Edwardian culture. People who, like my mother, grew up listening to recitations of Kipling's 'Mandalay' and the 'Green Eye of the Little Yellow God' in west of Ireland parlours that otherwise optimistically anticipated Home Rule (which Kipling so famously opposed).

The Edwardian ambiance is deeply embedded in the work of James Joyce, and his quintessentially Edwardian work, *Ulysses*. It is in the popular music that Joyce favoured that this shared Edwardian culture of England and Ireland comes through most strongly. Many of James Joyce's best-loved songs – which often appear in his texts – were the self-same ones enjoyed by all Edwardians: 'Oh! Oh! Antonio!', 'I Dreamt that I Dwelt in Marble Halls', 'Has Anybody Here Seen Kelly?', 'The Last Rose of Summer', 'After the Ball', 'Macushla', and, most merrily evocative of all, 'The Man Who Broke the Bank at Monte Carlo'. This last was Joyce's party piece[90] and a great favourite with my own father and uncles. And, indeed, also much-loved by Albert Edward, King Edward VII, known to his family as Bertie.

Chapter Three

GEORGE V:
REVOLUTION AND PARTITION

We will yet defeat the most nefarious conspiracy that has
ever been hatched against a free people.
(Sir Edward Carson on Irish Home Rule, 1911[1])

With all my heart I pray that the blessing of God may rest upon you and
upon the Ministers of the Irish Free State.
(King George V's message to the first Governor-General of Ireland,
read out to the Oireachtas, Leinster House, Dublin, 1922[2])

George V was in practice the last king of the 32 counties of Ireland, and the last British monarch to pay a state visit to what is now the Republic of Ireland. He and his wife, the ramrod-straight Queen Mary, came to Dublin in much splendour in 1911, in what turned out to be a valediction.

George reigned during the most revolutionary period of the twentieth century. And considering how he loathed revolution of any kind (he shared with contemporaries such as Winston Churchill a horror of 'Bolsheviks') he presided to the best of his ability over the most radical change in British-Irish relations since Henry II.

GEORGE V: REVOLUTION AND PARTITION

Like his father before him, George was a Unionist – he believed absolutely in the unity of the United Kingdom and Ireland – but he also strove dutifully to 'hold the ring', as he put it, and to be as fair as possible in dealings with both Irish Unionists and Irish Nationalists. He felt he had a mission to conciliate Ireland and sought to do so, within the limitations of a constitutional monarch's role (to advise and to warn). He was a meticulous constitutionalist – overly so, in the eyes of the Ulster Unionists, who thought him indulgent to Home Rule politics *and* too carefully constitutional at the same time.

George worried so much about Ireland that at one point he admitted to thinking 'of nothing else by day & by night'. Brooding about Ireland caused the King sleepless nights and, according to one of his biographers, the King had tears in his eyes when he contemplated the horror of a possible civil war between Ireland, north and south.[3]

He was so obsessed with Ireland even in 1914 that he barely noticed the warning signs of the First World War, and registered in his diary, almost casually, the portentous assassination of Franz Ferdinand at Sarajevo.

*

When Edward VII died in 1910, his son wrote: 'I have lost my best friend & the best of fathers.' Only once in 45 years did George ever criticise anything that his father did (and that was a footling matter over an extension made to Sandringham).

And yet they were so different. Edward VII was absorbed by foreign affairs, travelled incessantly, was at ease speaking French, German or English, and mingled cordially with international statesmen. George was bored by foreigners and uninterested in diplomacy. His was the English-speaking world of the Empire and Commonwealth: he seldom visited Continental Europe. Whereas his father had loved champagne, and bridge, and mistresses, George was strictly uxorious and his main hobby was collecting stamps (on which his own image appeared so copiously). He liked staying at home in the evening and reading aloud to his wife.

He certainly had his critics among the intellectuals. George's court was described by H. G. Wells as 'dull and alien'. The King retorted, with some spirit –'I may be dull, but I'm damned if I'm an alien!'[4]

George struck contemporaries as the epitome of the Norfolk squire. He preferred domestic gatherings of friends to grand dinners. He preferred a modest country home, described as a 'cottage', to a palace; he liked gardening better than tiger hunting. Like other country squires he liked to shoot, and was an excellent shot. In sexual matters, he was strait-laced (as was Queen Mary – she once had a peeress expelled from Ascot for sporting a saucy sailor's cap marked 'HMS Good Ship Venus'[5]). George looked horrified when it was suggested that Lady Headfort (the former chorus-girl Rosie Boote who had married an Irish peer) should be presented to him at court.[6]

Whereas Edward VII had intervened behind the scenes to help homosexuals in trouble with the law, advisers shrank from raising this question with George V. 'Good heavens,' he once exclaimed, when a homosexual matter arose, 'I thought fellows like that shot themselves!'[7]

George was not adventurous in taste: he did not like abstract painting or experimental literature or bobbed hair or cocktails – all innovations of his reign. Some of his more reactionary observations turned out to be surprisingly prescient: he called Cambridge University 'a nest of Bolsheviks' just about the time Kim Philby and Guy Burgess were flourishing there.

Yet he could be decent. For example, he disliked the suffragettes – they were regarded as dangerous and violent.* During this period art galleries were guarded lest they should slash paintings, and in Dublin an English suffragette threw a hatchet at Prime Minister Asquith, hitting John Redmond on the ear.[8]

---

*The King was appalled when a suffragette with a history of mental instability, Emily Wilding Davison, threw herself under his horse, Anmer, at the 1913 Derby. She died a few days later.

Nevertheless, the King protested against the practice of force-feeding the militant feminists in prison when they went on hunger strike. He expressed his outrage to Prime Minister Asquith, calling the practice 'shocking' and 'cruel'.[9]

Emmeline Pankhurst had been greatly influenced by Irish politics in her formative years: she had been politicised as a girl by the 'Manchester Martyrs'. The compliment was not returned and every member of the Irish Parliamentary Party voted against allowing women the vote – perhaps fearing hatchet-throwing activists.

George's upbringing was, in the early years, intensely domestic. If he adored his father, he had the most intimate bond with his mother, Queen Alexandra. As a grown man in his twenties, he would finish his letters to her 'Your loving little Georgy'. In his forties – now King and Emperor – he would address her as 'my own darling Mother-dear'.

It is sometimes said that men inherit their intelligence from their mothers and George's mother was a simple soul. One historian has described Queen Alexandra as 'intellectually retarded'.[10] But she was family-minded and loving and she had a compassionate nature: she taught her son to read the Bible every day of his life and always to have care and respect for the poor.[11]

Until he was 26 years old, George was the second son, on whom no great hereditary responsibility was expected to descend. He had virtually no early training for the role of constitutional monarch, and little knowledge of politics. He had been sent off to sea, and had done well as a sailor, and the experience had developed his character (and his stamp-collecting hobby during the *longueurs* of sea life).

But his elder brother, Prince Albert Victor, known as Eddy, Duke of Clarence, suddenly died from a fever of the lungs in January 1892. 'To me, his loss is irreparable, as you know how devoted we always were and we had never been separated until I was eighteen,' George wrote to a shipmate.[12] George now became the next in line to the throne after his father, who was still, in the 1890s, waiting in the wings as an ageing Prince of Wales.

Eddy and George had been born only 18 months apart – Eddy in 1863, George in 1865 – and as little boys they had done everything together. Eddy was difficult to teach, lethargic and indolent, whereas George was diligent and biddable, and possessed what the Victorians called 'healthy animal spirits'.

It is clear that Eddy would not have measured up to the challenging circumstances awaiting the reign that followed his father's. Yet George's fraternal attachment was strong: he kept momentoes of his dead brother all his life, always remembered Eddy's birthday in his diary, and signed most documents with a pen that had been Eddy's. He grieved: but he accepted, and got on with life. He also soon took to his brother's fiancée, May of Teck, who was in time to become the formidable Queen Mary.

George visited Ireland five times before he came to the throne: in 1887, 1891, 1897, 1899, and 1905, and always proclaimed himself very pleased to be there.

The 1891 visit had been personally significant. Prince Eddy had been stationed in Dublin (as part of the 10th Hussars) and his younger brother came over to join him. On the last day of their visit, the brother princes visited Parnell's grave in Glasnevin, which would not have pleased their grandmother, Queen Victoria, had she known about it.[13]

However George's visits in the 1890s probably helped to pave the way for Queen Victoria's final, reconciliatory trip to Ireland.

Dublin made a special impression when he first went there. 'I well remember the pleasure it gave me,' he wrote. As with other royals, the Irish people did not fail to extend a cordial welcome, although, by the turn of the century the civic authorities had ceased to give British royalty a formal or 'loyal' address. Because of his pleasant experiences in Ireland, George believed the Irish liked him: he did not quite understand the circumlocutions of the Celtic mind, which can both like and dislike simultaneously.[14]

He imagined the Irish Nationalists would be delighted when he offered ceremonially to open Dáil Éireann, when the Irish Free State came into being in 1922–23. The offer was brusquely rejected (a Dáil decree had described the Crown as the Irish people's 'traditional enemy'), but George, remembering his welcome in Dublin, persisted in sending his (and God's) blessing on the Irish Free State. [15]

As Duke of York, George had sat in the Commons to listen to Gladstone, before the Grand Old Man's death in 1898. George noted what Gladstone said about Ireland and took it all in. Yet George was conservative by inclination, and he was frightened of the rise of socialism, especially after Keir Hardie entered parliament in 1892 wearing a cloth cap and accompanied by a miners' brass band – for Hardie had led an attack on royalty in 1884.

George wrote nervously to his father after the famous Liberal landslide election of 1906, in which Labour gained 29 members: 'I see that a great number of Labour members have been returned, which is rather a dangerous sign, but I hope they are not all Socialists.' He need not have fretted. Labour politicians generally turned out to be more compliant with the monarch than the Tories.

Since the death of Parnell in 1891, the Irish Parliamentary Party at Westminster had been quiescent: there had been a famous split after Parnell's downfall and time was needed to reorganise (and recover). Then, under the Liberal administration of Lord Rosebery (1894–95), the 'Irish question' was simply parked.

For the Tory Prime Minister, Salisbury (1895–1902), and his nephew Arthur Balfour, Prime Minister from 1902 to 1905, Ireland was not a significant player at Westminster. Plenty was happening in Ireland and the place was feverish with cultural activity: but Home Rule politics at Westminster was insignificant.

However with the dramatic landslide of 1906 the Liberals won an extraordinary 377 seats against the Conservative tally of 156 and, perhaps as importantly, the election brought to power new men from a meritocracy, who would gradually replace the grandees of the aristocratic caste.

The new Liberal administration would promote men like Herbert Asquith, the son of a non-conformist Yorkshire wool trader, and David Lloyd George, a brilliant and radical solicitor from a modest Welsh background, whom King George couldn't stand (the feeling was mutual).

Winston Churchill, grandson of the Duke of Marlborough who worked for his living as a mere journalist, was a star of the new intake. Outside of Parliament the feminists, the Fabians, the trade unions, the social reformers, the Bloomsbury group, abstract art, and (increasingly) the mass media (the *Daily Mail* was now outselling *The Times* ten-fold[16]), were changing the country as much as the new brand of politician.

Yet Ireland remained in the background during that Liberal administration. The government's majority was so great that they could govern without the 83 Irish members.

The January 1910 election, just before King Edward's death in May, returned a fresh Liberal administration: and this time the numbers were on a knife-edge. Under Asquith (Campbell-Bannerman had died in 1908) the Liberals had 275 seats, while the Conservatives commanded 273: Asquith could only govern with the support of, now, 82 Irish Home Rulers (and Labour's 40 members). Ireland held the balance of power at Westminster.

As King George V stepped up to the throne, Ireland was at the heart of British politics. The Irish Parliamentary Party's leader, John Redmond, was keenly aware of his command of political power. Home Rule was the price that Redmond and the Irish Parliamentary Party justly demanded in exchange for their support of the Liberal government – and the House of Lords would be made to swallow it.

Herbert Asquith was a sincere Home Ruler and a matchless parliamentarian – but he always tried to work by stealth rather than confrontation.

As king, George's baptism of fire involved a complex constitutional crisis over the House of Lords, directly linked to the Irish question. The Liberal government needed to pass a Parliament Bill to curb the veto power (John Redmond's phrase) of the Lords. This would make the will of the Commons supreme.

And it touched the King in a way that worried him – he was a worrier anyway. Asquith obtained from George an undertaking that he would, if need be, create a large batch of new Liberal peers to 'flood' the Lords. This would secure the passage of the Parliament Bill to end the upper house's veto. Otherwise the King would be asked to use his royal prerogative to also ensure the Parliament Bill went through.[17]

Though the King did not personally care for such stratagems, he agreed to follow his Prime Minister's advice from a sense of constitutional correctness. Throughout 1910 and 1911 there was intense political excitement over this House of Lords question, since the Lords itself rejected the bill to curb its own powers three times in the course of these years – which meant that the responsibility to force through the political will of the elected House devolved upon the King.

George did his constitutional duty, and the Parliament Bill was duly passed in 1911: never again would the hereditary House of Lords, with its great landowners and fabulous aristocrats, frustrate the will of the elected House of Commons. They could henceforth delay, but never destroy, legislation.

The Leader of the Conservative Unionists in the Lords was an Anglo-Irish landowner, the Marquess of Lansdowne, who had started out as a Liberal, but had quarrelled with Gladstone over Irish Home Rule. He was promoted by Arthur Balfour, who had been his fag at Eton (an English networking opportunity that has never yet failed.)

Lansdowne was to pay dearly for his leading role in obstructing Home Rule: his cherished house at Derreen in Co Kerry was burned down by Republicans in 1922. He never got over the loss.[18]

Since the Lords' veto had been a mighty obstruction to Home Rule (as had Tory and Unionist opposition in the Commons), the Irish Parliamentary Party and their allies in the Labour and Liberal parties now felt the way ahead was clear for a successful Home Rule Act.

In accordance with both his own and his father's wishes, King George had the words known as 'The Protestant Declaration' removed from his first parliamentary speech.

This was the declaration which had caused Edward VII so much embarrassment in 1901 – the one that repudiated 'Rome and all her superstitions and idolatries'. Salisbury had not permitted Edward to alter the formula, but before his accession George had instructed Prime Minister Asquith that he would not agree to open parliament unless a more tolerant formula were devised.

Despite some rumblings about 'papal despotism', Asquith and the King worked out a new statement whereby the King simply declared, 'I am a faithful Protestant and will uphold the Protestant succession'. Both houses of parliament passed this formula, on 3 August 1910 and 6 February 1911, King George duly read it from the throne.

The coronation itself took place on 22 June 1911 at Westminster Abbey, with the usual splendour and ceremony. The standards of England, Scotland, Ireland and Wales were raised as George and Mary proceeded towards the altar – Ireland's standard being carried by The O'Conor Don, descendant of the high kings of Ireland.

In his coronation oath, as with the parliamentary statement, George had the anti-Catholic clause annulled. Instead of repudiating the 'idolatry and superstition of the Papist faith and its invocations of the Blessed Virgin and Saints', George again simply pledged to 'maintain the Protestant religion and the established church' and to 'govern the people of this United Kingdom of Great Britain and Ireland, and the Dominions thereto belonging, according to the statutes in Parliament agreed on and the respective laws and customs of the same'.[19]

True to his character, having been crowned in the morning, George worked during the afternoon, showed himself on the balcony in the evening, then did a little more reading and writing, before retiring 'rather tired' at 11.45pm. He was always conscientious in keeping his diary: it is a careful and dutiful journal of record, if sometimes a little wobbly on spellings – and occasionally rather 'Pooterish' (as in 'Good old 1911!'). As a consequence he has provided history with every last detail of his first state visit to Dublin.

Because of the importance of Ireland in the dynamics of the United Kingdom, a state visit to Dublin was arranged soon after the coronation. Indeed, within a fortnight, the King and Queen were on their way, accompanied by their elder son, David (who would briefly be Edward VIII, and then, after abdication, the Duke of Windsor), and their shy daughter, Princess Mary (who to everyone's embarrassment, Countess Markievicz would later accuse of planning to marry Michael Collins). The King's elderly Uncle Arthur, the Duke of Connaught, also accompanied the party.

George and Mary sailed into Kingstown-Dún Laoghaire harbour on the morning of Saturday 8 July 1911. The King, writes his biographer Harold Nicolson, 'could not have conceived it possible that he would never visit Dublin again.'

> We reached Kingston [sic] at 7.30 [pm] & anchored inside the harbour,' George wrote in his diary, having also noted that the previous day was their 18th wedding anniversary. 'The whole of the Home Fleet, who were anchored just outside, saluted & cheered as we passed them. The break-water & harbour was [sic] crowded with people. My little old gunboat, the *Thrush* is here, she is doing fishery work now.[20]

The former sailor always noted naval matters. The monarchs dined with six admirals aboard the royal yacht and were next morning drawn to land by a pulling barge.

After various ceremonials 'we started our long drive to Dublin', reported the King. 'The streets were beautifully decorated & were lined by hundreds of thousands of people who gave us a wonderful reception.' At Monkstown Church and at 'Ball's Bridge' addresses of loyal welcome were presented: these were traditional royalist redoubts.

At Ballsbridge an escort of the 1st Life Guards relieved the 5th Royal Irish Lancers, and the party reached Dublin Castle at 12.30 pm 'after a most successful but hot drive'. The King was pleased that 'dear old Uncle Arthur' made it all the way without feeling faint. George and Mary were lodged at Dublin Castle, rather than at Viceregal Lodge in the Phoenix Park.

The Castle, in the centre of the city, was less scenic than the park, which Queen Victoria had so liked for its views, but it provided many conveniences – in several senses of the word.[21]

With the prospect of hosting the royal party, officials at the Castle had had new, superior lavatories installed – this was *the* age of loo improvements. So the King found that 'our rooms in the Castle are most comfortable'.

His first appointment – escorted now by the 5th Dragoon Guards – was to open formally the Royal College of Science in Merrion Street, where his father, Edward VII, had laid the foundation stone in 1908, now the office of the Taoiseach.[22] Thence to Trinity College Dublin where Lord Iveagh presented a loyal address and, following that, to the Phoenix Park races – 'large crowds all the way, the heat of the sun there was tremendous & there was a very large attendance,' noted George. Later on during the Saturday afternoon the royals paid a visit to the 'Lord Iveagh play centre …where we saw the poorest RC children sing & dance, quite delightful, the Iveaghs & family were there. These children are of the very poorest & they feed them & look after them,' the King recorded.[23]

On Sunday the royal family went to church at St Patrick's Cathedral: 'a beautiful service. The Archbishop of Armagh preached an excellent sermon.' More crowds in the street and again a cavalry escort.[24] In the afternoon George and Mary went by 'motor car' to Maynooth, where all the Catholic Bishops of Ireland awaited and gave the King an address of welcome. This was correct rather than effusive. 'They then showed us round the College & the beautiful chapel. There were a great many people there.'

The crowded schedule went on: visits, addresses, tea parties, dinner parties. Everything was recorded in detail by King George: a levee held by the King; a 'drawing-room' by the Queen; and the trip to Leopardstown Races, with an escort of the 20th Hussars and the 1st Life Guards, where there were 'cheering crowds all the way. We got a tremendous reception on reaching the course, the place was crammed.'

The King ran two horses (Devil's Dyke and Mirabeau) in two races, '… & I am sorry to say they were only second, both being beaten by a short head … that is the luck of racing.' Back to a state banquet at the Castle: '… we sat down 121, every thing beautifully done.' And then an investiture: Lords Shaftesbury and Kitchener made Knights of the Order of St Patrick.

The selection of two such candidates sums up a core problem with British rule in Ireland: the visible failure of the ruling caste to confer upon mainstream Irish people the honours of an allegedly Irish order, the Patrick. The *Irish Catholic* newspaper repeatedly complained that 'no one from the majority religion' was ever chosen to join the Order of St Patrick.

The 9th Earl of Shaftesbury, Anthony Ashley-Cooper (42, Eton and Sandhurst), had been a Lieutenant Colonel in the North Irish Horse, a Commissioner of the Congested Districts and the Lord Mayor of Belfast (an office then closed to Catholics, or to anyone married to a Catholic). His mother had been the daughter of the Marquess of Donegall. His links with Ireland were entirely confined to the Ascendancy.

Lord Kitchener of Khartoum had been born of English parents at Ballylongford in Co Kerry. Kitchener was a Unionist and an imperialist: his contemporary fame now rests upon the iconic recruiting slogan 'Your Country Needs You'. But his entry into the world at Ballylongford was an accident of birth, and he had scant attachment to Ireland. The historian Léon Ó Broin wrote that Kitchener looked upon the Irish with 'unconcealed contempt' – a rather strange candidate on whom to bestow the honour of St Patrick.[25]

It is true that the King or his government offered a knighthood to William Martin Murphy, the Cork-born magnate and transport millionaire, and a man who has been disparaged in the canons of Irish history as the cruel capitalist who caused the 1913 Dublin lock-out. (Recently, there have been efforts to re-assess Murphy as an Edwardian version of a Celtic Tiger entrepreneur *avant la lettre.*[26])

Murphy refused the honour: such baubles did not interest him, and he sensed that the rising tide was Nationalist. But it is still evident that although King George himself did his best to be fair-minded and to 'hold the ring' between Irishmen of different backgrounds, his court advisers failed lamentably to reach out to Irishmen of any persuasion different from that of the Unionist and Ascendancy caste.

*

Yet there certainly was no shortage of ordinary Irish applicants to attend a royal garden party at Viceregal Lodge. The Lord Mayor of Dublin, Mr Lorcan Sherlock, who had sat rather painfully on the fence over the usual Dublin Corporation arguments on whether the monarchs should be given a formal address of welcome (they voted against doing so), nevertheless found time for the event.

The Irish Parliamentary Party also held itself aloof from contact with the royal visit. As in the time of Edward VII, they declared they would rather wait until Ireland had its own Parliament before formally welcoming the royals.

And yet a great crowd attended the King's garden party – and another throng turned up for the royal reception at St Patrick's Hall in Dublin Castle. Indeed, the Lord Lieutenant received over five thousand letters from Dublin society requesting invitations for the Castle reception to meet the King and Queen: no more than 1,500 could be accommodated at the very maximum. Lord and Lady Aberdeen had the unenviable task of selecting the lucky 1,500 from the unlucky 3,500 rejects – a task that they quickly delegated to their chamberlain and his staff, so as to escape the obloquy of the disappointed. It turned out to be a very brilliant evening, and the King duly shook hands with all fifteen hundred present.

Lady Aberdeen (eccentric owner of 40 pet Scotch terriers, campaigner against tuberculosis, and a Home Rule enthusiast who had once entertained James Larkin at Viceregal Lodge) had the bright idea of organising a special welcome address from the 'women of Ireland' to the Queen.

The suffragists may have been disliked by polite society. Yet an extremist movement often stimulates a more moderate imitator in its wake. Women's groups were springing up everywhere.

And so, in a gently feminist spirit, Lady Aberdeen organised the women's welcome to Queen Mary, county by county. Lord Aberdeen wrote:

> All the ladies in charge of the counties sent most
> pleasant reports as to the general desire to sign, and

> also as to the spontaneous way in which the women gave their little contributions [which were to range from a halfpenny to one shilling]. ... It was often quite a difficulty to persuade poor people to give only a penny, for they said they did not like to give anything but silver for the Queen.[27]

There were 165,000 signatures 'gathered from all sections, creeds and parties, and [they] may be held to be truly representative of the women of all parts of Ireland.' The 'Address of Welcome from the Women of Ireland' was richly illuminated by 'lady students' at the Metropolitan School of Art in Dublin: the style chosen was 'Book of Kells', designed by James Ward, with intricate Celtic ornamentation, 'tooled in silver and inlay', and bound in six volumes in St Patrick's blue morocco by Messrs Galway, Printers of Dublin (now preserved in mint condition at the Royal Archives at Windsor). Queen Mary's arms and monogram, adorned with May blossoms, were artistically intertwined in the binding. Miss Eleanor Kelly, the binder of the Address, presented the gift and the sum of money subscribed by the women of Ireland, being £1,873.7s.3d.[28]

In many cases, the poorer Catholic counties, such as Clare and Mayo, matched or outdid the more affluent parts of Ireland associated with the Ascendancy class.

Despite the rising tide of 'Irish-Ireland' nationalism, there remained in Dublin a substantial group of Irish Catholics who thought of themselves as thoroughly Irish and yet were still quite happy to show loyalty to the Crown. This group was later to be stigmatised as 'shoneens' – lickspittles to the British – and marginalised by history.

Helena Molony was one of the Nationalist-separatist women protesting vehemently against the royal visit and wrote to the *Irish Independent* to voice her disapprobation at this 'Irishwomen's Address' to Queen Mary: it only represented 'the Garrison Party', she said. But one Mary O'Connell of Roman Street, Cork, replied, complaining that Miss Molony's attitude was 'small'. 'What harm is there in presenting a kindly person, though he or she be royal, with an address of welcome when they come from another country?'[29]

*

And so the King continued with his busy schedule during this last visit to Dublin. On Tuesday 11 July – a 'beautiful day, but very hot sun' – he worked over his boxes, as he did every day, with his private secretary Lord Stamfordham; then he drove in state to Viceregal Lodge and embarked on a morning's reviewing of military and constabulary, mounted on his horse Derby for some of the time.

Then, along with Lord Aberdeen and 'Uncle Arthur', he rode out into Phoenix Park and reviewed 16,220 men 'under the command of Sir Neville Lytelleton': he rode past the lines and lines of Irishmen in the uniform of the King, and presented colours to five regiments. 'There was an enormous crowd,' the King wrote, 'who cheered tremendously, we could hardly ride back to the Viceregal.'[30]

That night they held court at St Patrick's Hall in Dublin Castle, and the next day (which he noted was the sixth birthday of his mentally handicapped youngest son, John – little Prince John was epileptic and was to die aged 14) the royal party prepared to depart.

The King said goodbye to 'Mr Birrel' (the Chief Secretary, Augustine Birrell) and made to depart from 'Westland Road' (Westland Row, now Pearse) Station, accompanied by the 1st Life Guards, and again 'large crowds in the streets, who gave us a very hearty send off.'

They sailed away from Kingstown-Dún Laoghaire in the early afternoon, with the 1st Division of the Home Fleet escorting them for ten miles out of the harbour: the King recalled that 'they looked splendid steaming 16 knots'. The sea was a 'flat calm all the way' – and we now know that as George and Mary watched the Irish coast receding, they were the last reigning monarchs of both England and Ireland to look upon the lovely curve of Dublin Bay.

King George was well pleased. Once again, despite political opposition to the 'Crown', the ordinary Irish people had given the monarchs a fulsome welcome. Repeating history, the moderate Nationalist newspapers referred to the unprecedented welcome accorded to the King: the *Irish Independent*, now the dominant newspaper for middle-class and Nationalist Ireland, printed many fine and innovative photographs of the welcome committees.

As he departed from Westland Row, the King indicated that he hoped to come back soon to Dublin – which greatly pleased the press.

> I cannot leave Ireland without at once giving expression to the feelings of joy and affection inspired by the wonderful reception which the people of Dublin have just given to the Queen and myself. Wherever we have gone we and our children [sic] have been welcomed with a spontaneous and hearty loyalty that has greatly touched our hearts and made a permanent impression upon us ... without restraint, and in obedience to what seemed a natural impulse of goodwill, the entire populace, men, women and children, came out into Streets and the Parks to give us a true Irish welcome. We shall never forget it.[31]

He also said that he 'greatly admired' the street decorations, and felt 'grateful' for all the efforts made in all parts of the city. And he looked forward so much to returning and seeing other parts of the country. The *Church of Ireland Gazette* remarked that:

> No British Sovereign has ever had such a reception as King George has received from his Irish subjects. Dublin shows her cheeriest smiles and has put on her brightest dress; the dingy, if beautiful old city is looking her very best, and many of the squalid streets of her poorest quarters reflect the gaiety of her welcome.[32]

The King's impression that 'the entire populace' had come out to greet him was understandable: the crowds were terrific. But the influential spirits who were forging Ireland's future – the artists, the revolutionaries, the poets – were not among the welcoming throng. Countess Markievicz, along with Helena Molony, had set fire to a British flag in protest against the royal visit, receiving an ovation from the surrounding crowd.[33]

And it was hardly coincidental that, just as the King and Queen arrived in Ireland on 8 July, the Abbey Theatre had been running both Yeats' *Cathleen ní Houlihan*, in which Ireland is personified as the true Queen who will stir Irish hearts, and *The Workhouse* by Lady Gregory, a play underlining the poverty and the fear of poverty that was so much part of Irish rural life.

*

The King returned to London and to the discomfort of Home Rule politics in the middle of what was to be the hottest summer in centuries, with the temperature sometimes reaching 115 degrees Fahrenheit.

For George now faced serious trouble with Irish Unionists. After the nullifying of the House of Lords' veto by the Parliament Act, the King was exposed to the full wrath of those Conservatives and Unionists who were willing to go to any lengths to halt Home Rule. Since the Lords could no longer obstruct, the diehard Tories and Ulster Unionists turned to the King, hoping that he would personally withhold consent from the Home Rule Bill that had been introduced on 11 April 1912. Alternatively, they hoped that the King might dismiss his ministers and appoint others more obliging to the Unionist cause.[34]

Three men of like mind now banded together to lobby – and even to threaten – the King in a desperate attempt to stop Home Rule. These were Edward Carson, James Craig and Andrew Bonar Law, the last of whom quite unexpectedly, and to the King's dismay, became leader of the Conservatives and Unionists in November 1911.

Bonar Law was born in a Canadian manse, of Ulster Protestant parents: he had grown up in Orange Glasgow. Edward Carson, who became the charismatic leader of the Irish Unionists in 1910, was a Dublin-born lawyer in the southern Unionist tradition – a quirky, passionate Irishman (or so he considered himself) who seemed to apply the rebel streak to the Orange cause. James Craig, the Ulster Unionist leader who would become Viscount Craigavon, was a canny if unimaginative leader who would organise the Ulster Volunteers specifically to resist Home Rule.[35]

This trio shared a similar tradition of Bible-based Christianity, and a profound attachment to the Union of Britain and Ireland and the cherished cult of the legacy of King William III, victor at the Boyne, who 'gave us our freedom, religion and laws'. To these men Irish nationalism was anathema and sedition, and Roman Catholicism slavery to a foreign superstition and a continental power (although Carson, the Dubliner, was of a less sectarian cast of mind).

But now the trio prepared to lead their followers to 'die in the last ditch' rather than allow a Liberal administration to legislate for an independent parliament in Dublin. They would do all they could to use the King against Home Rule.

As soon as Asquith introduced the Home Rule Bill, Sir Edward Carson, fresh from an enormous anti-Home Rule rally in Belfast on 12 April, hurried to Westminster to warn that Ulster would *never* accept the measure. Asquith replied that it would be 'impossible to concede the demand of a small minority to veto the verdict of the Irish Nation.'[36]

That week in April was melodramatic. Within a few days, proceedings in Parliament were interrupted by the stunning news that the *Titanic*, the greatest moving object in the world, constructed in Belfast (then the greatest shipbuilding centre on earth), had hit an iceberg and sunk in under three hours.

The *Church of Ireland Gazette* reported that 'it would be impossible to describe the consternation in Belfast. The city may be said to reel under the shock. Belfast people feel as if a crushing, numbing personal catastrophe had fallen on them.' Even the 'Home Rule danger has been, for the time being, superseded.'[37]

Yet even the shock of the *Titanic*, the pride of Protestant Ulster, could not for long hold back the political tempest emanating from Ulster Unionism. By September 1912, Edward Carson was presiding over a solemn Covenant signed at City Hall, Belfast, which declared that Ulster Unionists, as 'loyal subjects of His Gracious Majesty King George V', were convinced in their consciences that Home Rule would be 'subversive of our civil and religious freedom, destructive of our citizenship, and perilous to the Unity of the Empire'. And thus beseeched the King to 'use all means which may be found necessary to defeat the present conspiracy to set up a Home Rule Parliament in Ireland ... and to refuse to recognise its authority.'

By the end of November 1912, some half a million men and women in the province of Ulster had signed Carson's sacred covenant, many in their own blood.[38]

The poet Rudyard Kipling turned out a characteristically brilliant, if somewhat blood-curdling, poem to mark the occasion of 'Ulster 1912', which promised Ulster Protestants that Home Rule meant they would be ravaged in their beds by the hordes of Romish zealots. Kipling came near to the note of rebellion and sedition with which, paradoxically, the Ulster Loyalists were threatening the Crown: 'If England drives us forth / We shall not fall alone.'

Over the next year, this situation was to bring King George to despair. He felt he was being propelled by the Ulster Unionists to obstruct the will of the House of Commons. Carson had few inhibitions about invoking the possible assistance of the German Emperor – that is to say, treason, in the name of 'loyalism'.

The King lamented to the Prime Minister that 'no Sovereign in generations has been placed in so difficult & anxious a position as that in which I find myself today.' He was to repeat this plaintive cry many times over. He wished to use his influence 'to avert the catastrophe which threatens Ireland' but 'Whatever I do I shall offend half the population.' Again he repeated his lament: 'No sovereign has ever been in such a position ...'[39]

As Ulster Unionists threatened to sabotage Home Rule and Irish Home Rulers resisted, the King pledged that 'I shall continue as long as I can to persuade the parties concerned to come to an agreement & shall certainly do all in my power to prevent civil war & bloodshed in Ireland.'

But he felt continually 'embarrassed' and 'uncomfortable' all the same. 'I shall be placed in a most awkward & disagreeable position.' And again, came his *cri de coeur*: 'no Sovereign in this country has ever been placed in such a cruel predicament.' Sometimes he reiterates this with emphasis: '*Never* has a British Sovereign (in more recent times) been placed in such an odious & mortifying position.'

George's own inclinations were both conservative and unionist, since he was himself both the personification of the Crown and the apex of the United Kingdom. Yet still he strove, as best he could, to be 'constitutional' and to 'hold the ring' between differing parties.

Sir Edward Carson was sometimes exasperated with George's 'constitutionalism'. 'I am told he is saturated with the idea of "constitutionalism",' he wrote disparagingly, 'which he translates into doing everything the Prime Minister tells him.' Carson adds sarcastically, 'What a good King!'[40]

The King was bombarded with letters supporting the Ulster Unionist cause, and telling of the extreme measures to which Ulster Unionists would go to defend their heritage. On the other side, George had hardly any personal contact with Irish Nationalists, and only the very slightest connection with the parliamentary Nationalists led by John Redmond of the Irish Parliamentary Party. Indeed, he did not meet Redmond on a personal basis until July 1914.[41]

Ireland's case for Home Rule was represented by the Liberal Prime Minister Asquith, in his compromising, moderate English way (egged on to more affirmative action by his more outspoken second wife, Margot, whom the King privately thought should be banned from public expression); and also by the Irish Chief Secretary, Augustine Birrell, an Englishman who had 'gone native' in Ireland and was regarded by some in England (and by Irish Unionists too) as 'complacent' on the Irish issue. But Birrell underestimated the resolve of the Ulstermen – thinking their threats were 'all bluff and blackmail'.

Birrell was indeed favourable to Home Rule for Ireland, and was more inclined to be sympathetic to Irish Nationalists than to Ulster Unionists – he preferred, as he wrote jocosely, 'the Babylonian Whore to Sir Edward Carson'.[42] But he was also, from 1913 onwards, struggling with a painful private problem – his adored wife Eleanor was suffering from a fatal brain tumour, which caused him ineffable anguish, and brought her a form of insanity. He told few outside his family about this matter, though it must have distracted him seriously from his political task.

Otherwise, the Unionist aristocrats, establishment grandees and conservatively-minded courtiers had the greater access to the monarch. The names of the King's regular informants and correspondents on the matter of Ireland are revealing: Lord Crichton, Lord Morley, Lord Grey, Lord Haldane, Sir Francis Hopwood, Lord Halifax, the Archbishop of Canterbury, Lord Curzon, Lord Charles Beresford (who would become the Marquess of Waterford), A.V. Dicey (the noted jurist who had written a book arguing strongly against Home Rule), Walter Long (who had been a stern, though effective predecessor to Birrell), and Bonar Law – the last three being particularly committed to Ulster Unionism. Plus F. E. Smith, later Lord Birkenhead, a Unionist particularly committed to making mischief who would later prosecute Sir Roger Casement. Admittedly Morley and Haldane were former Liberal statesmen, but they could scarcely be said to represent grass roots Irish Catholics.

Some of George's advisers were men whose sources of information came from the landlord class in Ireland, and had little understanding of what was happening in a wider perspective. They often sent to Windsor information and advice that was wrong-headed or beside the point. One informant told the King that ordinary people in the south and west of Ireland were 'comparatively speaking, content and well-to-do' and 'no longer enthusiastic' about Home Rule. This information had come from a local landlord in the south west of the country.

The King was also assured that the Catholic Church in Ireland was 'indifferent' to Home Rule, and 'probably at heart would be glad not to come under the power of an Irish parliament'. The most cursory reading of a devotional magazine or newspaper would have revealed that the Catholic Church was largely in line with John Redmond's thinking – he *was* a Clongowes boy – while some of the younger priests were veering towards Sinn Féin. Charles Fitzmaurice, kinsman to Lord Lansdowne, the Unionist leader in the Lords, also reported rather erroneously that 'the priests' feared Home Rule because they feared losing power.[43] Contrarily, several of the King's correspondents underlined the danger of 'priestcraft' if Home Rule should be granted.

Sir Robert Charles, one of the most distinguished surgeons in the land and the King's own personal physician, informed the King from Belfast that 'The fight [by Unionists] is *not* against their fellow countrymen but against the priestcraft that sows the seeds of dissension amongst as worthy a people as there is in the world.'[44]

Lord Stamfordham, the King's Private Secretary, had daily access to the monarch: when he died in 1931, George V said of him 'he taught me how to be a king'. But Stamfordham, who wrote many of the King's letters and acted as regular adviser, was a strong Tory and patronisingly interpreted the Nationalist movement in Ireland in a personal memo to King George in April 1912:

> The men who really are at the back of the nationalists are the keepers of those endless stores in every village which sell boots & shoes on one side of the counter – whisky on the other. 'Gombeens' I think they are called. They are the curse of the country & their owners pull the strings.[45]

This was again off the mark: the 'gombeen' men – shopkeepers and *commerçants* who sometimes came to dominate small-town business – were indeed becoming more prosperous in Ireland. Although the word means 'usurer' in Irish, and was always employed disparagingly, it had no political connotation.

Admittedly the 'gombeens' had connections with organisations such as the Ancient Order of Hibernians, who were forming a Catholic-Nationalist commercial base challenging the cultural monopoly of the Orange Order in the North of Ireland, and the trading and mercantile monopoly of the Freemasons' Lodges in Dublin and the south.

The King also received long and sometimes vehement letters from the Ulster-Canadian Unionist Andrew Bonar Law – whom George did not personally like – about the 'outrage' of 'coercing Ulster' under a Home Rule policy.

'If the Home Rule Bill passes through all its stages under the Parliament Act & requires only the Royal assent, the position will be a very serious and impossible one for the Crown,' came Bonar Law's message, touching on King George's most obsessive worry.[46] The Unionist party would hold, he insisted, that the Constitution was 'in suspense'; if there were the least doubt that the government had the support of the country, the sovereign should use his prerogative to ask his ministers to proceed with a fresh general election. He concluded by requesting that the King consult Lord Lansdowne, Mr Balfour, and himself before taking further action.

In subsequent letters he claimed that the Liberal government 'know that the country is against them': that there would be 'civil war' in the North of Ireland, and that the King should use his constitutional position to withhold consent to the Home Rule measure. That is, the King should use the royal prerogative to veto the Home Rule Bill which Bonar Law regarded as unconstitutional.

Walter Long, former leader of the Unionists – although described as a 'gullible' man – was another correspondent informing the King that he was in a perilous position if he did not obstruct Home Rule:

> I do not believe the gravity of the situation can be exaggerated. I am myself immensely distressed at the weight and prevalence of the opinion that to force these Bills upon the country by the aid of the Sovereign would be to precipitate Civil War, and prejudice – if not destroy – the position of the Crown.[47]

Yet another feverish lobbyist on behalf of the Ulster Unionists was the Editor (and proprietor) of *The Spectator*, John St Loe Strachey, a cousin of Lytton Strachey, and arch-Conservative author of books such as *Practical Wisdom of the Bible* and *Problems and Perils of Socialism*.

Strachey published influential articles in *The Spectator* claiming that the King would be acting unconstitutionally if he assented to Home Rule (suggesting that the Parliament Bill, which removed the House of Lords' veto, had illegally altered the British Constitution). At one point the Ulster Unionists, prompted by St Loe Strachey, were even suggesting that the King might abdicate rather than append his signature to a Home Rule Act.[48]

Some, like Chief Secretary Birrell, thought the Ulster Unionists were 'bluffing', but the King was assured this was not so. An experienced diplomat, Sir Robert Kennedy, retired in Co Down, sent a despatch to the King on Easter Sunday 1913, which reflected how sincere those convictions were:

> I know that every effort is being made by advocates of Home Rule to represent the opposition of Protestant Ulster to be mere Orange Bluff. I have lived in many foreign Countries and I have had many opportunities of witnessing political and national movements during the last forty years, and I affirm with conviction that I have never seen men of all classes more grimly in earnest than the Protestants of Ulster in their determination not to submit to a Dublin parliament.[49]

For a long time, Sir Robert told the King, he had laughed at all the 'tall talk', but he laughed no longer. There was no longer so much talk, now it was 'all drill'.

The drilling and the mustering and the monster meetings in Northern Ireland, the covenants signed in blood, the threats from the Ulstermen to bring the Crown down with them, the hints that they would appeal to Germany, the blatant importation of guns to Larne, the mutiny in the Curragh when a group of army officers said they would not draw swords against the Ulster Unionists (which angered King George, who believed that it was not a military man's job to hold any political opinions at all) did not affect the King's actions or decisions.

He was too level-headed and too cautious – and perhaps too shrewd about protecting his own position. He was advised by wiser counsels, such as Lord Cromer, the former Evelyn Baring, that it would endanger the Crown to be seen to oppose the will of Parliament. Lord Cromer's directive was firm: the King should certainly *not* refuse assent to the Home Rule Bill. He would have done his duty if he had advised his Ministers 'of the risk of Civil War in Ireland'. Soldiers should obey orders and the King should insist on their obedience. The King should not show 'the smallest animosity against the Home Rule Bill on its own merits'. He should make it quite clear that there was no question of reviving the royal right of veto over Home Rule, though he may suggest an election as a means of 'consulting the country'.[50]

The King would be repeatedly lobbied by his Unionist correspondents into suggesting to Asquith that it might be useful to hold a fresh general election on the specific subject of Home Rule. The Conservatives and Unionists were convinced they would win such an election, and the bill could be thus defeated at the last ditch.

Yet George, though anguished, continued to be prudent. He worried that whatever he did he would be blamed: whether he stood by the will of the Commons on Home Rule, or whether he was guided by Bonar Law into recommending a dissolution, he would be 'blamed by half the population'.

While the King agonised, the militarism of the Ulster Unionists was having a profound impact elsewhere in Ireland. It could be argued that the real founder of modern Irish separatism – paradoxically – was Edward Carson, the driven, emotional and inspirational leader of the Ulster Unionists.

Until Carson mustered his million men and women in defence of Ulster's cause, most Irish Nationalists were constitutional. Men like Patrick Pearse and Eoin MacNeill were supporters of John Redmond's constitutional Irish Parliamentary Party at Westminster. Patrick Pearse had started off as a monarchist and was making speeches in favour of Redmond's Home Rule movement as late as 1912, while Arthur Griffith of Sinn Féin had originally advanced a 'dual monarchy' for Britain and Ireland, based on the Austro-Hungarian model.

The current of separatism – rather than moderate nationalism – was already gathering pace, but the excitement of the Ulster Unionists must have been hugely infectious. The passion in their correspondence alone still throbs with that excitement.

The example of the Ulster Volunteer Force inspired a parallel Irish Volunteer Force. In March and April of 1912, Home Rule fever ran high in Dublin: within six months, the tide was turning towards more direct action, as an inflamed response to the sight of Orangemen readying themselves to fight.[51]

In an excitable – and influential – article, Pearse wrote, 'I am glad that the Orangemen have armed, for it is a goodly thing to see arms in Irish hands … We must accustom ourselves to the thought of arms, to the sight of arms, to the use of arms.' In a much quoted and rather chilling sequel he added, 'We may make mistakes in the beginning and shoot the wrong people; but bloodshed is a cleansing and a sanctifying thing, and the nation which regards it as the final horror has lost its manhood.'

Would Pearse have written this if he had not been aroused to a state of excitement by the sight of the marching, drilling, arming and rebellious Orangemen? After all, what Irishman could not admire those who were willing to fight for their values, their heritage, their 'faith and fatherland'? Patrick Pearse proclaimed – and his fellow Nationalists heard the message – 'An Orangeman with a gun is a far less ridiculous sight than a Nationalist without a gun.'[52]

The militias in Ireland were also picking up the Zeitgeist of the European age: war fever was rippling across Europe, in Balkan and Turkish wars that were but preludes to the Great War of

1914–18. The Ulster Unionist women had caught the spirit of the age in full. The King's surgeon Sir Robert Charles wrote:

> The power in this movement is the Ulster woman. Woe betide the man who shows slackness. ... They will allow neither love of children, husbands, brothers or sweethearts to stand in the way. They will sacrifice all. They believe they are in the right and work for conscience's sake. ... They are fully prepared to die & they expect that when many of them have been killed England will wake up and at length see the remainder righted. They will fight – they will face the regulars.[53]

In this heightened atmosphere, one of the more steadying counsels came from Winston Churchill, who saw King George in September 1913. Churchill was 'hopeful of a solution' in Ireland. He had always admitted that:

> Ulster *has* a case, and that if Ireland has the right to claim separate Govt from England, Ulster cannot be refused similar exemption from Govt by an Irish Parliament. But he [Churchill] strongly resents that Ulster should talk of 'Civil War' & do everything in her power to stir up rebellion before even the Home Rule Bill has passed, let alone before the Irish Parliament is set up.[54]

Ireland, Churchill told the King, 'has been earnestly waiting for the fulfilment of their dream [sic] for the past 30 years. Is it likely that she can now stand by & see the cup, almost at their lips, dashed to the ground?' It would be fatal, he warned, if the Home Rule Bill was killed off.

By 1913 it was becoming accepted that 'Ulster' (as it was commonly called in the official papers) would be exempted, at least temporarily, from Irish Home Rule. In other words, that partition would be inevitable. This also worried the King. He asked F. E. Smith, just back from Belfast, 'if Ulster were left out [of Home Rule], the Protestants would give a promise not to molest the Roman Catholic minority?' The ebullient F. E. said he was confident 'this could be arranged'. But he was not confident about everything: first he had said that Carson was 'bluffing'; then he said he took that back.[55]

Meanwhile, in Belfast, some of the grass roots Loyalists were worried about the King's compliance with Home Rule: 'Surely he won't sign the Bill. His Majesty will never hand us over to the Pope.'[56]

*

There had been so much talk about civil war in the North of Ireland, and so many alarming reports about the drilling and the mustering and the armed rebellion for which the Ulstermen were preparing, that the imperial authorities were bracing themselves to deal with such disorder.

Sir Francis Hopwood sent a *very confidential* memo to the King's secretary in March 1914, to say that 'I hear secretly that two small ships are under orders to go to Belfast tonight ... only stoops probably – & ostensibly to guard a magazine or magazines – but there is a flutter of excitement & disaffection here for any such job ...'[57]

On that very day, 20 March, 57 officers at the Curragh military camp in Co Kildare (out of 70 stationed there) had declared they would resign their commissions rather than be used to enforce Home Rule against the wishes of Ulster. This was known thereafter as the 'Curragh Mutiny'.

The King was furious that he had not been properly informed about this incident, and had had to read it first in the newspapers; furious that soldiers should take it into their heads to effect rebellion, and furious that they should feel driven to rebel in the first place. And then *livid* when the 'radical and socialist' newspapers blamed him for allowing it to happen.

'I am grieved beyond words at this disastrous and irreparable catastrophe which has befallen my army,' he wrote to Asquith, 'which, whatever may now happen, will tarnish its long and glorious history. It is deplorable to think that gallant Officers have been driven to take such fatal steps.'

George complained that he had been kept 'in complete ignorance' of the events. He had learned of the mutiny from the morning papers, and from a letter to Queen Mary from an officer's mother 'who had been ordered to choose between dismissal or to fight against Ulster'. He instructed that he should be more fully informed about anything else that was going on, particularly 'any proposed employment of the Navy in connection with Ulster'.[58] Asquith pleaded innocence: but Bonar Law wrote to the King specifically to 'ask whether the officers who have risked everything for a cause in which we believe should be allowed to suffer?'.

There is a likelihood that at least some of the men were victims of 'peer pressure', and were pushed into this gesture of resigning their commissions; and also that the Unionists had over-inflated the hypothetical theory that British Army officers would be shortly opening fire on their 'kith and kin'. But the Curragh 'mutiny' certainly had the desired effect of alarming everyone.

By the spring of 1914 the North gave every sign that it was bursting to fight. Sir Robert Charles, the King's physician, reported from Belfast on the 'united front of all [Unionist] workers and classes.'

It was suggested at this point by an Irish Home Rule backbench MP, Sir Thomas Esmonde (a grandson of Henry Grattan), that if only John Redmond and Edward Carson could be brought together by the King, perhaps a solution could be found.[59]

Unfortunately, the King had little contact with John Redmond – only one very brief and formal letter exists from Redmond to King George – and was wary of this correct and constitutional Irish Nationalist. Nevertheless, there is evidence that George had some sympathy with Redmond's position, and he did eventually tell the Irish Home Ruler that he understood the need for Home Rule.[60]

Redmond's career is a warning to moderates: you will be rejected by both extremes. Redmond believed that a Home Rule Ireland would take her place among the Dominions of the British Empire (Redmond's first wife had been Australian and he was comfortable with the links that Australia and Canada maintained with the imperial parliament). But some members of the British establishment saw him as a dangerous and recalcitrant Irish Nationalist, and he was described, on one occasion, as 'ugly' and 'squat'.[61]And, in the fullness of time, John Redmond would be spat upon in the street by the genuine Irish Nationalist rebel C. S. Andrews who despised the compromises of constitutionalism.[62]

When Redmond resisted partition, the King thought him unreasonable, though Redmond could not possibly have conceded this outright. George complained to Asquith that 'although Mr Redmond said "there were no lengths to which he was not prepared to go towards a settlement", he at the same time refused to agree to the permanent exclusion of Ulster or to go beyond the six year limit. This is not encouraging.' Trying to be even-handed, the King added: 'On the other side, Sir E. Carson's & Mr Bonar Law's speeches were not much more conciliatory.'[63]

By April of 1914, the King felt that 'the time is slipping away': he could hardly have realised just how little time was left. At the end of the day, said King George, the Irish really do have to sort out the problem between themselves. But 'It will be my duty to leave nothing undone which lies within my power to save Ireland from Civil Strife'.

A 'Buckingham Palace' Conference on Ireland was held on 21 July 1914. This was the King's initiative: he believed, perhaps naively, that talking could patch matters up. But it was too late for all that. It failed, although the King's gesture in including the Irish Home Rulers acknowledged their legitimacy, as James H. Murphy points out.[64]

The Great War was now but a fortnight away.

In September 1914, after the First World War had begun, the King gave his final assent to the Home Rule Act. However, the question of excluding the Six Counties remained unresolved, and by agreement between Ulster Unionists and the Irish Parliamentary Party, the Act was suspended for the duration of the war and until special provision could be made for Ulster.

Although George V had agreed to the principle of Home Rule (he believed it would make Ireland a more contented member of the British imperial family), in the end he could not but feel a wave of ruefulness in breaking up the United Kingdom.

'I do not conceal from you my regret at having to give my Assent to the Home Rule Bill, which has now been placed upon the statute Book', he wrote to his advisor Sir Francis Hopwood on 17 September. He felt that despite the compromise reached 'the question is still far from a settlement. ... Time alone will show whether the blessings which they [Asquith's government] promise from the passing of the Bill are fulfilled or not.'[65]

To the Prime Minister the King wrote that in giving his assent he hoped that Asquith would understand 'how deeply I feel the gravity of the political outlook as evidenced by the recent debates in both Houses of Parliament.'[66]

Civil war had been averted, but George couldn't help regretting the bitterness that remained. 'So far as Ireland is concerned I can only trust that by the end of the war there may be a marked change for the better in the attitude [of the different political parties].'

His secretary Stamfordham observed that 'It was almost pathetic to watch the King actually signing the instrument by which the Bill becomes an Act. For one's thoughts go back more than a year and recall how during that period His Majesty had devoted quiet, patient, unremitting work to help in arriving at a peaceful and honourable settlement.' Yet Stamfordham 'suspects the whole thing is unsatisfactory'. 'Thus the curtain falls upon, not as we have always suspected, the final, but practically only the first act of the Drama or Tragedy, according to the political colouring of our opera glasses!'[67]

The Government of Ireland Act was to become law on 18 September. The parliamentary session closed with a 'remarkable demonstration of loyalty & affection to the King, the singing of the National Anthem in the House of Commons, having been started by Mr Will Crooks, the Labour Member for Woolwich, and heartily joined in by Mr J. Redmond.'

But the Ulster Unionists stormed out of the chamber.[68]

*

George V: Revolution and Partition

The King had been so involved with Ireland that war in Europe almost seemed to take him by surprise. But once it was under way, Britain's concerns moved swiftly away from the sister island and towards the involvement of the entire Empire in the conflict.

King George had rather erroneously given the impression to his cousin, Prince Henry of Hesse, that in any such European conflict his country would stay neutral. It is possible that this intelligence prompted the Kaiser to greater belligerence in continental Europe.

Almost a century later, the course of the Great War retains a strong imaginative hold in novels, films, and television. It was entered into with great gusto on all sides, and the many Irishmen who voluntarily joined up did so with the common belief that 'it would all be over by Christmas'. Some joined for adventure, some for steady work and pensions for their families should they perish. The Catholic Church did not disfavour this war against what it regarded as a brutal regime (that of Prussia) and it still had a score to settle with Germany for Bismarck's 'Kulturkampf' ('Culture War') against Catholicism.

Perhaps some 200,000 Irishmen responded to the call for recruits. John Redmond, the leader of Nationalist Ireland in 1914, encouraged Irishmen to do so, believing (naively, as it turned out) that in serving 'King and Country' the Irish volunteers would also serve Ireland.

Redmond entertained high hopes that an all-Ireland regiment would be created within the British Army that would knit together Catholic Nationalists and Ulster Protestants (something on the model of the Anzac corps that united Australia and New Zealand) and that common Nationalist and Unionist participation would lead to all-Ireland reconciliation. But in this, as in much else, Redmond was to be frustrated.[69]

Although Home Rule was on the statute books, Redmond was gradually sidelined by the rise and rise of the more radical form of Irish separatist nationalism that went under the general banner of 'Sinn Féin'. But it can also, with justice, be said that Redmond was seriously let down by the British.

Andrew Bonar Law (who would become Prime Minister briefly in 1922, dying of throat cancer in 1923) treated John Redmond shabbily, even refusing to share a platform with him when Asquith visited Dublin. He described Redmond as 'implacable' in correspondence with the Archbishop of Canterbury, Randall Davidson, which was very far from being the case.[70]

Edward Carson rebuffed Redmond's overtures in bringing all Irishmen together in the war effort: he refused to join Mr Redmond in addressing a recruiting meeting at Newry, although the Dublin-born Carson outwardly declared that he always wanted to see Irishmen together under the King's colours. (By the time Redmond died in 1918 Carson's personal feelings – often volatile anyway – had mellowed. 'I cannot recall to mind,' he said, 'one single bitter personal word that ever passed between John Redmond and myself.'[71]

But then, by the last year of the Great War, suffering had mellowed many.

John Redmond felt that he was treated patronisingly by the War Office, and that Irish Catholics were not given equal treatment by the brass hats; they were certainly contemptuously regarded by Lord Kitchener, that native of Ballylongford, Co Kerry and Knight of the Order of St Patrick.

By contrast, Edward Carson (who was the leader of Ulster Unionists, as Redmond was of Irish Nationalists) was taken into the coalition British Cabinet of Asquith in 1915, while Redmond was not in a position of parity. To some degree, this was John Redmond's own choice: Paul Bew tells us that Redmond's servant slammed the door on the official emissary offering a Cabinet position.[72]

But Carson's promotion to political power seemed like yet another manifestation of unequal British attitudes towards the two parts of Ireland. It was also a curious example to give to Irish rebels: Carson had been close to sedition in 1911–13, threatening a civil war, and hinting at seeking treasonable assistance from Germany. Whereas, as Alvin Jackson points out, Redmond had always behaved with impeccable constitutionality.[73]

Redmond made personal sacrifices for Ulster. He believed –
after all the parliamentary differences with Ulster Unionists over
Home Rule which nearly brought Ireland to a civil war – that it
could in some way be healing for Irishmen, south and north, to
face a common enemy together.

Some of the Ulster regiments did fight side by side with their
southern and Catholic comrades: John Redmond's younger
brother, Willie Redmond, was to say in a poignant valedictory
letter from the Western Front: 'My men are splendid and we are
pulling famously with the Ulster men. Would to God we could
bring this spirit back with us to Ireland.'[74] Willie Redmond was
killed, and John Redmond was to die a broken and disappointed
man: he who believed he had won Parnell's dream, and who had
thought that Ireland could stand with Britain in a great conflict,
and would be rewarded.

On the Unionist side, Edward Carson was also to experience
sharp sadness, as the 'Ulster' that he had been so proud to see
armed and ready to fight for its own defence went forth to die
in such numbers on the Somme. On 1 July 1916, the 36th Ulster
division attacked the German lines, and held a sector of the front
by Thiepval wood. But they lost more than half their men, and
the loss was felt to be a devastation.

The Great War would mark a significant divergence between
British and Irish interests, though this would not become immediately apparent. In the spring of the very worst year of the war
– 1916, the year that was to bring the terrible losses of the
Somme (19,000 men slaughtered in one morning, 60,000
wounded) – a rising against the Crown occurred in Dublin.

For many decades afterwards, this was seen as a 'stab in the
back' in Britain.[75] And yet the Irish view would be that after 25
years of parliamentary delay Britain deserved this reaction: as
Winston Churchill had said, Ireland's claim to nationhood was
of long standing.

When it occurred, King George did not make too much of the 'Sinn Féin rebellion'. (Neither did many people in Ireland.) He thought it a very minor matter. On Monday, 24 April, he noted in his diary that 'At 4.0[pm] Capt Hall came to tell me they had caught Sir Roger Casement in Ireland, where he had landed from Germany in a submarine; he has been a traitor since the beginning of the war.' King George had personally knighted Casement, so he was not best pleased by such a change of heart.[76]

The King's focus, like that of most people that week, was on the war on the Western Front. 'I mounted our horses,' he noted two days after the Easter Rising, and while Dublin was in the throes of fighting, 'I rode 'Delhi' & inspected the 41ˢᵗ Division under Major General Lawford; a very fine lot of men, they go to France next week. Glorious day, quite hot, 76 in the shade.'

Later in the day, Lord Crewe came to inform him about the disturbances in Dublin. 'I held a Council at 5.15 to declare Martial Law in Dublin, where the Sinn Féiners [he writes 'Feinners' initially and crosses out the first 'n'] rose two days ago & have barricaded themselves in some of the houses, there are several thousands concerned. Two Brigades have been sent to Dublin from Liverpool which will make 12,000 troops there besides the police.'

Thursday, 27 April was even hotter – '80 [degrees] in the shade, no wind' – and the King sat out on the terrace at Windsor Castle reading *The Times*. On the Friday, he 'motored to London after luncheon. Both the Prime Minister [Asquith] & Kitchener came to see me & I discussed the rising in Ireland with them, we have about 50,000 troops there now.' He expressed at this point his support for 'compulsion' (enforced military conscription) all round: 'it is the only possible thing now'.

By Saturday, Lord French – whose political judgement was wobbly at the best of times – came to inform the King that the situation in Dublin was 'well in hand now'. What he didn't confide to the King was that his own sister, Charlotte Despard, a committed Irish Nationalist, and Maud Gonne's best friend, was in the thick of it all. Lord French would be appointed Lord Lieutenant of Ireland in 1918, where he would proceed to entertain his mistress in the Viceregal Lodge, also unbeknownst to the strait-laced King George.

On Wednesday, 3 May (which the king also noted was the 23rd anniversary of his engagement to Queen Mary) he wrote that 'The rebellion in Dublin is practically over, they have already tried & shot three of the ringleaders. Mr Birrell has resigned.'

Indeed so. Augustine Birrell, who as Chief Secretary for Ireland was held responsible for 'allowing' the Easter Rising to occur. He had, from the British point of view, been too indulgent and liberal with the Irish. He, too, had originally seen the 1916 Rising as not much more than a skirmish, largely confined to Dublin.

But in truth, it is unlikely he could have prevented the events of Easter 1916. He had several times sought to resign before, especially when it became clear that Ulster would be excluded from Home Rule, but Asquith had persuaded him to remain – and drink the poisoned chalice. An honourable, witty man, and a consummate lover of books, Birrell retired into private life: he was a widower now, but close to his two sons, one of whom was mentally handicapped, and the other of whom was a conscientious objector, at the time when to his embarrassment his father was being asked to conscript Irishmen for the Western Front.

The leaders of the Easter Rising were idealistic men and women: poets, writers, schoolmasters, visionaries: James Connolly, the Communist who was said to have died a Catholic martyr's death: Seán Mac Diarmada, the crippled tram driver suffused with humble altruism. They believed that the time had come for Ireland to wrest her independence from the prevailing power.

It was predictable – and perhaps, from his viewpoint, natural – for King George to express disgust at Roger Casement's 'treason', but for Casement his commitment to Irish nationalism was part of his search for a true self (and perhaps admixed with his struggle to come to terms with his sexuality, which fixated on adolescent boys).

Several of the 1916 men equated the Rising with a kind of graduation to 'manhood', and perhaps it was necessary for Ireland to affirm an independent virility thus. However, Roy Foster's view is surely right: that the Easter 1916 was not something apart from the First World War — it was within the spirit of the age.[77] Patrick Pearse's images about irrigating the good earth with the red blood of youth were not so very different from the speeches of the generals on the Western Front: or, indeed, the songs being sung by young Serbs, young Arabs — and young Russians.

It was not coincidental that the Bolshevik revolution took place in the following year, 1917: the French call 1917 *l'année fatale*, when war and revolution engulfed Europe from end to end — Russia, the Middle East, Italy, the Balkans.

It was also the fatal year of change in Ireland when the vision of Home Rule (with the Monarchy as a 'golden bridge' between Britain and Ireland) died, and the inexorable advance of Sinn Féin signalled that the future would be, not only an independent Ireland, but an Ireland separated from the Crown.

In March 1917 John Redmond told the Prime Minister, David Lloyd George, that he was so alarmed by the rise in Sinn Féin's influence that he 'intended to stage a demonstration in the House of Commons, and to issue some sort of appeal to the Dominions, the US, and neutral countries'. Lloyd George was a wily, energetic, and often duplicitous politician, who had risen to the top from modest beginnings (a notorious womaniser, but also a successful one) and he pre-empted Redmond's warning, quickly offering Home Rule 'to that part of Ireland that wants it'.

He then added that Ulster could never be handed over to the rest of Ireland against its will. The King endorsed Lloyd George's statement to be made in the House of Commons: and, in response, John Redmond and his party walked out of the Commons to demonstrate that they would never accept the partition of Ireland. [78]

The Irish Parliamentary Party was never again to return to Westminster. Many of its members ended up living in very reduced circumstances – some in near penury – in bedsitters in Pimlico and the Elephant and Castle. This band of more than eighty men had served the cause of Ireland in a constitutional manner, and in the footsteps of Parnell: but they were rebuffed by the subsequent Free State, which was dominated by the heirs of Sinn Féin, and their contribution to the Irish political process was never acknowledged. Reporters said they were missed in the Commons: the Irish Members had added a lively, entertaining and often provocative element to the House that was never quite replaced.[79]

In May of 1917, Lloyd George called an 'Irish Convention', which was to consist of 101 Irishmen, representing Irish Nationalists, Ulster Protestants, southern Unionists, the Catholic Bishops, and the Church of Ireland Archbishops of Armagh and Dublin. Also included were several non-party individuals recognised as *notables,* such as the Provost of Trinity College Dublin, Mahaffy, and the poet and mystic George Russell (known as AE). No women were present. It was chaired by Horace Plunkett, pioneer of the agricultural and cooperative movement – a decent and diligent man, but lacking in political shrewdness.

It was just about possible that the Convention might cut a deal, as between the stubborn Ulster Unionists, the flexible Home Rulers and the insecure Southern Unionists, but Horace Plunkett fatally faltered, and, instead of pressing home a moment of opportunity, deferred a crucial vote to further committee examination and general blather.[80]

The moment passed, and the Convention failed. Within five years Sir Horace would be exiled from Ireland, his beautiful home in Foxrock, Co Dublin, 'Kilteragh', burned out by Republicans as a penalty for having been a Southern Unionist, and then a Free State Senator.

The King, supporting peace and concord, endorsed the Irish Convention. Perhaps surprisingly, he also approved of the release of Irish prisoners held at Frongoch, and elsewhere, consequent upon the Rising of 1916: 'Very glad that the Government are going to grant an amnesty to the Irish prisoners as it ought to help the Convention.'[81]

He was mildly miffed that his opinion had not been sought on the matter, as he would have made it known that he endorsed it. But Lloyd George regarded the King as a stuffy old Tory (and the King thought Lloyd George 'hopeless'). Eventually their relationship would mellow: the King might be a stuffed shirt, but the politician came to see that he was also a *canny* old party, and was capable of eliciting enormous popularity from the people.

The release of Irish prisoners did not help the Convention at all. Sinn Féin, the rising power, refused to attend: those who hold the power do not need to compromise and negotiate. The release of the Irish prisoners – which would include one Michael Collins – fuelled the rebel cause, rather than supporting the Convention, which soon came to be seen as a talking-shop of the impotent, filled with 'yesterday's men'.

The First World War proceeded on its weary way, eating up men's lives at a terrifying rate, and changing perceptions. Between 30,000 and 50,000 Irishmen died serving the Crown, each family receiving that dreaded telegram with the words: 'The King commands me to assure you of the true sympathy of his Majesty and the Queen in your sorrow.' The King was not lacking in sympathy – he had visited the battlefields of France and Flanders on several occasions – but he still believed in 'pressing on' with the war against 'these brutal Germans'.

So as to remove any remaining dynastic link with Germany, he changed the family name from Saxe-Coburg to Windsor, which caused him no repining. George never had the affinity with Germany felt by his grandparents: he was emotionally closer to his Danish mother.

A dramatic impact also came with the Bolshevik revolution of October 1917 (November in the Western calendar) – those 'ten days that changed the world', and fired the imagination of so many radicals for the rest of the twentieth century. Even among soldiers, a fashion grew up to establish mutinous 'soviets' in imitation of the Bolsheviks. One was even tried in Limerick.

The British Labour Party sympathised with the Bolsheviks: conservatives (and many Christians) were horrified, and saw this sympathy as a threat to the established order of property, monarchy and religion.

King George sent his cousin, Tsar Nicholas II (to whom he bore a striking physical resemblance), a sympathetic telegram deploring events, and assuring his kinsman that 'my thoughts are constantly with you and I shall always remain your true and devoted friend'. In fact, the Provisional Government withheld the message, and cousin Nicky never received it. Lloyd George, meanwhile, sent a message of support to the more moderate revolutionaries, Kerensky and Milyukov.

There was a plan to give the Tsar shelter in England which fell through. While protesting his esteem for his cousin, George worried 'whether it is advisable that the Imperial Family should take up residence in this country'. And in the end, he advised against it, out of sheer caution – and self-preservation.

One of the reasons that he gave was that he 'received letters from people in all classes of life' and that he was aware that 'working men' and those in the Labour movement regarded the Tsar as a tyrant. But there was also a deep concern that the virus of revolution might be imported into Britain – and Ireland. By 1918, the British authorities in Ireland saw 'bolshevism' as part of the insurrectionary influence.

Blood is not always thicker than water. Self-preservation is uppermost. This failure to make a special effort to save his cousin did not reflect magnanimously on George, but the prudent move to protect his own position was rather characteristic.

As everyone knows, the Tsar and Tsarina, their four daughters and only son, the haemophiliac Tsarevich – whose illness had caused his frantic mother to allow such power to Rasputin – were brutally murdered in a cellar in Ekaterinburg, in the Urals.[82]

*

The 'fatal year' of 1917 was most significant for Ireland. Sinn Féin began to win by-elections, and there was a moment of trans-ference when Éamon de Valera won the East Clare by-election – occasioned by the death of Captain Willie Redmond, John Redmond's younger brother fighting alongside the Ulstermen. The appearance of Éamon de Valera on the national scene was the omen of a new state arising.

All over Ireland, the young people were joining Sinn Féin, sporting Sinn Féin ribbons, appearing at sporting events with Sinn Féin regalia. Yet the war in Europe continued into its last, wretched phase.

In early 1918, so depleted were the ranks of fighting men on the Western Front that Lloyd George, supported by the Tories, determined to enforce conscription on Ireland, where voluntary enlistment had fallen off after 1915. This brought out the one power in the land that could always cause apprehension in British (and Unionist) circles: the Catholic Church.

The Church had been reserved on the matter of the Great War: at the beginning, there had been many sermons supporting the fight against 'Prussian' Germany – and the many priests, particu-larly in France, who joined the ranks. But by 1917 the influence of Pope Benedict XV was being felt: he was preaching peace, and warning that any cessation of hostilities should be done with honour, and not by enforcing humiliation on the vanquished.[83]

In Ireland, there was no mistaking strong opposition to con-scription. An Irishman may choose to fight in a war, but he's damned if he will be made to. Not only were the anti-conscrip-tion meetings overflowing: in the devotional magazines many accounts appeared of novenas to Our Lady of Lourdes 'against the conscription'. Hundreds and thousands of prayers were said, and candles lit, against 'the conscription': this was a true, grass roots movement.[84]

Although coercive conscription in Ireland was technically passed through the House of Commons, it was never imple-mented. It was the conscription issue (writes John A. Murphy) that above all delivered Ireland into the hands of a more militant Sinn Féin.[85]

George V: Revolution and Partition

Finally came the long-awaited day, in November of 1918. In London the people swarmed onto the streets to celebrate, and their focal point of celebration was Buckingham Palace with King George and Queen Mary appearing on the balcony.

But in Dublin, significantly, there were also anti-Armistice demonstrations, when Irishmen who had fought for the Crown were attacked by Sinn Féin supporters. This denoted the divergence of values that was now entrenched between the Crown and Nationalist Ireland. Only in 1994 did the Irish state officially acknowledge those who had gone to the battlefields of France and Flanders, often in good faith, and often as patriotic Irishmen.

In Great Britain, just as plans began for post-war reconstruction — and war memorials in almost every town — in Ireland began the Anglo-Irish war. As is well known, in the General Election of 1918 Sinn Féin swept the board in what was then called 'Southern Ireland': it won 73 out of the 105 Irish seats. There were accusations of electoral personation and allusions to the dead registering their vote: 'vote early, vote often' was one mocking jibe. But if Sinn Féin resorted to personation practices, so in all probability did everyone else concerned.

Famously, too, Countess Markievicz won a seat as the first woman to be elected to Parliament, though Madame Despard — Lord French's sister, Irish Nationalist and Bolshevik sympathiser — who had also stood for election, did not. The Irish Parliamentary Party was routed: John Redmond was dead, and his successor, John Dillon, lost his seat. At Westminster, the withdrawal of the Irish Parliamentary Party left Lloyd George's Liberal–Tory Coalition in a supreme position of power.

In January 1919 the victorious Sinn Féin representatives met at the Mansion House in Dublin and elected Éamon de Valera as President of the Irish Republic, which was as yet notional.

The Crown at this point ignored the gesture. It was not 'official' and, moreover, Britain was somewhat preoccupied elsewhere. Aside from coping with a demobbed army, immense problems of employment and housing shortages, the Spanish Influenza (which was to kill more people than the Great War), and the popular — and ugly — clamour to 'Hang the Kaiser',

Britain remained responsible for (or at least involved with) policing in Palestine, Mesopotamia (Iraq), Siberia, India, Hong Kong, Singapore, and Constantinople/Istanbul.

The King, who had been so preoccupied with Ireland from 1911–1914, now does not mention Ireland in his diaries. All his focus is elsewhere – not least on personal sorrows. In January 1919 his youngest son, John, suddenly died from an epileptic fit. Because of John's illness, George and Mary had always kept their youngest son, born in 1905, in seclusion at Sandringham. This may have partly been because of the stigma then attached to epilepsy. But it may also have been protective.

King George always noted John's birthday in his diary, and when the boy died, aged 14, George and Mary felt the loss deeply, although Queen Mary also felt grateful that it had been a peaceful passing. 'For him it is a great release,' she wrote. 'I cannot say how grateful we feel to God for having taken him in such a peaceful way, he just slept quietly into his heavenly home, no pain, no struggle, just peace for the poor little troubled spirit.'[86]

George's experiences of visiting the trenches in the Great War had turned him into something of a pacifist: his experience of losing his son helped him to identify with so many families who had lost theirs.

Meanwhile, in Ireland, despite the non-violent elements of original Sinn Féin, and the pleas of the Catholic clergy not to allow the 'idealism' of 1916 to descend into violence, that is precisely what happened. Men like Dan Breen and Seán Treacy – who launched the Anglo-Irish war by shooting dead two policemen at Soloheadbeg in Co Tipperary – paid little enough attention to the clergy, unless they could manipulate them. Michael Collins' view about asserting independence for Ireland at this point was simple: you had to fight the British for it.

By April, Sir Hamar Greenwood was appointed as Chief Secretary for Ireland: in July he announced that because the Royal Irish Constabulary was so constantly under attack, and so many of them were by now resigning their posts, he would send a supplementary force to Ireland, dressed in khaki uniforms with black hats and armlets.

These were to be known as the 'Black and Tans', and the savagery of their – often drunken – military tactics were to be legendary in Ireland for the rest of the twentieth century. It is no mitigation of their actions to say that many of the Black and Tans were shell-shocked and brutalised from hellish experiences on the Western Front.

They had returned to Britain in 1918, often to less than a hero's welcome: in many cases they did not even qualify for unemployment benefits. In her memoir of the 1920s, Barbara Cartland recounts the story of a cheerful but penniless boyfriend, who would do anything for employment: he thought his luck had changed when hired to do a job in Ireland. Only later it emerged that he had been sent off as a 'Black and Tan'.[87]

The King was anxious to make the point that innocent people should be protected in any military or police endeavours in Ireland. He was assured by Andrew Bonar Law, now a Minister in a Tory-Liberal Coalition, that all was under control.

King George, perhaps naively, regarded himself as 'the protector of the Irish', stubbornly holding on to his view that all of 'his people' deserved equal concern. This was not the way in which Sinn Féin and the new Irish leadership viewed the Crown – de Valera in fact raised strong objections when the King called the Irish 'my people'.[88]

King George could not approve of the Irish rebels, but in an interesting reprise of his attitudes to the suffragettes, he also objected to what he heard about the strategies of the Black and Tans. It was said that the King was appalled by some of the reports he heard. The King's attitude was 'leaked' via Lord Northcliffe, proprietor of the *Daily Mail*, on a visit to the United States. It was claimed that the King had said, 'I cannot have my people killed in this manner', referring to the Black and Tans' Irish victims.

Subsequently, Northcliffe disclaimed this, in one of those clichéd I-was-quoted-out-of-context excuses. And Lloyd George – who was himself ultimately responsible for the conduct of the Black and Tans – called the leak 'a complete fabrication'. And yet, significantly, it was not denied by palace sources, and George V's authorised biographer says that it was a broadly fair representation of what the King had said.[89] The King thought the Black and Tans should be disbanded, but that the police should be subjected to military discipline under Sir Nevil Macready (who himself was uneasy about the Black and Tans, and did not agree with Hamar Greenwood's hard line).

In May 1921 Stamfordham had written to Sir Hamar Greenwood on behalf of the King saying, 'The King does ask himself, and he asks you, if this policy of reprisals is to be continued and, if so, to where it will lead Ireland and us all? It seems to His Majesty that in punishing the guilty we are inflicting punishment no less severe upon the innocent.'[90]

It has also become evident that the King and Queen were very concerned about the hunger strike and subsequent death of Terence MacSwiney, the Mayor of Cork, in November 1920. But how far could a constitutional monarch go in expressing opposition to his own government's policy?[91]

It is a strange paradox, as the historian Alvin Jackson has pointed out, that Ulster Unionists, who did everything to wreck Home Rule for Ireland, in the end benefited from Home Rule themselves. The Government of Ireland Bill would establish a partitioned state of six counties in Northern Ireland, and received the royal assent in December 1920. The Belfast Parliament was to be opened in the early summer of 1921, with Sir James Craig as Northern Ireland's first Prime Minister. Significantly, Edward Carson – who really wanted the entire island of Ireland to stay united, within a United Kingdom – stayed away from proceedings.

During the Home Rule crisis of 1911–13, King George's effigy had been jeered at by Belfast Orangemen because his careful constitutionalism was interpreted as sympathy for Irish nationalism. That was all forgotten and the Ulster Unionists were now anxious to bring George V to Northern Ireland for the state opening of their parliament – to take place at Belfast City Council. (The absurdly grand Stormont – bigger than Washington's White House

– would not be opened until 1932.) Craig wrote to Stamfordham in February 1921 saying that the King's presence, and that of premiers of the Dominions, would be 'most desirable for every reason and especially on political grounds'[92]

Stamfordham replied that if the Ulster parliament was to be opened by the monarch, 'so must be the Southern Parliament', in accordance with George V's continuing desire to be even-handed: there were still plans to have an equivalent southern Irish parliament of Home Rulers in Dublin also provided for in the Government of Ireland Act.

Craig wrote back shrewdly saying that the Dublin parliament should only be opened by the King 'if *asked* to do so'. Craig knew the way the wind was blowing in the 26 counties. 'If a Republican Majority is elected, they would not wish the King to open their Parliament – or again there may be no Members returned and no Parliament.'

He was right on every count: the 'Southern Parliament' that the British sponsored in Dublin turned up just four members and was immediately perceived as a total fiasco. Nationalist Ireland wanted to establish its own parliament, not one 'granted' by Britain. Even John Dillon, deputy to John Redmond in the Home Rule Party, had now thrown in his lot with Sinn Féin.

In May, Stamfordham saw the Lord Mayor of Belfast, William Coates, who would be rewarded with a baronetcy during the King's visit. Coates was 'anxious to convey to the King the intensely strong feeling in Belfast and Ulster generally that Their Majesties should visit the Province this year and open their Parliament'.

Lord Londonderry – later to be known as 'The Londonderry Herr' for his appeasing attitude to Hitler's Germany (and the model for the aristocrat played by James Fox in the film *The Remains of the Day*) – piled on the pleas. He told Stamfordham that 'there was a very strong feeling in Belfast that they had been neglected by the Royal Family during the War – that His Majesty had visited all the great shipyards in England, whereas Belfast has been ignored, although her shipyards turned out as much if not more than any other yard in Britain. He pointed out what an enormously good effect such a visit would have.'

The King's private secretary was concerned about the sovereign's safety, while George himself continued to feel that if he went to Belfast he should also go to Dublin. Londonderry told Stamfordham he was absolutely sure that His Majesty's personal safety 'could be assured in both places'.

Towards the end of May Stamfordham was still stalling, and still telling the Lord Mayor of Belfast that the matter was uncertain. In the final analysis, it would depend on 'His Majesty's Ministers' and, in a letter marked 'Secret', he informed Craig that 'there is a very strong difference of opinion about the King going to Belfast, and many Irishmen, including those residing in that country, tell me that His Majesty is running considerable risk in going.' Although, he added, personal risk 'has not entered into His Majesty's calculations'.

Yet it looked by now as though the visit would take place: it was, he went on, his absolute duty to impress upon Sir James 'the importance of taking every human precaution for the protection of His Majesty's life.' Stamfordham had been informed by a newspaper editor of some importance that 'Irish Orangemen' thought it [the advisability of the visit] question-able.[93]

Craig swallowed the insult and assured the King's secretary that George V's life would be perfectly protected. 'No one is more alive than I am to the compliment being paid to us. The people here will themselves repay it in their own way.' And so arrangements were put in place for King George's state visit to Belfast on 21 June. Precautions were taken to send a phalanx of politicians and government personnel along.

Craig then boldly pressed his advantage further, and suggested that Queen Mary should accompany her husband. Surprisingly, after all the concern about the King's safety, this was quickly agreed: George V probably appreciated the presence of his consort on this assignment.

So did the press: the modern media was evolving, and Queen Mary's presence helped to provide women reporters with the chance to describe her various costumes: the female angle on celebrity frocks being an enduring fact of media life.

King George then started working on his speech for the opening of the northern parliament, in which he was assisted by General Smuts, the South African leader, and probably by one of his secretaries Edward Grigg. There were several drafts of this text, all of which had to be submitted to the Prime Minister, Lloyd George. In one draft of an address that he planned to give to the Lord Mayor, the King wrote:

> Since my boyhood I have loved Ireland and the Irish people and it grieves me to stand by while the spirit of murder, outrage and revenge dominates a certain (?large) [sic] portion of the community. With a yearning heart I pray that my coming to Ireland may prove to be a first step towards the ending of the din of strife and violence and the gradual return to peace and goodwill.[94]

Aside from the troubles in the south, there was continuing sectarian strife in Belfast, with the Catholics very largely on the receiving end. His draft went on: 'I appeal to all – irrespective of class, social, political, religious differences – to pause, to stretch out the hand of forbearance and conciliation: to forgive and forget and finally to join in one common cause – the happiness and prosperity of a United Ireland.' A watered down version of some of these sentiments eventually appeared in George's formal address.

The King's visit to Belfast to open Stormont was regarded as a triumph: he and Queen Mary were showered with praise by the press when they returned to London, for their courage, initiative, and Christian gesture advocating peace and reconciliation. A. J. P. Taylor later wrote that George's speech in Belfast was 'By far the greatest service performed by a British monarch in modern times.'[95]

Even among Irish Nationalists, King George's speech was regarded as being high-minded and well-intentioned, partly because it was seen as a veiled reprimand to the Orangemen. Although, naturally, it is couched in the imperial language of a king and emperor, it could be seen as decades ahead of its time, since it pre-figured many of the sentiments expressed in the Belfast Agreement of 1998; sentiments that underlined the peace and reconciliation then heralded as such a breakthrough.

> For all who love Ireland, as I do with all My heart, this is a profoundly moving occasion in Irish history. My memories of the Irish people date back to the time when I spent many happy days in Ireland as a midshipman. My affection for the Irish people has been deepened by successive visits since that time, and I have watched with constant sympathy the course of their affairs. I could not have allowed Myself to give Ireland by deputy alone.
>
> My earnest prayers and good wishes in the new era ... and I feel assured that you will do your utmost to make it an instrument of happiness and good government for all parts of the community which you represent.'[96]

He meant this: he had written privately to several prominent Unionists saying that the new Six County government should represent all the people, and should take care not to act unfairly against Catholics. He went on:

> Few things are more earnestly desired throughout the English-speaking world than a satisfactory solution of the age-long Irish problems, which for generations embarrassed our forefathers, as they now weigh heavily upon us.

In a warning to the new state that fair play should prevail, he said he was:

> confident that the important matters entrusted to the control and guidance of the Northern Parliament will be managed with wisdom and with moderation, with fairness and due regard to every faith and interest, and with no abatement of that patriotic devotion to the Empire which you proved so gallantly in the Great War ... I speak from a full

heart when I pray that My coming to Ireland to-day may prove to be the first step towards an end of strife amongst her people, whatever their race or creed.

In an oft-quoted conclusion, he said with special emphasis:

In that hope I appeal to all Irishmen to pause, to stretch out the hand of forbearance and concilia-tion, to forgive and to forget, and to join in making for the land which they love a new era of peace, contentment and good will. It is My earnest desire that in Southern Ireland too there may ere long take place a parallel to what is now passing in this Hall; that there a similar occasion may present itself and a similar ceremony be performed. May this historic gathering be the prelude of a day in which the Irish people, North and South, under one Parliament or two, as those Parliaments may them-selves decide, shall work together in common love for Ireland upon the sure foundation of mutual justice and respect.

Although George had done his best to emphasise the need for reconciliation and, in his own manner of speaking, inclusive-ness, the ceremonial surrounding this occasion could not but be monarchical and Unionist. And for all the King's fine words, Catholics and Nationalists were in practice absent from the occasion.

The *Daily Telegraph* reporter, Harold Spender, wrote that prayers were read 'by each head of the church, except, I regret to say, the Roman Catholic'. [97] The Catholic hierarchy had held itself aloof from the occasion. The Editor of the *Catholic Herald*, Charles Diamond, considered something of a maverick, complained that the ceremonial and honours had deliberately excluded Catholics. [98]

The King's postbag burst with congratulations. He received many sweet letters, cards, and momentoes, as well as lucky symbols, such as a four-leafed clover and miniature horseshoes. But there were notes of caution and of criticism too. C. J. O'Donnell – a former member of the Irish Parliamentary Party

– wrote to the King to ask him 'not to be identified with the partition of Ireland'. A Mrs Pope-Hennessy, matriarch of the literary Anglo-Irish (and Catholic) family of that name, saw the King's endorsement of Stormont through the other end of the telescope: 'to identify Monarchy with the North is tacitly to admit the claim of Independence in the South', she told the monarch in a letter.

A Mr J. F. Manning of New Malden in Surrey wrote to King George saying that either Queen Mary or Princess Mary should now visit 'the South of Ireland', to bring about a final peace, and described himself as, 'A Sinn Féiner, loyal to the Crown'.[99] Mr Manning surely was the last of his breed.

Chapter Four

FROM ALLEGIANCE
TO ABDICATION,
1921–37

I do solemnly swear true faith and allegiance to the Constitution of the
Irish Free State as by law established, and that I will be faithful to His
Majesty King George V, his heirs and successors by law, in virtue of the
common citizenship of Ireland with Great Britain, and her adherence to
and membership of the group of nations forming the British
Commonwealth of nations.
(Oath of Allegiance to King George V in the Constitution
of the Irish Free State, 1923)

I am opposed to this declaration of fidelity to an alien King because it is
an outrage on the memory of our martyred comrades … and an open
insult to the heroic relatives they have left behind.
(Deputy Seán T. Ó Ceallaigh (later President of Ireland),
Dáil Debates, December 1921)[1]

K ing George V's speech opening the parliament in
Belfast was considered so brave and so radical in
Britain, that, according to the *Daily Sketch*, 'the very
newsboys' voices vibrated with excitement'.

His speech '... coming from the King had an enormous impact,' recalled Barbara Cartland in her unusually sharp memoir of life in the 1920s. Dame Barbara and her fashionable London set (which included Noel Coward, Lady Diana Cooper and Tallulah Bankhead) believed the King had personally brought peace to Ireland by his words, inviting Irishmen to stretch out the hand of friendship to one another. 'A fortnight later hostilities ceased. The rebel leaders from the South came to London for negotiations, to which Lloyd George brought all his wizardry of persuasiveness. Before the year's end a treaty was signed – the Irish Free State came into being.' And for the fashionable Mayfair set, that seemed an end to the damnable 'Irish question'.[2]

Oh, not so hasty, Dame Barbara. Although the King celebrated the Anglo-Irish Treaty of December 1921, signed by Arthur Griffith and Michael Collins (et al), with Lloyd George and Winston Churchill (et al), and pronounced himself delighted with the peace that it seemed to promise, the new Irish state was within a few months plunged into a civil war.[3]

It is a commonly held fiction that the Irish Civil War of 1922–23 was fought over the partition of Ireland and the consequent loss of the Six Counties of Ulster to the Irish state. But the Civil War was essentially about King George V's position in the Irish Constitution, and the Oath of Allegiance to the King that was part of the Anglo-Irish Treaty of 1921. According to this, Irish parliamentarians must swear fidelity to 'the Constitution of the Irish Free State ... [and] His Majesty King George V ...', in the words that introduce this chapter.

This declaration was to be the subject of impassioned debate in the new Dáil Éireann. For some, the oath was the most hated of all symbols of 'flunkeyism', and the most passionate opponents of the Treaty – led by Éamon de Valera – formed the anti-Treaty faction in what would become the Civil War.

For more practical men, like Michael Collins, the Oath of Allegiance was just a formula, which would fade away in the fullness of time, while the more urgent task of state-building now beckoned. For Collins, it was Irish independence that mattered, not the precise form of government: he once said that if Britain had been a republic, Ireland would have insisted on being a monarchy.

The Oath of Allegiance was also a part of the Treaty package which the British had insisted upon. Winston Churchill believed it was a necessary part of the defence of the realm and that, without it, Ireland would be free to side with a foreign power, which could imperil the United Kingdom. During the Second World War, when Éire was neutral (and a minority of Irish citizens were pro-German), some of Churchill's deepest fears were aroused.

However the more uncompromising Irish Republicans said they would rather die a thousand deaths before they would swear an oath of fidelity to His Britannic Majesty King George V.

The much-esteemed writer Daniel Corkery said that the Oath of Allegiance bound the Irish nation to the British Empire, and 'if we go into this British Empire, we will go in there as a prop to hold up a rotten Empire'. Collins, who had worked in London as a young man, did not have the same visceral hatred of the British Empire: and neither did the thousands of Irishmen and women who had found more opportunity within that same British Empire than they had done in their native land.

And so the Dáil debate on the Oath was fierce, robust, passionate, and often impressive. It was high-flown and deeply felt: it was Danton and Robespierre all over again: it hardly touched on bread-and-butter issues.[4]

Cathal Brugha, the uncompromising Republican whose portrait today hangs in the foyer of Dáil Éireann, opposite the portrait of Michael Collins, argued that allegiance to the Crown was submission to the hated English authority in Ireland, and every Irishman should resist to the very last.

'If ... our last cartridge had been fired, our last shilling had been spent, and our last man were lying on the ground and his enemies howling round him and their bayonets raised, ready to plunge them into his body, that man should say – true to the traditions handed down – if they said to him: 'Now, will you come into our Empire?' – he should say, and he would say: 'No! I will not.' Like many another committed Irish patriot, Cathal Brugha was by inheritance an Englishman: more specifically, a Yorkshireman by the name of Charles William St John Burgess, which perhaps accounts for his obstinacy and fearlessness.

Much anxiety was expressed about the powers that the King of England might exert over the Irish nation, once an Oath to the monarch was put in place. The Oath, said Éamon de Valera in 1921, 'makes British authority our masters in Ireland'. To swear allegiance to an English king was to 'subvert the Republic' (that is, the idea of a republic, since no official republic existed at this time).

To pledge allegiance to King George would mean that 'the Ministers of Ireland will be His Majesty's Ministers, the Army ... will be His Majesty's Army. ... the Ministers of the Irish Free State will be His Majesty's Ministers and the Irish Forces will be His Majesty's Forces.'

Count Plunkett movingly opposed the Oath, and spoke of seeing his son die in the 1916 Rising, and his other two sons sent away for penal servitude after rebelling against British Rule. Could he be faithful to the memory of his boys and accept the writ of the English Crown, after all that had been done in its name, he asked?

Likewise, Kathleen Clarke – one of a trio of *jusqu'auboutiste* female deputies,[5] along with Countess Markievicz and Mary MacSwiney – spoke of witnessing her husband, the veteran Fenian Tom Clarke, go to his death for Ireland. With the poetry of an O'Casey drama she recalled her pride in that moment when he said, 'we have saved the soul of Ireland', as he went before the firing squad. 'And though sorrow was in my heart, I gloried in him, and I have gloried in the men who have carried on the fight since.'

Inconceivable to forsake this powerful memory for an Oath of Allegiance to the King of England! (Indeed, when Mrs Clarke became the Lord Mayor of Dublin in 1940, her first action was to remove all royal portraits – and most especially Queen Victoria – from the walls of the Dublin Mansion House.[6])

In response to the diehard Republicans, Michael Collins, Arthur Griffith, and Kevin O'Higgins argued coherently for accepting the Oath to the King: it was a contractual part of the Treaty agreement that had been signed with the full authority of all representatives, including Mr de Valera.

It was an evolution towards nationhood. The Irish Free State was to be part of the British Commonwealth of nations, and the other nations in this wider family – Canada, Australia, New Zealand and South Africa – had similar arrangements, whereby the King was recognised as the titular head of the Commonwealth network.

Kevin O'Higgins, who, after the death of Collins and Griffith, was to emerge as the most dominant personality in government, pointed out that the Oath in the Constitution of the Irish Free State was of a milder variety than that which obtained in the other Dominions. It was little more than a starting point for a constitution that would give the Irish Parliament, and the people, the real power. The King's position was even a kind of fiction, O'Higgins maintained: in England itself he had less power than the lowest elected Member of Parliament. This was true in a strict political sense, though not in the symbolic one. And symbols count.

Those who argued for accepting the Oath tended to minimise the importance of the King, or kings. An eloquent young Cork councillor Liam de Róiste (a close friend of the late Terence MacSwiney) who supported the Oath and the Treaty, opined that 'the days of kings and Kaisers are almost ended and will soon be as obsolete as the theory of their divine right to rule; and the day of the rule of the sovereign people has begun, whatever the form in which it will take expression ...' The coming abolition of monarchies was a commonly held belief among progressives: the modernising Americans had greatly influenced the Versailles Treaty, and Germany, in particular, did away with its patchwork of princelings

In a long and subtle speech, Michael Collins claimed that those who made such a song and dance about the King were in fact *more* in the grip of the 'slave mind' and its adherent flunkeyism. The obsessive fear of falling into this royal 'flunkeyism' implied, at some level, a lack of confidence in their own values.

Eoin MacNeill, the Celtic scholar who had recruited Patrick Pearse into the leadership of the Gaelic League (Wimbourne, the Lord Lieutenant in 1916, wanted MacNeill shot) made much sport of the fears that the Irish Free State would have

> His Majesty's Ministers all over the place, and His Majesty's Officers all over the army ... a Governor-General and a Gold Stick in Waiting and I don't know what else. An appalling picture! We will be overawed by these people, perfumed, in uniform, and dressed up in their court dress, and the rest of us will all be rubbing our foreheads in the dust before them, as flunkeys! A terrible picture indeed![7]

Of the Governor-General representing the king (as it would turn out, his own brother, James, would later be appointed the last Governor-General of the Free State) Eoin MacNeill said he would call him the Grand Panjandrum if it so pleased the House. 'What's in a name?'

With sarcastic humour, he proceeded to conjure up 'a second appalling picture' – for Republicans – of the King's Governor-General holding 'Drawing Rooms and Levees and Garden Parties, and giving Balls and Dances. And our poor girls! Their nationality will evaporate because they go to these functions.' There had been some anxiety expressed that the tender vulner-abilities of young women would be seduced and exploited by the flummery and flunkeyism of even a titular attachment to the British monarchy. Protect the women! – from their own soft-headedness!

This was in answer to Mary MacSwiney's concerns that the 'drawing-rooms, levees and honours and invitations' might be 'bait' to wives and sisters and mothers, and might turn the heads of young girls growing up in 'this so-called Free State'. Miss MacSwiney, sister of the iconic Mayor of Cork, the late Terence MacSwiney, represented the most 'sea-green incorruptible' voice of Irish Republicanism and of high-minded Catholicism (she was as concerned about the influence of Dr Marie Stopes as of monarchical flummery).

And most bitterly opposed to the Oath to the King (and all a monarchy represented) were the two Anglo-Irish deputies, Erskine Childers and Countess Constance Markievicz.

Childers, a highly principled and remarkable character (perhaps most accurately described as an English radical) warned that the Governor-General would be at the centre of the British government in Ireland, and how dangerous, how very threatening was England's proximity to Ireland. The Oath to the King would mean that the King's authority and the King's forces would occupy Ireland.

Constance Markievicz was the first woman ever to be elected to the British Parliament, though she refused to take her Westminster seat; she was a spitfire revolutionary whom the Catholic bishops had denounced as an outright Bolshevik. She castigated Arthur Griffith for having any truck at all with the 'privileged' Anglo-Irish 'Southern Unionists' who had represented the old order.

In a masterly riposte Griffith outlined the meaning of 'inclusiveness', as we call it today: 'I met them [the Anglo-Irish] because they are my countrymen; and because, if we are to have an Irish nation, we want to start with fair play for all sections and with understandings between all sections.'

To this there was much applause. Griffith continued: 'I would meet to-morrow on that basis the Ulster Unionists, to seek to get them to join in an Irish nation' – cries of Hear! Hear! – 'I met these gentlemen [the Southern Unionists] and I promised them fair play; and so far as I am concerned they will have fair play [applause].'

Countess Markievicz, née Gore-Booth, was one of the Anglo-Irish herself. She had very successfully disobliged the Gore-Booths (eccentric though they were) by 'going over to the rebels'. Just to rub in this rebuff, she also converted to Roman Catholicism (as did Maud Gonne).

Lily Yeats, sister to W. B., considered Constance and the entire Gore-Booth family 'cracked'. 'What a pity Madame Markievicz's madness changed its form when she inherited it,' Miss Yeats remarked drily. Constance's father, Sir Henry Gore-

Booth, an Arctic explorer, had once set off for the North Pole in an open boat.[8]

Among the general populace, according to the Free State historian Denis Gwynn, most people were indifferent to the Oath issue: they cared neither when the King was mentioned in the Irish Constitution, nor later, in the 1930s, when he was removed. Yet the anxiety among Republicans about flunkeyism and flummery and levees and drawing-rooms was not without some justification: for society continued to yearn for some element of social ornamentation.

The first Governor-General of the Irish Free State was to be Mr Tim Healy: he and his wife, née Erina Sullivan, were in considerable demand to preside over social occasions. Democracies have to be built, politically: but social intercourse has to continue, too!

Presently, even the ardent Republicans would find a vehicle for the pomp and ceremony that every society either derives from tradition or re-invents: the Holy Roman Catholic Church would soon fill the vacuum left by the departed pageantry of His Majesty.

And so in 1922 Mr Timothy Michael Healy, born in 1855, was selected to be the first Governor-General of the Irish Free State, also known as Saorstát Éireann. The Governor-General was the representative of the King in the new Irish state, as the Anglo-Irish Treaty had stipulated.

Tim Healy came from a strong County Cork clan: his wife was one of the Sullivans associated with stirring books of Irish patriotism in the nineteenth century. Healy started life as a self-educated shorthand clerk in a railway company, moved on to journalism, became a secretary to Parnell, and finally an MP for the Irish Parliamentary Party.

He fell out with Parnell for a number of reasons, including Parnell's questionable support of his mistress' husband, Captain O'Shea, for a Galway parliamentary seat. Later, Healy came to support Sinn Féin as it rose to prominence in 1917. He was regarded as a political 'gadfly', who, in his mellow years, suited the office of Governor-General, since he could be said to have a finger in every pie.

He was a broad and general Irish Nationalist: he was liked by the Catholic establishment (he had denounced Darwinism as 'the monkey theory', and a cover-up for sexual promiscuity); he was supportive of monarchy; and he had wide experience. He was also the father of six, and an uncle of Kevin O'Higgins. Indeed, it was O'Higgins' idea to nominate him in the first place.

Healy's appointment was not London's choice, although Lord Birkenhead supported his candidacy. The 'Imperial Government', as the British government was called, would have liked a belted earl of their own nomination – 'a distinguished peer' – but the Irish politicians insisted that they would nominate their own man.[9]

London came to see the wisdom of accepting this, although they still wanted power of approval. The unreconciled Republicans referred to Mr Healy in abusive graffiti as 'King George's batman'.[10] And Tim Healy did find favour with the Duke of Devonshire (then His Majesty's Secretary of State for the Colonies and a considerable Irish landowner) who was touched by Mr Healy's annual practice of putting flowers on the grave of Lord Frederick Cavendish, victim of the Phoenix Park murders of 1882 and the Duke's kinsman.[11]

There was some concern about the cost of maintaining a Governor-General, and warnings were expressed that he should not be seen to be a spendthrift, or to entertain lavishly. The builders of new nations are puritans and do not approve of extravagance or show.

The Leader of the Labour Party (which, between 1924 and 1927, formed the main opposition) proposed that the Governor-General's remuneration should be reduced from £10,000 to £7,000. It was a question of setting standards. There were to be none of the 'lavish displays' associated with the ancien régime.[12]

The Minister for Posts and Telegraphs, Ernest Blythe, an Ulster Protestant with a Calvinist bent, certainly did not want to see any displays of 'lavishness' or high living. Did the Governor-General have to live in Viceregal Lodge (the splendid Palladian Mansion which had been occupied by the Viceroy, and is today the official residence of the President of Ireland, Áras an Uachtaráin)? Could he not be lodged in some more modest quarters?

Mr Healy's position was saved by the intervention of a deputy speaking for the Business Party (subsequently called the Businessmen's Party, subsequently called Independents), one John Good, who expressed the view that if foreign persons were to be attracted to Ireland, and to form a favourable impression of the country, the Governor-General could hardly be expected to offer hospitality on a shoestring.

Moreover – and even Ernest Blythe saw the point – if you paid the Governor-General in a niggardly way, then only very rich men would be in a position to take up the post, and that would hardly serve the public interest. Anyway, it was calculated, there were only 20 rich men in Ireland at the time.

And so Mr Healy was given a position commensurate with his peers in Australia and Canada, and he fulfilled his duties correctly. Only once – towards the end of his term – did he allow himself to fall into a political rant against those he disparaged: that is, the followers of Éamon de Valera and the extreme Republicans, whom he considered to be wreckers for refusing to enter the parliamentary process because of the Oath to the King.[13]

He also thought de Valera mean-spirited for trying to spoil Armistice Day each November, when Dev protested against First World War veterans remembering their dead in a Dublin ceremony.

*

During the Civil War – from June 1922 until April 1923 – it seemed to some that anarchy was let loose in Ireland. It was not anarchy: it was the terrible but, alas, inevitable struggle between two alpha-male leaders – de Valera and Collins – and the settling by war of the question as to which state of Ireland would prevail.

After Michael Collins and Arthur Griffith died in August 1922 (Collins by an opponent's gun, Griffith from a stroke), Lord

Desart, one of the old gentry, reported to King George that 'Greater anarchy there can hardly be … Griffiths [sic] was the only man who realised that there ought to be any consideration for minorities, or had a conception of Government & administration.' Desart deplored the 'gush' about Collins' death (most of the London papers had reported the death of Michael Collins with sensational headlines and a rush of sympathy), saying he had in mind 'the deaths of British officers, British soldiers & Police where he [Collins] was responsible.'[14]

Lord Desart expressed to the King his sense of abandonment by the Crown, as he observes the condition of so many of his fellow gentry, attacked by Irregulars (anti-Treaty Republican forces), burned-out, told to clear their houses within ten minutes. 'I have been relatively fortunate – as they have only, so far, taken about £300 worth of my cattle, and my clothes & boots, and frequently raid my garden.'

The anarchy of Ireland, he repeated, was complete. 'No police, no magistrates, no courts.' And he is sad to have read in one of the papers that the King now planned to abolish 'the Patrick', that is, the Order of St Patrick. It was such a symbol of the loss of 'British Protection and & its law': and the Free State, should it ever come into existence properly, would certainly forbid all British honours. 'Leaders in Ireland, whether Free State or otherwise, are Republican in all but name, and wish to obliterate everything that preserves any tie, symbolic or otherwise, with the Crown.'

Lord Castletown, who thought of himself as an Irishman, spoke Irish, and was proud to be a cousin of the patriotic poet and author Emily Lawless, took a similar view: 'The land is now in possession … of what may be called a lot of boy bandits, fanatics & gunmen,' he wrote in 1922.[15]

Stamfordham replied that he entirely shared Desart's doubts about the establishment of the Free State. He also quoted Bishop Bernard that 'Adult Suffrage' would favour a Republic in Ireland.[16] Adult suffrage meant including women in the vote, and women voters were expected to be radical. Stamfordham continued:

> do not pray imagine that there is any sympathy here
> with the exaggerated, but almost universal, gush

173

about Collins. You may have noticed that no message was sent from the King who, while recognising Collins' bravery and honest endeavours to fulfil his engagement with the British Government, did not forget that, rightly or wrong, Collins is accused of having personally arranged, if not actually committed, murders of loyalist Officers and civilians.[17]

Stamfordham (and the King) may have had in mind such acts as the liquidation of Field Marshal Sir Henry Wilson, killed by two IRA men – while in full regalia, having just unveiled a monument to the war dead at Liverpool Street station – on the steps of his London home, and probably with Collins' approval. But Wilson, as Ulster security chief and a vehement Unionist, was regarded as being responsible for the deaths of Northern Irish Catholics shot in cold blood.[18]

The King did not abolish 'the Patrick', but restricted it to members of his own family. (In 2007 Bertie Ahern, as Taoiseach, suggested reviving the Order of St Patrick, but the heraldic aspect is complex.[19])

After 1922, King George was less focused on Ireland. There were repeated rumours that some member of the royal family might visit the Free State – the Prince of Wales (afterwards briefly Edward VIII) expressed some interest in doing so – but Dublin intimated that it would not be acceptable, although some individuals might like to welcome the Prince, regarded at the time as dashing and glamorous.

George must have been disappointed that his peace gesture for Ireland had ended in what seemed like mayhem. Yet the turbulence in Ireland was part of a pattern after the Great War. George had seen the thrones of Europe tumble – there had been a popular cry in England, much encouraged by Lloyd George, to 'hang the Kaiser', who was fortunate merely to get away with living in disgrace in the Netherlands.

The Ottoman Empire was no more, and in Vienna the Hapsburgs had fallen less brutally than the Russian Romanovs, but the Hapsburg dynasty had come to an end just the same. In Britain the Labour party and many radicals sympathised with the Bolsheviks: to the consternation of the King, the British government was among the first to recognise Bolshevik Russia.

Moreover, a shocking social revolution was happening before the King's eyes: women's skirts went from ankle to knee, their hair was bobbed, they smoked, wore lipstick, danced to jazz and stayed up all night drinking cocktails. Birth control was the new fad, although in the aftermath of many millions of lost lives, not widely approved of – Barbara Cartland had to keep secret a meeting with Marie Stopes.

The King not only read about these social revolutions in the popular press: he and the Queen were worried about such influences within their own household. From around 1922, it was becoming clear that their son and heir, David, the Prince of Wales, was himself part of these changes – the night clubs, the cocktails, the craze for dancing, the rejection of much that a more decorous world had respected.

In Dublin, my mother – aged 21 in 1923 – was also excitedly aware of cocktails and cigarettes, and movie stars and jazz, of short skirts and painted fingernails, and the development of the motor car (a craze among young men, including her own brothers). But this was not the mood embraced by the politicians building the new Ireland. Kevin O'Higgins, the Economics and Home Minister who forged the new state with such zeal, introduced legislation to curb the liquor trade. O'Higgins refused to drink a bottle of champagne which had been presented to him on his appointment to government on the grounds that imbibing champagne was 'unbecoming' to a minister of a new and impoverished state.[20]

The Civil War had come to an end in 1923, with the pro-Treaty forces victorious: backed by Britain, and especially by Winston Churchill. The Free State was endorsed by a majority of the electorate – and the Catholic Church. A Free State government was formed by Cumann na nGaedheal (or the Society of Gaels, later Fine Gael), under the quiet leadership of W. T. Cosgrave, who was more like a civil servant than a political leader; this charisma vacuum brought O'Higgins to the fore.

When it came to values, both Republicans and Free Staters shared the same puritanical ethos – de Valera's Republicans being even more lofty and anti-materialistic, affirming their oft-stated belief that it was better to be poor and virtuous than prosperous and worldly. Much was said about the 'Irish soul', which had to be guarded in its spiritual integrity.[21]

Almost the first act of the Irish Free State was the Censorship of Films Act. Divorce also fell under a prohibition – Mr Cosgrave agreed with the Catholic hierarchy that there should be no provision for the dissolution of marriage. King George V does not record his reaction, but his attitude scarcely differed from an Irish bishop. He and Queen Mary deplored divorce and would not meet divorcées.

Irish Protestants had mixed feelings about the prohibition on divorce, as the correspondence in *The Church of Ireland Gazette* reveals: some felt (as Yeats did), that this was an intolerable intrusion upon private conscience. But others wrote that 'the Romans' were upholding Christian values in marriage and family life.

In the end the Anglican Archbishop of Dublin, Dr Gregg, came to support the Catholic state. Some commentators considered this over-pliable, but the Irish Protestant leader's speeches reveal a genuine tussle of conscience, and we must bear in mind that to orthodox Anglicans at this time (as the abdication of a King would subsequently dramatically illustrate) divorce was indeed abhorrent. This official Anglican stigmatisation of divorce would also be manifest thirty years later, when Princess Margaret considered marrying a divorced man.

In the 1920s there was much to be done in constructing a new state. Ireland was devastated by the Civil War, which had done an enormous amount of material damage to the country – bridges were broken, roads in ruin – let alone the loss of life and the enduring enmities begotten. Yet many of the civil and political structures Britain had bequeathed were left in place, as was the civil service and, with some amendments, the judiciary.

Controversially, Kevin O'Higgins decided that women would no longer be called to serve on juries. Feminists then, and later, objected, but the new administration blamed women themselves for their reluctance. So many women pleaded exemption from jury service – it was claimed that nearly 90 per cent of women summoned asked to be excused – that it was administratively simpler to abolish jury service for women altogether. As a sop to critics, the regulations were amended to allow women to serve if they requested to do so: few made the request.[22]

A new police service, the civic guards or An Garda Siochána, was inaugurated as the old Royal Irish Constabulary was disbanded. The Garda were unarmed on a point of principle: they were civic guardians, not a militia. One veteran southern Unionist noted that the Garda Siochána now swore allegiance to the Sacred Heart rather than the King, but observed philosophically that they seemed none the worse for it: men have to venerate *something*.[23]

The new state's programme of works included the reorganisation of education, agriculture, and the poor law; and a senate was devised to extend inclusion to those southern Unionists who had done their best to serve Ireland, and perhaps to compensate them for their chagrin in losing the connection with the Crown.

Men such as Lords Mayo and Dunraven (who had been conciliatory towards Home Rule), the Earl of Granard, Sir Horace Plunkett, the poet W. B. Yeats, old soldiers of the Anglo-Irish tradition such as Sir Bryan Mahon and Major-General Hickie, as well as whiskey magnates like Andrew Jameson – all gave dutiful service to that first Free State Senate. The Senate's remit stated that 'citizens ... shall be proposed on the grounds that they have done honour to the Nation by reason of useful public service or that because of special qualifications or attainments they represent an important aspect of the Nation's life.'[24]

The old relics of the Ascendancy may not have relished the task of painting the letter-boxes green from their original royal red, but they accepted it, and, to this day, most of the postboxes erected by the Crown still stand and serve in the Irish Republic, green-hued – Edward VII's reign having provided more than any other.

There was also the process of replacing the coinage, and substituting the sterling coins bearing the head of King George with one of an Irish design. In an enlightened initiative Senator Yeats was appointed to preside over the commission to design a set of Irish coins. Yeats outlined his ideas for the new Irish coins: they were to have a harp on one side, and some 'simple symbols' on the other – a salmon, a horse, a bull.[25]

Piquantly, an Englishman won the competition for carrying out this design, one Mr Percy Metcalfe –and, as the coins were to be minted by the Bank of England, perhaps this was not inappropriate. Yeats' muse and dear friend, Maud Gonne MacBride, again objected to this.

Senator Yeats succeeded in giving the Irish state a monetary system of aesthetic charm. The pound notes carried a portrait of Hazel Lavery, the Irish-American beauty married to the Belfast painter Sir John: a woman who had been mad about Michael Collins, and with whom, subsequently, Kevin O'Higgins also fell deeply in love, despite (or because of) his austere and priestly character. Lady Lavery indeed earned her place on the Irish currency, and until 1971 we cherished every note that she adorned.[26]

The first phase of nation-building came to an end with the murder of Kevin O'Higgins in July 1927, as he was on his way to midday Mass. True to his Christian ideals, he forgave his assassins as he lay dying. As his life ebbed away, he jested about being reunited with Mick (Collins) in the hereafter – 'playing the harp on a damp cloud'[27]

He had worshipped Collins and sought to fashion the Irish Free State as he believed Collins would have wanted it. O'Higgins was resolute and stern: and his government's order to execute the former best man at his own wedding, the Republican Rory O'Connor, remained a terrible example of the ferocity with which the new state implemented its authority.

Yet, as Ronan Fanning has pointed out in his superb history of independent Ireland, by this tough stance the Free State survived and established the rule of law. The IRA called off their fight.

Éamon de Valera declared himself shocked by O'Higgins' murder; and no one was ever apprehended for it. But this death left a political vacuum from which Dev benefited. He abandoned the political wilderness, took the constitutional route (or 'slightly constitutional' as Seán Lemass put it) and entered the Dáil in 1927, naming his Republican party 'Fianna Fáil' (the romantic 'Soldiers of Destiny').

And what of that hated Oath of Allegiance which de Valera and his fellow Republicans had so anathemised? As Henri of Navarre reasoned when he changed religions for the Crown of France: 'Paris is worth a Mass'. For a man driven by power what is a ritual gesture in exchange for access to power? So de Valera and his cohorts found a way to accept the Oath, while exercising their 'mental reservations': eventually meaning to destroy both the Oath and the binding elements of the Treaty of 1921.

Éamon de Valera and Fianna Fáil came to power in February 1932, after winning 72 seats out of 138 in a general election (although the Dáil majority depended on support from the Labour Party and Independents.)

King George V had been privately worried that this de Valera victory might indeed occur: as were Irish Protestants, who again voiced their dismay in *The Church of Ireland Gazette* that a type of Irish Bolshevik would altogether wipe out what remained of the old order. The King remarked to the Irish High Commissioner in London, the socially and politically adroit John Dulanty, that Dev was 'not an Irishman at all', as far as he could see. Certainly, Dev had escaped execution by the British on the grounds that he was an American.

George's view of de Valera had not always been negative. In 1921, he had described Dev as a 'dreamer and a visionary', and yet he had also recommended to Lloyd George that the Irish leader had some 'good points', and that he was worth listening to.[28]

On coming to power, one of the first targets of de Valera's regime (as promised in the party election manifesto) was the abolition of the Oath to the King.[29] By 1932 most members of the Dáil, including the outgoing administration, thought the Oath was outdated. Even Kevin O'Higgins had found it 'distasteful'. And yet the Oath – being the password that ensured membership of the Commonwealth (as the British Empire had been renamed, partly to pacify the Irish) – had in some ways bolstered the Irish state in the ten years from 1922 to 1932.

The Irish Free State had expanded its influence and proved itself a leader among the core group of nations in the Commonwealth: Australia, New Zealand, South Africa, Canada.[30] When Éire made a démarche, other members of the Commonwealth would often follow her lead: for example, after the Irish insisted on choosing their own Governor-General rather than having a representative appointed from London, both Canada and South Africa claimed the same entitlement.

The Statute of Westminster (enacted in 1931, again partly to mollify the Irish) had extended further independence and equality to all the Dominions: Canada, New Zealand, the Australian Commonwealth, the Union of South Africa and the Irish Free State were now all recognised as states independent of Great Britain. Their only link was their common recognition of the Crown. By this Statute Britain renounced all power to pass laws that affected a Dominion – unless with the consent and request of that Dominion.

And although the Oath to the King was disliked by Irish administrations, it did bring the satisfaction of being able to tell the King that he must obey them, one of his own Commonwealth governments.

One of Mr de Valera's first actions, on forming his Fianna Fáil administration in March 1932, was to issue instructions to High Commissioner Dulanty. He was to inform the British authorities that the Oath of Allegiance was to be abolished and that land annuities to Britain were to be withheld[31]. (The land annuities were monies payable to the British Exchequer by tenants of Irish estates who had purchased their tenancies, on a mortgage system, under a series of land acts. They were collected – with difficulty – by the Irish state on behalf of the Crown.) John Dulanty showed the King a memorandum sent by de Valera, putting the case against the Oath, explaining that its abolition had been an election promise.

Dev's memo stated that 'The abolition of the Oath was the principal and dominating issue before the electors. It has been the cause of all the strife and dissension in this country since the signing of the Treaty.' *All* the strife and dissension seemed a little overstated: Ireland did have other problems, which were quite unaffected by parliamentary oaths. Furthermore, the King was told by the High Commissioner, on behalf of Dev:

> The people, and not merely those who supported the policy of the present Government, regard it as an intolerable burden, a relic of mediaevalism, a test imposed from outside under threat of immediate and terrible war. ... the British Government must realise that real peace in Ireland is impossible so long as the full and free representation of the people in their Parliament is rendered impossible by a test of this character.[32]

Even if the British government took the view that the Oath was mandatory in the Treaty, Dev maintained, 'they must recognise that such a test and imposition on the conscience of the people is completely out of place in a political agreement between the two countries.'

This missive was aimed at the Dominions Secretary, Mr J. H. Thomas, but naturally the King had to read it and consider its implications.[33]

*

The Dominions Secretary, J. H. ('Jimmy') Thomas, was an engaging character, and became a great favourite of the now ageing King George.

Jimmy Thomas had been born the illegitimate son of a domestic servant and was raised by his impoverished grandmother, a washerwoman. In his *Who's Who* entry, Jimmy Thomas proudly wrote, 'Education: council schools. Commenced work at nine years of age as an errand boy: from that to engine-cleaner and stage to stage as fireman and engine-driver.' Apparently he once told a grandees' dinner, 'When you were huntin' and shootin', I was shuntin' and hootin'.'[34]

Through the railway union Jimmy Thomas had worked his way up from trade union delegate to Member of Parliament and, by 1932, His Majesty's Secretary of State for the Dominions. Thomas' rise was described as a 'product of exuberant spirits, native shrewdness, broad populist sympathies, and keen assessment of the achieveable.' In conversation he mixed 'reason, invective, sentimentality, anecdote and repartee.'

The King was always cheered to see him. George rarely, if ever, mentioned the personal attributes of any of his Ministers in his usually prosaic diary, but for Jimmy Thomas he made an exception. 'Jimmy Thomas is very good company,' he remarked.[35] Thomas' critics were caustic, but he possessed that rare quality in a politician: a sense of humour.

Thomas had always supported Irish Home Rule and was sympathetic in general to Ireland. But he was also a loyal defender of the Crown and the Commonwealth. He clashed with de Valera over the Oath: Thomas believed that it was a contractual part of the 1921 Treaty between Britain and Ireland. He praised W. T. Cosgrave for 'his wonderful fidelity and determination to be loyal to the Treaty'.[36]

He felt even more strongly about the question of land annuities (repayments of loans for land purchased under the succession of land reform acts called the Wyndham Land Acts). The annuities were not popular with the Irish farmer (understandably), but Thomas regarded them as revenue due to the British taxpayer.

When he set up a negotiating meeting with de Valera over this question, Dev employed a strategy he often used with British politicians: he began a long lecture on the ills that Britain had inflicted on Ireland over the centuries. He concluded with the calculation that, far from Ireland owing Britain five million pounds per annum, Britain owed Ireland at least four hundred millions, including interest, in historical compensation.[37] De Valera would have had plenty of support for this view among his electorate.

The King was kept informed of all this, as Jimmy Thomas strove to show that abandoning the Oath of Allegiance would be a breach of contract between Ireland and Britain. Yet Thomas received conflicting legal advice from the civil service mandarins and treaty experts he consulted, who, when they examined the small print, ventured to suggest that while it might be technically a breach of the Treaty, legally it might not. Or that 'it would be a breach of the Treaty, but it would not in itself be a repudiation of allegiance or an act of secession.'[38]

The King was grateful for this advice and said, through his secretary, now Clive Wigram, 'We can only wait and see what Mr de Valera intends to do, and whether he may propose to abolish the Oath while maintaining allegiance in accordance with the Constitution and Articles of Agreement with the Irish Free State.'[39]

Mr de Valera's message issued in March 1932 was repeated on 5 April 1932, and presented to the King forthwith: it was more aggrieved than before. It was clear that he was resolved to undo the Treaty of 1921 that he had despatched Michael Collins and Arthur Griffith to negotiate.

The Oath was 'an intolerable burden to the people of this State', he repeated, 'and ... they have declared in the most formal manner that they desire its instant removal.' Moreover, de Valera complained that the Treaty agreement of 1921 involved 'no parity of sacrifice as between Great Britain and Ireland. This agreement gave effect to what was the will of the British Government. It was, on the other hand, directly opposed to the will of the Irish people and was submitted to by them only under the threat of an immediate and terrible war.'[40] Dev also implied in communications that he resented the notion popularised in the British press that King George had somehow 'brought peace to Ireland'.

In meetings in London and Windsor Irish High Commissioner Dulanty interpreted Mr de Valera's agenda to the King's secretary, Clive Wigram, in lofty terms. He explained that 'de Valera was rather like Gandhi, an idealist, and at present he seems to be a Dictator as well and is taking everything into his own hands. He is quite obsessive about the Oath, which he says is subversive and humiliating ...'[41]

However, Dulanty assured Wigram that Dev 'does not wish to break away from the Empire': he especially valued the Canadian connection. This was true enough: Dev did not want to break with the Commonwealth. He wanted it both ways – to be part of the club, but to be a lone voice at the same time.

*

When it came to the land annuities, Mr de Valera complained that Britain had 'extracted from us a financial tribute which, relative to population, puts a greater burden on the people of the Irish Free State than the burden of war reparation payments on the people of Germany.'

The land annuities question was to become a central issue in Anglo-Irish relations during the 1930s, especially as Dev embarked on an 'economic war' with Britain. But land annuities did not involve the King directly, although he would have read all the state papers pertaining to it.

Mr de Valera's next complaint was about the Governor-General of the Irish Free State. Dev was determined to extinguish this post, which he regarded as archaic and feudal, though he planned to do so by stealth rather than by a guillotine.[42] Tim Healy had served his term and, after a full and long life, died. When de Valera came to power, the Governor-General was the scholarly James McNeill (brother to Eoin, who spelt his name 'MacNeill'.)

Mr McNeill had been a successful civil servant in India who had become a supporter of old Sinn Féin: he was the first High Commissioner for the Irish Free State in London in 1923 and thus a pro-Treatyite (though he had lost a son in the Civil War fighting on the anti-Treaty side.)

The King was apprehensive about who de Valera might now appoint as the King's representative. George V was advised by his Attorney-General, Sir Thomas Inskip, that de Valera 'may propose some person wholly unacceptable to His Majesty for appointment and may try to force his nominee upon the King. He may propose himself.' Sir Thomas advised that the 'King is entitled to satisfy himself as to the qualifications of a nominee and entitled to withhold his approval.'[43]

The King was relieved to be advised that Ministers could intervene and protect His Majesty in the event of Mr de Valera seeking to nominate himself as Governor-General. 'Doubtless', went on the King's secretary, in communication with the Assistant Under Secretary at the Dominions Office, Sir Harry Batterbee, 'if it ever came to the point of de Valera putting forward the name of some rebel or murderer to become Governor-General of which the King refused to approve, His Majesty's Ministers here would be equally ready to support the King if he appealed to them.'[44]

Jimmy Thomas noted in his private talks with Dev and his colleagues (Dev was often accompanied by Seán T. O'Kelly, his faithful lieutenant, whom Thomas found to be 'an excellent representative of his country and a most cordial and happy companion') that the root of Fianna Fáil resentment was in their desire for a united Ireland. But, Thomas concluded, 'if that desirable end is ever accomplished it will not be by force or coercion from this country or even from the Irish Free State, but it must come by the goodwill and co-operation of Irishmen themselves, north and south.' It would take another sixty years before that penny would drop.[45]

The de Valera newspaper, the *Irish Press*, founded in 1931, pursued an energetic campaign throughout the spring of 1932 against the hated Oath of Allegiance. Seldom did a day pass in those spring months without castigating the perfidious Oath, with many quotations from Mr de Valera to the effect that Ireland 'cannot tolerate outside interference'. Even the small ads took up the theme: 'No more oaths! No more swearing of anything. Get a "Faulat" collar & do not be trying to strangle yourself before your time!'[46]

Finally, on May 30, the Dáil passed an 'Oath Removal Bill' in a midnight division, and the *Irish Press* went into swoops of soaring lyricism: 'The decision will live in the memory of our people forever, and all associated with it will be kindly thought of by the generations … for national freedom it means a turning of the tide and coming out of the valley of the shadow.' This was certainly de Valera's sentiment: he thought the Oath 'evil'.

In fact, the oath issue was not over yet: it would still have a struggle in the Senate, where, in the words of the *Irish Press*, it would come up against the 'anti-national tendency' (that is, anyone who dissented from the politically correct Fianna Fáil line). It would eventually be deleted from the Irish Constitution in 1936, in dramatic circumstances.

However, the Oath was temporarily put to one side while Mr de Valera and, indeed, all Ireland, prepared for the great Eucharistic Congress of June 1932. Dulanty reported to Wigram in April that matters would be quiet for some time: 'de Valera is concentrating upon the Eucharistic Congress'.

In Dublin people were speaking of little else but this globalised Catholic festival. Mr Dulanty now reassured the King's secretary that there was now more debate 'as to the wearing or not of top hats' than over the Oath. (Adroitly, Mr de Valera would avoid the dress code dilemma by donning his academic robes as Chancellor of the National University of Ireland.)[47]

Before parting from Clive Wigram, John Dulanty asked him if there was any chance of the King's household getting hold of a couple of decent tickets for Ascot?[48]

*

It is a cliché to refer to the 1932 Eucharistic Congress held in Dublin as a riot of 'triumphalism', brought about by the combined power of Church and State. But there was very little for the new Irish State to be 'triumphalist' about. It was still a small, unsure, unconfident, and sometimes chippy national entity. Some ordinary Irish people were even beginning to grumble that life had been better under the British.

The Eucharistic Congress was desperately needed by the stewards of the Irish Free State to impart some sense of purpose, dignity and ceremonial to the country. The Free State was as poor in ceremonial as it was in resources. Anything linked with imperial power was banished; and the dilemma that has ever arisen for revolutionaries arose: when you do away with something old, what do you put in its place?[49]

The Eucharistic Congress, as planned by the Irish state, followed in almost every detail the format previously used for royal visits and royal events in Ireland. Excitement mounted from the end of April, and the press was in a high state of anticipation as they reported the meticulous preparations for the event.

The Eucharistic Congress was designed to be 'an international gathering, presided over by a papal delegate, which, by means of solemn services and other religious exercises, together with addresses and discussions, gives honour to the Sacrament of the Altar and increases devotion thereto.'[50] The first had been held at Lille in 1881, and subsequently at a number of important locations, including Paris, Jerusalem, Lourdes and Rome.

What is striking about the 1932 Congress is the pleasure that the poor seemed to have taken in a sense of jubilation that had been denied to them for decades. Dublin had lived through war and revolution and civil war and austerity – but little public celebration. Even given the grainy photographs of the day, one can make out that the slums of Dublin were a fiesta of flags and bunting (Clery's store had been selling 'national flags, papal flags and congress flags' for 1s.11d. each from April onwards).

The touching banners declaring 'God Bless Christ the King' provided more than an echo of a divine form of monarchy – and the theme was often taken up in newspaper headlines proclaiming 'Christ, the King of Kings'. Conveniently, the Feast of Christ as King had been inaugurated in Rome in 1925.

Mr de Valera – the political leader (the title was 'President of the Executive Council') who had denounced flummery towards the King of England as a 'relic of Mediaevalism' – now took a somewhat adulatory approach to an institution with even deeper roots in tradition than the English monarchy. He proceeded, from May of 1932, to mark the Eucharistic Congress as the greatest and the most splendid ceremony that the Irish nation had ever experienced. He and his minister Seán T. O'Kelly (always the First

Mate to Dev's Captaincy in the 1930s) would be the leading canopy bearers for the Pope's representative.

A million people would attend the Congress and there would be both cheering and kneeling in the streets. There would be gorgeous Masses in the Phoenix Park and a magnificent altar atop O'Connell Bridge. There would be processions, massed bands, massed choirs, a public subscription for a towering crucifix in the Dáil, temporary arches and round towers erected at the gates of Dublin; and Grafton Street would be a blaze of religious regalia. There would be a special cavalry of hussars with gold braid, and frogged jackets, and fur headgear. This regiment was togged out with great care and much thought.

The newly launched Irish society magazine, the *Irish Tatler and Sketch*, especially praised the new cavalry regiment:

> We must congratulate the artistic sense of the Free State Army authorities on the splendid uniforms of the Irish Cavalry, which took part in the procession and formed the bodyguard to the Papal Legate on his arrival. The enthusiasm of the crowds knew no bounds when the Hussars came riding by in their glossy busbies and smart St Patrick's blue-and-gold befrogged uniforms.[51]

The hussars' costumes were finished off with military boots and a sabre: although the uniforms (and even the horses' draped saddle-covers) had to be scraped together with extreme economies —with, it was said, the help of the theatrical outfitters, Ging's.[52] But they did indeed look very dashing by all accounts, and I rather regret that the Irish state has no such colourfully attired regiment in our times. Mr de Valera himself was seen proudly inspecting the Congress' Irish cavalry.

The arrival at Dún Laoghaire of the Papal Legate to Pius XI, Cardinal Lorenso,[53] was in direct imitation of previous visits by British monarchs to Ireland. The port was packed to the gills, as Dev and his ministers awaited the ship carrying the Pope's representative into Dublin bay. A 'glittering cavalcade' met the SS *Cambon* as she sailed into shore: above the vessel, the Irish Air

Force provided an escort flying in cruciform pattern, making a cross in the sky.[54]

Mr de Valera, and the Lord Mayor of Dublin, Alfie Byrne (an old Home Ruler, and not averse to the British monarchy), riding in his Lord Mayor's coach, welcomed Cardinal Lauri and his retinue. Lauri was inevitably described as 'radiant' – a favourite word of royal reporters.

The party then moved in procession towards Dublin city, the route lined with welcoming crowds proclaiming by their presence the 'Unbroken Allegiance of People's Loyalty to the Holy See.'[55] Not coincidentally, words and phrases previously applied to the monarchy were attached to the papacy: 'allegiance', 'loyalty' and 'kingship' (of Christ).

*

At Merrion Road, Ballsbridge – always a great halting point for Royal processions – special gates had been erected; heralds bugled the approaching progress of the legate and there was praying on the streets.

There was praying also in the many Dublin churches, with different rites and variations of Catholicity in various locations: the Slav rite, the Oriental rite (referring to Abyssinians, Armenians, Chaldeans, Copts, Maronites and others), the rite of the Syro-Malankara church. If the imperial power could boast of a 'multi-national' empire – Catholicity's universality could rival it!

The cardinals, bishops, archbishops came from Malta and Australia, from India and Canada, from France, Germany, Czechoslavakia, Spain, Italy, America, and from China – from 20 different countries in the world in fact, and many of these princes and prelates had a direct link to Ireland.

'Every English-speaking cardinal', gloried de Valera's *Irish Press*, 'visiting us is of Irish parentage, England's included. Canada sends four Archbishops of Irish blood and name. Six of the seven prelates from Australia are Irish – Kelly, Killian, Byrne, Ryan, Norton, Dwyer. From the British West Indies comes

Archbishop Dowling OP. Ten of England's own Bishops and Archbishops are Irish.'[56]

The roll-call proceeds: the Fijian bishop is an Irishman, as is the Bishop of Danzig; then there is Dr O'Rourke, the Archbishop of Simla; Kennealy, from the Philippines; O'Doherty and every other bishop in Nigeria, an Irishman; Broderick, Leary, O'Rourke, Shanahan. From Scotland, McCarthy. From South Africa, MacSherry, O'Reilly, O'Leary. Two Irish bishops came from Zanzibar: and 19 of the visiting American bishops and archbishops were of Irish families. This was 'Ireland's Spiritual Empire' – the globalised influence of the Irish through the agency of the Catholic Church.

There was also an element of pride that a new, fledgling nation could competently run such a show – despite British sneers, real or imagined.

The *Irish Press* did not fail to contrast Britain's lack of trust in Irish competence, with Irish ecclesiastical efficiency. 'See how well [Irish churchmen] administer their provinces. And yet Mr [Jimmy] Thomas and Mr Lloyd George … [57]presume to interfere with us in our own land and when we object, denounce us as incapable visionaries and fanatical dreamers. Apparently Ireland has produced the miracle among the races – one that can rule all nations but itself.'[58]

De Valera pointedly did not invite Governor-General McNeill to the formal ceremonies arranged by his government – he was very obviously being marginalised. Indeed James McNeill and his clever wife, Josephine, had been made to feel fairly miserable by Dev's administration: there had been an unmannerly incident when two senior Fianna Fáil ministers (Seán T. O'Kelly and Frank Aiken) walked out of a reception at the French legation because the Governor-General was present. Dev was constantly trying to reduce McNeill's salary and, wherever possible, the King's representative was excluded from state occasions. This dismissal by stealth was in a way more personally wounding than an outright sacking.[59]

Yet the government's attitude did not inhibit the *Irish Tatler and Sketch* from gushing over the Governor-General and Mrs

McNeill at other, non-state, events. Mr and Mrs McNeill appeared at a delightful garden party held for the Congress at de Valera's Alma Mater, Blackrock College, to the magazine's obvious delight: '… the gorgeous robes of the multi-coloured gowns of the women created that happy scene as Churchmen and people met to welcome the representatives of the Congress.'[60]

The society magazine was equally enraptured in its description of Eucharistic receptions at Dublin Castle:

> For the first time in the history of Ireland, Dublin Castle, the seat of British Government in Ireland for centuries, was thrown open to the Irish people for the State Reception to the Cardinal Legate in Dublin. It was a wonderful sight to stand in the old St Patrick's Hall, which the Government has so wisely retained in all its beauty with the standard emblazoned and with arms and trophies telling the history of the past. The beautiful chandeliers lit up the scene of glorious colour with the dais crowded with the Princes of the Church – the messengers of peace to Ireland.

Where previously the King had held levees and the Queen drawing-rooms, now 'passed four thousand guests, and as they approached the Legate they bowed reverently in twos. Then they moved to the marquees and gardens:

> a great mass of humanity drawn from all creeds and classes of people. Handsomely clad officials from foreign countries, Churchmen, University professors in their robes mingling with Friars and black-soutaned clergy, the old men and young leaders of various parties, poor and rich, fashionably dressed women and simple folk from all parts of Ireland – one of the greatest democratic gatherings seen in the heart of the Irish capital … It is a happy omen that this first function in the old Castle should be given to honour the Prince of Peace.

If the Congress strikes twenty-first-century commentators as 'sectarian', that notion would seldom have occurred in Ireland in 1932. As the *Irish Tatler and Sketch* put it, the celebrations all seemed quite remarkably 'democratic', by which it meant that people were not selected on grounds of social rank.

In its own way, the *Irish Press* sought to strike an inclusive note to Irishmen of other faiths, or none, at least by way of a coda: 'Nor can we forget the non-Catholic section of our people. They may not join in the religious festivals, but we know that they too extend to the great churchmen and the simple pilgrims who have come amongst us the Irish welcome, the welcome of friends.'[61]

There were dissenters: the Theosophist, George Russell (known as 'Æ'), an early campaigner for an 'Irish Ireland', stood on a mountaintop and called for rain and tempests to fall upon the Congress.[62] The gods of Theosophy did not oblige and it was splendid weather all through. Dublin, said the *Irish Independent*, choosing a significant image, was like a queen restored to her domain. The *Irish Press* preferred the image of Cathleen ni Houlihan, the personification of Ireland whom Yeats had so celebrated as having 'the walk of a Queen', brought to life by the legendary Maud Gonne MacBride.

The Congress – just like a royal jubilee – was also an excuse for an uplifting experience in the troubled decade of the 1930s. George V was in the last phase of his reign and he and his wife Mary were now increasingly concerned about the character of their heir, David, Prince of Wales. George had fallen seriously ill in November 1928 (with septicaemia) and for a time he was not expected to live.

The Prince of Wales was at this time on safari in Africa and had to be brought back hurriedly in case his father should die. The King pulled through, but the illness lasted five months and the scare concentrated the palace's mind on the fact that this jazz-loving, cocktail-mixing Prince of Wales was to be the next King of Great Britain, Ireland and the Dominions overseas.

The Prince of Wales loved everything his father did not, such as America, and the cinema, and cigarette smoking: and, much to the anguish of his parents, the company of married women. King George V would have matched – or surpassed – any Irish ecclesiastic in his disapproval of divorce (and homosexuality).

He and Queen Mary would not receive divorced or separated persons at court (or at the Royal Enclosure at Ascot, a royal prohibition which lasted until 1968).[63] Winston Churchill had to write to the King to implore him to allow his cousin, the Duke of Marlborough, to attend lunch at Windsor after a chapter meeting of a ceremonial order: Marlborough had been barred because he was separated from his American heiress wife, Consuelo Vanderbilt. The King relented by downgrading the ceremonial.[64]

A Scottish aristocrat who pleaded that his divorce had been acceptable to the Church as an annulment – he had been allowed to remarry ecclesiastically – was informed: 'That may well get you into the Kingdom of Heaven, but it will not admit you to the Palace at Holyroodhouse (the Edinburgh royal residence).'

The King would not be represented abroad by divorcees: he would not accept an ambassador to the Court of St James who had been divorced twice. 'They want to send me a man who has three wives alive, but we shall refuse him. I will not have a man with three wives.' He succeeded in barring the candidate.

George and Mary had four sons living and one daughter. Two of the sons were serious and conscientious – Bertie, Duke of York and Henry, Duke of Gloucester (the latter described by a biographer as 'somewhat dim'). The other two were less orthodox: David, the Prince of Wales, and George, Duke of Kent – who did marry Princess Marina of Greece, but was known to have had a homosexual affair with Noel Coward, not to mention having dabbled in cocaine.

Of such cavortings by young Kent, King George had no knowledge – he and Queen Mary were so focused on David, the heir. What would become of England, and the Empire, under David? 'Can't do a thing with the fellow,' George used to mutter.

The elderly parents were most distressed at David's attachment to Mrs Thelma Furniss and Mrs Dudley Ward – both married women.

Yet publicly, the Prince of Wales was adored. People liked him for being 'modern'. He himself liked the 'modernising' aspects of the Irish Free State – he especially praised Irish politicians and ministers for being of the younger generation.

Desmond FitzGerald (father of Garret) had written to his wife, Mabel, in 1931 that the Prince of Wales had congratulated an Irish minister, Patrick McGilligan, on the youthful appearance of FitzGerald, Patrick Hogan, and McGilligan. The Prince was informed that the trio were actually the oldest ministers in the Irish government: the Prince was duly impressed that Ireland's politicians were generally so youthful.[65] In London, by contrast, there were still ministers serving the Crown who had risen to prominence under Queen Victoria: Austen Chamberlain, aged 68 in 1931; and Lord Crewe, aged 73.

The Prince also pumped McGilligan on whether Éire was planning to dump the monarchy. 'To hear you refer to my Father, I thought you or at least your people wanted to cut him out.' McGilligan 'suggested that though some might have thought about various forms of government and decided against monarchy that the real thing had always been against English control and that what we were occupied with [was] the getting rid of every form of seal or apparent power of British government.'

The Prince asked, had not the last vestiges of British power already gone? McGilligan said that 'a few other things occupied us still'. David confided to McGilligan that, as he might one day be in the position now occupied by his father, George V, these things interested him. He said he was glad that McGilligan would be there as his advisor and that he would be getting good advice. Fitzgerald took from this that the Prince of Wales felt the Irish were on the 'right lines in our constitutional demand.'

But politics – and sometimes monarchy – are unpredictable, and neither McGilligan nor the Prince would ever be in the anticipated positions of power. Yet Patrick McGilligan seemed to have made some personal impression on his royal interlocutors, as King George later asked about his financial situation when he had lost office – in the days before generous political pensions, Mr McGilligan had to go back to the Bar to make his living, but he had meanwhile lost ground in the legal hierarchy. King George was equally worried when Ramsay MacDonald, sometime Labour Prime Minister, was so badly off when out of office that he was reduced to earning a crust as a journalist.

*

David, Prince of Wales, visited Northern Ireland at the end of 1932 to open the Stormont parliament and he received a rapturous welcome: the 'loyal addresses' presented to him were written out and illustrated with a love and care that is poignant to see today – exquisitely handcrafted manuscripts from 117 loyal organisations.

Ecstatically cheering crowds carried public banners with such messages as 'Welcome to our Beloved Prince. The Protestant religion we will maintain'. There were private messages from some Ulster Catholics, too, affirming their loyalty to the Crown. A retired sea captain wrote to say, 'Let me tell you, you have hundreds of thousands of Catholics as loyal to you as any Protestant.' An army captain of Irish Catholic background assured the Prince, 'Please don't think we are all de Valeras – mad as hatters.' A correspondent from Queenstown, Co Cork, wrote to warn: 'Don't say anything about religion when up North.'[66]

David's speeches were carefully constructed for him – he found the straitjacket of palace control oppressive anyway. Left to his own devices, it is likely that the Prince of Wales might have made remarks regarded as politically sensitive (just as he had said about the unemployed miners of Wales: 'something must be done!'). David saw very little difference between Irishmen north and south. He dropped hints that he would like to visit south of the border – but he was directed to concentrate on the 'loyal' part of Ulster.

The conservative journalist G. Ward Price sent back a private report to Windsor after the Prince's Belfast visit saying it had gone very well, and there was much interest in the Prince of Wales from the Free State:

> The Prince's popularity, from the point of view of his personality, stands high in the Free State, and a woman ... who is a close friend of de Valera, assured me that if it were ever possible for him to come to Dublin, the southern Irish would give him just as enthusiastic a reception as he got in Belfast.[68]

Ward Price went on to say that he thought this was perhaps an 'overstatement': he himself was no great admirer of the Free State and described it, politically, as akin to 'moving about in an open-air lunatic asylum.'

Nevertheless, Ward Price reported to the Palace that the leader of the Opposition, Mr Cosgrave, 'told me that HRH had asked him to tell his successor [de Valera] that he would like to come to Southern Ireland, but that as he [Cosgrave] was not on speaking terms with Mr de Valera, he had been unable to do so ...' This was true – astonishingly, de Valera and Cosgrave, sitting opposite each other in the Dáil Chamber, did not encounter each other, socially, for 40 years.[69]

Doubtless the Prince of Wales would have been received well had he visited the Irish Free State at that time. He was regarded as a rather dashing and romantic bachelor figure, who inspired the popular song: 'I danced with a man who danced with a girl who danced with the Prince of Wales.'

There was to be a significant constitutional link between David, as Edward VIII, and the Irish Free State, but it was in a more sombre context than anyone could have imagined during his Belfast visit of 1932.

*

And so the old King, George V, moved towards his closing years: the 25th anniversary of his accession was celebrated as a jubilee on 6 May 1935. It could be said that the festivities were a mirror image of the Eucharistic Congress, with many street parties and bunting – most especially in poor areas.

King George was deeply moved at the love that he felt from his people. '… I thank you from the depths of our hearts for all the loyalty – and may I say so? – the love, which this day and always you have surrounded us.[70]

The Papal Legate, despatched to Ireland, had sent a message in similar language: 'Go And in My Name Say: "The Pope Loves Ireland",' as the banner headline in the *Irish Press* proclaimed.[71]

But at King George's Jubilee, Prime Minister Ramsay MacDonald noted mournfully the absence of Ireland from the ranks of the Empire. 'Reception of Dominion Premiers the most touching and homely triumph of ceremony and loyal homage ever held. Ireland was out and the gap lay like a shadow of smallness over a ceremony of bigness and graciousness.'[72]

MacDonald, who had been born poor and illegitimate in Scotland, and had been a radical anti-monarchist in his youth, had become devoted to the King. 'The King's reply was a perfect expression of Sovereign affection and solicitude … everyone deeply moved.' Here the Empire was a great family, the gathering of a family reunion, the King a paternal head.

Again, Irish attitudes towards the monarchy were inhibited by the political overview. Mr de Valera wrote to the Dominions Secretary, Jimmy Thomas, that 'my Government sincerely rejoices that His Majesty has been spared to rule his people for almost a quarter of a century.' (An interesting slip, overvaluing the role of a constitutional monarch, who reigns but does not rule and is so politically powerless.)

'We would gladly share in the Jubilee celebrations', he went on, 'if it were possible to do so without giving rise to serious mis-understanding.' He then went on to enumerate Ireland's grievances, which necessarily restrained any participation in the Jubilee:

> Ireland has been incorporated in the Common-
> wealth by force; her territory has been partitioned
> against her will without regard to justice, and we feel
> that we would be false to our duty as a national

Government, and lacking in frankness, if, by our presence at an occasion of Commonwealth rejoicing, we made it appear that we voluntarily accepted a position which is in fact contrary to the national aspirations of our people.[73]

Taking his cue from Dev, High Commissioner Dulanty sent a suitably austere account of how the Free State would hold aloof from the celebrations. 'I have, so far, declined to allow myself or this Office to be associated in any way whatsoever with the forthcoming Jubilee Celebrations,' he told his chief in Dublin, Joseph P. Walshe.

While the other tenants in his Piccadilly building were preparing decorations, Mr Dulanty was giving orders that no such decorations should occur in the part of the building associated with Saorstát Éireann. He had been offered six seats at the thanksgiving service in St Paul's Cathedral, he added, but he had 'urbanely declined'.[74]

At this point Dublin softened its policy slightly, and Joe Walshe wrote again to say that, 'without doing anything exaggerated', perhaps the High Commissioner could conform to whatever every other ambassador and minister accredited to the Court of St James was doing.

It might perhaps seem a bit churlish if there were no decorations at all in the Irish quarters of Piccadilly House – which the Irish High Commission shared with other tenants who displayed riots of bunting and flags. It was sufficient that the government itself was staying away from the main event: for the rest, Dublin instructed that Dulanty should not show discourtesy, but could use his judgement on bunting matters. And by the way, if there was any celebration at Westminster Cathedral, he should certainly attend that.

The Roman Catholic Cathedral in London was, after all, the Pope's domain. And that was Ireland's.

By this point in 1935, Governor-General James McNeill had departed from his thankless role: he had offered his resignation to the King in October 1932, although de Valera's *Irish Press* made it clear, in reality he had been forced out of office by Fianna Fáil.[75]

De Valera's contempt for the office of Governor-General was evident when he nominated Domhnall Ó Buachalla – described even by sympathetic historians as a 'nonentity' – as the next Governor-General.

Ó Buachalla was a grocer from Maynooth, born Donal Buckley in 1866: nothing wrong with being a grocer, although Dulanty tried to enhance his status to the King by spin-doctoring him as 'the owner of a substantial emporium in Ireland's ecclesiastical capital.'[76] He was an enthusiast for the Gaelic League who had had rather a thrilling time in the 1916 Rising, operating from the roof of the General Post Office, under the direct command of James Connolly, and killing two crackshot snipers. In 1918 he was left a widower with four sons and three daughters, but remained active on the anti-Treaty side. He took a seat in Dáil Éireann with Fianna Fáil in 1927, losing it in 1932, and retiring, for the moment, quietly to Maynooth.

Mr Ó Buachalla had no personal desire to be even a farcical Governor-General, but he knew de Valera required his service as a step to abolishing the role altogether. Ó Buachalla, a religious man, also wrote to a priest friend that he hoped God would give him 'grace and strength of will to perform the functions of the position according to His will and for the sake of Ireland'.[77]

He never set foot in Viceregal Lodge, the Governor-General's formal residence. He was sworn in at his brother's suburban home, 108 Rock Road, Booterstown, Co Dublin, on 26 November 1932, and continued to live there until early 1933, when he moved to a house in Dún Laoghaire. He continued to travel by bicycle – a low-emission official before his time. He performed no social functions whatsoever, though he did sign letters patent and other documents put before him by Mr de Valera's administration.

The King's officials were not at all pleased by this development, but in the end they had to swallow it. The King had to take the advice of his ministers, and the ministers of the Irish government were also *his* ministers. King George drew the line, however, at being forced to sign documents in Irish.[78]

Relations between Britain and Ireland were tense and grumpy during the 1930s: the annuities question had led to an 'economic war', and Britain restricted Irish agricultural imports, which penalised Irish farmers more than it hurt the British exchequer.[79] (At the end of the economic war, in 1938, the Irish negotiated a one-off payment of £10 million to wipe out the annuities debt.)

There was, of course, much else going on in the world during these years. There was India and its rising nationalism; conflict in Spain; the rise of the dictators and of Fascist and Communist parties all over Continental Europe; not to mention Stalin's famines in the Ukraine (which *The Irish Catholic* press reported surprisingly well, considering the communications difficulties).

During the last days of his life King George's worries were focused on all of this brewing trouble in Europe – as well as the character of his son, David. He had often expressed the hope that David would never be King and was certainly appalled to learn of David's growing obsession with Mrs Ernest Simpson.

From the beginning of 1934 onwards the Prince of Wales had become hopelessly smitten by Wallis Simpson, a witty, intelligent, and elegant American from Baltimore, who already had two husbands still very much alive. The relationship was known about in royal and society circles: at first Mrs Simpson had appeared everywhere the Prince happened to be, in the company of her second husband, Ernest. Then Ernest faded away, and Mrs Simpson gradually assumed the role of David's constant companion.[80]

Throughout 1935 she was pictured with the Prince of Wales on various social occasions, and while this was the subject of speculation in the American and Continental papers, not a word appeared in the British – or indeed the Irish – newspapers while King George lived. This did not preclude the King from predicting to the Conservative Prime Minister, Stanley Baldwin (who succeeded Ramsay MacDonald in June 1935), 'After I am dead, the boy will ruin himself in twelve months'.

George V died on 20 January 1936, writing his diary almost to the end. It would be more accurate to say that his physician performed a deliberate act of euthanasia on him: Lord Dawson of Penn, the King's personal doctor, admitted in clinical notes that were only released in 1986, that at 9.25 on the night of 20 January, he administered to King George a cocktail of morphine and cocaine, which duly brought about a peaceful death about ninety minutes later.[81]

The King was suffering from a heart condition – not a terminal illness – and Lord Dawson administered the fatal dose not merely to relieve the patient of a death struggle, but, more purposefully, to catch the deadlines for the next day's *Times* newspaper.

At King George's funeral five monarchs walked behind his coffin: Christian of Denmark, Haakon of Norway, Carol of Rumania, Boris of Bulgaria and Leopold of the Belgians. Only three of these were to survive as kingdoms after the Second World War.

In Ireland the death of King George was to be approached 'with dignity and respect', according to the secretary of the Irish Department of External Affairs, Joseph P. Walshe.[82]

But once again a tension arose between Windsor and Dublin as to how condolences were to be treated. Lord Wigram (formerly Sir Clive), the King's secretary, wished to acknowledge letters and condolences directly from Windsor Castle. The Irish government wished to take charge of this task. This was all part of de Valera's policy of controlling Ireland's sovereignty and frustrating, wherever possible, 'Palace intervention' in matters of procedure.

Lord Wigram's attitude and actions, Dublin said, 'would be regarded by the ordinary Irishman as irritating propaganda, and they might – in some cases certainly would have – the effect of rousing anti-monarchist passions.' This threat was frequently made: if the monarchy did not bend to Dev's wishes, there would be rioting in the streets.

Yet most of those who sent messages of condolence from Ireland belonged to Protestant Loyalist groups, formerly called the Southern Unionists. The list of condolence-senders included: The North Dublin Branch (Women's Section) of the British

Legion; the Royal Irish Yacht Club; The Royal Dublin Fusiliers Old Comrades Association; the Protestant Orphans Society; The Central Committee of the YMCA; the Killarney Branch of the British Legion; the Masonic Lodge No 62, Tralee; the Royal St George Yacht Club, Kingstown (sic); the Guinness Athletic Union; the Parishioners of Glenageary; the Chapter of Christ Church, Dublin; and many others of similar ilk.

There were also some non-affiliated groups, such as the Literary and Philosophical Society of University College, Cork, the Guardians of the Coombe Lying-In Hospital, and the Royal Hibernian Academy of Arts, but they were in the minority. Furthermore, there were individual messages from 'many Free State loyalists'.

Many of these self-described 'Free State loyalists' would surely have preferred an acknowledgement directly from Buckingham Palace or Windsor Castle, rather a reply through the medium of de Valera's government. Some 'Free State Loyalists' specifically mentioned, in letters to the King's household, that they were posting their letters in Holyhead in Wales for fear that the Free State authorities would not actually handle a letter addressed to royalty.[83]

The handling of letters was continually disputed between the Irish government and Lord Wigram. The private secretary complained in a memo to the King – who would now be Edward VIII – of the repeated manner in which the 'Irish Free State refuses to conform to the procedure followed by other Dominions.'[84]

Apart from the letters of condolence, there was an ongoing row about those diplomatic letters of credence and recall in connection with the Irish Free State that were addressed to the King: these were constantly being opened by Mr de Valera – 'in spite of frequent remonstrances dating from May 1933' – and then forwarded to HM via the Irish High Commissioner.

Wigram carpeted Mr Dulanty in March 1936, explaining that 'gentlemen did not open letters not addressed to them': Mr Dulanty promised he would smooth matters over with Dublin. But such matters were never resolved. In November 1939, the row still continued: the Free State was still affirming the right to handle this matter in its own way, and His Majesty's private secretary was still complaining.

Diplomatic procedure may only be a matter of form. But we can imagine that the Guardians of the Protestant Orphans Society in Dublin might have liked to think their correspondence with the royal household was unmediated by Mr de Valera's administration.

*

For Éamon de Valera, the passing of King George was another opportunity to enlarge Ireland's independence and affirm her sovereignty.

Early in the reign of the reluctant King Edward VIII, Mr de Valera cleared the final hurdles to abolish the Oath of Allegiance, on 29 May 1936: 'his favourite piece of legislation', as Tim Pat Coogan calls it. The amendment had taken since 1932 to pass both Dáil and Senate, and now the Constitution (Amendment No 24) Act neatly abolished the Senate as well as the Oath.[85]

Throughout the summer of 1936, as a civil war started in Spain and Éamon de Valera worked on his preparations for a new constitution for Ireland, British officials grew anxious about the character of the new King of England, Edward VIII.

David, Prince of Wales, had automatically acceded on the death of his father, but was not yet crowned – a coronation would normally take place the year following the accession. This new King was liked because he seemed such a contrast to previously stuffy royal protocol. He was photographed in shorts and bathing costumes, was seen drinking from a bottle of lemonade, appeared naked in a Turkish bathhouse – moreover he was 'Americanised' in the style that was thought go-ahead and progressive.

He seemed to be able to reach out across the classes, and when he visited working-class locations he would do something simple and beguiling, such as ask a construction worker to show him how to mix cement. Towards the Irish he displayed not only a courteous approach, but also a human touch.

In the second month of his reign, in February 1936, King Edward made a dutiful tour of a trade show in which goods from the Irish Free State were on display, and seemed to be particularly interested in the Irish system of egg-testing and egg-grading. He then detached himself from the accompanying official and spoke privately to the Irish High Commissioner, John Dulanty, saying 'how glad he was to have received the messages from the Seanad and the Dáil [on the death of his father]. He was also grateful, he said, for the telegram which Mr de Valera had caused to be sent to the Queen [Mary, George V's widow].'

The King then made mention of the tragedy of Brian de Valera (Mr de Valera's 20-year-old son) who had been killed in a riding accident in February 1936. He asked if Mr de Valera's son had been an experienced rider? Dulanty said that he was. Was it, asked the King, that the horse had run away with him? Dulanty went on to explain the circumstances of the accident, which took place on a Sunday outing at Phoenix Park.

King Edward said 'he could feel more deeply than most people the tragedy of a death in such circumstances since he himself had had two escapes from a similar ending – escapes which were almost in the nature of miracles.' (He had loved dangerous sports, both in England and on safari in Africa.) Once again, he repeated to John Dulanty his deepest sympathy for Mr de Valera's loss.[86]

The British Prime Minister was the Conservative Stanley Baldwin, whose morals were as middle-class as his background. He looked upon King Edward's flighty circle of friends with deep suspicion. Throughout 1936 he was increasingly aware of Edward's fixation with Wallis Simpson. Baldwin was also worried that David might confide state matters to Wallis: he seemed absolutely dependent on her.

The British press was famously discreet about Edward's association with Wallis, but within political circles it was known via the American media. In the summer of 1936 the King took a Mediterranean cruise, on which he was much photographed with Wallis. On returning to London in September, Wallis Simpson proceeded with her divorce from her second husband, Ernest.

Alarm grew in political circles that the King would insist on marrying Mrs Simpson once she was free. The leader of the

Opposition, Clement Attlee, made it quite plain to Baldwin that the Labour party would have 'little sympathy with the King's favour towards Mrs Simpson.'[87]

The waves of rumour and gossip spread. In the Commonwealth most vehemently opposed to Mrs Simpson's ascendancy were the Canadians, who were privy to everything the American press was publishing: and with their Scottish Presbyterian background, most disapproving. Scotland too was unfavourable when it was leaked that the twice-divorced Mrs Simpson had paid a visit to Balmoral.

In the autumn the British Cabinet met to discuss the suggestion that King Edward might insist on marrying Mrs Simpson when she was free. They were so concerned to preserve secrecy that press statements were issued to the effect that His Majesty's government was deep in discussion about Spain (improbable in that Britain had decided to stay well out of the Spanish Civil War, much to the disapprobation of the Left).

Baldwin, despite being a 'sound Churchman', was prepared to consider 'the mistress option', in the style of Madame Lupescu, the King of Rumania's mistress. This outraged King Edward. 'Mrs Simpson is a lady,' he told his Prime Minister.

By the late autumn, the Irish government had been fully briefed by the indefatigable John Dulanty. Dulanty was a sociable animal and he went out to lunches and receptions in London, listening and making contacts, always reporting back to Dublin what he heard. He was given the lowdown on the King's romance from Dr J. J. Mallon, the Warden of Toynbee Hall. J. J. Mallon was a close friend of Queen Mary, who was in despair about her son's conduct, and thought him contemptible for not doing his duty and renouncing the American divorcée.

Mr Dulanty was reporting back to the Department of External Affairs, effectively run by Dev himself, under the direction of his faithful lieutenant Joe Walshe. Dulanty suggested that while clearly Mr de Valera would not be concerned with tittle-tattle about the personal lives of public figures, nonetheless it was coming to the point at which, he warned, a constitutional crisis loomed. Dulanty went on to provide a full profile of King Edward:

a first-class business man in running the Crown estates in the Duchy of Cornwall which have prospered under his direction. A complete modernist, he does not conceal his disregard for what may be described as traditional authority. He has a marked tendency on social questions to a liberal attitude almost unheard-of in the royal circle. He has always claimed complete freedom about the selection of his friends. Years ago, he was very much attracted by Lady Ednam who was a woman of ability and character, who, unfortunately, was killed in a flying accident. It is suggested that the Queen today feels some regret that that friendship was not encouraged.[88]

Queen Mary, the Archbishop of Canterbury and the Prime Minister, said John Dulanty, had all pleaded with the King over Mrs Simpson, 'but each has suffered a severe rebuke. He will allow no one to make even a distant reference to the question and Dr Mallon thought that he was therefore living in a fool's paradise.' Yet if the King decided to cast off the conventions of established tradition, he might have the sympathy and support of the younger generation. 'Some of the younger people certainly would take that line ….', Dulanty advised his government, 'but [Dr Mallon] felt that the country as a whole would be against such a marriage, and that his former popularity would begin to wane.'

This helpful memo probably did not come as a surprise to de Valera. He was indeed too high-minded to stoop to low gossip: yet he never missed a chance, especially in dealing with the British, to take advantage of a crisis. The crisis swirling around the British monarchy would be another opportunity to detach the Irish Free State from the tentacles of the old enemy.

And yet his personal approach was surprising. De Valera was an orthodox Roman Catholic, but he could be liberal when he chose. On the question of King Edward's paramour, and her two previous divorces, Dev was markedly liberal. (Countess Markievicz was now dead: how roundly she had denounced the

English for their 'immorality and divorce laws' in the original Treaty debates!)[89]

There was Machiavellian reasoning behind Dev's liberal attitudes. He told Sir Harry Batterbee of the Dominions Office that the Irish Free State had no 'personal' interest in the King. However, if Commonwealth opinions were sought, he, Dev, was inclined to favour the King's choice of bride, if that was what the man desired.

King Edward was popular, said Dev, 'including in Ireland', and surely every avenue should be explored in solving this problem? Divorce, added Dev, was not recognised in Catholic countries: but King Edward was a Protestant and Protestants could presumably do as they liked?

Dev even romantically added that he thought many young people would be attracted by the idea of a King ready to give up his throne, if necessary, for the woman he loved. This was a true reading of popular reactions.

The pros and antis often lined up according to their concern for the monarchy. Those who felt that the institution of the monarchy had to be respected and preserved disapproved of the Mrs Simpson connection. Those who cared little for monarchy tended to say the man should do as he pleased. Communists and Fascists both supported the King's 'personal choice'.

The Communist leader Harry Pollitt made a speech denouncing the government for its meddling: 'The spectacle of the national government laying down a code of morals and behaviour for the King is indeed a sight … Let the King marry whom he likes. That is his personal business.' Like Harry Pollitt, Dev had no interest in defending the British monarchy. Irish Protestants, on the other hand, worried that the scandal would harm the Crown.

By December 1936, the political classes were fully aware that the King was likely to abdicate: and the great drama of the King's love life was to become fully public on December 3.

It had to be explained to Dev that a king's abdication was not a simple matter of resigning his post: there was a complex constitutional procedure in which the King would sign 'the Instrument of Abdication' in favour of his brother Albert, Duke of York. All of the Dominion governments would have to recognise and endorse this procedure, including the Irish Free State.

*

When the story broke in the newspapers, the romance of the King's illicit relationship with Mrs Simpson was, predictably, rather more enticing to the average reader than the constitutional procedures involving the Dominions. The horrors of the Spanish Civil War receded in the public imagination: a French journalist complained that the deaths of Spanish children were ignored because of a King's love affair.

The Dominion governments were consulted over the King's dilemma, with the suggestion that he might contract a morganatic marriage (in which he would be legally married to Wallis, but she would not be Queen).

While Mr de Valera was indulgent of the King, the Canadians, the South Africans, the Australians – and New Zealand public opionion – ruled out a morganatic marriage because it would damage the good name of the Crown. The Canadians wanted the king to abdicate voluntarily: the Australians said there was 'no possibility of compromise' – the King must either abandon the idea of marrying Wallis, or abdicate.

The Dominion, New Zealand's leading newspaper wrote, 'It is almost incredible that in less than a year from King George's death, the throne should be shaken to its foundations by indiscretions which age, experience and cognizance of the obligations attached to his exalted office should have warned King Edward to avoid: it is a tragedy that he appears to have failed to realise what this may mean to the idea of Kingship throughout the British Commonwealth and the Colonial Empire.'[90]

Catholic voices were also disapproving on moral grounds: Dr Daniel Mannix, the Irish-born Archbishop of Melbourne said that the King's marriage to a divorcee was unacceptable to HM's Catholic subjects. The *Irish Catholic* newspaper was at one with the Anglican Archbishop of Canterbury, and almost all of the

Christian churches in taking this opportunity to disparage divorce (which they regarded as an American fashion picked up from Hollywood movies, treating the dissolution of wedlock as a fit subject for comedy).

The *Irish Catholic* deplored, too, the popular press interest in Edward and Mrs Simpson and 'the amount of space devoted by certain newspapers which claim to represent Ireland's Catholic press to the trivial detail of a sordid love affair with which the present King of England is involved.'[91]

Why were so-called Catholic Irish newspapers flaunting 'this disgusting story of royal lust'? It seemed that people in Ireland were as fascinated by the story as people anywhere else. However much divorce might be officially deprecated, it was the human element that caught the imagination, as many older Irish people recall. 'Divorce, at that time, was not widely accepted, especially by Catholics,' Eileen Clare remembers. She was then a young girl from Ireland attending convent boarding school in England run by Irish nuns.[92]

Yet when the story of the King and Mrs Simpson was formally explained to the schoolgirls, no judgement was passed by the Mother Superior. When Eileen returned to Co Wexford for the Christmas holidays, she was met by her Uncle Pat, a local farmer, in his pony and trap. 'And the first thing he said was "what kind of people are they in England – they won't let the poor King marry the woman he loves?"'

Neasa McEnery's recollection was that 'most Irish people were sorry for King Edward, and even more so in Dublin itself. ... My aunt in Dublin said it was time that women of 40 were put on the map!' (Wallis was then 40 – possibly 41.) To Neasa, then a young schoolgirl, 'Edward VIII was young and handsome and ranked second only to my adoration of Michael Collins!' This ecumenical jostling of republican and royal emblems was not unusual in Irish households.

Maeve O'Connor from Dalkey, Co Dublin, recalls that her father, a civil servant in the Irish Customs & Excise, expressed 'sadness and regret, as, like many of his friends & colleagues, he respected Edward and his attitude towards Ireland which was decidedly friendly'. Maeve's father had 'heard suggestions of offering the Prince of Wales a high position in Ireland.'

It seems that every twist and turn of the fateful romance – once it was openly reported, and even when there were rumours and repeated gossip from American magazines – was followed closely, particularly by women. For the first time since Parnell – and in less painful circumstances for Ireland – it gave people permission to discuss the human aspect of divorce.

The mother of Marie Sheridan from Co Clare worked in the Irish Sweepstakes at the time, which employed many women as ticket clerks. There was an American employee among their number who brought in all the latest gossip. The Sweepstake ladies were enthralled by the whole saga, and Marie's mother recounted it to her like a novel, or an epic legend of old. 'They kept hoping the King would see sense, and they also felt that the American lady [Wallis] had too much power over him. Eventually their fears were realised. Edward put the love of his life before duty. Some of the staff cried openly & asked for prayers for the other shy prince, Bertie, married with two little girls – who must steel himself to be King, reluctantly, it was thought.'

Sharon Griffith in Co Dublin also recalls much storytelling around the King and Mrs Simpson. Her mother would recount the story to her – 'she spoke dramatically and thoroughly enjoyed the tragedy of the King's abdication speech'. Ms Griffith's mother had mixed feelings about the participants in the narrative:

> She was of the opinion that Wallis Simpson 'set her cap at him' … She felt Wallis Simpson was a social climber, and having had her husband give up the throne, failed to give him children. (My mother always blamed the women.) But equally she felt he was so devoted to her that it was a *major* love story as he gave up the throne and indeed had to go into exile and ultimately take up a token position in the Bahamas.

Mary Lodge, who later became a renowned journalist for the *Sunday Press*, came from a well-to-do-family in Tramore, Co

Waterford: her mother's health was fragile and baby Mary had a
Nanny. Nanny had to be given the day off for Edward's abdication, because:

> she was very upset and could not stop crying. Her
> feeling was that Edward would have been a fantastic
> king and her hatred of that 'awful American Wallace
> [sic] Simpson' was intense. Nanny then astounded
> my Mother by confessing that on that free day she,
> a staunch Protestant, had spent hours in the Catholic
> church in Tramore, praying for Edward.

Mary's mother also 'admitted to her admiration for Edward
whom she thought had amazing charisma', though Mrs Lodge
took care to be discreet as 'Tramore would have had a strong
Republican ethos and she was nervous of the fact that she had a
very close cousin who had served with the Prince David and had
liked him enormously.'

It is sometimes claimed that committed Irish Nationalists
were 'passive' and 'aloof' from these royal stories, rather than
actively hostile, while the strong Republicans preferred to focus
their anger on the issue that the King had any link at all with the
Irish Constitution.

Irish Protestants and southern Unionists, on the other hand,
recall feelings of anxiety that the debacle might imperil the
Crown. Maurice Bryan, born in 1929, from a Protestant family in
Dublin, felt that his family's attitude was disapproving, with
allusions to Wallis as an American – 'slack morals, don't you
know!' He also picked up a sense of 'considerable disappointment
that the king had not 'done his duty' – especially as he had been
such a contemporary pin-up, and a feeling that he was letting
down the side.

'This was a generation that had been nourished on Kipling
and Bulldog Drummond …', Adrian Somerfield (who attended
St Columba's, the prestigious Church of Ireland school) recalls,
and goes on, 'My father did not really approve of the Prince of
Wales … considered him a 'bounder'. I expect my mother had a
sympathy for Edward and thought of him as a victim of silly old

male politicians and the stodgy Archbishop of Canterbury.' Archbishop Cosmo Lang was himself an unmarried Anglican bishop with stern views on the indissolubility of marriage.

But not all Irish Protestants took this view. Rosemary Mathews of Dublin describes her own father as a 'free-thinking former Anglican' who 'admired Edward for putting the love of his life as top priority. He also admired Edward for his sympathy for Welsh miners who had gone on strike.'

Some Irish Catholics thought that the Church of England was being hypocritical: 'the opinion in the country in Wexford was that Protestant England was founded on Henry's [VIII's] Divorce & that once again the English made up the rules to suit the moment,' recalls Eileen Clare.

But many onlookers just had a romantic involvement in the story of Edward and Mrs Simpson. Marilyn Keogh of Limerick still has in her possession an American magazine, dated 1936, 'devoted entirely to Wallis Simpson and her life and loves and romance with Edward VIII and a great collection of photographs of her mother, his family and all the social set of the day'. It was pored over by her own mother and aunts and kept carefully almost as 'a family heirloom.'

Among the romantics who supported Edward was the poet W. B. Yeats.[93]

*

And so the Dominion parliaments quickly passed the Instrument of Abdication through their respective chambers. But something quirky occurred in Ireland: owing to certain procedural difficulties the legislation went through Dáil Éireann a day later than elsewhere. By that strange anomaly, King Edward VIII remained King of Ireland while he was no longer King of the United Kingdom or the Dominions overseas.

The delay, according to Mr de Valera, was because he was unable to gather all the Dáil deputies together in time. In fact he deliberately kept his plans under wraps as he feared that the press might use information as propaganda against him. His game plan was, naturally, to use the event to distance the Irish Free State ever more from the Crown, and to weaken Ireland's link with what had been the British Empire.

Deputies were only summoned to the Oireachtas at the last moment, and there were some heated objections to the way in which deputies were deprived of sufficient information while facing a parliamentary guillotine – most particularly vehement from Professor John O'Sullivan, the Professor of Modern History at University College Dublin (UCD).

But Fianna Fáil deputies replied 'we've got the numbers', and the Irish External Relations Act was passed in the Dáil on 12 December 1936, reducing the King's role to an exclusively external one: to act on 'the appointments of diplomatic and consular representatives and the conclusion of international agreements' on the advice of the Irish government.

On the previous day, 11 December, the Constitution (Amendment No 27) Act had removed the King from the Irish Constitution, paving the way for the abolishment of the Governor-General, which post had already been, de facto, a nullity.[94]

King Edward VIII abdicated on December 10. The Abdication Act which had been passed at Westminster received the assent of Canada, Australia, New Zealand and South Africa as required by the Statute of Westminster: it was de Valera who ensured that Ireland was out of step with the rest of the Commonwealth.

This has led to pedants of historic anomalies claiming that the defunct Edward VIII – who died as the Duke of Windsor in 1972 – remained technically King of Ireland until his death: and Wallis, Ireland's legal queen until her death in 1986.[95]

But events moved on. The man who had been the glamorous Prince of Wales and a popular king with the young and the dis-affected, made a radio broadcast in which he explained that he 'could not undertake the heavy duties of kingship without the support of the woman I loved'. People all over the world crowded around radios and listened raptly, sometimes in tears.

My husband, Richard West (aged six in 1936, and at his English prep school), heard a children's bowdlerised version of

Wesley's Christmas carol that year: 'Hark the herald angels sing / Mrs Simpson's bagged our King!' In Cavan, Peadar Cassidy's parents heard a Protestant neighbour say something similar: 'Mrs Simpson pinched our King', and concluded that Unionists resented the American femme fatale.

In Glasnevin, north Dublin, Patrick Fleming heard the street urchins singing a popular chant about King Edward's abdication:

> Who's this coming down the street?
> Mrs Simpson, smelly feet!
> She was married twice before,
> Now she's knocking on Edward's door.
> 'Edward will you marry me?'
> 'Yes, my dear, at half-past three.'
> 'That will be much too late.'
> 'Marry me at half-past eight.

In Sandymount, south of the Liffey, my brother, Carlos Kenny (then aged 8 and attending an Irish-speaking national primary school), heard a slightly more genteel version of the ditty:

> See her coming down the street,
> Mrs Simpson, ain't she sweet?
> She's been married twice before,
> Now she's knocking on Eddie's door!
> Tra-la-la-la-la-la-la, Tra-la-la-la-la-la-la.

Sweet or not, Mrs Simpson had played her part in the evolution of Irish sovereignty.

Chapter Five

GEORGE VI AND
'LEAVING THE FAMILY',
1936-52

In the last six years, look how we horse-whipped John Bull
every time. We whipped him right, left, and centre, and with
God's help, we shall do the same again.
(Election speech by Seán T. O'Kelly in May 1938[1])

Must you leave the family? (King George VI to Ireland's envoy on the
declaration of the Irish Republic, 1948[2])

In December 1936, King Edward VIII of Great Britain and
Ireland laid down his Crown: his abdication was made public
with a sensational radio broadcast. In Sandymount, Dublin,
my brother Carlos remembers family, friends and neighbours
crowding around our large German wireless, particularly effective
in relaying overseas broadcasts. Then the announcement came
from Sir John Reith of the BBC that the King would now speak
directly from Windsor Castle.

And so Edward VIII began, in a steady but solemn voice: 'At
long last I am able to say a few words of my own. I have never

wanted to withhold anything, but until now it has not been constitutionally possible for me to speak.' He had, he said, just discharged his last duty as 'King and Emperor' and he had been succeeded by his brother, York. 'My first words must be to declare my allegiance to him.'

The handkerchiefs came out when the abdicating monarch came to the often-quoted passage: '.... But you must believe me when I tell you that I have found it impossible to carry the heavy burden of responsibility and to discharge my duties as King as I would wish to do without the help and support of the woman I love.'

Even today, more than seventy years on, my brother becomes quite emotional as he recalls the impact that had on the company assembled around our family radio: neighbours and friends ranged from old Empire Loyalists to Free Staters to passionate Republicans. Poor King Edward! So sad! The man who had been the pin-up Prince of Wales and a well-liked king among the young and the disaffected was renouncing it all for a woman.

My mother, then a woman of 34 with three young children, thought it was simply the most romantic story in the world: she also saw it as a tribute to women in general that a *woman* could wield such power over a king. It meant much more to her – in terms of female empowerment – than carrying placards and placing bombs in letterboxes, as the suffragettes had done.

The former King had ended his broadcast with the traditional words: 'God bless you all. God Save the King.'

The former Prince of Wales and the former King Edward VIII then drove away from Windsor Castle as the Duke of Windsor and, after that, to a life of exile with the bewitching Wallis, Duchess of Windsor (who was never to be 'Her Royal Highness').[3] The Crown passed to his younger brother, the Duke of York, known in his family as 'Bertie' (like his grandfather, Edward VII), and subsequently crowned as George VI.

Some of the Irish who followed the royal narrative with that sense of family involvement worried that Bertie, with his awful stammer betraying his bad nerves, might not be up to the task.

George VI succeeded to the throne of what was still 'Great Britain and Ireland', but from 1937 onwards (under its new Constitution) Ireland, whose name would be changed to Éire, effectively became a republic with an elected President. A popular Irish song in the 1920s had described de Valera as 'the King of Ireland' and now, in a way, he was.[4]

The Oath of Allegiance to the King had been abolished by the Dáil in 1932, and the abolition bill was approved, despite the Senate's opposition, in 1936. After Mr de Valera introduced Éire's new Constitution in 1937, the King would have no further internal connection with Éire.

But Ireland still remained a member of the Commonwealth, and de Valera repeatedly said he did not wish to change that. He saw two advantages to retaining membership of the Commonwealth, with the King at its apex: it offered a 'bridge', of sorts, with the Ulster Unionists, and the opportunity for Ireland – and Dev – to have a role upon the world stage. He greatly relished his appearances at the League of Nations, and the British Commonwealth (so recently the Empire) certainly represented another important international forum.

It was no small thing to be on a par with Canada, Australia, New Zealand, and South Africa, and to exercise some influence over these nations, as Éire now did. In fact the other Dominions often followed Éire's lead in areas of policy and administration: Ireland had advanced the principle of equality within the Commonwealth, and her ministers and people were regarded as 'the constitutional masters' when it came to statecraft.[5]

From the end of the 1930s, the monarchy was not only less relevant to Anglo-Irish relations, the monarch was less significant within the British political framework, too. George V had been a very correct constitutional monarch: he had never interfered in politics, but he had been continuously involved, and he had had an influence. Edward VIII, for all his charm, had little taste for the more tedious aspects of constitutional duty. Officials complained that the red boxes of state papers that the King was obliged to scrutinise came back stained with wine-marks.

George VI would be exceptionally dutiful as a monarch, but in his reign the monarchy would develop in a new and different direction: it would become a comforter in time of war, representing the symbol of a united family in the face of all threats.

Yet at the start Bertie seemed unpromising material. He was scoffed at for being 'thick': at his naval college of Osborne he came 68th out of 68 cadets, and at Dartmouth Naval Academy, 61st out of 67. He was so painfully shy that he would sit in a darkened room rather than summon a servant to fix a light; he stammered because, as a young boy, he had been forced to write with his right hand, although naturally left-handed (a practice commonly inflicted on left-handed children by educationalists in the first half of the twentieth century).

He was prey to a number of phobias, including vertigo. As a child he had been forced to sleep with his legs tied to wooden splints to correct knock knees. He was bullied and assaulted by a nursery maid, who pinched him and his brother David until they cried. He was also mercilessly bullied at school, which was the custom of the times, when a dose of bullying was thought a healthy antidote to mollycoddling. He was seldom, if ever, kissed by his mother, Queen Mary, who thought physical affection softened the character, and he was constantly reprimanded by his father. He was subjected to physical chastisement, on one occasion given six strokes of the lash.[6]

Bertie was often disparaged by the brainy British political class, products of Oxford, Cambridge, and the London School of Economics. He was variously described as 'colourless', 'weak', and 'stupid'. R. A. Butler called him 'a dull dog' and Lloyd George described him as 'a nitwit'. The Surveyor of the King's Pictures, Kenneth Clark (known afterwards as 'Lord Clark of *Civilisation*'), called the King 'a very stupid man': this did not inhibit Clark from flirting with the Queen, whom he said had a good eye for pictures. Even the French Prime Minister Daladier had a go, calling King George 'a moron'.

Small wonder that Bertie occasionally flew into private, irrational rages, known in the family as 'gnashes': the anger he must have banked up from childhood, the frustration of his shyness and stammer, and the resentment he felt (and certainly his Scottish wife, Elizabeth, felt) at being thrust into the role of monarch by the abdication of his elder brother were bound to produce outbursts.

Whether he was disappointed not to beget a son we do not know: in any case, he was deeply attached to his daughters, Elizabeth (to succeed him as Elizabeth II) and Margaret Rose. The Queen was instructed by her doctors, after the birth of Princess Margaret, not to have any more children, since she had difficult labours and had to undergo delivery by Caesarean section. At that time it was considered dangerous to have more than two Caesareans.[7]

When it came to politics, George VI's thinking was very much on the same wavelength as Prime Minister Neville Chamberlain's (de Valera's favourite British leader). The King (and Queen) have been described as 'appeasers' towards Germany in the late 1930s – although it should be borne in mind that most people, everywhere, were at this time in favour of 'jaw–jaw, not war–war', ironically, in the phrase coined by Winston Churchill himself.

John Dulanty, the indefatigable Irish High Commissioner in London, reported back to Dublin very favourably on the character of the new King. 'Whereas the late King George [V] was inclined to be rather brusque, [and] the Duke of Windsor to be slightly over-anxious to please, the present King seemed to me to be simple, frank, free from affectation, and to have neither the brusqueness of his father nor the sign of the cinema 'star' that marked his brother,' he wrote.

King George was clearly aware of some of the criticism about him, and confided to Mr Dulanty, with humorous self-deprecation that, according to some of the newspapers, 'I am consumptive, I stammer incessantly, I am a dull dog, and in short a complete wreck'. Dulanty noted that the King had only stammered three times during the course of their conversation: he seemed to be relaxed with the High Commissioner, though he smoked incessantly (even during his coronation, he managed a 'gasper').

The new King George amiably asked to be remembered to Mr de Valera, whom he 'hoped he might meet'. He added to the Irish envoy that if ever he, George, could be of help to the Saorstát he was 'at our service'.[8] Piquantly, the King with whom Ireland finally 'broke the connection' was perhaps temperamentally the best suited of all British monarchs to communicate with Irish political leaders. Bertie was so mild and anxious to please – very far indeed from the imperious British bulldog type – at a time when Irish leaders were so prickly about the context of British-Irish relations.

In fact they never met, although Mr de Valera was not personally hostile to George VI, and in his correspondence with the monarch was always punctiliously correct, even to the point of extreme deference, signing himself, 'Your Majesty's obedient Servant, Éamon de Valera'.

Yet de Valera was always aware of his own, more extreme, Republican wing, who were constantly pushing for a full republic, shorn of all links with Britain, and with the province of Ulster fully restored to Irish jurisdiction. Before the decade of the 1930s was out, the IRA would declare a terrorist war on England, carrying out a bombing campaign on innocent passers-by at Broadgate in Coventry.

De Valera's own newspaper, the *Irish Press*, tended to play *up* to the sensibilities of extreme Republicans, and play *down* any of Dev's more nuanced attitudes to the King. On the day that King George and Queen Elizabeth were crowned in Westminster Abbey, the *Press* ran an approving headline story announcing, 'Crown A Foreign Institution'.[9] This was an approval of white South Africa's denunciation of the monarchy: fundamentalist Dutch Calvinists regarded monarchy as a form of 'idolatry'. Among Irish Nationalists, there was still that sentimental link with the Boers – or, as they now were, the white Afrikaners.

The *Press* was also pleased to highlight a story about a Glasgow ship in Dublin port which came into harbour flying the Irish tricolour[10]: while, in contrast, only a few public buildings, such as Trinity College Dublin (unfailingly identified as a residue of the old Ascendancy), flew flags to mark the 1937 coronation. There were also a couple of Union Jacks on display in 'some houses in Monkstown' – another old Loyalist redoubt – and Northumberland Road, Ballsbridge. There was a 'Protestant Coronation Service' held at Christchurch Cathedral – and at TCD.

Significantly, the Dublin Stock Exchange was closed for the day. Since London was not doing business, neither could Dublin – indicating that however much Nationalists might break the symbolic links with the Crown, the economic tentacles were still deeply intertwined. Even if Mr de Valera had declared that the British market for Irish goods was 'gone forever'.[11]

Then, the day after the Coronation of George VI in London, a statue of King George II was blown up in Dublin.

On the same day, May 13, the *Irish Press* reported that in Ireland itself 'the Last Function of the Crown [is] abolished', as the Governor-General's office was now officially obsolete. The bicycling Governor-General, Domhnall Ó Buachalla, was glad to be informed that his position was now to be scrapped. He had only taken it as 'a step in the direction of abolishing the post altogether. I would greatly prefer not to have to bother with it, but since it was [de Valera] who asked me to take it for the good of the country, I told him I would do what he wished.'[12]

If this was good news for Dev's independence agenda, it was bad news for the *Irish Tatler & Sketch* who lost a notional figurehead of status for their social rounds, although Mr Ó Buachalla had resolutely refused to be seen in grand places – a tribute to his austere Republicanism (and equally austere form of Catholicism). Increasingly they had to rely on the doings of lady golfers and lady foxhunters – often cutting quite a dash in figure-hugging pants and streamlined jodhpurs – to feature on their pages.

All through the 1930s the ideal of a plain-living, but high-thinking peasantry (devoid of the folderols of an 'alien power') was promoted through the official culture. Bishops of the Catholic Church joined in, no less than politicians, by praising the ideals of the simple, even monastic, life. The Gaelic Athletic Association was of the same mind and banned 'jazz dances' or all 'dances not in harmony with our traditional Irish culture'. In pursuit of the higher things of the spirit, Mr de Valera laid it down that no person should earn more than £1,000 a year.

*

The coronation date of May 1937 had originally been set for the uncrowned Edward VIII: Bertie – as George VI – was crowned on the day arranged for his brother.

Plans proceeded for the coronation at Westminster in London – while in Ireland different arrangements developed, almost in parellel, with the drafting and launch of the new Irish Constitution of 1937, which remains the legal framework for Irish law, values, obligations, and rights to this day.

At a legal and political level, the publication of a new constitution (the draft was first issued on 1 May) was the more significant event: whereas the coronation of George VI is but a memory on a commemoration teacup. Yet a coronation is a mighty pretty occasion, and appeals to the instinct for pomp and circumstance which seems to be part of the popular psyche.

Irish official attitude to the coronation (as prescribed by Mr de Valera) was to be one of lofty 'detachment'. Although invitations had been issued to all Commonwealth members, no official from the Irish government was to be present. The independent-minded TD James Dillon chose to attend the event and was mocked by his peers in Dáil Éireann as a 'shoneen' (lickspittle) for such an 'anti-national' gesture. Another attender was the Fine Gael TD for Wicklow, Dermot O'Mahony, who went at his own expense, much to his daughter's lifelong pride.[13]

High Commissioner Dulanty (who secretly longed to attend the Abbey pageant, and privately asked the Dominions Secretary if he could sneak in as an 'observer') was given instructions by Dublin to explain to the King why the Irish attitude must be one of such 'detachment'.[14]

It was not, said Mr Dulanty at the meeting with King George VI, intended as a rebuff to His Majesty. It was just that 'until recently in Ireland the King and nearly all associated with the monarchy had been a kind of stage property of the old Unionist political party': to which observation the mild-mannered George gave 'ready assent'.

Mr Dulanty went on to give the new King a tutorial in Irish history (a common experience in Anglo-Irish meetings: one British politician thought it a triumph of communications if, in conversation with de Valera or his emissaries, Cromwell was not mentioned once.)

The Irish people, Mr Dulanty went on, could not, in the light of history, have the same feeling for the King as the English had. However, he quickly added, it was not, of course, *personal*: any hostility was 'towards [the King's] office of the titular head and front of a foreign system which they had only lately broken down.' In his reserved way the King 'made no demur' while the discourse continued in the same vein.

Bertie must have liked John Dulanty – and perhaps Éire's very 'detachment' helped him to be more open – because he spoke with disarming frankness about his attitudes to the coronation.[15] (They also chatted amicably about the difficulties of raising children in the modern world.[16])

'How would you like,' said the King to the High Commissioner, 'to pass through throngs of people for four and a half hours and to know that all the time thousands and thousands of people were staring at you?' For a man of such a nervous disposition, it was truly an ordeal:

> Hang it, you can't keep smiling all the time. It is
> fatiguing too because, as I said to my wife, all that is
> to happen throughout this long ceremony happens
> to me, everybody else gets off scot-free. I have to
> dress and undress three times and I have to be not
> only word-perfect, but I also have to be foot-perfect
> because if I turn to the left instead of the right the
> whole show will get hopelessly tangled up.

Mr Dulanty sympathised: and no doubt wished all the more that he could be present. But Dublin was unbending. Not only were Irish officials barred from being present at the ceremony, they were instructed to abstain from participating in any form of decoration that was going on in the building they then shared in Regent Street. And they were *not* to attend any parties or receptions, either, in connection with the coronation.

The Dominions Minister in London, who was responsible for all Dominions within the Commonwealth, was now the usually accommodating Malcolm MacDonald: but he refused John Dulanty's request to come along to the coronation itself as an observer. Mr Dulanty could either attend in an official capacity, or stay away: no sneaking in at the back. But Mr Dulanty was forbidden by de Valera himself to go along in any kind of official capacity.[17]

While maintaining austere Republican 'detachment', de Valera still saw in the coronation a good opportunity to annoy the British by spelling out his objections to the ceremony. Malcolm MacDonald (son of Ramsay, educated at the progressive Bedales School, patient diplomatist and ornithologist) was informed by the Irish Department of External Affairs that the specifically Anglican character of the coronation ceremony, as well as the issue of partition, had resulted in a *froideur* towards the ceremony on the part of the majority of the people:

> Mr MacDonald should know that the attitude of the Government of Saorstát Éireann towards the Coronation as a whole can only be one of detachment and protest, so long as our country is partitioned and the religious service implies discrimination (to put it mildly) against the faith of the majority of the people of this country.[18]

Malcolm MacDonald was to bend over backwards to please Mr de Valera in the coming times – they shared an interest in bird-watching – but it was not in his power either to disestablish the Church of England – or to bring about a united Ireland overnight.

There was also quibbling over the question of flags and regalia. At the previous coronation of 1911, there had been a Lord High Constable of Ireland and a Dublin herald among the ceremonial attendants. These had been declared obsolete. Mr MacDonald obligingly tried to demote, or even terminate, the office of Ulster King-at-Arms.

This was not something calculated to go down well in the province itself, so the Ulster herald stayed. And the Lord High Steward of Ireland would be expected to attend, purely as a hereditary procedure.

Then there was the awkward matter of the Standard-Bearer of Ireland at the coronation. The Irish quarter of the Royal Standard, featuring the harp, was carried by the traditional heraldic bearer. Dev dismissed all this as 'feudal' and of no importance, but he still wanted to have his say about it. He sent a message, through the ever-assiduous Dulanty, that this individual could *not* be said to represent the people of Ireland: in truth, the people of Ireland had not been consulted on the matter.[19]

And actually, the people of Ireland might well have been intrigued and positively diverted by a bit of pageantry and feudal rigmarole in an era before TV: we need hardly doubt that had there been a *Hello!* magazine at the period, details of the coronation ceremony would have been snapped up. As it was, the ceremony was secretly followed with much interest in the Irish Free State, and souvenirs and memorabilia were eagerly pounced upon. The remotest Irish connection was relished. And I have been told by older women that young girls in Ireland of a like age often felt personally drawn to 'the Little Princesses', Elizabeth and Margaret Rose.

Nonetheless, Mr de Valera suggested that the British government should advise the King against including any Irish element in the Royal Standard, assuming that the King would then have to take the counsel of his Ministers. It was left to Malcolm MacDonald to point out, in his painstakingly progressive and affable way, that decisions on matters of ceremonial remained the King's prerogative and were not part of political procedure.

The question was settled by everyone agreeing that Mr de Valera had not been 'officially' informed about the presence of the Standard-Bearer of Ireland at the coronation: as so often, the most sensible course being to turn a blind eye to that which one does not 'officially' know.

De Valera, as ever, used this exchange to his advantage: he even gained some ground from it – and probably influenced the other Dominions too. The Commonwealth countries were generally realising greater self-determination, in any case, proceeding from the Statute of Westminster, so there was a patchwork of constitutional re-arranging to do.

'Much complicated haggling had taken place between the various Dominions and … Malcolm MacDonald,' writes the King's biographer Sarah Bradford, 'with South Africa and Éire – as usual – being the most troublesome.' A coronation oath read out by the Archbishop of Canterbury was devised to reflect the greater autonomy of the Dominions: 'Do you solemnly promise and swear to govern the peoples of Great Britain, Ireland, Canada, Australia, New Zealand, and the Union of South Africa, of your possessions, and the other territories to them belonging or pertaining and of your Empire of India, *according to their respective laws and customs?*'

Dev's religious objections also bore some fruit. Originally the King was to swear to maintain the Protestant faith, but de Valera ('naturally' adds Bradford), as well as the Canadian Prime Minister (thinking of French-Catholic Quebec), and the Catholic Prime Minister of Australia, requested that this denominational reference should be limited to the United Kingdom. On behalf of the Dominions the King was to make a general promise to maintain 'the true profession of the Gospel', which seemed very ecumenical at the time.

Having won some ground, Dev graciously consented not to object any further to those ancient ceremonial roles that were matters of custom rather than law, even if they touched on an Irish dimension. Certain procedures were 'traditional' and not 'legal', he declared. And he returned to being 'detached'.

He would also graciously allow the Protestant (Anglican) Archbishop of Dublin, Dr Gregg, to attend the coronation, but, while he would continue to maintain his exquisite detachment, he nevertheless insisted that the invitations to the said Protestant Archbishop must be processed through him, Mr de Valera, and should not be sent directly to the ecclesiastic from Windsor. Control was all.

The coronation duly took place in London, and was considered a very splendid occasion. The procession to and from Westminster Abbey was, according to one report 'a brilliant cavalcade ... a tableau *vivant* of past glories, a shining reminder under grey skies that a quarter of the globe was still painted red on the map, a picture of mediaeval romance in the midst of the devil's decade.'[20] The diversity of the British Empire and Commonwealth was emphasised with gorgeous costumes from India and Pakistan, brilliant colours from Africa and servicemen in every conceivable military dress from the scarlet Canadian Mounties to the neat khaki Gurkhas.

Those onlookers who thrill to the sight of marching men in uniforms would have witnessed the masquerade of 'frogged tunics, aigrettes, bearskins, leopard pelts, kilts, striped turbans, scarlet coats, plaid pantaloons, gilt cuirasses and waving plumes – all the pageantry of impracticality wherein England's genius for poetry and empire equally thrive'. But official Ireland remained resolutely 'aloof' from it all: and some ultra-Republicans protested.[21]

In Cork a group claiming association with the IRA broke into *The Irish Times'* offices and demanded the removal of pictures of King George and Queen Elizabeth that had been on display in the front window for the coronation day. The manager at first refused 'then relented not to cause trouble'. No gesture was made to uphold the rule of law, under which business premises may display whatever pictures they choose without being subjected to threats of violence. However, in Dublin a planned IRA meeting at College Green 'to repudiate the Coronation of an English King as King of Ireland' was banned. Eleven shop windows were smashed just the same, and a fracas between Gardaí and protesters resulted in Tom Barry, Frank Ryan, and three Gardaí being treated at Jervis Street hospital.[22]

*

The drafting of the new Irish Constitution of 1937 was the main political preoccupation in Dublin while King George and Queen Elizabeth were being put through what was, for him, the ordeal of his coronation.

High Commissioner Dulanty in London was forthwith instructed to refer to the monarch as 'the British King': since it was unlikely that he was thought to be speaking about the King of Norway this seemed a somewhat artificial construct for the envoy in London. But it made a point.

De Valera had told Malcolm MacDonald in advance that the new Irish Constitution would make no mention of the King. MacDonald apologetically said that he was 'most anxious to avoid any words which might suggest that he was 'pushing the Crown' at [the Irish Free State], but if they had not recognition of the Crown he did not see how the Commonwealth could continue.' Also, the other Dominions were now not happy about the way the Irish Free State was moving, which they accurately perceived as a half-in and half-out position.

King George had examined the draft of the new Irish Constitution – which is among the royal papers at Windsor, in its English and Irish-language version – and made no comment that all reference to His Majesty was now dropped. His only objection was being referred to as an 'organ' in official papers. It was bad enough to be called an 'instrument', he said, but even that was better than 'organ', which seemed to him an unhappy epithet. Since 'organ' can also be slang for the male sexual member, an understandable point.[23]

But if the King did not personally protest at being deleted from the 1937 Constitution, Irish Protestants did not like it: 'The removal of the King's name from the Oireachtas is a further sop to the extremists in Mr de Valera's party ...' wrote the *Church of Ireland Gazette*. They thought de Valera a hypocrite:

> Mr de Valera, in fact, wants to have it both ways. Inside the country every trace, every suggestion, of allegiance to the Empire must be eradicated. Outside, the Irish Free State will rank with Australia, Canada and the other Dominions and will share

equally in the common rights and privileges of the other members of the Commonwealth. Such is the extraordinary position in which the Government has now placed the country, a position which would tax the ability of the greatest of international jurists to comprehend.[24]

The usually measured voice of the Church of Ireland also expressed concern that there were insufficient checks and balances in the Irish polity. 'The present Government has far too little respect for constitutional methods of law-making. Bills are being rushed through the Dáil, now the only national representative body in the country, and are being placed on the Statute Book before a proper study is made of their probable implications.'

Independent Oireachtas members had sought to make this point repeatedly: that the government pushed through its own programme whatever the objections. The Senate, which had acted as a kind of brake on the Dáil, was now abolished. And with it had gone some of the last useful vestiges of the old Anglo-Irish gentry: for instance the input of experienced businessmen such as Andrew Jameson and dissident squire Sir John Keane, both of whom had staunchly opposed the creeping hand of narrow-minded censorship.

'A great deal of the Government's professed hostility towards Britain has been eyewash,' proclaimed the *Gazette*. The whole agenda was being driven by 'the extreme element among the Fianna Fáil', which 'had to be placated at all costs, and the best method of doing so was to proceed towards a constitutional, but mythical, independence.'

Irish Protestants of the mercantile class were always aware of how fragile was the economic 'independence' of the Irish State. De Valera's 'economic war' with Britain during the 1930s had been catastrophic for poor farmers.

Agrarian radicalism – like collectivised farming – has seldom been a successful system, and many visitors to Ireland in the 1930s commented on the abject poverty of the countryside. Nicolette Devas, step-daughter to the painter Augustus John, described

1930s Ireland, in a staccato phrasing of miserabilist nouns, as 'a poor land with poor crops – malnutrition – tuberculosis – barefoot children in homespun shifts – poteen'.[25] By the later 1930s, de Valera's younger lieutenant, Seán Lemass, would push the country towards a more realistic grasp of economic reality – especially with regard to trade links with Britain.

The constitution that Dev produced in 1937, though greeted with a meaningful silence at Windsor and Buckingham Palace and criticised by the British press, was accepted by the British government by the end of the year. (It had been ratified by referendum in July 1937, although not overwhelmingly: votes in favour numbered 685,105, with 526,945 against.)

Yet it has proved a skillful and a modernising document, and flexible enough to provide both change and continuity. And, although criticised at its inception by some historians as 'too Catholic' (much as the coronation ceremony was seen as 'too Protestant'), some Irish Catholics during the 1930s thought it not Catholic *enough*.[26]

The Constitution begins: 'In the name of the Most Holy Trinity, from Whom is all authority and to Whom, in our final end, all actions both of men and States, must be referred ...' Some of the more fervent Catholic citizens suggested that it should start with 'In the name of Our Lady', or 'In the name of God and his Blessed Mother', this being a traditional Irish greeting in the western islands of Ireland. The Trinity allusion was seen by some as a Protestant emphasis: consider Trinity College Dublin, founded by Elizabeth I to make Ireland Protestant, and the many Anglican churches and institutions bearing the name 'Trinity'.

But the Trinity had been chosen as an inclusive Christian symbol: and it is not without historical and legendary resonance. Did not St Patrick himself select the shamrock as the natural metaphor to explain the Trinity of three persons in one Deity? That gave it an emblematic significance with a long Irish pedigree.

To be sure, the Constitution acknowledged the 'special position' of the Catholic Church as the faith of the majority (subsequently deleted in December 1972), but it also recognised the Church of Ireland, the Presbyterian and Methodist churches, and other nonconformists such as the Quakers, the Jewish faith, and those of other persuasions – and those of no faith.

It was not quite Catholic enough for the Holy See either. When a draft of the Constitution was shown to the Pope's representative at the Vatican, the Cardinal in question smilingly, but meaningfully called it 'heretical': a properly Catholic constitution would only recognise the 'One True Faith'. Neither was the Vatican inclined to praise the prohibition on divorce: for the Holy See, marriage and its annulments were a church matter, not one for the state at all.[27]

In 1937 the Pope's comment was (to the disappointment of de Valera's chief civil servant, Joseph Walshe) 'Ni approvo ni non disapprovo; taceremo.' 'I neither approve nor disapprove: we shall maintain silence.'[28] In accordance with guidelines given by Jesus Christ about rendering unto Caesar what is Caesar's, perhaps it is appropriate for the Church authorities to neither approve nor disapprove in the normal run of political arrangements. However, twenty years later, Pope Pius XII did praise de Valera for the constitution he had so carefully crafted.[29]

But active criticism came from other quarters: there was outrage among Ulster (and some southern) Unionists that Articles 2 and 3 of the Irish Constitution should lay claim to the territory of the whole island, against the wishes of the majority in the North.

Feminist groups such as the Women Graduates' Association, the National Council of Women and even the Anglican Mothers' Union were critical of the clause, stating that women should be respected within the home, where they had a 'special position'. Some of de Valera's most steadfast female followers such as the author Dorothy Macardle regarded the Constitution as repressive and patronising.

Some of the senior Fianna Fáil wives were also less than admiring. Margaret McEntee (married to Seán, and herself a cultivated woman who was a specialist in Balzac's works) was critical of such notions of female domesticity.[30]

Noticeably absent from the list of protesters were ordinary housewives and mothers: to some women the fact that the article referred to 'homemakers'seemed a nice touch, since it confirmed that women were entitled to a dominion, and to respect and authority (even sovereignty) within it.[31]

Palace officials in London and Windsor certainly did not approve of deleting all mention of the King from the new Irish Constitution. The King was still linked to Éire as head of the Commonwealth and he still had a role in relation to external affairs, as spelt out by the External Relations Act of 1936. But now the constitutional arguments were left to the politicians. Like the Vatican, the courtiers at the Court of St James chose – 'taceremo', maintaining silence.

Within Ireland the 1937 Coronation and the 1937 Constitution were often juxtaposed against one another, particularly in newspaper reports. Although one was a sacrilised ritual steeped in feudal pomp, and the other a political construct for the development of a modern state, they did have a purpose in common: both George VI and de Valera were, in their separate ways, seeking legitimacy.

De Valera had but ten years previously embraced constitutional politics: from a position as rebel leader of a lost civil war he had climbed to the top of the political ladder, but he still needed to stamp upon the Irish people his legitimate right to power and governance. George VI, too, came to the throne in the shadow of his brother who had been adored and idolised as Prince of Wales, and, for the brief year of 1936, King. He was in many respects (or at least he felt himself to be) a less gifted person than David, now Duke of Windsor.

David had been fluent and good with people. Bertie was, literally, tongue-tied, and worried that he came across as a nervous wreck, smoking incessantly for comfort and support. The 'king across the water' – the Duke, and even more the Duchess, of Windsor, residing in Paris – remained a hovering presence for the rest of his life. However, George VI did have the support of a wife who was, in the long run, even better at public relations than her charismatic, abdicated brother-in-law. By the time she became 'the Queen Mum', she could do no wrong, as far as the British public was concerned.

Less than a month after the coronation, the Executive Powers (Consequential Provision) Act legally transferred all functions of the Crown representative – the Governor General – to the Free State Executive. The bicycling Domhnall Ua Buachalla was pensioned off with the sum of £500 per annum, £10 a week being a more than adequate pension at the time.

De Valera 'crowned' his own legitimacy by creating the office of President (Uachtarán) of Ireland, and by installing the impeccable Dr Douglas Hyde in the ceremonial office on 4 May 1938 (although his first choice was his own ever-faithful supporter Seán T. O'Kelly.)

Dr Hyde, aged 77, was the founder of the Gaelic League and an outstanding scholar, but a Protestant (and even possibly a Unionist).[32] The former Viceregal Lodge was, after all, put to use as Áras an Uachtaráin – the President's Residence – and has served its purpose more than splendidly ever since.

After accompanying the new Uachtarán to the former Viceregal Lodge, Mr de Valera took Dr Hyde to afternoon tea with the Papal Nuncio, Monsignor Pascal Robinson, which was, in a way, another kind of coronation.[33]

The Irish Constitution of 1937 was of course deplored by that part of Ireland whose Prime Minister had described it as 'a Protestant state for a Protestant people' – Northern Ireland. Neither divorce nor the position of women in the home troubled the Ulster Unionists: what they especially detested were Articles 2 and 3 which laid claim to the whole territory of the island of Ireland.

It was this, as Conor Cruise O'Brien has written, which entrenched and inflamed their siege mentality and convinced them that they were in danger of being claimed by a dangerous Fenian autarchy, whose puppet-master was the Pope of Rome.

By contrast, in their eyes the coronation was a ritual of great significance, and it was an even greater joy that the King and Queen planned to visit Belfast just two and a half months after their crowning, in July 1937.

In preparation for the royal visit, the Duke of Abercorn (chief of the Orange Order) took charge and many loyal addresses were prepared. Mindful of his bashfulness and the anguish he suffered over his stammer, the King asked if he might be spared from making too many speeches in response.

Neither did he wish for too much ceremonial. Perhaps some visiting with ex-servicemen, children, and youth. But there would be addresses of welcome from the three principal Protestant churches. 'Unfortunately', the Palace was informed by Government House in Belfast on 8 July, 'the Roman Catholic Church has not accepted the invitation to present an Address.' The Catholic Church felt itself to be excluded from the 'Protestant state for a Protestant people'. Moreover, royal visits sometimes provoked attacks on Catholic Nationalists in the North by triumphalist Orange yobs. Yet the failure to reply to an invitation to participate seemed a little churlish, and perhaps overlooked an opportunity for dialogue.

It was reported to the Palace that 'many persons were coming from the Irish Free State' to witness the royal visit. Letters of welcome were sent to the King and Queen by southern Unionists. Tony Gray reported that 'thousands of Dubliners travelled to Belfast on July 28 for a ten-hour visit to the Northern Ireland capital by George VI and Queen Elizabeth.' A William Harvey of Booterstown, Co Dublin, informed the King, after the event, that it was a 'privilege and great joy to come and see your Majesties in Belfast on the 28th ... I can assure your Majesty that there are many thousands of your loyal subjects in the Irish Free State.'[34]

The visit was declared a great success, and the King received many messages of thanks afterwards. 'On all sides I have received reports that their Majesties' charm and obvious pleasure at their welcome has pleased all the people,' wrote Oscar Henderson from Government House, Hillsborough. 'I have heard no word whatsoever of adverse comment and you will be particularly pleased to know that … this morning all is quiet.'[35]

But George VI's visit had not passed off without incident: the IRA had destroyed 30 customs huts along the border and a bridge just north of Dundalk just as the royals departed. Trains between Dublin and Belfast were held up for many hours. Although Governor Henderson strove to assure the King that 'these sporadic outbreaks are carried out by an irresponsible minority who have little, if any, feeling for Ireland, either North or South', it was a foretaste of events to come.

Irish Protestants living south of the border continued to write to Buckingham Palace and Windsor Castle throughout the 1930s. The correspondence is not particularly copious, but there remained a steady minority of people in Éire who felt a link with King George. Some were wary that the Irish state might be monitoring their correspondence. There was also continued bickering between the Palace and Dublin over the matter of royal correspondence – the Palace personnel affirming that they should have the right to correspond directly with those who sent them letters, while Dublin government officials insisted that all correspondence should be routed through their authority.

Some southern Unionists in the late 1930s felt that they were under hostile surveillance by what they saw as an anti-British Irish state. When the King again visited Belfast in 1939, letters from Ireland mentioned this fear specifically. Some correspondents to the King, as mentioned on several occasions, went to the trouble of posting their letters from Holyhead in Wales, as they believed that a letter posted from the Irish Free State to the King of England might not be handled, or might be confiscated by the authorities.[36]

In retrospect, it may be judged that Éamon de Valera was right in his overall strategy of constantly affirming Ireland's sovereignty and enlarging the Free State's sphere of control; especially since the Free State had had to back down over the Boundary Commission in 1925, and had lost all claim and authority over

Northern Ireland, which contained a substantial Irish Nationalist minority.

The majority of the Irish people undoubtedly did want management of their own affairs, and in this Dev represented the majority in the Irish state. One is compelled, moreover, to admire his chutzpah in taking on the Imperial power – never missing an opportunity to tweak the lion's tail.

Yet all political manoeuvres have their cost, and the cost of constantly distancing the Crown, even in small matters, was to alienate those Irishmen and women who still cherished a sense of historical connection with the monarchy, and who were made to feel as aliens in their own land.[38]

And it may be that the price of constantly rebuffing the Crown cemented Partition ever deeper, and, by gesture and signal, egged on extremist Republicans to violent actions.

The second half of the 1930s was a turbulent time in the world at large, with a civil war in Spain (which Sir James Craig, Prime Minister of Northern Ireland, did not hesitate to suggest could so easily be replicated in the Free State), the invasion of Abyssinia, the rise of the European dictators, to list but some of the political events of the period. Maurice Manning, the historian specialising in this period, has claimed that the 1930s were the high point of anti-British feeling in Ireland. Aside from the 'economic war' with Britain, there was generally a more authoritarian approach to the Gaelicisation of Ireland, implementing a rigid policy of compulsory Irish at school and in all government or semi-state services.

Presciently, the independent (later Fine Gael) TD James Dillon had said that the compulsory policy would ensure that 'the Irish language, which we are most anxious to see revived, will come to stink in the nostrils of the people'.[39] My brother, at his all-Irish language primary school in Marlborough Street, Dublin, was beaten savagely for failing to speak Irish, since it was compulsory not only within the school, but within a one-mile radius of the location (a mean-spirited busybody having reported him to the school on hearing him converse in English). Twenty years later, in the 1950s, at my own convent school in Dublin, the unconsciously negative attitudes of many of the teachers (Irish was a government diktat, but a low priority in terms of education proper) was clearly signalled by attitude. It is my great regret that I was not introduced to the language with greater affection and respect.

Towards the end of the 1930s, the economic relationship between Ireland and Britain improved – the 'economic war' was brought to an end, and a coal-and-cattle deal was signed in 1935 whereby we sent them cattle and they sent us coal.

Under a happy combination – for de Valera – of Neville Chamberlain and the obliging Malcolm MacDonald, whom Professor Lee has suggested was 'psyched' or somehow bewitched by Éamon de Valera's personality,[40] the Treaty ports of Cobh, Berehaven, and Lough Swilly were handed back to the Irish State in 1938, thereby ending the 'economic war'.

This was a significant political triumph for Dev, and he enjoyed strong support from the Irish electorate for this démarche. But Winston Churchill never accepted that it was the right thing to do, and always maintained that Britain's inability to operate from the Irish ports (to which Britain had been guaranteed access under the 1921 Treaty) during the Second World War cost British lives in the battle of the Atlantic.

Neville Chamberlain was de Valera's favourite British Prime Minister, and Dev always spoke with great affection for the man (and his wife Annie, who was, apparently, especially engaging).

The Crown itself was not involved with the matter of the Irish ports.[41] King George VI was not a political animal and, in any case, he greatly liked, trusted, and approved of Neville Chamberlain, his first Prime Minister. (By contrast Bertie would be quite hostile towards Winston Churchill – who had loudly sided with Edward VIII during the Abdication crisis – when he succeeded as Prime Minister in 1940.)

King George felt that if Mr Chamberlain wanted to give the Irish back their ports, then that was all right by him. Some historians have thought that the King was 'unconstitutional' in this approach – that he should have exercised his prerogative more actively to warn and to counsel.[41]

Andrew Roberts has described King George VI as an 'appeaser' in his support of Chamberlain, and his attitude towards Hitler's Germany. But from 1938 until 1940 the majority of people were 'appeasers'. There were almost forty organisations in Britain dedicated to dealing with Hitler through peaceful means: organisations that ranged from pro-Nazi, such as William Joyce and John Beckett's National Socialist group, to the high-minded and pacifist Quakers, and left-wing feminists of the Women's Peace Pledge Union.[42]

In the period before the Second World War, King George backed Neville Chamberlain wholeheartedly in his quest to negotiate with Hitler. When Chamberlain, in effect, sold out Czechoslovakia at the summit with the Fuehrer at Munich in 1938, the King (and the Queen) were wholly supportive of his endeavours. They simply thought it was a sincere effort to win 'peace in our time': and, to do him justice, the King also knew that Britain's defences were quite inadequate to meet a German challenge in the autumn of 1938. George VI had been of the generation marked by the First World War, and was very keen to avoid a repeat performance: he had served at the Battle of Jutland and was in France to witness the armistice of 11 November 1918, which brought an end to the horrors of the trenches.

When Chamberlain arrived back from Munich in September 1938 the King sent the Prime Minister a personal letter praising his 'courage & wisdom in flying to see Hitler in person'. A few days later, Mr Chamberlain went back to Germany and on 29 September he was again in Munich to sign the famous 'piece of paper' that guaranteed 'peace in our time'. The King asked Neville Chamberlain to come straight to Buckingham Palace on his return, and the royal family appeared on the balcony with the Prime Minister, to the sound of cheering crowds, relieved that there would be no war. For now.

Dev, too, was a 'man of Munich' – and, like the King, he backed Chamberlain wholeheartedly. He had made a broadcast from Geneva (under the aegis of the League of Nations) praising

Chamberlain for 'putting peace before pride'. When the Prime Minister flew off to see the Fuehrer, Dev sent a cable saying that this was 'the greatest thing that has ever been done'.[43]

Chamberlain had agreed to yield the Sudetenland to National Socialist Germany, and de Valera was especially delighted that Germany had 'repossessed' this part of Czechoslovakia, since it was, arguably, Germanic in culture.[44] Dev drew a direct parallel between the six counties of Northern Ireland and that disputed Czech territory. Thus it was that the King of England, the Prime Minister of Great Britain, and the Taoiseach (as he now was) of Ireland were quite of one mind – at least in 1938.

It could not last, since Hitler planned so much worse to come. The King would have to face the fact that there would be a European war: even Chamberlain came to see that, and himself issued the ultimatum to the Reich over Poland. And of course it was to be Chamberlain himself who finally declared war on Hitler's Germany in a sonorous broadcast over the BBC on 3 September 1939.

Éamon de Valera would retreat from the theatre of all these activities to protect the neutrality of Ireland, as the Irish Free State was now called.

But both the King and de Valera remained loyal to Chamberlain to the end of his life, which was not much more than a year after the outbreak of war. Labour leaders refused to serve under Neville Chamberlain in May 1940, and, already afflicted with the stomach cancer that would kill him, he resigned as PM, giving way to Winston Churchill.

He might have died a bitterly disappointed man if the King and Queen had not shown Christian compassion towards the Prime Minister they had liked so much, and supported so heartily in his honest – if naïve – efforts to achieve peace. For, shortly before he died in November 1940, Neville Chamberlain was deeply gratified to be visited by King George and Queen Elizabeth, who showed much kindness and sympathy.

After he died, Dev sent a warmly-worded telegram to his widow expressing not dissimilar sentiments, at least from his point of view: 'Mr Chamberlain will always be remembered by the Irish people for his noble efforts in the cause of peace and friendship between the two nations.'[45]

De Valera always kept a cherished memory of Neville Chamberlain. Though he had harried Chamberlain in 1938 over Partition – constantly nagging the British PM, in the course of Anglo-Irish talks, to use 'moral force' to push the Ulster Unionists into a united Ireland – nevertheless he spoke appreciatively ever after of the Prime Minister whom history had, perhaps unfairly, discredited.

Chamberlain had been obliged to refuse de Valera some requests – notably a reprieve for the execution of the Coventry bombers, Barnes and McCormack, in February 1940, nonetheless he was the PM who gave Ireland back her naval ports.

Peter Barnes and James Richards (known as McCormack) were the instigators of an IRA bombing campaign in Britain in January 1939, focused mainly on Coventry. More than 200 people were injured and five people were killed, including a 16-year-old youth, John Arnott, and a 21-year-old young woman, Laura Ansell, who was preparing to get married. Aside from the humanitarian damage, Coventry was a serious setback to Anglo-Irish relations, which had finally begun to improve.[46] The Coventry bomb was placed on a bicycle – which survived oddly undamaged and is still kept at a Coventry museum.

Barnes and McCormack were ultimately sentenced to death for the killings. The IRA bombing of Britain was publicly deplored by the Irish government, which was privately deeply disappointed by the episode.

De Valera had initially released IRA prisoners because he hoped that once he had abolished the Oath of Allegiance to the King, and enacted his new Constitution, dissident Republicans would follow him down the route of constitutional politics. But quite the contrary: the rump of the extremist Republicans resented de Valera for his move to constitutionalism (and for his

Edward and Mrs Simpson. George V was briefly succeeded in 1936 by Edward VIII, a popular and glamorous Prince of Wales. His subsequent Abdication in December of that year provided a convenient constitutional turning point for the Irish state. © The Granger Collection

INSTRUMENT OF ABDICATION

I, Edward the Eighth, of Great Britain, Ireland, and the British Dominions beyond the Seas, King, Emperor of India, do hereby declare My irrevocable determination to renounce the Throne for Myself and for My descendants, and My desire that effect should be given to this Instrument of Abdication immediately.

In token whereof I have hereunto set My hand this tenth day of December, nineteen hundred and thirty six, in the presence of the witnesses whose signatures are subscribed.

SIGNED AT
FORT BELVEDERE
IN THE PRESENCE
OF

Edward R I

Albert

Henry.

George.

Edward VIII's instrument of Abdication, which had to be endorsed by the Dáil and the other Commonwealth Dominions. The Dáil's measure was out of synchronisation with the other Dominions and some constitutional lawyers still maintain that technically Edward VIII remained King of Ireland until his death in 1972 (as the exiled Duke of Windsor).

During the Second World War, Britain and the Irish state took different paths. In London, the quiet George VI and his Scottish queen, Elizabeth, subtly changed the image of the monarchy into a family emblem of comfort and concern.
© The Granger Collection

When Éire was formally declared a Republic in 1949, many veteran Irish unionists – in effect, mostly southern Protestants – were saddened that the monograms of the Kings and Queen were removed from some letterboxes (now painted green). However, many still retain their old monarchical motifs – especially those of Edward VII, in whose reign so many Irish letterboxes were put in place.
© Collections

The statue of Queen Victoria, which resided outside Leinster House (here seen with the National Library and Dáil and Seanad in the background) from 1908 until 1948. It was removed, significantly, shortly before the Irish state broke the last link with the monarchy and was declared a Republic. All statues of British royalty have now been removed from the Irish republic, with the single exception of Prince Albert, whose figure is mounted on a plinth at the back of Leinster House, discreetly surrounded by bushes. © National Library of Ireland

In the 1950s, beautiful Catholic processions and ceremonies answered the people's desire for – and participation in – public displays of dignity and ritual. © Topfoto

Princess Grace of Monaco
visited Ireland in 1961. There
was a rapturous welcome for a
royal figure genuinely 'one of
our own'. © Topfoto

Princess Margaret visited Birr in 1965 – it was not her first visit, but it was her first public appearance: and she was the first British royal to set foot in the Republic of Ireland. © Topfoto

The death of Princess Diana in 1995 seemed to unite all sections of Irish people.
Many Sinn Féin Republicans also signed the book of condolence in Belfast. © Getty Images

Queen Elizabeth meets Uachtarán Mary McAleese in Belfast in December 2005. Both President Marys – Robinson and McAleese – have had graceful and friendly meetings with the monarch, who has reigned since 1952. © Getty Images

initial acceptance of the Oath of Allegiance). They consequently increased their commitment to 'physical force'.

To some extent the anti-British rhetoric that had been part of Irish politics in the 1930s fertilised IRA activity. Mr de Valera's obsession with Partition – and his repeated insistence that this Partition was solely the fault of 'Perfidious Albion', and had nothing whatsoever to do with the choices of the majority of the Northern people – had perhaps unwittingly even prepared the ground. Dev always thought he could control events: but events often outrun even the most iron-willed control.

The bombings produced resentful and anti-Irish feelings in Britain – hardly surprisingly. In Ireland, the death sentences meted out to Barnes and McCormick produced even more resentment against Britain. The tragic event set at naught de Valera's oft-repeated affirmation to British ministers that Ireland would never be used as a base for an attack against Britain.

The Second World War was a cause of deep differences, once again, between Britain and Ireland, and led on to a final – if final it be – 'parting of the ways'. Britain was materially devastated by the war, while Éire, although it suffered one German aerial bombardment – apparently in error – was not. Yet the more lingering differences were evident in social change and an absence of shared memory.

When I first started work as a young journalist in London in the 1960s (born, myself, in 1944), I came to realise that 'the war', even twenty years on, was the defining experience for most British people. I had had a glimpse of this while living previously in Paris, but French memories of the war were more ambivalent, and carried, perhaps, more intimations of humiliation; so the experience was not so consistently invoked in everyday popular consciousness. In Britain, it was: everything went back to 'before the war', 'during the war', or 'after the war'. In Ireland, 'the war' was a bit of a blank. It was not even 'the war' at the time, but 'the Emergency'.

Growing up in Dublin, I had heard passing references to wartime rationing – Éire having been subject to some rationing, though less than in Britain – and shortages of imported food products and petrol. There were some Dubliners who, when in London and other British cities, had had direct experience of the Blitz, and a couple of my brothers' contemporaries had seen action in north Africa. But it all seemed rather marginal compared to the British experience. I realised that 'the war' narrative was something I did not share with British common memory. For, while Britain battled, de Valera had led Ireland in a neutrality that was (it must be said) fully supported by both parliament (Oireachtas) and electorate.

In their separate ways, both de Valera and George VI emerged from the Second World War with enhanced reputations, since both were perceived as standing fast and representing the sovereign values of their people. De Valera became – in Bew and Patterson's phrase[47] – 'the philosopher-king' of the Irish state.

As is well-established, the war was the making of George VI and his wife, Elizabeth. The nervous, stammering figure of the coronation of 1937, and the friend and supporter of Neville Chamberlain, was transformed by war into Winston Churchill's favoured confidant – a King who was something akin to a war hero.

In 1940 many English families – convinced that Hitler would invade successfully – evacuated their children abroad if they could afford it. Because of this fear, my husband and his brother were both despatched to Canada in 1940, where they shared a swimming-pool session with the future queen of the Netherlands, then the Princess Beatrix. Evacuation was also suggested, on ministerial advice, for the Princesses Elizabeth and Margaret Rose, but the King and Queen would not hear of it, and the royal family remained in London, though sleeping at night in Windsor.

In a fit of Scottish feistiness, Queen Elizabeth took up rifle and pistol practice, ready to meet the invading Germans with a gun: 'I shall not go down like the others,' she declared, meaning some of the European royals who had succumbed (although in most cases they did not have much choice).[48] That unbending matriarch Queen Mary, the King's mother (a strong appeaser right up until the start of the war), also took to carrying a pistol – an elegant little mother-of-pearl design. If threatened by a German, Queen Mary was determined to 'take one with her' – despite her own German family connections.[49]

The Blitz began in earnest in the late summer of 1940 (puzzlingly, Goering switched from his Battle of Britain onslaught, which was to be a prelude to Operation Sealion, to the aerial bombing of cities, notably London). Each night in September 1940 some 600 Luftwaffe bomber planes swarmed over Britain, and frightful casualty figures were announced. In London, the working-class parts of the city took the initial hits: the poorer but more industrialised parts of the East End, such as Poplar, Stepney, Bethnal Green, Bermondsey, Lambeth. Then, in September, a bomb fell on Buckingham Palace itself while King George was working in his study: the bomb took another day to explode and, when it finally did so, demolished the King's study and the palace swimming-pool.

Queen Elizabeth famously said that she was glad that Buckingham Palace took the hit: 'Now we can look the East End in the face.'

And, at looking the East End in the face, the King and Queen were splendid. They toured the bombed-out sites and met the people with an impressive sense of naturalness. King George's nervousness and stammer virtually left him, as he lost all self-consciousness to concentrate on talking to the victims of the bombing. If Goering believed that it would be a propaganda victory to attack the 'stammering King', the effect was quite the contrary: it bound the royals to the people ever more strongly, a fact recognised subsequently even by the anti-monarchist *Irish Press*, when it acknowledged what a solace and a morale-booster it was to the British people to have the monarchs go 'walkabout'.

Here was an example of one of the main benefits of having a monarch – someone who can be visible, and who can bring comfort – strange as it may seem – to the afflicted. It was a vivid demonstration of the functions of monarchy, as defined by the constitutionalist Walter Bagehot: that it should have a 'dignified' as well as a constitutional purpose. If historians have sometimes claimed that George VI was not sufficiently politically sophisticated to play an active constitutional part, he proved to be inspiring when playing the 'dignified' role.

As did his Queen. Elizabeth was shrewd, intelligent, and had a good ear for music, which proved to be a morale-booster, for she helped to instigate one of the most uplifting events of the war years – the lunchtime piano performances of Dame Myra Hess at the National Gallery in London. Myra Hess would perform faultlessly each day, and Londoners in their thousands came to listen, despite the Blitz. The Queen described the sessions as 'some of the happiest hours of the dark times': that Dame Myra (as she later became) was a Jewish refugee made a poignant point.[50]

Elizabeth, the future Queen Mother, was scoffed at by the ultra-thin, ultra-chic Wallis, Duchess of Windsor, for her round, soft shape – Wallis nicknamed her 'Cookie', saying she looked like a fat Scottish cook; she was nevertheless just the comforting maternal figure to provide succour under strain. And she developed her own fashion style, which turned out to be just what an East End, working-class Londoner might imagine a 'Queen Mother' *ought* to be – in fact later satirists would portray the Queen Mum as a Cockney 'Pearly Queen'.

It was widely reported – to much approval – that at Buckingham Palace, the King, Queen, and young Princesses Elizabeth and Margaret Rose were voluntarily submitting to wartime austerity. The King famously drew a line in the bathtub, above which no level of water was to rise: and the little Princesses busied themselves knitting gloves for the troops. Queen Elizabeth instructed her costume designer, Norman Hartnell, to employ certain restrictions, for reasons of fashionable austerity: ostentation was to be avoided. But a little ostentation was surely permissible: it was cheerful.

Some scepticism has been expressed about the true amount of privation that the royals endured. But if there were some sceptics, there remained a high level of general approval that the royal family were trying to share in the experience of war with their subjects. Older people in London still remember feeling a sense of confidence, and warmth, that the King and Queen were sharing in the Blitz experience. And when the Duke of Kent, the King's very handsome younger brother and husband of the beautiful Greek Princess Marina, was killed in a wartime plane crash in 1942, there was certainly a feeling of 'parity of sacrifice'. The loss of Kent added to the King and Queen's popularity.

If Winston Churchill was Britain's warrior leader – roaring with that particular aristocratic confidence and leadership that was his birthright – King George and Queen Elizabeth played the complementary role of family emblem of the nation: and, in this, the unwritten British Constitution showed a useful division of labour as between the political and the symbolic.

Ireland's path had starkly diverged from Britain's from September 1939, when de Valera solemnly declared the country to be neutral – evoking a solid sense of national unity as he did so. In parallel with King George, though in quite a different way, the Second World War also enhanced Éamon de Valera's status. Twenty European countries had declared themselves neutral at the outbreak of hostilities: only five succeeded in maintaining that neutrality. Ireland owed much to de Valera's single-minded stewardship (and something to her geographical position too). And yet, Dev played a canny game of open defiance of the 'outside world', while often subtly cooperating with the Allies.

Many – maybe most – Irish people were fiercely proud of Dev for defending Irish neutrality with such fortitude (and for standing up to Winston Churchill's 'bullying' rhetoric against the Irish state). And if Anglo-Irish relations – during the Churchill-de Valera linguistic sparring match – were scratchy, Irish-American relations declined seriously too, especially once America entered the conflict in December 1941. Roosevelt considered that de Valera lived in a 'dream-world', and an insular one at that.[51] Roosevelt's minister to Ireland, David Gray, was far more hostile to de Valera and his administration than the British representative to Éire, Sir John Maffey. (Incidentally, the poet John Betjeman, also posted to Ireland during the period, was a lyrical Hibernophile.)

De Valera, in defending Irish neutrality, constantly returned to the theme of Partition – which Roosevelt considered pettifogging and petty-minded. Dev formally complained when American troops landed in the Six Counties in 1942, saying that Éire should have been consulted. As both the United States and Britain desperately needed the ports and bases of Northern Ireland in fighting on the Atlantic front, it was unlikely indeed that Éire would have been consulted.

The Ulster Unionist regime in Northern Ireland was *certainly* not going to consult Dublin about defending the cause espoused by the Union. At the end of the war Churchill (who, strange as it may seem, believed in a United Ireland – 'you must get those fellows from the North in' – he told John Dulanty in 1948) especially praised the support received from Northern Ireland, in contrast to Éire's detachment.[52]

Yet Ulster people from Catholic and Nationalist backgrounds did not necessarily feel drawn to support Britain in her hour of need. Frank Aiken, de Valera's closest cabinet colleague in the 1940s (who ruled over the draconian political censorship during the war), and Cardinal MacRory, the Catholic Primate of Ireland, both Ulster Catholics who had experienced the unfair treatment of the minority in the North, were no fans of British policy anywhere.

In an interview in February 1943 Cardinal MacRory 'voiced strong anti-English sentiments, saying that he would prefer to have a peace dictated by Hitler rather than by the British.'[53] The interviewer, an American journalist called Frank Matthews, said that he thought the majority of Catholics in Ireland would take the opposite view, and that while he (Matthews) opposed the Partition of Ireland, it was nonetheless true that the British, with the Americans, were at that moment engaged in a life-or-death struggle.

The Cardinal 'made no rejoinder' and sat in 'sombre silence'. When the Archbishop of Dublin, John Charles McQuaid, was apprised of this conversation he remarked that the Cardinal 'was probably almost alone in Ireland in the views he expressed'.

Cardinal MacRory had been very agitated about Winston Churchill's suggestion of introducing conscription to the North of Ireland – mercifully never implemented. He was probably also concerned about the number of Republicans imprisoned in the

North at this time 'for political reasons': some 476 men and 14 women.

Some were almost certainly simply victims of discriminatory policing, although some were held on serious charges. In 1942 an IRA man, Tom Williams, had been hanged for murdering a policeman. His accomplice, Joe Cahill, was pardoned but imprisoned: he subsequently developed a long and active career within the IRA, including devising the appalling bombing of Warrington in 1993, when two little boys were disclosed to have been the main victims of such 'physical force' strategies.[54]

Until 1940 – despite the government's project of Gaelicisation – social aspirations in Ireland still preserved a certain continuity with the *ancien régime*. The 'Social and Personal' pages of the *Irish Independent* – the middle-market newspaper for Irish and Catholic Nationalists – continued to carry court reports of the King and Queen, sometimes of quite extraordinary insignificance. 'The King and Queen, Princess Alice and the Earl of Athlone and Princess Elizabeth of York went for a walk in the private grounds of Windsor Castle yesterday. The Castle grounds were open to the public by special permission of His Majesty.'[55]

A close genealogical interest was sometimes manifest: 'Princess Helena Victoria who celebrates her birthday today is the eldest daughter of the late Prince Christian of Schleswig-Holstein and Princess Christian who was the 3rd daughter of Queen Victoria. Princess Helena Victoria is thus a cousin of the King. She resides with her sister Princess Marie-Louise at Schonberg House, Pall Mall.'

Alongside the doings of Their Majesties and the complex tentacles of their kinship system, came the activities of the Anglo-Irish gentry: 'The Earl of Antrim arrived on Saturday at his ancestral home, Glenarm Castle, Co Antrim, where he will stay for a few days. ... Viscount Clifden will arrive in London today from Cornwall ... Lady Denny of Tralee Castle who underwent an operation for the removal of her tonsils at Guildford last week is progressing satisfactorily'.

Following seamlessly came the activities and appointments of various church dignatories: 'His Grace the Archbishop has made the following appointments: Very Revd Patrick J. Ryan, PP, Clondalkin, to be Vicar Forane [Dean] to the Deanery of Maynooth. Very Revd John McGurk PP, Rush, to be Vicar Forane to the Deanery of North Fingal ...' Significantly, the Irish papers at this time assumed that an 'archbishop' implied a Catholic archbishop, whereas British – and Belfast – newspapers would assume that an 'archbishop' was of the established Anglican church.

In Ireland, where the notion of clan has an ancient value, these notices might also have served to illuminate kinship relations. I could well imagine my mother deconstructing the kinship network of Princess Helena Victoria, Lady Denny of Tralee, and the Very Revd Patrick J. Ryan of Clondalkin, quite without any political discrimination between the various notables.

Blended in with the King, the gentry, and the ecclesiastics, were the aristocracy of the Irish independence movement – the heroes of 1916 – and their every commemoration was marked, usually without party rancour, at least among the media. Although it was known that someone like Austin Stack sided with de Valera against Michael Collins over the Treaty of 1921, the paper that supported the Treaty still honoured Mr Stack's memory as a patriotic Irishman.

All this was to change during the Second World War, when a fierce censorship, imposed by the state, put the country into isolation. Along with far more serious matters of war news that might be suppressed to preserve neutrality, the social activities of royalty and gentry were forthwith dropped. After the war, the doings of the Court of St James would fade from the 'Social and Personal' columns, and little by little, the old gentry would appear no more. The radiant daughters of earls and old clan chiefs advertising their flawless complexions due to the regular use of Pond's Cold Cream would be succeeded by film stars and international celebrities. The copious press and magazine photographs of distinguished ecclesiastics (who also became a kind of *gratin* in independent Ireland) would eventually be supplanted by pop stars, TV personalities and the rockocracy.

The political censorship in Ireland during the 'Emergency' rendered the British monarchy – as well as a lot of other things – much less visible in the public realm. Yet there remained, within the Irish state, a covert interest in the royal family. A Dublin nun, Sister Marie, remembers most vividly her childhood fascination with 'the little Princesses', because Princess Elizabeth was her own age. The Princesses had broadcast to 'the children of the Empire' and the engaging radio feature had been heard everywhere, with Elizabeth saying 'Good-night, children everywhere!' in her high girlish voice, and then urging her little sister, Margaret Rose, to join her, in a more childish pitch. 'Come on, Margaret!'[56]

Whatever the politics, the 'royals' now had an appeal because of the 'family values' the wartime events had solidified, especially in a country like Ireland where family networks had such a strong appeal. Even if so much of this royal interest was *very* discreetly concealed.

After a great war is over, the world is immediately very different: and not necessarily in ways that people expect it to be. And, in the same way as the experience of war conditions in Britain was very much in contrast to the kind of edgy, and sometimes isolated, sense of neutrality experienced by people in Ireland, so also, by the same token, was the aftermath of the Hitler war a markedly different experience in the two countries.

More than twenty years after the end of the Second World War, in the late 1960s, I was involved in founding a feminist movement in Dublin. Many of the changes that we demanded as young Irish feminists were precisely those changes which had already taken place in Britain during the war – and very specifically, *because* of the war.

At a serious level, these included the entitlement of married women to work in government services, including the right of married women to work as teachers. At a less serious level, the acceptance of women wearing trousers in respectable society – or even wearing lipstick. My family lived in Herbert Road, near Sandymount, Dublin: next door lived a family with a southern Unionist background (although they were Catholics).

The southern Unionist family despatched a son to fight in north Africa with Montgomery – the lad was a nervous wreck afterwards, though enormously nice – and a daughter to marry an Englishman and live in England. The daughter was, in the early 1950s, the talk of the neighbourhood when she returned on visits because she *dyed her hair* quite unapologetically, and wore 'slacks' quite brazenly. Later, it was no surprise to the local gossips that she got *divorced*.

Irish state radio did not accept advertisements for lipstick until after 1950: decent Irishwomen were not expected to be 'painted trollops'.[57] (Percy French's traditional and popular ballad, 'The Mountains of Mourne', disparages London girls because, when kissed, 'sure, the colour will all come away on your lip'.) But then, the Ireland of the 1950s was, in essence, still a pre-war society: Ireland in the 1950s was as England in the 1930s. My brother James went to London in 1952 and reported back on the comical sight of the 'clippie': the female bus conductor, an unknown and unconceived idea in Dev's Ireland. The social changes that had occurred in the countries that had experienced war had simply left neutral Ireland untouched.

And thus it was that, from about 1945 until the late 1950s, Ireland still remained in so many respects a traditionally hierarchical society, under the control of those in authority. In the main, this meant the political and administrative classes, the courts of law, the Gardaí, and, most dominantly, the Church. The Catholic Church and the political class were often hand in glove, although this was not necessarily thought malign at the time. For one thing, most of the leading politicians had brothers, sisters, uncles and aunts, and cousins galore among the clergy. (Seán MacEntee, one of Dev's most trusted lieutenants, had three brothers-in-law in Holy Orders: all men of scholarship, as it happened.)

The Church–State axis did not derive from constitutional arrangements, but from shared values, shared backgrounds: de Valera had been virtually brought up by the clergy (including an Irish-speaking priest and uncle of Conor Cruise O'Brien's), and was probably at his most comfortable in the company of priests and bishops. He often thought he was, by natural inclination, more a bishop himself than a politician.

The ease with which Irish politicians mixed with ecclesiastics could perhaps be compared to the manner in which the English upper classes became connected through intermarriage and kinship, mediated by old institutions like Eton, Harrow, and other public schools, Oxbridge, sometimes military service – and even London's clubland. Why, the very idiom for a successful outcome – '… and Bob's your uncle' – came from the nepotism of the Balfour and Cecil families, a phenomenon manifest in London social and political networks to this day.

Nevertheless, in Britain, as in France and Italy, the post-war world seemed like a more radical one. In England, many, if not most, leading post-war intellectuals were committed socialists – or indeed Communists.[58] The Labour Party gained a landslide victory in the summer of 1945, and Winston Churchill – shockingly, to some – lost office. King George had grown fond of Winston during his tenure – they had enjoyed over two hundred meals together, often without any servants present, merely helping themselves to a buffet supper.

Churchill's departure caused no tears in Nationalist Ireland: he had been loathed for his sally that Éire was 'neutral, but skulking'. Indeed, he did not believe that Éire was entitled to neutrality at all since, being still a Dominion, it was legally 'at war, but skulking'. Relations between Britain and Ireland reached a nadir in May 1945 when Éamon de Valera paid his respects to the German minister in Dublin, Eduard Hempel, on the death of Adolf Hitler – against his civil servants' advice, but following his own rigid mathematical formula of 'protocol'[59] – and Churchill hit back in a devastating speech castigating Ireland's neutrality, and indeed blaming that neutrality for the perilous situation Britain faced on the Atlantic front. Had it not been for 'the loyalty and friendship of Northern Ireland', Winston said, Britain would have been forced, in effect, to invade Éire

> ... or perish for ever from this earth. ... However, with a restraint and poise to which I say history will find few parallels, His Majesty's Government never laid a violent hand upon them, though at times it would have been quite easy and quite natural, and we left the de Valera Government to frolic with the Germans and later the Japanese representatives to their heart's content.[60]

This caused rage in Dublin, especially since help had indeed been given to the Allies (though not, admittedly, the use of the naval ports). De Valera gave a controlled, measured, and adroit response, pointing out that might was not right, and it would be a poor outlook for international relations if such a principle were upheld. 'It is indeed hard for the strong to be just to the weak. But acting justly always has its own rewards.' Cleverly, Dev praised Winston for not yielding to the urge to 'lay a violent hand' upon Éire. The nation had 'never been so proud of him', write Longford and O'Neill.[61] Churchill's electoral defeat was duly celebrated in Ireland with whoops of joy. Dev had blamed Churchill for the deterioration in Anglo-Irish affairs during the war.

It was an example of how the Crown was now quite out of the picture: hostilities were engaged between politicians.

Churchill – who was inclined to emotional outbursts, sometimes later regretted (and, as the historian Diarmaid Ferriter has said, prompted by too much fine brandy[62]) – must subsequently have regretted wielding the linguistic stiletto quite so sharply, especially after the war was over. Later in 1945 Randolph Churchill, Winston's son, had a long conversation with John Dulanty in which he said that 'his father's reference to Ireland and the Taoiseach [in the famous Maytime speech] was a piece of folly ... His father was the first to accept it.'[63]

But if Irish Nationalists imagined that the new Labour Prime Minister, Clement Attlee, would be more amenable in matters of Irish national sovereignty, they were to be soon disabused of the illusion.

*

Mr Attlee – the first person I interviewed as a young reporter on the *Evening Standard* – was then a very old man, very deaf and had retained his reputation for few words. He was personally fond of Ireland, and spent several holidays on the west coast. It says something for the relaxed attitude to security at that time that the British Prime Minister could (his wife at the wheel, driving 'idiosyncratically', in the euphemistic phrase used about her erratic motoring) take his Morris Minor from Dublin to Mayo in the 1940s quite undisturbed.

But if he was fond of Ireland for holidays, he was nevertheless as committed to the Union of Great Britain and Northern Ireland as any Tory. And, like other Labour ministers before him, he was especially respectful to the King – Labour Prime Ministers, who were once feared for incipient Bolshevism, have often turned out to be the most respectful of the monarch.

At the end of the Second World War, Labour and Left-wing values were everywhere in the ascendant: in some countries more prominently, in others more recessively.[64] France and Italy both had powerful and populous Communist Parties – and it might be argued that, at a cultural level, the Left had begun to assume a dominance that it has retained ever since.

Ireland was not immediately affected by the socialist ideas sweeping through Europe: partly because it was still culturally a pre-war society, and partly because the Catholic Church had too firm a grip on matters. The Left would become culturally ascendant in Ireland during the later 1960s – when the Catholic Church itself would become, at least economically, socialistically minded, swinging from condemning state welfare to suggesting ever more of such welfare (and higher taxes).

But in the 1940s and early 1950s the Irish version of post-war radicalism was a renewed flush of nationalism, focused on a fresh crusade against Partition.

The Partition of Ireland – which had existed since the foundation of the state, and which was never accepted by Nationalist Ireland – now became the abiding motif for Irish post-war administrations. Partition was the *fons et omega* of all the evils affecting Irish society: it had replaced the Oath of Allegiance as a fixed point of resentment.

The hostility to Partition was not without just cause: the Boundary Commission that had been due to examine the workings of Partition in 1925 was never permitted to complete its remit. Yet Dublin's relentless focus on Partition was also to some extent a displacement activity.

There was much that needed to be addressed in Irish society, from the modernisation of education to the renewal of housing; from the perpetual problem of emigration (which was to haunt Ireland in the 1950s with fears that the Irish people would disappear, 'like the Mayans', from their own terrain), to the equally perpetual problem of unemployment. Many social problems remained unaddressed.

All political energies seemed to focus on the campaigns against Partition, and a kind of national dream persisted that all worries would be solved by the reunification of the country. Ireland's cause was also taken up by English radicals, and the British National Council for Civil Liberties began to issue pamphlets and to launch speaking events about the discrimination and injustices against Catholics within Northern Ireland (in itself, to be sure, a just cause).

And then there came into government in Ireland a man whose heritage by blood and kind would force the pace more radically than ever before: one Seán MacBride. MacBride was the alluring and sophisticated son of the great beauty, Maud Gonne, and her mismatched husband, John MacBride (whom the poet Yeats had famously called a 'drunken, vainglorious lout' in his poem, 'Easter 1916'). Maud Gonne it was who had promoted the very expression the 'Famine Queen' about Queen Victoria. Major John MacBride had fought valiantly for the Boers against the British Empire in 1899–1900, and had been executed in 1916. Maud was still alive – a venerable and nationally respected old lady, still utterly staunch in her Republican ideals – and would live until 1953, when she died aged 87.

With that inheritance, Seán MacBride was likely to be anti-British and anti-Imperialist, and he was: he had also been an active member (and subsequently chief of staff) of the IRA in the 1930s. He had spent his early years in France and spoke English, all his life, with a French accent. This was among the reasons that my mother, who adored anything French, voted for him and his new political party, Clann na Poblachta (Family of Republicans). As did many of her fashionable friends in south Dublin.

In the Dublin of 1947, Seán MacBride was the very epitome of radical chic – a reputation he may be said to have retained all his life, being the only man ever to have been awarded the trio of honours of Nobel Prize for Peace, the Lenin Peace Prize, and the American Medal for Justice. In the last quarter of the twentieth century, he adroitly developed into an ardent international champion of human rights, though he remained socially conservative in his Catholic faith, supporting the 1983 referendum against abortion in Ireland, and opposing the 1986 referendum for the introduction of divorce.[65] In the early 1950s he was to show just how faithful he was to Mother Church in the celebrated 'Mother-and-Child' controversy.[66]

It was MacBride (not de Valera) who was the driving force behind the final break with the Crown in 1948. The state papers covering the 1948–49 period in the Irish National Archives make this evident, though it was already clear in published historical sources, notably Ronan Fanning's ground-breaking 1982 study on London and Belfast's response to the declaration of the Irish Republic.[67] MacBride caused British officials some dismay by asking to be excused from drinking the health of the King. He was an interesting example of a character that had no difficulty bending the knee to a bishop: but great difficulty in saluting a king.

To be sure, the phenomenon also occurred in reverse order: commentators such as Nancy Mitford who were sticklers for precedence and idiom among the aristocracy and upper classes, but hooted with laughter at any respect shown to the clergy, especially in Ireland.

*

The changing post-war world also brought about the end of empire: Burma left the Commonwealth in 1947, a straw in the wind (though it has hardly proved itself to be a beacon of progressive democracy since). It was inevitable that India should become wholly and legally self-governing (it already was, in effect), and Lord Mountbatten, the King's cousin, was despatched to India ('the jewel in the Crown') as the last Viceroy, who would usher in Indian and Pakistani independence in 1948.

Mountbatten was the agreed choice of both King George VI and the Prime Minister, Clement Attlee. Mountbatten's wife, Edwina, was the granddaughter of the wealthy philanthropist Ernest Cassel, who had been Edward VII's closest friend: on her father's side she was also descended from Lord Palmerston and the crusading Earl of Shaftesbury, who had so admirably put an end to the practice of sending small boys and girls up Victorian chimneys.

Mountbatten saw himself as a kind of radical — he told a political canvasser who turned up at his home, Broadlands, that only the servants voted Tory. He spent the last night of British rule in India with Éamon de Valera and Frank Aiken, who were out of office and on a world tour, raising consciousness about Partition.[68] Tragically, Mountbatten would meet his death at the hands of the IRA in Sligo in 1979. He had cherished the belief that he was 'too Left-wing' for the IRA to attack him: not being apprised of the fact that the IRA made no distinction between the voting habits of British aristocrats.

India's independence was to be declared on 15 August 1947, to the private sadness of King George VI and the even greater regret of his mother, Queen Mary, who greatly mourned her son's loss of the title 'Emperor (of India)'. She tenderly kept the last letter he sent to her on which he was entitled to affix the signature 'King and Emperor'. Still, India remained within the Commonwealth.

Ireland, and particularly Nationalist Ireland, was cheered and delighted by India's independence: even 35 years later Dr Noel Browne would refer with admiration to the 'smooth transfer' of power from Great Britain to an independent India.[69] This in spite of the fact that the transition was accompanied by partition, bloodshed (anything between one and two million people were killed), and that the transfer of populations was, and is still, a simmering source of resentment. In Britain itself, Muslim anger over Kashmir has fed into latter-day Islamic terrorism.

George VI was careful not to show any public regret about the loss of India: for to do so would have marked him amongst that group of 'imperialistic reactionaries' who were out of fashion in the post-war world. He accepted, even if privately he did not greatly like, the changes being wrought by Prime Minister Attlee, who had embarked on a programme of nationalisation of assets and sociali- sation of public services, including the National Health Service (also much opposed by the medical profession at its inception in 1948.)

But the King *did* mind – very much indeed – when it came to Ireland and the decision by the Irish government in 1948 to repeal the External Relations Act (which still retained a last, tenuous link with the Crown), and to quit the Commonwealth. This decision was made by the coalition government of Fine Gael, led by John A. Costello, and Clann na Poblachta, led by Seán MacBride, with MacBride as Minister for External Affairs.

Whether Éire was a full member of the Commonwealth was not really established, but there had not been an Irish attendance at Commonwealth conferences since before the war. Winston Churchill, in a surprisingly benevolent – if unprophetic – passage about Ireland in 1947, said that no one was quite clear what the Irish people's relationship with Britain was: 'They are neither in nor out of the Empire.' (And then added benignly: 'But they are much more friendly to us than they used to be. They have built up a cultured Roman Catholic system in the south ... the bitter past is fading.'[70] These thoughts may have originated in Winston's approval of Ireland's Catholic anti-Communism.)

The manner in which Ireland went on to become a republic was quixotic – even, perhaps, comical – but MacBride's intention to break definitively with the monarchy was deliberate. The British had anticipated that de Valera's administration might make the break, but were surprised when it was done by a coalition government in which the senior partner was the pro-Treaty Fine Gael.

Aside from all the talk about Burma and India and the rising tide of post-colonialism, a statue of Queen Victoria – admittedly, of exceptional ugliness – had been removed from the front of Leinster House in July 1948 – unceremoniously, but emblematically. And in some cases the still functioning British letter-boxes (now painted green) were having their royal insignia scraped off.

And in July 1948 Seán MacBride, as the new Foreign Minister in the coalition government, declared that Éire was *not* a member of the British Commonwealth, and Taoiseach Costello echoed that a week later. In August of 1948, the leader of the Irish Labour Party, William Norton, discussed dissolving the External Relations Act – which would drop the link with the King completely.

It was in October of 1948 when the Taoiseach, John A. Costello, was present at a Commonwealth conference in Canada, that it was suddenly and publicly made known that Éire would henceforth be a republic, and the link with King and Commonwealth finally, absolutely, repudiated.[71]

There was some speculation that 'drink had been taken' at the Ottawa party – so eccentric did the proceedings seem. There is no evidence of excessive drinking, but the Commonwealth dinner given in Mr Costello's honour by the Canadian Governor-General, Lord Alexander, would normally have been a convivial occasion.

But according to Noel Browne, who was Minister for Health in the Irish government at the time, Mr Costello felt rebuffed: he felt 'there was a certain coolness' displayed towards him, and an 'intended discourtesy' towards his wife, Ida. It would not have been the first time, either. Mr and Mrs Costello had been 'snubbed' by Lord Alexander at a Montreal tea party, when the Earl had avoided greeting the Taoiseach and had rather pointedly ignored the couple completely.

'Later', wrote Dr Browne, referring to the formal dinner for Commonwealth notables, 'a silver replica of "Roaring Meg" was placed in front of either Costello or his wife. "Roaring Meg" was a famous cannon used by the Protestants in their defence of Derry's walls against the Catholics during the Siege of Derry.' Costello told Dr Browne that 'I was so insulted by these things that I lost my temper and declared it [that is, the repeal of the External Relations Act].'

Obviously the change from Free State to Republic was brewing, but the manner of its announcement was unorthodox; and although the signs had been evident, the surprise was considerable. The Canadian historian, Don Akenson, called it 'a startling announcement', which 'caught everyone by surprise'. [72]

My uncle Jim, who voted for Mr Costello, thought the episode disgraceful. Many Irish Protestants, too, were appalled. Senator David Norris recalls that his Irish Protestant family in the midlands was desperately upset, and vowed never again to vote for Fine Gael or its coalition partners: Irish Protestants had believed until then that Fine Gael was the more 'moderate' Nationalist party, and would stand against the more emphatic nationalism of de Valera.

Mr de Valera himself, then in opposition, also thoroughly disapproved: *he* said he would have retained the link with the King to preserve relations with Northern Ireland, and he was subsequently to stay away from the main celebrations marking the Republic. Did Dev really believe it was wrong for the 26 counties to be a republic? To do him justice, he had on several occasions rejected suggestions of breaking with the Commonwealth.

But the Alpha-male explanation may also have to be factored in: he did not approve of it, because it had not been *his* initiative.

And did Earl Alexander of Tunis, the King's representative in Canada, really show 'coolness' and 'discourtesy' towards Mrs Costello, a Galway doctor's daughter of impeccable respectability? There certainly would have been little love lost between Lord Alexander and Irish Nationalists. Harold Rupert Leofric George Alexander was the son of an Ulster aristocrat, the Earl of Caledon and grew up on the family estate, Caledon Castle, in Co Tyrone, an area which had a reputation for being anti-Catholic in employment practice.[73]

Alexander's early life had been formed by the Ulster of loyal Britishness. He might well have thought it a lark to tease the Catholic Nationalist John Aloysius Costello – who was also described as an 'uneasy socialite' – with the replica of 'Roaring Meg'.

On such incidents, sometimes, do the fate of nations turn.

*

Just like my uncle Jim, the King was most upset by the developments at Ottawa: though it is not known whether he ascribed any blame to Earl Alexander's manners. While he had accepted that India's independence was inevitable, the King 'minded a great deal more', according to Sarah Bradford, about 'the final departure of Ireland'.

At a Buckingham Palace party, 'the King and the Queen had made a determined personal effort to stop the Irish breakaway'.[74] The King turned specifically to John Dulanty and said plaintively: 'Why leave the family?' And afterwards Mr Dulanty confided that 'the King was distressed by the whole business. He had been so glad to see relations with Éire improving; he had looked forward to the day when he would visit Dublin; now it was impossible.'

The still shy and unassuming King then asked if it was anything *he* had done wrong? Was it his personal fault? 'Dulanty assured him that "even the angel Gabriel" could not have prevented it.'[75]

King George, however, was, as always, extremely cordial with the Irish envoy, and both he and the Queen lingered with Mr Dulanty in a welcoming way during a reception for Commonwealth delegates. Although Éire's position was even more ambiguous by the end of October 1948, John Dulanty, who was a great fixture on the London diplomatic scene, was included in the beano.

Dulanty made a little joke about the situation, saying, 'with what I hope was the right sort of light in my eye', that in the 'present circumstances, it was good of them to ask me to their party!' The King laughed in response and said that he had been tempted to make the same observation, but 'it was better that you and not I said it'.

Despite there being a number of other guests to attend to, the King deliberately walked along with Dulanty and confided his regret about the repeal of the External Relations Act. He said that both he and his father had always entertained a great liking for the Irish people, 'and they [the King and Queen] would have been glad to have been able to have a residence in Ireland.'

Dulanty gave a quick summary of his government's case, and hoped it would never be an obstacle to the 'good neighbour' relations that they earnestly wished to pursue. Yet the King could not help thinking the proposed change rather sad, 'since it was a pity we were about to leave a circle in which the British and the Irish could help each other so much.'

The following evening another exchange took place, which illuminated the theory that the Scottish Queen had a rather sharper take on Anglo-Irish relations than the modest King. Mr Dulanty found himself at another reception given by the Prime Minister of Ceylon (Sri Lanka), and, once again, the royal couple 'stopped in their progress through the party and went out of their way to come and talk to me'.

There was no further reference to the political situation, the King saying 'with a gay flourish that– "we had all that out last night".' There followed a bit of banter from the Ceylon High Commissioner, describing Dulanty as the 'absent doyen' of the London High Commissioners, since he was by now the longest serving, but would be forthwith absent due to the change in Ireland's status.

Another High Commissioner remarked that Mr Dulanty had been in London so long that 'very likely the Irish Government had forgotten [he] was still here'. The Queen followed this up with a very quick riposte that brought gales of laughter, so that Dulanty did not quite catch the witticism.

It transpired that she had said that she 'did not think the Irish Government was given to forgetting'.[76]

Although Dulanty reported to his department chief that he found 'a friendly atmosphere' towards Ireland nearly everywhere in London, the Queen's little dart was a meaningful allusion to the Irish reputation for never forgetting any of the long griev-ances of history. British government ministers had, after all, long lamented the history lectures they were so often subjected to by (especially) Mr de Valera. Churchill once recounted that after two and half hours, Dev had still only got to Poynings' Law (enacted in 1495).[77]

*

Ireland's passage from Free State, with a residual link to the Crown and the other Commonwealth nations, to independent Republic, with no further links to the monarchy, was enacted in December 1948 and came into effect on Easter Monday 1949, the 33rd anniversary of the outbreak of the 1916 Rising. There was some sadness among the other Dominions. The Australians expressed 'deep regret that the association of Éire with the Dominions should be broken', but added that it was 'a matter for Éire'.

But, when it came to the formalities, in the end all was done with proper protocol and correctness. When the Republic finally came into being in April 1949, Prime Minister Attlee drafted a message in the King's name to be despatched to Dublin, with a special coda to those men and women in Ireland who had served the Crown:

> Mindful of the neighbourly links which hold the people of the Republic of Ireland in close associa-tion with my subjects, I send you my most sincere greetings and good wishes. The Queen and I hold in most grateful memory the services and sacrifices of the Irish men and Irish women who rendered gallant assistance to our cause in the recent war, and who therefore made a notable contribution to our victory. I pray that every blessing may be with you today and in the future of your country.[78]

It was Attlee's suggestion (in conjunction with Lord Rugby, formerly Sir John Maffey, Britain's wartime representative in Éire) that 'a message from the King will transcend all questions of politics, and will help to destroy the rebel significance of Easter Monday'. The Republic was to be finally celebrated on Easter Monday of 1949. Some remember it as a joyful occasion: some recall it as muted. Éamon de Valera, in opposition, made a minimal appearance, and declined to join the more jubilant aspect of the celebrations.

Attlee was right about the King's message transcending politics, but not about it helping to dissolve the rebel significance of Easter Monday.

In fact, the King himself deleted his wife's name from the formal communication: perhaps she did not care to celebrate a republic. His message, as finally amended by himself, went:

> I send you my sincere good wishes on this day, being well aware of the neighbourly links which hold the people of the Republic of Ireland in close association with my subjects in the United Kingdom. I hold in most grateful memory the services and sacrifices of the men and women of your country who rendered gallant assistance to our cause in the recent war, and who made a notable contribution to our victory. I pray that every blessing may be with you today and in the future.[79]

This final message had had the prior approval of Sir Basil Brooke, Prime Minister of Northern Ireland, whose opinion the King had sought.

The King's message elicited a warm response from Dublin, and the British representative in Dublin was told that the government could scarcely have hoped for such a 'generous act on the part of His Majesty'. The President, now Mr Seán T. O'Kelly, the former firebrand who had boasted of whipping John Bull at every turn, seemed genuinely affected, and reacted by saying:

> ... how greatly he had been touched by His Majesty's message and how grateful he was for it and

for the kind terms in which it had been expressed. It was a most generous and imaginative act on the part of the King and its sensitive and moving terms had been deeply valued. … it was in sharp contrast with the dry and formal terms of President Truman's message. When the English did a thing, they did it generously and well.[80]

Indeed, Seán T. (a short man and, for all his rebel bluster, kindly and enthusiastic – widowed once, married twice to two handsome sisters, regretfully childless) sent a warm telegram back to the King, expressing fully his appreciation, and wishing 'Your Majesty health and happiness'.[81]

Taoiseach Costello, who had himself proclaimed the Republic in Canada, also expressed his appreciation towards the King's 'gracious act'. He noted that General Sir William Hickey, Chairman of the British Legion in Éire, was particularly pleased with the reference to the Irishmen who had fought with the Allies. It was the first time that there had been official recognition from an Irish leader of the Irish who had fought for the Allies.[82]

So all ended (outwardly) on a friendly note, it seemed. But in a rectory in Irishtown, Ringsend, Dublin, a poignant little post-script was added.

Many Irish Protestants were, as mentioned, sad at breaking the last link with the Crown: but as a group they were committed to the rule of law and duly prepared to alter their liturgical services to reflect the change. Henceforth, from Easter 1949 onwards, 'God Save the King' would no longer be sung in the Anglican Church of Ireland in the Republic; henceforth, prayers would be offered for the President of Ireland rather than the monarch.

Mrs Doris Weir, the rector's wife at St Matthew's Church in Irishtown (a beautiful eighteenth-century gem, a short walk from the Lansdowne Road rugby stadium, and very near to where I grew up) wrote a letter to King George to describe the valedictory service conducted at St Matthew's:

> On behalf of many loyalists in Southern Ireland, may I thank you for the recognition which we feel was conveyed to us in your message to the new State, of services gladly rendered by our people to your Majesty and to the Empire in two wars?
>
> We may not now use in Church the prayers for Your Majesty and for the Royal Family. In our Parish Church, once the royal Chapel of St Mathew, Irishtown, on Easter Sunday evening we sang with sorrow, for it was the last time, the National Anthem. It was a prayer from all our hearts – God Save the King. Legislation does not kill love and loyalty. We will ever continue to pray for you and for all your family, and to hold you in deep affection.[83]

The King directed his private secretary to say how greatly he appreciated Mrs Weir's letter. For there is little doubt that the King, too, felt something of the same sadness. When he had heard that Ireland was leaving the Commonwealth, he had said mournfully, 'I'll never go to Ireland now'.

Chapter Six

MONARCHY AND REPUBLIC: PARITY OF ESTEEM?

Popular Irish interest in the British royal family is huge, but is accompanied by political hostility to the Crown as a symbol of Irish oppression. (Olivia O'Leary and Helen Burke, *Mary Robinson: the Authorised Biography*, 1998)

We heard in awe the news of King George VI's death in 1952, but otherwise it had little impact on us, as O'Connell's [school], like all Christian Brothers' Schools, passionately expounded Irish Republicanism. (George Rowley, *A Memoir: Original Writing*, 2007)

The death of King George VI was not, perhaps, of great significance to nine-year-old boys in Dublin's fiercely nationalistic Christian Brothers' school, but it was an occasion for the Republic of Ireland, declared in 1949, to affirm its new and proud status. The de Valera newspaper, *Irish Press*, devoted a prominent front-page box relating to the King's death (which took place on 6 February 1952), drawing attention to 'Ireland's Sympathy'.

'The President yesterday sent a message to Her Majesty, Queen Elizabeth, expressing sympathy with Her Majesty and the

266

Royal Family on the death of King George VI. The President also sent a message of sympathy to Her Royal Highness, Princess Elizabeth.'[1] Strictly speaking, Her Royal Highness was now Queen, following the tradition of monarchy whereby one monarch succeeds as soon as another dies, as in the phrase: 'The King is Dead, Long Live the King'.

Messages were sent from the Taoiseach (de Valera) to the British Prime Minister, Dev's sometime adversary, Winston Churchill, 'expressing sympathy with him and the British Government'. How protocols can smooth over the ripples of politics.

The protocols also underlined Ireland's newly established legal detachment from Great Britain: now, as it were, being just neighbouring islands, the former relationship of imperial power to dominion was swept aside. De Valera called to the British Embassy to 'tender his sympathy', as did the Minister for External Affairs, Mr Frank Aiken (whom British Intelligence had regarded as pro-German during wartime). Other callers to the British Embassy included the 'Most Revd Dr McQuaid, Archbishop of Dublin', and the 'Most Revd Dr Barton, the Protestant Archbishop'.[2] In Ireland the Catholic Church was an aristocracy and, by a rule of fair play, the other churches were at least minor nobility.

This diplomatic protocol was clearly relished. It showed the Republic as an independent neighbouring nation, no longer obliged to defer to the Crown: but graciously acknowledging the loss of a king who had been, in fact, a very nice man. The President of Ireland, Seán T. O'Kelly, had but a few decades earlier publicly snubbed the British monarch's representative in Ireland, and spoken aggressively about the pleasures of 'whipping John Bull'.[3] But time, events, and the dignity of office, had mellowed him.

The *Irish Press* editorial commented that King George 'will be deeply mourned, both as a man and as a monarch'. Bearing the stamp of de Valera's own authority, it noted that in Britain the King was no longer regarded 'as a ruler or superior, but rather as the head of the family, sharing the joys and sorrows of the ordinary man and woman whilst they share his, and typifying in his own conduct and in his family life the ideals that are held in common.' This was a particularly well-observed comment on the changing role of kingship.[4]

It went on to praise 'the unassuming manners of the late monarch, his simple tastes, and above all, the strong sense of duty that made him carry out his usual engagements even when weakened by a series of long and tedious illnesses ... [these] were qualities that caused the British people to regard the throne with deepened affection.'

Partition was not forgotten: that could never be overlooked. But in the shadow of the King's death, the drumbeat is muffled. 'It will be recorded that during his reign he made State visits to the Six Counties on three occasions, but the Irish people will not hold it against him personally that he came not as a welcome guest of the nation but as a symbol of an alien rule over part of our country.'

Yet, 'his sudden death, when it seemed almost that by patient courage he had conquered severe illnesses, touches our common humanity, and all who have ever mourned the passing of the head of a family will sympathise with his family and with the British people in their loss.'

The newspaper even took pride in the Irish connections of the King's speech therapist – who had done so much to help him diminish a painful stammer – Lionel Logue. He was of Irish origin (and a kinsman of the late Cardinal Logue). And the King's radiologist, it was reported, was Dr Peter Kerley of Dundalk.

With their special sensitivity about the Six Counties, Irish Republicans were watchful of titles and symbols that might be acquired by the new Queen. It was with some satisfaction that the *Irish Press* reported that Elizabeth II's title would be, 'Queen of this Realm, and her other Realms and Territories, Head of the Commonwealth, Defender of the Faith'.

This was in contrast to George VI, who had ascended the throne as 'His Majesty George the Sixth, of Great Britain, Ireland and the British Dominions'. At his death (and to this day in the authoritative *Dictionary of National Biography*) George VI's title in effect describes him as a last king of Ireland: 'King of Great Britain, Ireland and the British dominions beyond the seas and sometime Emperor of India.'

The Ulster Unionist Party in Belfast, speaking through Sir George Bellew, Garter King of Arms, wished the new Queen to continue with this historic title of 'Elizabeth the Second, by the grace of God, Queen of Great Britain, Ireland and the British Dominions beyond the Seas, Defender of the Faith'.[5]

There were to be questions in the Dáil about the titles accorded to the 'British Queen', led by the Republican Seán MacBride, who reported to the Minister for External Affairs, Mr Aiken, that he had heard the BBC describe her as 'Queen of Great Britain and Ireland', and would the government please register its protest against this?[6]

Mr Aiken, himself a Republican from South Armagh (a stronghold of Irish Republicanism), and also a former Chief of Staff of the anti-Treaty IRA, nevertheless gave Mr MacBride the brush-off. The BBC may have used such a phrase, he conceded, but it was not thus in the official proclamation from London.

Aiken's attitude suggested impatience with MacBride – that he was nit-picking over footling matters, while he, Aiken, had risen above such quibbling. Frank Aiken was now a senior member of the Irish government: he was 54 years old, about the age when politicians (and perhaps other individuals) often begin to perceive that the continuity of institutions has some merit; moreover, men in power have an interest in accommodating the existing order of established law and custom. The Queen would be proclaimed according to the correct legal formula: but Aiken had bigger fish to fry on a world stage.[7]

Aiken was a good deal more interested in re-branding Ireland as a respectable member of the western community, albeit a neutral one. He saw this as a far greater priority for the country than Elizabeth's titles.

Over the next few years, objections to Queen Elizabeth's titles continued from Nationalist sources in the North of Ireland, notably from the two anti-partitionist Members of Parliament for Fermanagh and Tyrone, Cahir Healy and Michael O'Neill, who repeatedly protested against 'Northern Ireland' being included in the royal title (or accepted as a political entity at all).[8] There were also critical letters to the *Irish Press*, frequently from a Canon

Maguire of Newtownbutler in Co Fermanagh (who proudly flew the Irish tricolour within the Six Counties when an occasion demanded it); but there were no reports of official objections from the Irish government.

Partition, rather than Crown nomenclature, continued to be a focus of Irish government policy until the late 1950s. Throughout the decade Irish diplomats and civil servants were instructed to carry out the anti-partitionist 'policy of the sore thumb' wherever they could: vexing Britain over the Partition issue, and explaining Ireland's neutrality in terms of this accursed Partition.

For discontented republicans within the Irish state, Partition became the grievance that replaced the grievance over the link with the Crown (finally removed in 1948–49); just as the link with the Crown had been the grievance that replaced the grievance against the Oath of Allegiance, removed in 1936. Now the partition of Ireland carried all the grievances in one basket.

At the same time, while Partition was a grassroots complaint (and solely blamed, of course, on Britain: in the Irish Republican catechism, Ulster Unionists are really Irish Republicans who have not yet been awakened to their 'true' sense of national identity), Irish foreign policy was feeling its way towards greater internationalism and expansionism. Ireland had itself rejected membership of NATO, but it had joined the Council of Europe: and it had applied to the UN in 1946, only to be rebuffed.[9]

*

If Ireland had reason to celebrate her own sovereignty (or at least the 26 counties could now proclaim themselves free from any further subordination, even symbolically, to the Crown and Great Britain), the years after the Second World War were internationally lonely for the new republic. Those countries that had fought so hard to defeat fascism were not inclined to give the neutrals an easy ride. Independent Ireland felt the cold air of disapproval from both the United States and the Soviet Union.

President Roosevelt, notably, had thought the Irish grievance about Partition was disproportionate. And though Roosevelt died in 1945, his critical attitudes towards the Irish state lingered.

The USSR (which had lost many millions in the 'Great Patriotic War') was determined to keep Éire out of the United Nations as a penalty for neutrality; it succeeded in doing so until 1956. From 1946, Andrei Gromyko, who would become a long-serving, powerful Soviet Foreign Minister, was making known his negative views on Irish wartime neutrality.[10] Russian attitudes may also have been coloured by the strongly anti-Communist views of the Catholic Church, views wholly supported, in Ireland, by the Protestant churches, who also anathemised Communist atheism.

Ironically, Winston Churchill (who had so abhorred Irish neutrality) waxed pro-Irish once the war was over. For Winston, once a quarrel was over, it was over. In 1948, he praised Ireland as a 'progressive Roman Catholic civilisation', by which he meant, perhaps, that it was anti-Communist.

He also took aside the Irish envoy John Dulanty (whom he had known as a friend since 1906) and reiterated how much he, Winston, supported a united Ireland. 'You *must* get those fellows from the North in,' he said.[11] In fact Churchill had supported a united Ireland since his Asquithian days as a Liberal, but he knew (and in this he was a realist) that you could not force the hand of the more vehement Unionists and Orangemen.

The gentle treatment that the *Irish Press* gave George VI's death extended to his funeral and mourning (they reported the rituals in detail over a period of 16 days), and may have reflected de Valera's sense that Britain was not now the biggest 'external' source of hostility for the Irish state. It may also have reflected an older Irish tradition of respecting the dead: Dev authorised representation at the funeral of the King, whereas he had refused Irish representation at the wedding of Princess Elizabeth in 1947.

The personal events associated with the monarchy have often provoked, in Ireland, discussions around apolitical issues of the human life cycle: marriage, divorce, relationships, pregnancy, health. The death of George VI triggered a discussion in my family kitchen about sickness and health. It was stated by my doctor uncle, P. J., that King George's death was precipitated by cancer, and by his incorrigible cigarette habit (although terminally ill with cancer, the cause of death was a thrombosis, from which the king died in his sleep.)

It was shrewd of Uncle P.J. to deduce that King George had cancer: other doctors also, apparently, read between the lines of the medical bulletins. The general public were informed that the King's illness had been 'a small catarrhal inflammation in the lung, following influenza'. Newspapers at this time seldom mentioned the dreaded word 'cancer': even when I started out in Fleet Street in 1966, the Beaverbrook papers still forbade the very word, as Lord Beaverbrook had regarded it as 'unlucky'. (Obituaries until the end of the century still described a death from cancer as 'a long illness', and cancer, which involved an arduous application of failed treatments, as 'a long illness bravely borne'.)

In 1952, young as I was, I remember hearing Uncle P.J. saying that the King's death would now establish the link between cancer and smoking, for doctors and public alike. As he spoke, the kitchen was a fog of cigarette smoke emitted by 'Sweet Afton', and 'Craven 'A'. Everyone seemed to smoke then, including the doctor himself.

In Britain the Second World War had left the country bombed and drained (and still on rations well into the 1950s). Life is often characterised as grey and repressive in that post-war era, especially for women and minorities: homosexuals were still sentenced to a prison term – perhaps the most famous case being that of the actor John Gielgud – if charged with an offence. Divorcees were still not admitted to Royal Ascot; class divisions were rigidly observed among the Establishment; and Blackpool landladies were said to have placed notices in their windows saying 'No coloureds, no Irish' (it is alleged that some added, 'and no dogs'.)[12]

Ireland in the 1950s reflected the values that obtained generally in the western world, with some cultural variation.

Censorship of books was notoriously more draconian than elsewhere, though it also existed elsewhere: *Ulysses* was banned in Britain, but not – quirkily – in Ireland. While censorship of plays existed in Britain (the Lord Chamberlain, who scrutinised plays in London for decency, was a servant of the monarch) there was no theatre censorship in Ireland – though pressures could be, and sometimes were, brought to bear.[13]

Divorce was prohibited in the Irish Republic, but the law against homosexuality was often more discreetly and flexibly interpreted – indeed, if there were no public scandal, ignored. Micheál MacLíammóir, a flamboyantly homosexual actor (and national treasure) could be seen regularly walking down Grafton Street wearing a thick application of Max Factor panstick make-up; Noel Coward's diaries about visiting Dublin in the 1950s are particularly appreciative – he found nothing but kindness and the warmest of welcomes. Bohemian Dublin pub life had a homo-sexual culture that was tolerated: Brendan Behan, who knew whereof he spoke, jocosely described an 'Irish queer' as a man who preferred women to drink.[14]

Unlike Britain or the United States, race was not an issue in the Ireland of the period. Catholic schoolchildren were taught to revere a black saint (then 'Blessed'), Martin de Porres, and there was a collecting box for the missions in every classroom featuring the Blessed Martin.

Economically, though, the early years of the decade certainly did represent hard times. De Valera's administration had returned to power in 1951 (after the fall of the inter-party government of 1948–51). Ronan Fanning describes the 1951 general election as the first genuinely 'pork-barrel' election in the Irish state, when the issues were those bread-and-butter questions which animate electorates: prices, wages, inflation, housing. No longer was 'the national question' to the forefront (for the electorate, at least) as it had been for so long.

The Irish state had achieved successes during its thirty years of existence: in land distribution, in a certain level of social care, and in the fight against diseases such as diphtheria, scarlet fever, typhoid and tuberculosis. The great baby-killer, gastroenteritis, was vanquished, and ricketts in children had become relatively rare. English visitors, such as Nancy Mitford (and one Antony Armstrong-Jones) remarked upon the almost Arcadian rustic simplicity found in Ireland, which they saw as a landscape dating from long before the Second World War. Ireland had not been changed, in the way Britain had been changed, by the war.[15]

But there were serious problems of unemployment and emigration, and the dole was desperately modest. Dónall MacAmhlaigh, author of a poignant and compelling diary of his experiences as an Irish navvy in England in the early 1950s, had received £1.2s.6d weekly as dole money in Ireland. And though his mother was heartbroken to part with him, she urged him to leave his native Co Galway and travel to Northampton, answering an advert for a stoker. As he leaves, a neighbouring man says to him: 'It won't be long till there's nobody left here at all. They're all going.'[16]

Once in England, MacAmhlaigh chronicles the life of the Irish emigrant: there were throngs of Irish incomers and Irish communities everywhere. Although a devotee of the Fenian tradition and a mellifluous Irish speaker, MacAmhlaigh admires much of what he finds in England, and far from grumbling about the English treatment of the Irish, he appreciates the opportunities that England is giving to Irish emigrants.

While Mr de Valera was to continue, all through the 1950s, to urge the Irish people to make 'sacrifices' for the sake of being a sovereign country, many an Irish working person was to become mightily tired of the 'poor-but-independent sermons'.

Dev reiterated metaphors he had taken up back in the 1920s and 1930s – that it was better to live in a humble cottage and be free, than to be attached to a grand mansion in the role of the servant, but the Irish navvies building the motorways and constructing the post-war houses in England were sceptical of such assurances. MacAmhlaigh takes Dev's point, but does not accept the excuse: 'It is understood, naturally, that we can never be as wealthy as England, but we're so far behind other countries such as Denmark that one can only conclude that something has gone wrong somewhere.'

Other Irish labourers were writing home in equally caustic terms, specifically asking what advantage it was to the working man that the Irish Republic should cut her last links 'with Crown and Commonwealth'. One Irish labourer in Surrey actually wrote to the Irish government to complain of the extra problems the Irish Republic had created for him:

> All the disadvantages are outlined for me and a very gloomy list it is for us, reporting to the Ploice [sic] station, having to return to Ireland, unemployment, a lower standard of living. Is the last doorway in Mr de Valera's wall being bricked up? As Seán Ó Faoláin so ably put it in his talk over the radio tonight, 'The only world open to the Irish soon will be the next one'. The Irish Government should be made aware that most of 'our Irish boy and girl emigrants … are backward and unable to fit into the more civilised mode of living here after the more cramped and less free standards prevailing in Ireland.'[17]

Ireland had gained her sovereignty, but economic self-confidence was a long way off. Ireland had ceased to have any link with a British monarch or the 'flummery' of a court, but intellectuals would bitterly complain that, instead, the Irish political class deferred with nauseating obsequiousness to the Catholic Church.

It is not cynical to say that a nation always needs both bread and circuses: and the Irish state did try to provide at least *some* of the circuses. In 1951, the United Kingdom had celebrated with a 'Festival of Britain', designed both to echo the great Victorian exhibition of 1851, and to boost popular morale after the Second World War.

The Festival of Britain, inaugurated by King George on 3 May 1951, had been declared 'a tonic to the nation', indicating that the nation needed a tonic: during that summer, eight and a half million people responded by visiting the Festival of Britain site on London's South Bank. The Welsh poet Dylan Thomas found the modernistic sculptures on display to be 'gay, absurd, irrelevant, delighting imagination', and the Archbishop of Canterbury, Geoffrey Fisher, described it, at the end, as 'a real family party'.[18]

Responding to the general idea, in 1953 the Irish state produced '*An Tostal:* Ireland at Home'. *An Tostal* was to act (like the Festival of Britain) as 'a raiser of our morale, brightening up houses, flowers, fountains ...' But whereas the Festival aimed to advertise British achievements in the arts and industry, *An Tostal* rather underlined Ireland's potential as a tourist location.

'*Tostal*', it was explained, was 'ancient Gaelic for "pageant, muster, array, display"' and it all began on Easter Sunday, April 5 1953.[19] At that time, it would not have been possible to launch it earlier, during the season of Lent, when St Patrick's Day was celebrated with '*prayer* and pageantry'. The festival had been unveiled by the President, Seán T. O'Kelly, with the Pageant of St Patrick, 'the most ambitious open-air pageant ever staged in Dublin'. There were events that underlined Ireland as 'a Paradise for the Huntsman', and 'the virile national games of Ireland'.

One modern commentator has pronounced it all a 'dismal failure', but actually it was rather a sensible investment in the development of the tourist industry, which would prove to be a big earner for Ireland.[20] Bord Fáilte, the Irish Tourist Board, had been established in 1952, and tourism was even then a source of some £32 million annually. The festival was repeated over several years and I remember being taken to an open-air pageant, as part of *An Tostal*, in one of the following years: it re-enacted the legend of Cuchulainn, the great Celtic warrior. I thought it was very exciting, infusing me with a lifelong enjoyment of theatre and display.

*

In the summer of 1953 Queen Elizabeth paid her coronation visit to Northern Ireland, accompanied by her private secretary,

Alan Lascelles, various dignatories from the Royal Navy and Air Force, and her Home Secretary, the flinty Scot David Maxwell Fyfe, who was the Nuremberg prosecutor said to have finally broken Goering.[21] There were protests from Nationalist (and Labour) sources: Belfast Corporation decided by 37 votes to 7 that no invitations to meet the Queen were to be issued to Irish Labour Party members. With a security cordon of between 60,000 and 70,000 Royal Ulster Constabulary, as well as 'B' specials and British troops, the ambience was highly militarised.

Galway Corporation, led by Alderman Lydon, passed a unanimous resolution protesting against the Queen's visit to the North.[22] The Anti-Partition Association condemned it and used the occasion to mount a slightly mean-spirited picket at Dublin's Amiens Street station, obstructing old soldiers who had served the Crown and who were travelling to Belfast for the occasion.

The Anti-Partition Association (sometimes called the Anti-Partition League) had had their appetite whetted by the controversy over the coronation films, described in the Introduction. De Valera's *Irish Press* fully supported the protest against the visit. The visit was, the paper maintained:

> ... part of the pretence in the English Queen's Coronation Oath, with its claim to Sovereignty over the Six Counties ... Queen Elizabeth's arrival in Belfast and her progress through the Six Counties is intended as a symbolical taking posses-sion of a part of her realm. ... [the Queen had] been given the ugly task of making an imperialis-tic gesture offensive to the Irish nation ... The organs of public opinion in Britain have endeav-oured to put the best face on it. They have tried to give the false impression that the Queen is being welcomed by a united people.[23]

The Irish newspaper was stung by the London *Times* writing of 'loyal Ulster' and the London *Evening News* reporting that 'the most loyal hearts in Britain beat in Ulster. ... to hear a National Anthem sung as only an Ulster crowd can, is an unforgettable experience.' Most insulting of all was the claim made by the London paper that Northern Ireland was 'as inseparable a part of the United Kingdom ... as Kent or Sussex'.[24]

A generation later Margaret Thatcher was to call the North of Ireland 'as British as Finchley', although nobody has yet glimpsed wall paintings of King Billy or Oliver Cromwell on the gable-end walls of Finchley, or its pavement kerbs decorated with Union Jacks.

In 1953 the *Irish Press* saw the Queen's presence in the North of Ireland as 'a symbol of foreign domination. Her visit is both an implementation of the British claim to sovereignty over the Six Counties and an opportunity for the Orange Party to strengthen this hold.' She was 'the symbol of bigoted sectarian rule'.[25]

These charges were not entirely groundless. Although Queen Elizabeth herself (only 27 years old at this time) was blameless, the management of such visits very clearly signalled not just the exclusion of Catholic Nationalists, which was to some extent self-chosen, but the triumphalism of the Orange state.

The Queen was photographed with two giant Lambeg drums: those terrifying tribal instruments which warned 'croppies' to lie down every 12 July. When beaten for the Queen in 1953, there was 'a tribal chant' and 'a ferocity, an aggressive quality' in the loyalty and 'wild beating of the Lambeg drums'. The speeches put into her mouth, though bland and ostensibly apolitical, nonetheless were clearly interpreted as being addressed only to the 'loyalist' section of the populace.[26]

Scant effort was made by the political establishment to reach out to Catholic and Nationalist sectors – so different from the careful itineraries of King Edward VII, who was so meticulous about visiting a Catholic institution every time he visited a Protestant one. Small wonder that in the Bogside area of Derry the *Observer* newspaper reported that the estates were silent and eloquently flagless for the visit.

Kenneth Harris of the *Observer* interviewed an Irish Republican man 'described as a terrorist' for the occasion: he told the reporter that there was 'nothing personal' in the silent reaction among the Catholic, Nationalist population. 'There is nothing personal against the girl. If she came here unofficially on holiday we'd roll out the red carpet for her and give her a great time at the races.' It was the monarchy's link with the Orange state that rankled.[27]

Twenty-five years later, in 1977, Queen Elizabeth would deliver a more emphatic message about the necessity of power sharing in the North: but only after much blood had been spilt, and indeed before even more blood was to flow.

There were mishaps on the 1953 visit, and de Valera's newspaper could hardly contain its glee.[28] The railway line between Belfast and Dublin was wrecked, deliberately: but there were also accidental moments of bad luck, as when the electricity system broke down and shut off all radio communications, isolating the royal party for 15 minutes, causing a panic among the authorities.

The 'parallel monarchy' of the Catholic Church was to produce (with the full backing of the Irish state) a different kind of ceremonial occasion for the Marian Year of 1954. From 1953 onwards – not coincidentally, from June 1953, alongside reports of the coronation of Elizabeth II – preparations were evident for the celebration of a year devoted to Mary, the Mother of God.

There were to be pilgrimages – many to Lourdes – and processions, many of them strikingly beautiful, with young women processing in file, dressed in long, white gowns, honouring the Blessed Virgin. There were many 'Rosary Rallies': in the small town of Loughrea in Co Galway, a Rosary Rally attracted an astonishing 30,000 people to honour 'Our Lady of Clonfert', a traditional local site of devotion.

Whether consciously or unconsciously, photographs of processions celebrating Our Lady were often juxtaposed next to photographs and reports about the royal family. 'Dublin Marks Marian Year with Solemn Procession' would appear next to 'Royal Procession – Elizabeth II in tour of Commonwealth'. The Marian processions – a phenomenon which has now totally disappeared in Ireland – were almost Spanish in their solemn pageantry, with a statue of the Blessed Virgin carried aloft by women in white, often accompanied by a military salute.

A strong theme in the Marian devotion was the participation of working people. 'Industrial Tributes to Our Lady' were an everyday feature during the Maytime launch of the Marian year, with Masses, Benedictions, and rosary rallies held in factories, foundries, and workplaces: '2,000 workers at Sunbeam Solemn High Mass'; 'Athlone's Tribute to Our Lady – 700 at Mass in Factory'; and 'Dundalk in Industrial Tribute to Our Lady – P. J. Carrolls [Cigarette] Factory'.[29]

The Corpus Christi processions each June were, in any case, wonderfully colourful and flamboyant, most particularly in those inner-city areas of Dublin some would have called slums. In this way the Irish people affirmed their values and heritage, just as the British people did through the ceremonial associated with the monarchy.[30]

All over Ireland to this day there are statues and grottos and shrines built in the Marian Year of 1954, and every house named 'Stella Maris', 'Cnoc Mhuire', 'Ave Maria', 'Santa Maria', 'Regina Caeli', 'Notre Dame', 'Lourdes', and every other variation on the Marian theme in English, Irish, Latin, Italian, and French, usually traces its naming to that year.

*

There was now no more contact between the British monarchy and the Irish state than there was between the British monarchy and the French state: less, since the monarchs of the United Kingdom made state visits to the Republic of France, but never to the Republic of Ireland. The indefatigable John Dulanty, the long-serving Irish Commissioner, was appointed Irish Ambassador in 1950; but, having served for many decades, he was to retire in the same year.

With Dulanty's retirement – and subsequent death, in 1955 – a whole chapter of political and social history passed away.[31] The confidant of de Valera, the long-standing friend of Churchill, the intimate of a string of British politicians and officials, and the regular interlocateur with three kings – George V, Edward VIII and George VI – he preferred the spoken word to the written memoir, much to our loss.

Dulanty was a social as well as a political animal: who but Dulanty could have chatted up Queen Mary on a subject that impassioned her – antiques? His early apprenticeship had not been through the discreet echelons of the civil service, but in the rougher world of commerce where he had started off as a manager in the John Lewis chain of stores.

Dulanty was succeeded by F. H. Boland, an outstandingly able civil servant (and the father of the poet Eavan Boland); a man often described as 'sagacious'. Though faultless as a public servant, Boland did not give the impression that he had much interest in the London posting. He saw Ireland taking on a role on a much wider stage; he was later to become president of the UN General Assembly, famously breaking his gavel when trying to call Nikita Khrushchev to order.[32]

Freddie Boland did report a significant social development taking place in 1955 – although, considering the rumours buzzing around the popular press for some time, rather tardily, and in a dry manner greatly in contrast to Dulanty's fascination with people and human events. On October 26 1955 the Ambassador sent Dublin a formal communication concerning Princess Margaret's love life. Margaret was romantically involved with – indeed, passionately in love with – her late father's equerry, Group Captain Peter Townsend. He was a divorced man, although it was emphasised (this being a significant point at this period) that he was the 'innocent' party in the divorce. It was Townsend's wife, Rosemary, who had committed the 'matrimonial offence': that is, adultery.

The romance had been the source of press gossip in the popular papers: but it had also been referred to in the influential left-wing *Tribune* as early as July 1953. The Irish newspapers re-iterated such reportage only where there was a 'political' justification, or a constitutional angle. In fact the Margaret–

Townsend affair had no constitutional implications, though it did have an eerie echo of Edward VIII's situation, and some British churchmen thought it to be deplored.

It was late October 1955 when Ambassador Boland informed Dublin that 'Princess Margaret has not yet made up her mind' [as to whether she would marry the divorced Townsend]. 'She is very conscious of her royal status.' The Queen had 'kept the Commonwealth governments in the dark', and they had not been consulted.[33]

The Ambassador, correctly as it turned out, singled out the Queen Mother as the source of the public problem. She was 'indulgent when the relationship began', thus allowing her daughter to walk into a controversy. He also correctly reported that 'popular opinion was in favour' of Margaret being free to marry whosoever she pleased. By contrast the aristocracy was against such a step, because 'the monarchy is a "mystique", resting on the idea that the Royal Family puts the interest of the country first. Otherwise [it would] weaken the monarchy.'

This was altogether a succinct and correct summing-up of the situation, as subsequent research has shown. The Queen Mother was not only 'indulgent' to Princess Margaret (who had had a crush on her father's handsome equerry since she was a teenager): the Queen Mum's way of coping with any unpleasant suggestion was to ignore it, and to 'brush it under the carpet'. Initially failing to confront Margaret about the romance, once it was out in the open, the Queen Mother took a strongly disapproving attitude: for a while, mother and daughter were hardly on speaking terms.

Queen Elizabeth's biographer, Sarah Bradford, also blames (to some extent) the Queen herself: she too had not wished to spoil her sister's romance, and had even entertained Margaret and Townsend to dinner together. But it might have been wiser to warn the younger sister that the relationship would, eventually, cause a problem.

The problem was not strictly constitutional, but it was nonetheless considered a serious difficulty at the time. The Queen was the Supreme Governor of the Church of England, which did not (in 1955) recognise divorce: indeed, it was an institution that abhorred the dissolution of marriage. If Elizabeth's sister should defy the rules of the Anglican Church, by law established, then Margaret would have to renounce her position within the succession. As Dr Leslie Weatherhead of the Methodist Conference pointed out: 'Clearly the status of the Princess raises difficulties in regard to a fiancé who is divorced and whose wife and two children are living.' If Margaret had inherited the throne, then 'her child would be the fruit of a marriage which many Anglicans would not recognise as valid. … If the state church approves this marriage it would break its own rules.'[34]

And then there was the question of example:

> Her example does not make it easier to uphold the ideal of Christian marriage in a land in which divorce is already too lightly regarded: homes [are] too readily breaking up and children too thoughtlessly deprived of the mental security of having two united parents, a security which surely is part of God's plan.[35]

As Mr Boland had pointed out to the Irish government, the ordinary folks on the road to Wigan Pier did not give a fig about royal example or the high ideals of marriage and morality: they just wanted the Princess to be happy. But the Establishment did care – and so did Margaret herself.

She certainly could have married the man she loved: but, had she done so, she would have had to sacrifice her privileges – and, more harshly, her income. Money was almost certainly a factor in Margaret's decision to renounce her lover. Townsend only had his civil service pay as an air attaché, on which he was supporting the two sons from his first marriage. Moreover, as a divorcée, Princess Margaret would not have been entitled to be invited into any of the Queen's palaces, to step onto the royal lawn at Ascot, or to go aboard the royal yacht.

And yet, when she finally made her choice – over a weekend that must have caused much heart-searching – that she would renounce Townsend, there was something touching and vulnerable about it, especially since the Princess claimed that she had reached her decision alone. 'Mindful of the Church's teaching that Christian marriage is indissoluble, and conscious of my duty to the Commonwealth, I have resolved to put these considerations before any others,' she said in a young, brave voice.[36]

Princess Margaret was, at this stage in her life, sincerely religious. She and Peter Townsend shared a sense of faith and had gone to church together: she was sometimes drawn to Anglo-Catholicism, and was seen attending a well-known high church in London's West End. Lady Glenconner, Margaret's close friend, claimed that it really was religious belief that swayed the decision for the Princess.[37]

The principal Irish newspapers reported Margaret's decision in a factual manner, without resort to comment – and, indeed, with a Republican austerity that would be inconceivable today. There was an evident feeling that this was not Ireland's business. The newspaper reports concentrated on the reaction – not altogether beguiling – of the Archbishop of Canterbury, Geoffrey Fisher, who seemed triumphant that the Church had won the day, and thanked the Holy Spirit for prevailing.

Five years later, when Margaret married Anthony Armstrong-Jones in 1960, I was a 16-year-old pupil at a convent school in Dublin. The mistress of studies, the practical and sensible Mother Margaret Mary – a wealthy farmer's daughter who made a considerable sacrifice in taking the veil, as her dowry would have attracted the cream of suitors – gave a group of us senior girls a talk on the theme of the Princess' decision. Within the decorous phraseology of the time, she addressed the question of the moral temptations for young women in the world of 1960. 'Princess Margaret is getting married tomorrow', she said, 'and she will be happy in her marriage because she has been *good*.' By this, we knew she intended us to understand that the Princess had renounced a divorced man. We also believed, somehow, that Princess Margaret entered her radiant marriage as a virgin. After all, she was dressed in white: and only virgins were entitled to wear white on their wedding day.

But how dangerous it is to make premature moral assumptions! Princess Margaret did not turn out to be at all happy, and her renunciation of Peter Townsend rankled until the end of her life. The marriage to Snowdon ended in divorce, after much bickering, and – as a subsequent biography of Snowdon has disclosed – much private humiliation. Subsequent biographical studies have not portrayed Princess Margaret as someone 'good', in the nun's sense.

Yet it was significant that Mother Margaret Mary had chosen Margaret's wedding day to speak about love and marriage. Once again, a royal narrative was, in the Irish Republic, an occasion for discussing aspects of personal life, sexual mores, health or morality. The morning after the Princess' wedding, a group of us schoolgirls sat around in the convent garden, with the mayflower, giggling and exclaiming: 'Now she *knows* what "it" is like! Now she's *done* "it".' It says a lot about our ignorance – or innocence – about sex, and the strange sense of wonder with which we regarded the conjugal act, that it never occurred to any of us that the Princess might have crossed that frontier well before her wedding night.

In 1956 the next Irish Ambassador, Con Cremin, presented his credentials to Queen Elizabeth in cordial circumstances. There was a brief audience afterwards, and the Queen strolled over to a balcony overlooking the lawn of Buckingham Palace. The Venezualan Ambassador, who had been with her the previous day, had remarked on how green the grass was. The Queen turned to the Irish Ambassador and said Ireland, the famous 'Emerald Isle', must be just like that.[38]

It might have been Mr Cremin's cue to reply, 'You must come and visit some time,' but he said nothing. When the Queen added, 'Ireland must be very beautiful,' he simply took it that the audience was now concluded.

He was correct not to issue any such invitation at that time – it would not have been his place to do so anyway. Feelings about

Partition were still inflammatory in the Irish Republic, and only the previous autumn a Union flag – fluttering among a collection of international flags – had been torn down at a dance organised for international Catholic students in Dublin. A typical student was quoted as saying, 'Nowhere in the world where Britain was in occupation would students tolerate a display of the Union Jack in such circumstances.'[39]

Queen Elizabeth continued to visit Northern Ireland, with and without Prince Philip, but such visits were visibly confined to the northern state, and hedged about with security restrictions. Some Nationalists have claimed that a royal visit at this period was generally an excuse to lock up anyone with either Catholic or Nationalist connections, since such persons were, by definition, a security risk. Elizabeth's visits therefore served to reinforce the Queen's image as 'Queen of Ulster Unionism', rather than an inclusive monarch for both communities in the North of Ireland.

And yet, despite Elizabeth being presented as the Queen of Ulster Unionists and not of Ulster Catholics, there were Roman Catholics – and even moderate Nationalists – in the province who liked and admired the monarchy. Surprisingly, Nell McCafferty, feminist and radical Derrywoman, recalls the Queen's early visits to the North quite warmly. 'We thought she was wonderful. We were only disappointed that she didn't wear a crown! We wanted to see a Queen in a crown!'

My mother's oldest friend (from her home town of Galway) was married to an Ulster Catholic, and practised dentistry in Banbridge, Co Down, in those days a hotbed of Unionism and, regrettably, some fairly bigoted attitudes. The daughter of this eminently respectable and politically discreet household – also called Margaret – had to pass through a taunting gang of schoolgirls shouting 'Fenian bitch! Fenian bitch!', on her daily route to her utterly respectable convent school. She was totally bewildered as a young schoolgirl, as she had never heard her parents allude to politics. (She only found out later that her upright and correct parents, Mr and Mrs Byrne, a lawyer and a dentist respectively, were never permitted to purchase their house in Banbridge because they were Catholic: each attempt to acquire property was mysteriously obstructed.) Finally, Margaret had to be sent to a boarding school in Dublin to avoid such bullying, to which the Banbridge Unionist authorities had turned a blind eye.

And yet when the Banbridge family came south to visit us, one of the treats they brought were magazines and special-issue picture-books illustrating the magical world of Buckingham Palace, adorned with the radiant photograph of the happy young Queen, in ermine and sapphires, wearing a diamond crown, and waving from a state coach. We pored over these pictures, and imagined the life of the Queen, the Queen Mother, Princess Margaret, and (very much in the background) the male members of the family. As little girls, Margaret Byrne and I even played out little dramas in which the Queen Mother and her two royal daughters starred: I seem to remember that sibling rivalry and other family narratives were a central feature of this home-made soap opera.

It was not just the glamour and family dynamics that drew us to this royal story: I think there was also an element of a matri-archy. The Catholic Church certainly provided us with the enchantment of religious processions on holy days, and the beauty of ritual with Latin Masses and Benedictions: but it lacked women in ermine and sapphires; and it lacked dynasty, and romantic stories about who would marry whom, and with what consequences.

Among Northern Irish Catholics, as in the south, there was ambivalence towards the British royals: sometimes (still) even sharp hostility. But there are always shades and nuances of opinion. Martina Devlin, the novelist and journalist from Omagh, describes this as a 'Jekyll and Hyde' approach: her father, an Ulster Catholic, was all for 'abolition and exile' of the monarchy. While her mother, admittedly originally from the south of Ireland, 'dreamed of the day she might curtsey to the Queen. Whenever a royal news item featured on TV, she'd insist the volume be turned up. He'd threaten to switch off – but he always gave in to her.'

'She drew the line at tea towels with the Queen's face on them, but the house was awash with glossy magazines and books about the monarchy. They sat – surprisingly easily – alongside Fenian songbooks and biographies of Collins and de Valera. Goodness knows what visitors made of the mix.'[40] Some visitors were probably used to this quite common pairing of the icons of Irish Republicanism alongside the celebrity pictures of the royals.

Other Irish Republicans sometimes kept mementoes of the monarchy for more cynical reasons. Elizabeth McCluskey, who grew up in the Fermanagh–Monaghan border region – always a strong area of Republicanism – recalls her mother keeping a coronation tea caddie in case a show of 'loyalty' was required by police or military searches. She also recalls the sweets distributed to the children in Northern Ireland on Coronation Day in 1953. There was, of course, disapproval from the Fermanagh Nationalists that Catholic children should accept royal treats. But strangely from the southern side of the border came quite a different reaction, 'Aren't you steeped in luck?', cried the Monaghan neighbours.[41]

*

In August 1957 a peer, Lord Altrincham (the author, John Grigg, whose father had been a secretary to King George V), issued a devastating critique of Queen Elizabeth, attacking her voice, her manner, and, above all, the 'tweedy entourage' of the royal officials. The sentiments put in her mouth were those of 'a priggish schoolgirl, captain of the hockey team, a prefect and a recent candidate for confirmation'.[42] It was a long time before Altrincham was forgiven in certain quarters: he was physically assaulted by an Empire Loyalist for his ungallantry, and Altrincham in Cheshire withdrew the town's name from his title. It took an even longer time before the 'tweedy entourage' began to rethink the issues raised.

Altrincham's commentary was intended, he said afterwards, to be helpful: but it seemed a very personal judgement on Queen Elizabeth. It was not the first time such remarks had been aired.

Monarchy and Republic: Parity of Esteem?

In 1952 the left-wing *New Statesman* had lambasted the monarch as the apex of an outdated system of landed aristocracy, and described the court entourage as 'the gang of costly and largely parasitic hangers-on whose interest is to perpetuate the starchy protocol of the court and the far-reaching symbolism of master and man.' Malcom Muggeridge, in radical voice, had also dismissed the monarch as 'dowdy, frumpish and banal', and the royal family a mere 'soap opera'. But such critiques were regarded as embittered socialist tripe when coming from left-wing sources. They were usually reported and repeated in the *Irish Press*, but not directly commented upon.

However Altrincham was a peer of the realm, his father had been part of the royal circle, and that was more shocking to the Establishment. The palace officials themselves made a point of ignoring it, but the proverbial 'storm of abuse' descended on his head and continued for some time. In Dublin my aunty Dorothy, who had loved the 1953 coronation, called the young peer (as he then was) a 'jumped-up young brat'.

Yet although perhaps not gracefully phrased, Altrincham's thesis was apposite. He had described the adulation accorded to the monarchy after the Second World War as 'something uncomfortably akin to Japanese Shintoism': in other words, regarding a sovereign as a kind of god. He also felt that the 'blandness and servility' of public attitudes towards the monarchy were 'quite alien to the British tradition', and thought there had been a lot of silly talk about 'a new Elizabethan age', when it was evident that Elizabeth II bore no political or cultural resemblance to her predecessor.

Altrincham's attack on the Queen, although greeted with such noises of horror at the time, was in fact a foretaste of the more critical attitude towards monarchy that would develop at a later period.

The very deferential attitude to the royal family in Britain (as to religion in Ireland) would pass, if not quite yet. The two major political events of 1956 – Britain and France's failed operation in Suez, and the USSR's distressing invasion of Hungary – signalled the crumbling of empire: Britain (and France) were no longer effective colonial powers, while Moscow's assault on Budapest triggered the gradual disillusionment of western intellectuals with the Russian Communist Party.

It is possible that there might have been more rapprochement between Ireland, north and south, and thus (in the larger picture) between Crown and Shamrock in the middle 1950s. John Costello, as Taoiseach in 1955, indicated that he was open to north–south talks, and Belfast indicated willingness also, provided that partition was not discussed. The matter ended there, but at least the idea had been mooted.[43]

But then, in 1956, the IRA once again opened hostilities against the northern state with a 'border campaign' of violence. And although such assaults on the North were pointless and self-defeating, still, the romanticism of self-defeating gestures could reach into something fatalistically self-sacrificing in the Irish psyche.[44] Ballads were written about Seán South of Garryowen – the Limerick man who led one of the border raids – and Fergus O'Hanlon, the 17-year-old IRA recruit who bled to death alone in an abandoned border cottage after yet another abortive effort to blow up an RUC barracks in the northern state. The ballad written about O'Hanlon, 'The Patriot Game', was to be sung in many a pub session over the next thirty years, and was a rousing background flavour to my youthful years.[45]

The IRA 'war' against Northern Ireland would continue from 1956 until 1962, and any reconciliation between Crown and Shamrock seemed a long way off. Although 'The Patriot Game' can be analysed as a sardonic denunciation of the way patriotism is manipulated, nonetheless I have often heard it sung as a mournful tribute to young men like O'Hanlon, and the lines 'I've learned all my life / Cruel England to blame' summed up rather well the political analysis of those caught up in this fatal game.

I turned 14 in 1958 and sensed the opening up of a new world – a world utterly changed from that of our parents, which we considered unique, just as every generation before us had similarly believed. This was indicated to us when the nuns at our convent school showed great excitement over the election of a new pope, John XXIII.

Whereas Pius XII, Eugenio Pacelli, had seemed aristocratic and remote (and, with his small round spectacles, like an Italian version of Mr de Valera), the new Pope was hailed as an entirely fresh phenomenon. John XXIII's relatively short pontificate would have a huge impact on Irish values – nuns, for example, discarded their seventeenth-century habits, which were crushingly repressive, from bosom-flattening bodice to chin-irritating wimple.

Values and political attitudes were changing anyway: finally Éamon de Valera was eased out of direct political power, and moved to the Presidency of the Republic, theoretically then (and much more so now) a non-political role. Seán Lemass, who had been kept waiting for at least twenty years, became Taoiseach in 1959 with an agenda of economic modernisation: what the new Vaticanologists called *aggiornamento*. This was a prelude to changing attitudes towards the monarch Ireland had regarded as truly legitimate – the Pope.

Yet in terms of values, Catholics and Protestants in Ireland were not that far apart. In the summer of 1960 I left school, aged 16, and (as was the practice in those days) was instructed by my family to go out and earn my keep. I worked first as a waitress in a lovely little restaurant on St Stephens Green called The Country Shop, run by the Irish Countrywomen's Association, which was, in its own brisk way, a progressive force. There was a tradition of Protestant young ladies from good families waitressing at The Country Shop, and I became friendly with a girl from Tyrrellspass in Co Westmeath.

She had been to London the previous summer, which was considered an exciting adventure at the time. But my! (She exclaimed in an astonished voice.) The English were so *forward* and so *indelicate* about private matters. She had been shocked to see *Evening Standard* vans buzzing about the West End – she was asking a policeman for directions to the Apollo Theatre at the time – with huge banners unblushingly proclaiming: 'The Queen – A Baby.'

Worse, in buses, at the tops of their voices, London girls were talking quite uninhibitedly about the Queen being 'preggers'. I listened with awestruck attention to this account of strident modernity: the Protestant girl from Co Westmeath had been brought up with exactly the same reticence about such matters as Catholic convent girls.

And indeed, reporting on the Queen's later pregnancies did signal a social change: the women's magazines had seldom used the word 'pregnant' until then – the acceptable phrase had been 'expecting a baby', or even the more euphemistic, if anthropo-logically quite subtle, 'in the family way'. A woman giving birth is usually contributing to the foundation of a family.

Queen Elizabeth, now in her thirties, was indeed expecting a baby (Prince Andrew) to be born in 1960. Andrew was the child she was 'determined to have', despite (it is implied) Prince Philip's inclination to stop at two. It has been claimed that Andrew is the Queen's favourite child, though how anyone can suppose such a thing is not clarified. In 1964 her fourth baby, Edward, would appear. By then decorum had been thrown to the winds. It will be recalled that sex was only invented in 1963: it was invented by the Beatles; by public discussion on the contraceptive pill; and, most pointedly, by the very open and (to the public) hugely enjoyable sexual scandal involving Her Majesty's defence minister, Sir John Profumo, and good-time girls Christine Keeler and Mandy Rice-Davies.

In 1961 a surprising and (to us) thrilling royal occasion occurred in the Irish Republic. There came a state visit by the most alluring princess we had ever seen: Her Serene Highness, Princess Grace of Monaco. She was not, of course, British royalty, but it was aston-ishing how proud the Irish were of Princess Grace's rank. The newspapers proudly trumpeted that she was 'the most titled woman in Europe', being 'twice a princess, four times a duchess, twice a marquise, eight times a countess, and five times a baroness'.

'All Ireland', wrote the *Irish Independent*, 'today greets two distinguished visitors, Their Serene Highnesses the Prince and Princess of Monaco. We join with Church and State and people in extending to them a sincere welcome.' There were many references to Grace's 'fairy tale life', along with the 'deep claims of race' that she had with her fellow Irish.[46]

She looked happy, beautiful and radiant, if sometimes a little overwhelmed by the huge crowds who lined the streets to greet her. Some 75,000 people waited to wave to her in the streets of Dublin, and there was such a jostling crush outside the Gresham Hotel when she stood on the balcony that – to her distress – more than a dozen people were injured.

Grace was compared to President Jack Kennedy, who also came of Irish emigrant stock, and who had made a fabulous visit to Ireland in 1963, greeted as 'one of our own'. He had been elected in 1960 as the first Catholic to get to the White House. But Kennedy represented more than the golden 'Camelot' of legend; he was seen, in Ireland, as the symbol of a 'risen people' – not in the sense of insurrection, but of resurrection – of a real Irish recovery from more than a hundred years of woe and want.

If Jack Kennedy had proved that an Irish Catholic *could* get to the White House (his religion and background were considered a serious issue during his election), Princess Grace represented old royalty in a new light, and her visit illuminated the needy public response to the allure that royalty still held. She was the first princess to visit Ireland on an official visit since the foundation of the state; and her visit may well have paved the way for that of another princess.

In May 1960, as already mentioned, Princess Margaret had married the photographer, Anthony Armstrong-Jones. In London the engagement had been greeted with mixed feelings. The novelist Kingsley Amis described Armstrong-Jones as 'a dog-faced, tight-jeaned, fotog of fruitarian tastes'.[47] But in Ireland Armstrong-Jones' Irish links were significant: he was the son, by an earlier marriage, of the Countess of Rosse, chatelaine of Birr Castle, Co Offaly.

The Earldom of Rosse was bestowed upon the Parsons family in the seventeenth century. Biographical details in early twentieth-century editions of *Who's Who* stress that the second earl spoke out against the Union in 1801. The third earl built the famous telescope, which can still be seen at Birr Castle. The family remains one of the most successful of the old gentry class who stayed on in Ireland after independence, adapted to the new Irish state, and went on improving their demesne to the greater service of heritage and education.

Annie, Countess of Rosse (née Messel), had been married briefly to a lawyer, Ronald Armstrong-Jones, and into this marriage was born Anthony. The marriage did not endure and Mrs Armstrong-Jones went on to marry the 6th Lord Rosse, and to have another family (their eldest son being Brendan, the present and seventh earl). Tony Armstrong-Jones grew up with the strong impression that he was an unwanted child: his mother referred to him as 'my ugly son'.[48]

As a schoolboy in the 1940s, he would travel back and forth to Ireland on the old mailboat that ploughed unsteadily between Holyhead and Dún Laoghaire, rocked by the choppy waters, and often odorous with the smell of seasick. From Dublin he would make his way to Birr. The Ireland of his childhood and youth is a country now long gone: he remembers, chiefly, quaint donkeys and children with bare feet and the curl of the turf fire rising from a cottage on the hill.[49]

And though his mother often treated him coldly, it was at Birr that he discovered his vocation. The castle had a pioneering Victorian photography studio and darkroom, bequeathed by a nineteenth-century countess, Mary Parsons, herself an acclaimed photographer. Tony's Eton reports had been dismal concerning any academic gifts, but this studio fascinated him and helped to develop his talents.

So it was natural that soon after their wedding in May 1960 Tony Armstrong-Jones – now Lord Snowdon – would take his bride to Ireland. That first visit was kept very quiet although the couple did manage a drinks session in Dublin with Brendan Behan, at which Behan told a racy anecdote that amused the

Snowdons (though it rather shocked Lady de Vesci, Tony Snowdon's half-sister).

Behan saw a priest passing by on a bicycle and said he knew the cleric. 'Says I to him, "Father, what'll you give me for a penance if I told you I fucked your fucking sister-in-law?" "So," says he to me, "well Brendan, just so long as you didn't fuck my fucking brother-in-law."' At this point the usually abstemious Lady de Vesci said, 'I think I'll have a large gin and tonic.' Princess Margaret thought Brendan Behan 'hilarious' — ironic, in that Behan had made his name as an indirect consequence of having been in the IRA.[50]

But it was the second visit, in January 1965, which made a public splash. The couple arrived at Dublin Airport on a cold January day, the Princess wearing a mink hat and camel-hair coat: hundreds of people (who, it was noted, had braved the bitter cold) cheered as she descended the steps of the Aer Lingus Vickers Viscount, the St Gall. The Princess smiled in response and entered the chauffeured car awaiting her.[51]

Also awaiting her was a protest by (it was presumed) Sinn Féin–IRA: trees had been deliberately felled on the expected route to Birr. But 150 Garda detectives soon cleared the way. There had also been protest meetings in Dublin and Abbeyleix objecting to the visit.

But, from the Snowdons' point of view, they felt that everything went wonderfully well. Margaret, says Lord Snowdon, 'loved Ireland'. She greatly enjoyed Birr Castle and its surroundings, and in general met with a kindly welcome. She socialised with the de Vescis, Desmond and Mariga Guinness, the Earl and Countess Mountcharles of Slane, the Marquess of Hamilton, Sir Alfred Beit, and Roddy More O'Ferrall, among others. There was a pleasingly comical episode when Queen Elizabeth made an attempt to telephone her sister at Birr Castle, but by some mishap got through to Dooley's Hotel in Birr town, where she found herself in communication with the local *Daily Express* correspondent.

The IRA also made an attempt to cut off the electricity to Birr Castle, but only succeeded in bringing a blackout, briefly, to the town, since the Castle had its own generator. As the

Snowdons were leaving Ireland, six days later, Margaret said 'we will always be coming back to Birr and Abbeyleix'. Asked about an explosion that had taken place in the vicinity, she laughed and said: 'We were not at all upset.'

At Dublin Airport there were waves of applause as the Snowdons' car moved along the approach. As they alighted, the couple were mobbed by a crowd of well-wishers, who shouted out 'come back again soon' – almost the exact words heard by Queen Victoria as she departed the shores of Ireland – and 'bring your mother and sister with you!'

Nine men were charged with damaging the trees and 'unlawful assembly'. They represented that minority of hardline Republicans who always had been (and perhaps always will be) opposed to anything associated with British royalty. The newspaper columns articulated some of their discontents: 'Would members of the British royal family have the courtesy to refrain from visiting a country which has suffered, and is still suffering, under their rule for centuries and spare us the protests which are made against such visits and the penalties which are incurred because of them?', wrote one M. Rodgers of 73 St Lawrence Road, Dublin 3.

A Micheal O Coisdealbh from Kimmage wrote to upbraid *The Irish Times* for an editorial saying that 'British Royalty are welcome here and will be so treated'. In response he wrote:

> I am appalled at such a statement. This sundered island may have side-stepped some of the memories of its patriot dead in the rat-race of materialism, but while British money continues to bolster the economy of the Six Counties and while British troops continue to occupy the North against the oft-stated wishes of the majority of the Irish people, British Royalty cannot be and never will be, welcome here.[52]

Even more alarmed, however, were those correspondents who worried that 'patriotic sentiment' was growing scarce in the Twenty-Six Counties, and that 'so engrossed are the Twenty-Six

County people in the "rat-race of materialism" that Queen Elizabeth, Mao Tse-tung and the devil himself might safely make a joint visit without provoking a protest of any consequence.' Con Lehane wondered if the normalisation of relations with Britain simply meant that Ireland was being re-integrated into the British economy? Was this what Mr Lemass had in mind? Indeed, Seán Lemass was to sign an Anglo-Irish Free Trade Treaty in 1965 (considered by economists as an enlightened step forward), and would even have an historic, well-publicised lunch date with the Prime Minister of Northern Ireland, Mr Terence O'Neill.

For many younger people Princess Margaret and Lord Snowdon represented not the Britain of old tradition, nor even the political mood music for Anglo-Irish trade treaties, but the new 'Swinging Sixties' Britain. Why, the Snowdons were friends with Peter Sellers and Peter Cook. Cool! Hip!

Coincidentally, the other visitors from across the water who came to Dublin in January 1965 were the Rolling Stones: this was what England represented now. And it was precisely what Kingsley Amis disliked about the Snowdons – that they were 'such a symbol of the age we live in … a royal princess famed for her devotion to all that is most vapid and mindless in the world of entertainment.' But it was also part of the times which were a-changing.[53]

The anxiety that issues like partition might be forgotten in the more 'materialistic' Ireland was well founded. A more 'material-istic' – that is to say, prosperous – Ireland would indeed take the focus off Partition. And that was just what Seán Lemass had in mind. The 'sore thumb' policy simply had not worked, and, like the characters in Aesop's fable about the sun and the wind, perhaps it was time to try a little sunshine. *An Tostal*, moreover, had not been barking up the wrong tree: tourism was an important source of revenue and of social change. Irish people were also travelling abroad more for their holidays.

Optimistic economists were claiming that eventual entry into the European Economic Community (Ireland first applied to join in 1961) would itself 'solve' the problem of Partition, especially since the United Kingdom and Ireland would enter the Common Market in tandem. The Anglo-Irish Free Trade area Agreement, signed by Seán Lemass and Harold Wilson in December 1965, did indeed create a common trade area between the two countries.

The formal meetings of Seán Lemass and Terence O'Neill seemed to make progress towards addressing the Partition problem through friendly contacts. Captain O'Neill's mother had come from a tradition of Irish Home Rulers, and, having lost his father during the First World War, his mother's influence was the greater.[54] I was, by this time, working as a reporter on the London *Evening Standard* and the Editor was convinced that the Lemass–O'Neill meetings had 'cracked' the problem of Ireland's alienation from Britain. Alas, matters regarding the North of Ireland are never that simple, and optimism is often misplaced: a year later P. J. Gormley, MP, was still announcing 'the beginning of the end of Partition'.[55]

But O'Neill was suspect among grass roots Ulster Unionists precisely *because* his mother had been a Liberal Home Ruler and his patrician background (Eton and Irish Guards) did not betoken a visceral commitment to the Orange Order. And then Lemass, in 1965, was already preparing for one of the most influential national events of his premiership – the 50th anniversary commemorating 1916, which would fall in 1966.

Every modern nation needs a founding narrative, whether in the style of the Icelandic sagas or Mandela's 'long walk' in South Africa. And that was the aim of many in Dublin who planned the 50th anniversary of the 1916 Rising. There were still men alive who had taken part in it: Lemass himself had not only been active in 1916, but had lost a much-loved brother in the civil war. He was keen to use the 1916 commemorations as an opportunity to 'modernise' Ireland: to underline his ambitions for prosperity in the south, and more co-operation with the North. And yet a great opportunity was missed to give the 1916 commemorations a broader base by including the 150,000 Irishmen who had fought for the Western Allies under the Crown in 1914–18.

Although progressive church leaders were keen on 'ecumenism' at the time (as were most ordinary Irish Catholics, who experienced a rush of kindness and fellow-feeling for their Protestant compatriots in the early 1960s[56]), the Irish state failed to insist, as it certainly should have done, on an ecumenical service to mark the 1916 Jubilee. In fact the draconian Archbishop of Dublin, Dr McQuaid, actually refused to share a blessing service with clergy of other faiths, and a golden opportunity to demonstrate tolerance and inclusivity was missed by allowing Dr McQuaid his unilateral terms.[57]

The 1966 celebrations for 1916 started off with a bang: in the early hours of 8 March, the IRA daringly blew up Nelson's Pillar in O'Connell Street, Dublin. My recollection of this event is that it was considered hilarious: it showed how clever the IRA were, in that they could effect such an operation without a single flesh wound to a living person.

We Dubliners had been fond of 'the Pillar' (as the wonderful song associated with Ronnie Drew illuminates[58]), which offered a unique view of the city if you paid sixpence and climbed up its more than three hundred steps in the interior of the Doric column, erected in 1801.

Earlier, in the 1920s and 1930s, there had been a suggestion that Nelson's Pillar might be replaced with a statue of St Patrick. Patrick would surely have been an acceptable candidate – and the most ecumenical too, since all the Irish churches accepted that Patrick evangelised Ireland and his cultural legacy included the significance of the shamrock. Had Plan Patrick been carried out, it is unlikely that the Pillar would have been attacked.

In the 1970s, there was a proposal to fill the empty space of the vanished Pillar with a smaller monument to Patrick Pearse, but it was eventually (and mysteriously) turned down by the city authorities, after its designer, Garry Trimble, was killed in a car crash.[59] Eventually, after an experiment with 'the Floosey in the Jacuzzi' (a Molly Malone in a kind of bathing fountain, which accumulated much debris), the Spire was erected in the centre of O'Connell Street, causing Dubliners to jest darkly that a giant heroin needle was a perfect visual metaphor for the troubled inner city.

However the destruction of the Pillar did amplify something about the 1966 celebrations, which would have the effect of reviving strong feelings of Irish nationalism. The suggested rapprochement with Northern Ireland was brought to naught as the flame of Irish separatism once again burned bright. Some writers have suggested that the official 1916 celebrations triggered the turbulence that followed in the North of Ireland. 'There is an awful logic in the proposition that if a small band of men and women could bring Britain to its knees in the years between 1916 and 1921,' wrote Peter Somerville-Large, 'why should it not happen again?' Conor Cruise O'Brien also wrote that celebrating 1916 in 1966 – and the way it was done – was bound to put the idea of 'violence, applied by a determined minority' into the heads of young activists.[60]

Historians such as Mary Daly challenge the claim that the 1916 Jubilee revived not only Irish nationalism, but also brought new recruits to the IRA. During the 1966 celebrations, there was more cooperation than ever between the British and Irish governments: Harold Wilson's administration was perhaps more pro-Irish than any London government had ever been. In a gesture of reconciliation, London returned to Dublin the green flag that had flown over the GPO in 1916, and had been retained at the Imperial War Museum.[61] And Roy Jenkins, the liberalising Home Secretary and biographer of Asquith, finally agreed to return the remains of Roger Casement to Dublin, something that Éamon de Valera had asked successive British administrations to do, without success.[62]

*

In July 1966 Queen Elizabeth paid a visit to Northern Ireland that, by the measure of later trips, seemed reasonably well received and lacking in tension. The entire schedule of the visit – each and every move the monarch would make – was published openly in advance and security was routine, but light.

True, a missile (described as a 'cement block bottle') was hurled at the Queen's car as she made to open the new Lagan Bridge named after her: a 17-year-old youth and a 44-year-old waitress from Salford and Lancashire respectively were subsequently charged with chucking the item, which did little damage. The youth, John Francis Morgan, said he just wanted to make some sort of protest, he did not wish to harm anyone, and the older woman was revealed to have a history of mental disturbance. Otherwise, the Queen's visit was reported benignly and her speech about moving forward to prosperity and mutual understanding was uncontroversial.[63]

Even her address at Queen's University commemorating the Somme was not the cause of much remark:

> For many throughout Northern Ireland, July 1 1916 was a day of bereavement. We should now remember it – with sadness, but also with pride – and pay a tribute to all who fell, and express our sympathy to the families who suffered loss. And at the same time it will be an occasion on which to rededicate ourselves to the cause of peace.[64]

It was a speech that her grandfather, George V, could have made: and indeed did make, saying that the losses of war should teach us about peace.

The Somme had not yet become an iconic date for Orangemen – or at least not *such* an iconic date. That only occurred as Ulster Loyalists gradually responded to the Republican celebrations of 1916.

Two days after Elizabeth spoke at the university, Cardinal Conway, the Catholic Primate, and Archbishop McCann, his Church of Ireland counterpart, received honorary degrees at Queen's University, and the Queen Mother made a visit to Omagh. This was one of the first really visible efforts made by the Stormont administration to show more 'inclusivity' towards Catholics. In a way, these years between 1964 and 1968 seemed to herald better times all round, and better times usually meant better Anglo-Irish relations.

Yet the Lemass–O'Neill meetings, which promised more co-operation and progress, also evoked ancestral voices.

As has been described many times, in many fine texts, the events in Northern Ireland began with a high-minded campaign for civil rights – which actually started at Caledon in Tyrone, the home ground of Earl Alexander of Tunis who had been the unwitting midwife to the 1948 declaration of the Republic. The struggle for civil rights seemed to indicate a move away from the sterile debates about partition: they were about equality of oppor-tunity within Northern Ireland.

But it all developed in an unforeseen way, and by the early 1970s the North was plunged into a cycle of violence coming from all sides. In 1963 someone had said that 'Anglo-Irish relations are at their best ever'. By January 1972 and the notorious 'Bloody Sunday' – when a paratroop regiment opened fire on unarmed Nationalists in Derry, killing 13 (one victim died later from injuries, which made it 14) – they had plunged to a new low.

The British Embassy in Dublin was burned down by an enraged crowd, as a payback for Bloody Sunday, and in middle-class south Dublin, glasses of champagne were lifted in celebration. 'To this day', wrote Peter Taylor in 1997, 'it is difficult to convince nationalists in the city [of Derry] that the killing of their fellow citizens was anything other than pre-meditated murder by the army, authorised by Stormont and the British Government.'[65]

During the 1970s Anglo-Irish relations were often pretty grim: at one point, Prime Minister Heath considered imposing sanctions on the Republic of Ireland, introducing identity cards for Irish people in England and freezing Irish sterling assets. And yet there were periods when cooperation seemed to move forward: the Sunningdale Conference of 1973 involved Dublin, and London, and the main democratic parties in Northern Ireland, and, even if it failed (in May 1974, under pressure from Unionist workers) the Irish government had established a good relationship with Ted Heath. Heath's own attitude to Ireland became much more positive after this experience.[66]

Like a lot of Irish people, I blew hot and cold over the whole question of the North: I felt by turns patriotically Irish and sympathetically Republican – and exultant when Stormont, symbol of partition, was abolished by Prime Minister Heath in 1972. I thought the Loyalist terrorists as much – maybe more – responsible for the overall deterioration of the situation during the 1970s.

All through the decade, the Troubles in the North of Ireland went on, with the Provisional and Official IRA, and INLA (Irish National Liberation Army) mounting a terrorist – or guerrilla, depending on your viewpoint – war against the northern state and the 'Brits' (who were now in charge of it, having replaced Stormont with direct rule): and Loyalist terrorists answering atrocity with atrocity.

When Queen Elizabeth visited Northern Ireland in 1977 for her Jubilee year, the parlous condition of Anglo-Irish relations was evident. This would be payback time for Bloody Sunday.

The Queen and Prince Philip could now only set foot in Northern Ireland surrounded by a formidable ring of steel. There were 32,000 troops – headed by the crack Spearhead Battalion specially flown in from England – engaged to protect the royal pair. It was 'possibly the biggest on-the-ground show of strength by the Security Forces ever seen in the North of Ireland'.[67]

The visit, moreover, coincided with the anniversary of internment without trial. The peace-making SDLP politician, John Hume, called the timing 'insensitive'. 'Buckingham Palace should have been reminded that August is a wicked month in this part of Ireland,' he said.[68] Ten people had been charged with 23 murders in the previous fortnight. Gerry Fitt (who would later accept a seat in the House of Lords) refused to attend a Hillsborough garden party for the Queen.

Queen Elizabeth and her family had been faced, in the past, with detachment, aloofness or even sullen withdrawal on the part of the Catholic, Nationalist population, but this time the Provisional IRA was visibly on the offensive. They announced that a 'Black Flag' march would take place from Andersonstown to Belfast City Hall 'in honour of Ireland's dead'.

The 'Relatives Action Committee' – a lobby representing Republican prisoners, largely composed of battleaxe mammies and grannies who were sometimes said to be fiercer than the Provos themselves – issued a statement saying 'We reject British rule in Ireland. We abhor the presence of the British Queen in our country. We call on all the Republican people of Belfast, all other anti-Imperialist groups and all other individuals and groups who resent the presence of the British Queen to support this March to the City Centre.'

Roy Mason, the Northern Ireland Secretary and one of the toughest politicians ever to take the job, considered cancelling the visit, but it seems that the Queen herself insisted on carrying on regardless. She told her private secretary, Martin Charteris, who had passed on Mr Mason's misgivings, 'Martin, we said we were going to Ulster and it would be a great pity not to.'[69]

Elizabeth arrived with Philip on August 10, on board the yacht *Britannia*, which she used to entertain the women who had started the Peace People, Mairead Corrigan and Betty Williams. All three women looked cordial in the photograph, but Mairead Corrigan would have been one of the very few Catholics that Her Majesty encountered at close quarters. Subsequently Betty Williams (who came from a Unionist tradition) was criticised for referring to the Queen as 'Our Sovereign Lady'.

The demonstrations against the monarch certainly were cor-uscating. A crowd of 3,000 marched down the Falls Road in Belfast carrying placards saying 'ER Queen of Death', showing a crown atop a grinning skull. A child carried a poster saying 'Queeny, Queeny, Who's Got the Bomb?' A mock Queen was sentenced to death in a Provisional Sinn Féin Rally. There were other posters and placards with hostile, if less gruesome, messages: 'Will Lizzie Visit H-Block?' (where internees were held); and 'Stuff the Jubilee'. Black flags mingled with tricolours in the Catholic and Nationalist areas.

The Queen solidly went on with her programme, wearing 'Kelly green' and smiling through. She was, of course, welcomed by official Ulster and the Unionist and Loyalist public, and Philip was a hit with the Harland and Wolff workers – his salty and sometimes robust humour has always gone down well with men, it being an appealing counterpoint to the feminine allure of royalty.

But it must have been the most trying part of a Jubilee that was otherwise hailed as a great popular success. The *Irish Independent* in Dublin (traditionally moderate in its politics, never Anglophobe, and never supportive of Provisional Sinn Féin) condemned Queen Elizabeth for setting foot in the North of Ireland.'The British Queen's visit to the North is one of the most unwelcome arrangements that the inoffensive woman has ever agreed to,' it editorialised.

It is clear that the paper was echoing some public nervousness that an attempt might be made on her life, which would certainly have been disastrous for Ireland's reputation globally: surely, the editorial suggested, even the Provos would have the sense not to contemplate such an idea – the monarch was a 'symbol' of rule and not its executor.

They hoped that the visit would pass off 'with a minimum of incident', but that 'no such visit will ever again be contemplated by the powers that be in London.' Strong words indeed from such a source.[70]

Even *The Irish Times* (once a Unionist newspaper and now liberal) was critical of the visit. That many Irish people would 'welcome or at least be tolerantly indifferent to the visit', it wrote, did not outweigh the possible consequences, which 'the people of the North will have to live with for a long time while the Royal party sails serenely back to base.' The paper went on to suggest that the Jubilee visit had been planned because 'someone stuck a pencil in a calendar at random. Some adjutant or equerry decided to coincide with the grouse season' (which famously begins on 12 August.)[71]

Neither July nor August, it is true, are the most tactful times for a royal visit to the North of Ireland – it is traditionally known as 'the marching season', when Orangemen celebrate their victory over the Papists. But the Queen's schedule had actually been planned two years earlier, in 1975, so it was not a random matter.

In all the controversy about the visit, little enough attention was paid to Queen Elizabeth's speeches. She would not have written them herself (they might even have been written by the Home Secretary), although she may have had some input. But they were constructive – and even prophetic. She called for 'power-sharing', building a better society for the future, and the need for 'friendship and forgiveness' for the common good of the whole community. Not only totally inoffensive to all sections of the community, but broadly describing what would actually happen 25 years later.

Following her 1977 trip the Queen did not return to Northern Ireland for another 14 years. The next visit would be in 1991, and all through the 1990s, whenever she visited, she would never remain for more than 24 hours in the province, and would then be protected by draconian security.

In that late August of 1977, long after the royal yacht had sailed home, there were splash headlines proclaiming: 'The King Is Dead'. But the mourning this time was for Elvis.

It was clear that a great fear prevailed among responsible Irish Nationalists that the IRA (or the more reckless breakaway group, the INLA[72]) would assassinate Queen Elizabeth or a member of her family. In July 1979 the INLA killed, in a car bomb at Westminster, the Conservative politician, Airey Neave, a mentor to Margaret Thatcher, and a veteran who had helped to liberate the Nazi death camps in 1945.

But in August 1979 the IRA indeed targeted a high-profile member of the royal family when they killed Lord Mountbatten (along with his grandson, a young 15-year-old boatman called Paul Maxwell, and, eventually, the Dowager Lady Brabourne who died of subsequent injuries) at Mullaghmore off the Sligo coast. In his diaries, the Labour veteran politician Tony Benn reacted in a somewhat detached manner, rating the killing according to the status of the victim. 'It may have the most tremendous repercussions,' he noted, almost enthusiastically. 'The murder of an international figure, the Supreme Allied Commander in South-

East Asia during the war, a Viceroy of India, a member of the royal family ... is going to make people think again about Northern Ireland. The whole world will discuss this particular event and I think it may be a turning point.'[73]

Although the assassination of Mountbatten might have been seen as another response to Bloody Sunday, the reaction in Ireland – certainly in the 26 counties – was very different from Mr Benn's calculating political analysis. In Dublin, even among the Nationalist papers (perhaps especially among the Nationalist media), the overwhelming response was outrage and shame. The word 'shame' is used over and over again as the pitiful scenes near Classiebawn in Sligo are recounted. 'Mass murder – merciless slaughter.' 'An Outrage! Lynch Condemns Horrors – and Slams the Provos.'[74]

Taoiseach Jack Lynch had immediately contacted Margaret Thatcher with the message: 'I was horrified and saddened at the news of the murder of Earl Mountbatten of Burma at the hands of the Provisional IRA who admitted responsibility'[75]: and President Patrick Hillery sent a message of personal sympathy to the Queen. Cardinal Tomás Ó Fiach – who hailed from Crossmaglen and who had known Republican leanings – condemned the killings with 'horror and revulsion'.

The *Irish Independent* drew quite a different conclusion to that of Tony Benn about the impact: far from this being a 'turning point' that would make people 'think again' about Northern Ireland, the Provisional IRA had *not* put 'the northern problem on the world stage: they have put Ireland in the dock.'[76]

Many condemnations of the tragedy flowed into the newspapers, not only on grounds of compassion, but so many carrying that note of shame that a visitor's trust had been so tragically abused. Cecil A. King of Ballyshannon said that Mountbatten had been a good friend to Ireland: 'I regarded Lord Mountbatten as a man who fell in love with Ireland and the Irish people. He took a very keen interest in Irish history and ten years ago joined the Donegal History Society and has since remained a subscribing member.'

A Sligo artist, Bernard McDonagh, who had painted Mountbatten, called the assassination 'the most tragic event in our history. We lost an ambassador [for Ireland] and we are disgraced before the eyes of the world.'[77]

Dónall MacAmhlaigh, the Irish navvy–writer in England, reported about the sense of Irish unease in Britain 'after atrocities'. There were calls for prayers and vigils and a day of mourning for such 'dastardly murder': Diarmuid O'Donovan of Boyle in Co Roscommon wrote to express 'utter abhorrence of the shameful and cowardly activities carried out in our land and supposedly in our name'. It was felt that 'people in their millions should stand up and be counted on this issue': and, 'if we don't condemn, we condone'. Ireland should use the Pope's visit and 'Christ's presence in our midst' to speak out firmly against the men of violence. The Pope himself would, as it turned out, beg 'on my bended knees', for a turning-away from such violence.

The Nationalist *Irish Press* published only one letter that hinted at justification: Councillor Patrick McCaffrey of Fermanagh District Council complaining of the 'pro-British' voice on RTÉ (identifying Betty Williams of the Peace People, Dr Cahal Daly, and Conor Cruise O'Brien). 'Violence continues,' he wrote, 'because there is an army of occupation in the Six Counties …' Britain must 'unlock her grip' on Ireland: we must live by the words of Pearse – 'Ireland unfree shall never be at peace.'[78] Councillor McCaffrey's voice represented, no doubt, those strong Irish Nationalists and Republicans in the border counties who felt (and will always feel) bitter resentment over the issue of partition.

But it was clear that attitudes had changed in the Twenty-Six Counties: a joint letter from four women in Dublin 14 (Carmelle Clarke, Noirin Slattery, Lorraine Doyle, and Aileen Kehoe) published in the *Irish Press* expressed most articulately what I remember sensing on those August days in Ireland:

> We are sickened and revolted by the senseless murder of Lord Mountbatten, members of his family and the young boatman. It makes us ashamed to be Irish … what kind of people are they who can justify murder and call it patriotism? We ordinary Irish people by our very silence are seen to endorse

> these murders ... We say to the men of violence:'*You
> Do Not Speak for Us. You Do Not Act in Our Name ...
> In the Name of God, Stop Now'*[my italics].[79]

The four women underlined their feelings of frustration, hopelessness and anger.

It was significant that the largely pro-Republican *Irish Press* gave this such play.

Two men were subsequently charged with the Mountbatten killings: Francis McGirl, from a very well known Sinn Féin family in Leitrim, was acquitted on appeal (and later died in a tractor accident); but Thomas McMahon, from South Armagh, was convicted and jailed for 18 years, then released in 1998. McMahon, described as a legend in the IRA, retired into private life as a carpenter. Paul Maxwell's father, John Maxwell (who had spoken poignantly when he had gathered up the shattered remains of his son) now said it was right that his son's killer should be released.[80]

Some historians claim that the Provisional IRA benefited from the murder of a royal like Mountbatten simply because it increased their profile: any publicity is good publicity. More advantage was certainly drawn from the sensational hunger strike, and death, of Bobby Sands in 1981 (after his surprise election to Westminster) and of the 10 IRA men who followed him to the grave.

The self-immolation involved was indeed a world event – Irish politicians were embarrassed to be proudly shown a 'Bobby Sands Street' in locations such as Uzbekistan: but it also showed Provisional Sinn Féin that they could win votes.

Yet the death of Mountbatten, and the innocent people who died with him, was another turning point. So many Irish people I knew (especially those living outside Ireland) felt, as the Dublin 14 quartet of women had put it, that the men of violence did not speak for Ireland. Murdering members of the British royal family was no way to move forward.

It was reported in the United States that Princess Margaret's response to the Mountbatten murder was to say 'the Irish are pigs'. This upset people in Ireland: it is still quoted as an accepted truth – and even without the context of the Mountbatten killing. There was a formal Palace denial that she had made such a remark (although the denial did not seem very plausible: it was claimed that Margaret had *actually* said, 'the Irish dance jigs'); and Tony Snowdon has insisted to me, most emphatically, that 'Princess Margaret never said that about the Irish. Absolutely not.'

*

Mountbatten's assassination prompted fears about the Pope's visit to Ireland, programmed for later in September 1979. Perhaps the trip would now be cancelled? Some commentators thought it should be, and it seems that it was decided to call off a planned trip by the Holy Father north of the border.[81]

But Pope John Paul II did indeed pay a historic visit to the Republic in late September 1979 and, in one way at least, it was extraordinary and memorable. Never before had a living pontiff set foot on Irish soil: before Paul VI it had been unusual, in any case, for popes to travel at all. But on 29 September 1979 a million people converged on the Phoenix Park in Dublin for the papal Mass, and millions more watched or listened to broadcasts around the country. Those who were present remember, in Joe Duffy's words, the 'outpourings of joy and fervour' generated by John Paul's visit. 'It was a truly miraculous day,' wrote Kevin Myers, himself an ex-Catholic. 'The spirits of the people were beyond description.'[82]

This was a 'royal' visit as had never been seen before.

And yet there was a change of tone. There was a glorious welcome, but the Pope was no longer there as a 'parallel monarch', as popes once were for the Catholic Irish. And, viewed in retrospect, a much sourer note emerged. It was seen, in retrospect, as 'the last throw of Catholic Ireland'. After 1979 the Catholic Church would go into a decline, and the papal visit would be remembered by some as an ironic curiosity. Frank McGuinness (playwright and author of the influential *Observe the Sons of Ulster Marching Towards the Somme*, the play that did so much to arouse the memory of Orangemen about their 1916 sacrifice) excoriated the whole enterprise. He thought it stank of 'sickening' hypocrisy; two of the clerics most prominent on the papal tour were later revealed to have had mistresses and secret children.

The disparagement of the Catholic Church in Ireland that followed through the 1980s and 1990s (with some justified cause, following clerical scandals) saw a kind of strange parallel in the experience of British monarchy. During the 1980s and 1990s the monarchy endured a long period of scandal, marriage troubles, accusations of hypocrisy, and a media that altered its perception of the institution from the fawning adulation described by John Grigg to a hectoring hostility.

Again the status of the Catholic Church has seemed to echo the status of the British monarchy: it is as though two historic institutions were found to be composed of flawed individuals, not guided by an exalted mystique.

Indeed a shift was taking place in the institution of the monarchy. What had been a revered historical institution was increasingly subject to very public criticism, and a series of family problems were to be portrayed in an increasingly unedifying light: the breakdown of Princess Margaret's marriage, in which she was seen as the offending spouse, photographed in her swimsuit in the presence of toyboys, and even fashionably chic gangsters; the constant parliamentary campaigns carried on by the radical Scot, Willie Hamilton, underlining the cost of the monarchy; the lack of transparency in their financial matters, and their exemption from taxation; not to mention various cavortings by fringe members of the Windsor family, such as Marina Ogilvy, rebel daughter of Princess Alexandra who swept the tabloids for a time in her conflicts with her family.

There were so many indications that the old unquestioning loyalty to the royals was on the wane. Moreover, the British royal family was also now entering the realm of globalised celebrity, and would be increasingly under the media microscope.

They had always lived, to an extent, in a goldfish bowl, but this was greatly magnified by the marriage of Prince Charles to Lady Diana Spencer in 1981. Suddenly, it seemed, everyone was 'Lady Di' mad. Working as a journalist in London (and writing also for the *Irish Independent*) I became acutely aware of the market appetite for any story at all about Diana.

A brilliant Irish photographer, John Minihan, working for the London *Evening Standard*, took some of the first published pictures of Diana in September 1980, wearing a diaphanous skirt while working at a nursery school. It was, through no intention of Minihan's, the beginning of a paparazzi obsession with Diana that would last for the rest of her short life.

Diana was stunning-looking, had a model's figure, a sweetly sympathetic face with a Bambi-like expression, and she loved children and animals; the royal wedding of 1981 seemed like a fairy tale romance. We all wrote the most tremendous gush about it, much of it quite sincerely meant. But, a little like the Irish faithful's relationship with the Catholic Church, when the marriage went wrong and both partners in the marriage were revealed to have been less than ideal in their conduct, the disillusion was all the greater.

Strangely enough, the more critical attitude to the monarchy in Britain actually dates from soon after the Charles and Diana wedding. In 1982 Penelope Mortimer (first wife of Rumpole author, John Mortimer) published the first critical biography of the Queen Mother. She described the experience of researching this biography as akin to 'swimming through treacle'.[83]

I have had a similar experience. In the 1980s I was commissioned by the *Sunday Telegraph* to write an obituary for Elizabeth, the Queen Mother, then in her eighties. I sat in the *Daily Telegraph* archive library and went through all the newspaper cuttings about the Queen Mum, assembled since 1923 (the only time she ever gave an interview). Swimming through treacle just about describes the tone: the degree of fawning self-abasement manifested by journalists and authors towards the saintly Queen

Mother over the decades was – even for someone who had a reasonable level of respect for the old girl – an experience of extreme 'treacliness'. I tried to take a more rational tone in writing the obituary, which eventually appeared twenty years later, in 2002, when she died. By that time, attitudes had changed.

The story of Diana and her impact on the monarchy, is now familiar. She was indeed beautiful, compassionate and sympathetic, as her biographer Sarah Bradford (by far the most authoritative of the Diana biographers[84]) allows. But she was also deeply damaged from a seriously 'broken home' in childhood, psychologically needy and destructively manipulative. We in the media wrote reams and reams of tosh on the subject: some of it accurate enough, but much of it invented, or guessed at. Since the royals rarely answer back, whatever outrageous claim one made would seldom be denied.

And so when Diana appeared on *Panorama* saying 'there were three people in this marriage', it was a media sensation. And Charles' admission to Jonathan Dimbleby that he, too, had been an adulterer was another source of media jubilation, as I recall.

As I wrote for both the London and the Dublin papers, I could measure the difference in the level of interest: and there was no difference. Every newspaper was avid for Charles and Di and Camilla stories. The focus was devoid of political or constitutional content: it was the human angle that mattered. Back in the 1950s Malcolm Muggeridge had called the monarchy 'a soap opera'. Now this truly had come to pass.

Yet that 'soap opera' contained both the useful, as well as the superficial, aspect of the genre: the narrative of human life, the way in which human actions connect into each other, the consequence of human choices, the interplay of family, sexual attraction, values, loyalties. When Prince Andrew married Sarah Ferguson in July 1986 I was told that entire towns in Ireland emptied for the duration, while the population sat around its TV sets (British television was now easily available all over Ireland through the medium of cable). But that marriage, too, turned out to be a source of soap-opera disasters. Before too long, three of the Queen's four offspring were divorced.

Again there was a parallel with the Catholic Church in Ireland, whereby the taboos most rigidly enforced come back to haunt. Extremely forbidding about aspects of sexuality in its heyday, the Church in the 1990s was humbled and found wanting after an avalanche of clerical sexual scandals. Extremely stigmatising on the subject of divorce, the British monarchy found itself at the centre of a rash of failed marriages, leading (in the case of Diana, Princess of Wales) to a needless and careless early death.

We are all familiar with the final chapter in the Diana story: finally, a separation from the Prince of Wales, a divorce settlement, and an unwise friendship with Dodi Fayed whose cocaine habit restlessly pushed them both to their tragic accidental death in Paris on 31 August 1997. True, the paparazzi played their part in hunting Diana: that goldfish bowl was the death of her.

I remember being in Dublin a couple of days after Diana died. The British Embassy on Merrion Road, Ballsbridge, was covered, wall to wall, with flowers and floral tributes to the late Princess. I had seen it bristling with guns and barbed wire, forever braced for an attack. Now it was blooming with flowers of remembrance.

A day or two later, I travelled to Belfast on a journalistic project. I stood outside Belfast City Hall, mingling with the crowds in a Republican rally, while a senior Provisional IRA veteran – Martin Meehan – prepared to address the people about Republican prisoners still held at the Maze.

Behind me, a group of women from west Belfast were talking about Diana – and Mother Teresa of Calcutta, who had died in the same week. 'Sure they're up there in heaven together, so they are,' one of the Republican mammies said. 'The pair of them together – a couple of wee saints, so they are.' The women spoke about having signed the book of condolence for Diana at City Hall. Then one of their number dissented, and said she had not felt inclined to sign.

I turned around and asked the lady (who was called Betty) why she had not signed. I thought she would give me an earful about being a Republican, and having no interest in royalty. But her answer surprised me. 'Ach, no, it's not that,' she said. 'But I'm on Charles' side.' In the Wales' divorce, her sympathies had not been with Diana.

Much was changing in Ireland in the late 1990s, and had been changing since the mid-1980s when the Anglo-Irish Agreement of 1985 was signed, to be followed by the Downing Street Declaration of 1993, leading to the Good Friday Agreement of 1998. Just as the death of Winston Churchill in 1965 was said to signify the end of an older England, perhaps in Ireland the death of Éamon de Valera in 1975 heralded the end of an era too; as had the death of the highly controlling, extraordinarily dominant Archbishop of Dublin, John Charles McQuaid, in 1973. By the 1980s, the peace process seemed to indicate a whole new range of attitudes to reconciliation, which, according to Roy Foster, were in some part due to a new generation of Irish civil servants and diplomats working hard behind the scenes in London and Washington to bring about the fruits of peace and reconciliation.[85]

A significant manifestation of this progress was President Mary Robinson's widely welcomed visit to Queen Elizabeth at Buckingham Palace in May 1993, the outward symbol of a turning-point for the better.

*

Mary Robinson, *née* Bourke, had been elected President of Ireland (Uachtarán na hÉireann) in November 1990. It was considered a breakthrough event: Michael O'Sullivan wrote in the first biography of the President that Mrs Robinson took the office of the Irish Presidency 'from a near-dormant constitutional symbol into an active working presidency.'[86]

There had certainly been some worthy and honourable heads of the Irish state, but, apart from de Valera himself, who resided in the Presidency for two terms of seven years each, few charismatic ones.

By contrast, Mary Robinson made a great splash. Not that she was a loud personality: far from it. I knew Mary when we were both founder members of an Irish feminist group, the Irish Women's Liberation Movement. She sat in my flat in Dublin 4 at 'consciousness-raising' sessions in 1970–71, a clever but correct presence who never lost dignity. She was an accomplished lawyer and a senator then, and she believed the way to change circumstances for Irish women was through the legal route, and through the astute use of the Constitution.

This was radically innovatory at the time. Irish lawyers had traditionally followed British tradition in terms of legislation: the politicians enacted laws in Dáil Éireann, and lawyers interpreted it according to case law. Young, liberal lawyers like Mary Robinson introduced the idea of changing law and practice through interpretation of the Constitution – perhaps more on the American model. When she became President, she developed the office more affirmatively as guardian of the Constitution.

When I was a child my Edwardian aunts used to say of a certain type of woman that 'you'd know she was a lady'. This fully applied to Mary: you would just know she was a lady. She came from Catholic gentry in the west of Ireland, and had attended Mount Anville convent school in Dublin, where she became head girl. (Her four brothers had all gone to Clongowes, 'Ireland's Eton'.) She had all the sense of responsibility, confidence and gravitas of the model Mount Anville head girl – that very school where Queen Victoria had spent a last happy sunny afternoon in Dublin in 1900, feeling so attuned to the ambience of a rising and respectable Catholic bourgeoisie. Mary's great-uncle, Sir Paget Bourke, had been a judge in the British administration in Kenya and Cyprus, and had actually met Elizabeth on that last dramatic trip in 1952 when George VI died and she became Queen.

In every particular, Mary Robinson was more than qualified to become President of Ireland, and faultlessly qualified, too, to become the first President of Ireland to call upon Queen Elizabeth at Buckingham Palace. She had the class, she had the background, she had the graceful self-assurance, and, as an extra, she had the brains. It was a triumph from the off.

Mary had also done something very radical in March 1993. There had been a horrible bomb attack in Warrington, in

Merseyside, on 20 March, in which two little boys, Tim Parry and Johnathan Ball, had been killed when they were out buying Mother's Day cards.

Paul Bew wrote that the Warrington bombing created 'a wave of revulsion throughout the British Isles against terrorist killings'. This was so. Throughout the Troubles there had been many bombs, in which many innocent people died – innocent people on all sides. But this, somehow, seemed a tipping point. Mary Robinson flew to Liverpool (she must have had the backing of the Irish government, headed then by Albert Reynolds, for an Irish President cannot leave Ireland without permission from the government) for the funeral.

It was typical of her courage and, more, her confidence in her own judgement. It was absolutely the right thing to do, and she was expressing by gesture just what those four women had expressed in the *Irish Press* after Mountbatten's death: 'Not In Our Name'. Indeed, Mrs Robinson's closest aide, Bride Rosney, had herself spoken of that sense of 'shame' about Mountbatten's killing. Subsequently, the Irish rock band the Cranberries made a protest song against the Warrington bombs: called 'Zombie', it became one of their biggest hits.

Two months later, in May 1993, Mrs Robinson made her visit to Queen Elizabeth, and it was hailed as a deeply significant conciliatory gesture. 'Mary Robinson reached across the division,' wrote the Belfast surgeon and Irish senator John Robb. Mrs Jennifer Lyons, widow of the great Irish historian F. S. L. Lyons, called it 'absolutely enormous' in significance. It was the first time this had happened in the history of the Irish state. It heralded a new era in Anglo-Irish relations.[87]

The meeting between Queen and President was, as these meetings go, a perfectly anodyne occasion in which two ladies take tea. And yet it was clear that it was the visible part of an iceberg of steady diplomatic activity over years, maybe decades. It was reported, with authority, that the 'historic visit to Buckingham Palace' was approved by both governments and had been 'carefully designed to improve relations between the countries and the prospects for talks with Northern Ireland parties on the three strands of relations in these islands'.[88] It was, in a sense, background music to the 'peace process' which was building nicely, if cautiously.

An Irish government source described the meeting as 'symbiotic, atmospheric'. 'The intention is to contribute to a warming of the atmosphere between the two countries ... Without overstating its importance, we hope it will be a useful symbolic gesture which will send a message of the two governments being prepared to set aside old differences,' said the 'source'.[89]

And indeed the following year, 1994, the IRA called a ceasefire: this was subsequently broken, but resumed again, rather as smokers make several failed attempts before finally quitting the cigarette habit.

*

In 1995 the Prince of Wales was to visit Ireland, generally regarded as presaging a visit by the monarch: members of the royal family were, in any case, now developing a habit of dropping in on Dublin informally, notably Princess Anne for sporting occasions.

Charles' trip to Ireland was a formal visit, much welcomed by the then Taoiseach, John Bruton, and his deputy, Dick Spring. He arrived at Casement Aerodrome in Baldonnel on the Queen's flight: how the shade of George V would have flinched at that 'Casement' Aerodrome.

Tactfully, no Union flags were displayed, just the Irish tricolour and the Royal Welsh Standard. It was all correct, but low-key. Miriam Lord wrote that a pinch of pomp and ceremony would not have gone amiss. 'A marching band and some square-bashing would have been nice.'[90] But the Republic of Ireland does not really do 'pomp and ceremony': that had been left to the Catholic Church, which by now had discarded such flummery.

Charles politely said he had been looking forward to coming to Ireland for quite a while. There was a high measure of security, and a group protesting against the visit: 'Dublin Against the Royal Tour', led by one Des Bonass. (As Colonel-in-Chief of the

Parachute Regiment, Charles was – unfairly, for him – associated with the events of Bloody Sunday.) Significantly, though, Provisional Sinn Féin had given instructions that there was to be no violence involved with the protests: it was to be dignified.

And there were plenty among old Dubliners to welcome him. A battery of older Dublin Mammies and Grannies turned out to extend the traditional *céad mile fáilte*. Mrs Winnie McKay, who had been brought to see the Prince in a wheelchair, said 'Give my love to your mother and grandma.' He was seized and kissed by a 65-year-old mother of five from Kilbarrack, exclaiming, 'Charlie is me darling – c'mere Charlie and give us a kiss.' Mrs Terry Earley, aged 40, from Drimnagh, called out to him (referring to Diana), 'You let a good woman go there,' and he replied, 'Yes, I did.' The 'aul wans' of old Dublin called out, 'God bless ye, son', and, whatever about anything else, he was the Dubs' delight.[91]

Charles departed feeling 'happy' and saying that he wanted to return. Perhaps the most poignant – and surely forgiving – aspect of the visit was that Lady Patricia Brabourne, daughter of Mountbatten, was also in Ireland at the same time. 'It is lovely to be back somewhere we love so much,' she said, 'and amongst people we love so much.'[92]

Even more remarkable, perhaps, considering Charles' special relationship with Mountbatten – he was the family counsellor to the Prince of Wales – was the speech that the Prince was to make on a brief visit to the Glencree Peace Centre in Co Wicklow seven years later, when he spoke of 'the long history of suffering' of the Irish people.[93]

He went on to say that Britain and Ireland should not be prisoners of the past and talked about Northern Ireland and 'the pain and resentment' involved in those troubles. Princess Margaret had just died, and it was thought that Charles would cancel his Irish visit in 2002 because of that: but officials 'said that the fact it did go ahead showed the importance the prince put on the trip'.[94]

Throughout the later 1990s and into the early years of the twenty-first century, all the mood music was that of peace and reconciliation. Prince Philip visited Dublin as part of the Prince's Trust (twinned with its Irish version, An Gaisce) in 1996 and

1998, and was officially – and unofficially – welcomed. Princess Anne, a keen sportswoman, began popping over to Lansdowne Road to watch rugby games, without any great fuss.

In June 1996 President Robinson paid an official visit to Queen Elizabeth at Buckingham Palace, and again the mood music was cordial. Mrs Robinson saw her visits to Elizabeth as part of a 'modernising mission': she thought it was time to 'normalise' relations between Britain and Ireland, time to 'drop the baggage, time to move on'.[95] 'The Soldier's Song' was duly played at Buckingham Palace – with a hundred guardsmen in full dress – as was the 'Siege of Ennis', the 'Galway Races', 'Carrickfergus', the 'Star of the Co Down', and Percy French's charming 'Come Back Paddy Reilly to Ballyjamesduff'. Queen Elizabeth apparently told the President that she would very much like to visit Ireland 'when the appropriate time comes'. But Dublin ruled that the appropriate time had not yet come.

President Mary Robinson was succeeded in 1997 by another woman, another lawyer, and another Mary: the clever, witty, articulate, and humane President Mary McAleese. A very special moment occurred on November 11 1998, when President Mary McAleese stood shoulder to shoulder with Queen Elizabeth at Messines Ridge in Belgium, together honouring the dead who had fallen during the First World War. The Irish historian Professor Tom Garvin said of this meeting that it truly was the close of old hostilities. 'The Empire is gone. The old dependency versus the Empire business is gone as well.'[96]

President McAleese and Queen Elizabeth were to have several more cordial meetings over the years, in Belgium, Britain, and Belfast. Mrs McAleese openly stated that Queen Elizabeth would love to visit Ireland, and that she, President McAleese, would also love such a visit, but that the event had to wait upon political agreement.[97]

Meanwhile, in the political arena, Taoiseach Bertie Ahern and Prime Minister Tony Blair established a special relationship: Mr Blair was the first British Prime Minister to address the Irish Parliament of the Dáil and Seanad; and Bertie, in his turn, was to be the first Taoiseach to address the Lords and Commons.

1998 certainly was an auspicious year: the Good Friday Agreement was sealed in Belfast, and the way was opened to a more 'reconciled' Ireland, with all parties participating in democracy. Referenda were held in Northern Ireland and the Republic of Ireland endorsing this agreement: it passed by 71 per cent in the North, and 94 per cent in the Republic.

The vast majority of the people of the Republic had also voted to remove Articles 2 and 3 from the 1937 Irish Constitution: the articles which laid claim to the entire island of Ireland. The British Prime Minister, Tony Blair, vouchsafed that Britain had no imperialist claim on the North of Ireland: changes were now to be agreed by democratic mandate.

So it seemed, from that time onwards, that Crown and Shamrock could go forward together. At the beginning of the twentieth century, the founder of Sinn Féin, Arthur Griffith, had used the example of the dual monarchy of Austria-Hungary as a template for the possible relationship between Britain and Ireland. Then the Hapsburg monarchy fell, and Hungary was drawn into the orbit of the Soviet empire instead.

However at the end of the twentieth century Austria and Hungary might again have been said to be models for Britain and Ireland: free and democratic neighbouring nations who have a special friendship based on a shared past. The Irish ambassadors who have served in London in the early years of the twenty-first century, Mr Daithí Ó Ceallaigh and Mr David Cooney, have both described Anglo-Irish relations as 'the best they have ever been.'[98]

A departing British ambassador to Dublin has written something very similar. 'I leave Dublin,' wrote Stewart Eldon, 'when relations between Ireland and the UK have never been better.' A whole host of factors had contributed to this entirely friendly relationship, he maintained: shared membership of the European Union, trade, prosperity (he might perhaps have added sport), and the joint efforts on Northern Ireland which had brought Ireland and the UK 'much closer … both governments are working closely together to take the agreement forward.'[99]

Another memorable moment occurred in February 2007 when the band at Croke Park in Dublin struck up 'God Save the

Queen' before the first rugby international between England and Ireland on the nationally sacred ground of the Gaelic Athletics Association. Some apprehension was voiced in advance: protests were expected, but it all went off with the greatest possible grace. This, wrote John Waters, was a 'healing balm', 'a proud acknowledgement that, together, our two nations have grown into a better way of living side by side.'[100]

And another 'healing balm' occurred when Taoiseach Bertie Ahern was invited to address the joint Houses of Parliament at Westminster in May 2007, which he did, standing in front of an ornate, arched door and between the portraits of Queen Elizabeth and Prince Philip, addressing a packed auditorium. Could Parnell ever have envisaged such a day, carried out in such a spirit of cordiality and good cheer?[101]

From the middle 1990s, the ambience between Britain and Ireland was continually cordial in the political and ceremonial dimension, and that included the royals. Indeed every time a member of the British royal family came to the Irish Republic (Charles brought Camilla, Duchess of Cornwall on a private visit to Lismore in 2004) it was heralded as a sign that Queen Elizabeth would make a state visit to Dublin, the first such occasion since 1911.

It was expected from 1995, and then from 1998, and then from 2005 – and then it was expected again in the spring of 2008. President Mary McAleese met Queen Elizabeth five times between 1998 and 2008, but still, there was a hesitancy. The Irish Ambassador in London, David Cooney (himself a Londoner from an Irish background), who described Queen Elizabeth as 'a lovely person' when he presented his credentials, said in the spring of 2008: 'We want this visit to happen, but we want everything to be right.'[102]

Perhaps, like planning a perfect time to have a baby, the time is hardly ever exactly right: perhaps, like having a baby, the most natural counsel is – *just do it!*

We have all come a long way since the Crown was placed on the head of Elizabeth II in 1953 and the film of her coronation had to be viewed almost secretly in the Republic of Ireland. But the past is part of who we are, and *every* element of the past contributes to the continuity of a nation's history.

Epilogue

SHOULD QUEEN ELIZABETH
BE INVITED TO IRELAND?

When I think of the monarchy, I think of a noose.
(Caller to Radio Foyle, Derry, 26 June 2008)

In time I grew to understand what it was about the House of Windsor to captivate my Mum. It wasn't just the frocks, the tiaras and the pageantry. It was Elizabeth. (Martina Devlin, *Irish Independent*, 2007).

D uring the Treaty debates in Dáil Éireann in 1922 a young Cork Councillor, Liam de Róiste (who had been a close friend of Terence MacSwiney), suggested that the Irish should not get too worked up about the question of monarchies, for 'the days of Kings and Kaisers are almost ended and will soon be as obsolete as the theory of their divine right to rule.' This had an element of the prophetic, and Mr de Róiste was later echoed by King Farouk of Egypt, who apparently said that by the end of the twentieth century there would only be five kings left in the world: the King of Diamonds, the King of Spades, the King of Clubs, the King of Hearts – and the King of England.

Certainly, as the twentieth century progressed, the number of monarchs in Europe dropped perceptibly. As we have seen, the last great, fabulous funeral of a monarch was Edward VII's in 1910, when more than a dozen crowned heads walked behind the coffin – so many of whom would be swept away by the First World War. Only five monarchs walked behind the coffin of George V in 1936, and only three of their thrones survived the Second World War.

Councillor de Róiste (who was himself to die in his forties) predicted modernising political trends when he said that, in contrast to kings and queens, 'the rule of the sovereign people' had begun by 1921. Comparing Britain and Ireland over the course of the twentieth century, Ireland seems, in this sense, to have been in the vanguard of modernity: moving early towards a republic with a written constitution, an elected president, and the democratic concept that Éamon de Valera always put forward – that the people are sovereign (at least in theory).

However, some constitutional monarchies have endured (or have even been restored, as in the successful example of Spain) and those that have survived and lasted tend to be in progressive and open democracies, such as the three Scandinavian kingdoms, and the Netherlands. (Belgium is a special case, and so bitterly divided by language conflicts that the King remains one of very few unifying elements in the country.) But, as the dissolute Farouk of Egypt indicated, the British monarchy still remains the world's best-known, and Queen Elizabeth II now is surely the doyenne of monarchs presently existing.

Elizabeth has visited nearly every country in the world – even the Soviet Union under communism. The Republic of Ireland, the nearest island nation, is one of the very few where she has never set foot. Although the Queen has, it seems, on several occasions expressed her willingness to visit Ireland, no invitation has been forthcoming.[1]

The invitation has, for some time, been expected. It was seriously expected from the mid-1990s when President Mary Robinson paid two visits to the Queen in London (one official, one merely friendly) during her tenure of office. Prince Charles visited Dublin (and the west of Ireland) in 1995, and that was generally regarded as a signal that the Queen would follow.

Before Taoiseach Bertie Ahern left office in May 2007, he indicated that the Queen's state visit would be inevitable – and probably quite soon.

However, the general political view has been that it must wait until the political situation is 'settled': especially in regard to Northern Ireland. I am not sure Northern Ireland will ever be definitively 'settled': like Kosovo or South Ossetia or any of these regions where there is a disputed fault-line of history, final settlements are necessarily elusive.

But it is reasonably clear that the Irish people in the 26 counties feel that a new contractual agreement has been entered into: whatever occurs in regard to Northern Ireland in the future times, it will be done by democracy and consent, not by bloody conflict.

So: should Queen Elizabeth visit Dublin and the Republic of Ireland, as envisaged? The event is both imminent and nervously deferred. There would be pockets of resistance. There would be people who object to Union flags, as they always have done: perhaps, as with Edward VII at Maynooth, where his racing colours adorned the flagpoles, some tactful and imaginative alternative may be found, just to avoid stirring up ancestral voices of animosity.

And then there is another prospect, so brilliantly articulated by James H. Murphy, the meticulous scholar of the Victorian relationship with Ireland: the fear is not that the Queen might be welcomed too little – but that she might be welcomed too much. 'The danger for large-scale, formal, royal visits to the Republic of Ireland [lies] not in the possibility that royal visitors might not be well received by the Irish people, but that they might be too well received.'[2] A flush of 'abject loyalty' might emerge: my friend and fellow-scribe Michael O'Sullivan swears that there are little old ladies all over Rathgar and Rathmines even now practising their curtseys (although of course only *subjects* curtsey). And in reaction to 'abject loyalty' might come a recrudescence in abject hate.

I would argue that the reason Queen Elizabeth should be invited for an official visit to Ireland is not so much for her sake

– in her eighties, I daresay that there is little that is new or surprising to this exceptionally experienced sovereign – as for ours.
The Americans talk about 'bringing closure' to certain feelings
and emotions, and an official royal visit by the long-reigning
Queen of England to the Irish Republic would bring a certain
'closure' to a long and often adversarial relationship.

We are – both as individuals and as nations – everything that
our past has made us. We cannot progress emotionally and psychologically by denying our past. We should seek to understand
it, bringing together both the negative and the positive and,
perhaps above all, the *paradoxical* in what makes us how we are. In
the past of the Irish nation, there were certainly Republican
voices that abhorred a monarchy, and especially a monarchy that
reigned over us, in England's interest. But there were also many
who did not take this view. O'Connell and Parnell were both
monarchists as well as Irish Nationalists. In their early days so
were Patrick Pearse and Arthur Griffith.

Historically, the majority of Irish Protestants, south as well as
north of the border, had a deep attachment to the Crown. For a
long time this was suppressed and sidelined, and a small
amendment is due in this regard, just as a larger amendment was
overdue to the Irish men and women who fought with the Allies
in the two world wars of the twentieth century.

The narrative of the Irish Republic is not exclusively
Republican: it contains a broad and catholic mixture of Irish men
and women with all shades of political and constitutional values –
and with none in particular, too. For a long period of the twentieth
century it was represented to us that only the Republican and
Nationalist version of Irish history was admissible: Wolfe Tone and
Robert Emmet were the *fons et omega* of our island story. They
were fine and heroic men who gave their lives for Ireland, but
theirs is not the only kind of Irishness. And *that* is the 'closure' that
is necessary, in a symbolic way: the acknowledgement that the
community of the Irish nation is a broad church, and that it has
included those who cherished the Crown, as well as those who
have had a multitude of conflicting feelings towards both
Republicanism and monarchy, and a range of nuances in between.

The personal is political in the sense that personal character-
istics and attributes are a vital part of the flavour of history.
History, as A. T. Q. Stewart has written, 'is about humanity and it
is about emotions and some historians write as if it were not'.[3] In
that sense, the personal is indeed political: what people are feeling
matters. When the Chief Secretary of Ireland, Augustine Birrell,
seemed remiss in his attentions to Easter 1916, his concern about
his very sick wife, and mentally handicapped son, must have been
a factor.

But at another level, the personal may not be political at all. So
many people have written to me (particularly, be it noted,
women, who are better at tolerating contradictions) saying that
their Republican household had pictures of royalty and Michael
Collins side by side. My own mother admired two local Galway
characters with equal ardour: Liam Mellowes, an extremely left-
wing young IRA volunteer executed by the Free State – and the
Earl of Clancarty, who married a beautiful music hall artiste and
nursed her faithfully as she died of breast cancer. Mother made
absolutely no political distinction between her two heroes, the
rebel and the aristocrat, because she reacted like a human being,
not a political automaton.

As a journalist I know it is 'the human angle' that speaks to
most people, not austere theories. So let us live with some of the
contradictions of our history and be tolerant of them, instead of
insisting that everything must fit into some preordained social or
political dogma. True, there are always Roundheads and Cavaliers:
there are always individuals who, by temperament, love the ceremonial around a monarchy, and there are always those puritans
and rationalists who deplore it as a form of frippery and frivolity.
But there are also those who can live with the contradictions in
between: among the most charming letters I received was one
from a woman who said she came from a mixed Catholic-Quaker
background, and she did not approve of monarchy: but by heaven,
she loved the pageantry!

Yet even among those who dislike monarchies, people will
often add, 'But I do admire the Queen, personally'. North of
Ireland Catholics, who are often the most outspoken in their

condemnation of monarchy, and can be bitter and coruscating in their denunciations of anything associated with throne and 'loyalty', will still quite often add that Queen Elizabeth is herself 'a decent Christian woman'. Elizabeth really is widely (and rightly) admired for her dedication to duty over her long, and sometimes trying, reign, as well as for her very evident effort to do her best for her country and the Commonwealth. The monarch was 83 in 2009, and (no more than the rest of us) will not live forever. It would, I think, be a matter of regret if the opportunity were not taken to offer her that *céad mile fáilte* that history, and geography, and the interlinking relations of ordinary families surely justify.

Notes to text

Author's Note: I have given sources where the information is very specific. I have not troubled the reader where data is well known and appears in standard history texts.

Introduction

[1] Literally, 'Little John' ('Bull', presumably).

[2] The Anti-Partition League (sometimes also called the Anti-Partition Association) was launched in 1947 and was, according to F. S. L. Lyons (*Ireland Since the Famine* (Dublin: 1971), 'the most vociferous' of a series of voluntary bodies campaigning against the border between the Free State and Northern Ireland. 'Neutrality', wrote Professor Lyons, 'had stirred deeper feelings against partition: Winston Churchill's 'Iron Curtain' speech highlighting the partitions in Europe probably also raised consciousness. Campaigns against the border have tended, however, to solidify it: campaigns for prosperity have done most to dissolve it.'

[3] Thanks to Brian Fitzelle for the note on Major Cosby of Co Laois.

[4] See Brian Barker, *When the Queen was Crowned* (London: 1976), for a report on the worldwide reaction to Elizabeth's coronation.

[5] *Irish Press*, 3 June 1953. There was also some emphasis on the conquest of Everest by Hillary and Tensing. Several male correspondents told me that they thought male readers at that time were more interested in the Everest exhibition than anything from crown or altar.

[6] Cathal O'Shannon, a distinguished reporter for *The Irish Times* and RTÉ television for over 50 years. His father, Cathal O'Shannon senior, was a celebrated trade unionist and Irish radical who was active in 1916. His mother was English and Cathal (Óg) served in the RAF during the Second World War. The editor

of *The Irish Times*, the great Douglas Gageby, addressed O'Shannon as 'a fucking traitor' for having been among the men who defended, in effect, the British Isles from fascism.

PROLOGUE

[1] James Loughlin, *British Monarchy and Ireland: 1800 to the Present* (Cambridge: 2007).

CHAPTER I

[1] Gladstone, quoted in Frank Hardie's *The Political Influence of the British Monarchy 1868–1952* (London: 1970).

[2] 'The most distressful country that ever yet was seen / For they're hangin' men an' women for the wearin' of the green.' The ballad also contains the line 'the shamrock is forbid to grow on Irish ground'. This was not strictly true, although Irish soldiers in HM Forces were banned from wearing the shamrock on St Patrick's Day until 1900. In his memoir, *Forty Years of Irish Broadcasting* (Dublin: 1967), Maurice Gorham recalls that after 1900 it became a great fashion in England to wear shamrock – until 1916.

[3] The statue of Queen Victoria was removed from the front of Leinster House on 22 July 1948. (Tony Gray, *Ireland this Century* (London: 1994).) Its removal could have been seen as an augury of Ireland leaving the Commonwealth and declaring a republic later that year. The statue, rather bombastic in style, depicted Victoria surrounded by allegorical figures, one representing Erin presenting a laurel crown to a soldier, symbolising Ireland's contribution to the Boer War. The sculptor was John Hughes, and it was unveiled on 15 February 1908 (*Irish Independent*, 16 February 1908). Rory Egan, who researched the subject of Victoria's statue for the *Sunday Independent* reported that Dubliners had dubbed the image 'the Auld Bitch'. There were calls to have the statue removed in 1929, but Dublin Corporation found the exercise too costly. After the 1948 removal the statue was taken to a disused part of the Royal Hospital, Kilmainham, until 1987, when Taoiseach Charles Haughey agreed to send it to Australia, where it was ceremonially unveiled by Prime Minister Robert Hawke on 21 October 1987 in Sydney. (My thanks to Rory Egan for historical detail.) There was also a long saga associated with a statue of Victoria at University College Cork. It had been erected on a gable end of the then Queen's College in Cork in 1849. In the 1930s the college authorities removed this image (which was at the eastern pinnacle of the Aula Maxima) and replaced it with St Finbarr, by the sculptor Seamus Murphy. Victoria's statue was stored at UCC until 1946 when it was lowered into a pit in the President's garden and buried there. In 1995 it was dug up and displayed for the 150th anniversary of the college's foundation. There were some protests against displaying the 'Famine Queen', but there was also much public interest in the historical aspect. Professor John A. Murphy of UCC

writes, 'The general reconciliatory climate of the mid-1990s was a help. The argument was effectively between those (like myself) who saw history as a record (and therefore the statue as an important exhibit), and those who regarded history as a nationalist chronicle (and therefore Victoria as the evil "Famine Queen").' (My thanks to Professor Murphy, who also provided me with his text from the *University College Cork News* of September 2006.)

[4] For the comparisons between Victoria's time in Scotland with her time in Ireland, see Stanley Weintraub, *Victoria: Biography of a Queen* (London: 1987). For her sole visit to Wales, see Christine Kinealy in Swift and Kinealy's *Politics and Power in Victorian Ireland* (Dublin: Four Courts Press, 2006).

[5] For Queen Victoria's religion, see Walter Walsh, *The Religious Life and Influence of Queen Victoria* (London: 1902).

[6] Algernon Cecil, *Queen Victoria and Her Prime Ministers* (London: 1953).

[7] Elizabeth Longford, *Queen Victoria* (London: 1964).

[8] The following provide interesting detail on Victoria's attitudes: she was against separating soldiers by race; she deplored the use of the word 'nigger';. For *racism* see Hardie, *Political Influence*, for *courtiers* see Cecil, *Victoria and Prime Ministers*; and for the *Dreyfus affair* see Weintraub, *Victoria*.

[9] Longford, *Victoria*.

[10] Catholic Emancipation followed an 1828 reform liberalising the situation for Nonconformist Protestants. Nevertheless, until the end of the 19th century, the United Kingdom's established faith, the Church of England, retained a privileged position in many official areas.

[11] David Cecil, *Lord Melbourne* (London: 1954). Cecil's volume has provided me with much of the detail for the relationship and dialogue between Victoria and Melbourne.

[12] Ibid.

[13] Ibid.

[14] The royal declaration affirming the Protestant religion, taken from Walsh, *Religious Life*.

[15] Ibid. Although these declarations have been dropped, the prohibition against marrying a Roman Catholic remains. In 2008, Princess Anne's daughter-in-law, the former Autumn Kelly, a Canadian Catholic, chose to convert to the Church of England before her wedding to Peter Phillips. Otherwise, he would have had to renounce formally his position as 11th in line to the throne. It was not widely criticised by the general public, but in Northern Ireland it confirmed some entrenched Nationalist views that the British throne is still anti-Catholic. However, in September 2008, Gordon Brown's administration announced that they would delete the prohibition against Roman Catholics marrying an heir to the throne in a future parliament.

[16] *Freeman's Journal*, 3 August 1849.

[17] Walsh, *Religious Life*.

[18] Philip Ziegler, *Melbourne* (London: 1976).

[19] For Anglican authorities against the re-establishment of the Catholic hierarchy, see Cecil Algernon, *Victoria and Prime Ministers*. For anti-Papist sermons and

cartoons see Michael Wheeler, *The Old Enemies: Catholic and Protestant in Nineteenth Century English Culture* (Cambridge: CUP, 2006).

[20] Desmond Bowen, *Paul Cardinal Cullen and the Shaping of Modern Irish Catholicism* (Dublin: 1983).

[21] Wheeler, *Old Enemies*. His bill turned out to be a dead letter, and was never operative.

[22] RA VIC/MAIN/QVJ/1849:10 Aug. Cecil, *Victoria and Prime Ministers*.

[23] See also Wheeler (*Old Enemies*) who states that Victoria was 'comparatively broad-minded' on matters of religion and disliked the Puseyites [High Church Anglicans] more than Roman Catholics. Victoria's close friendship with the Empress Eugenie, a devout Catholic, also may have had an influence on her personal feelings.

[24] Royal Archives, *Queen Victoria's Journal*, 10 August 1849.

[25] Walsh, *Religious Life*.

[26] Mike Ashley, *A Brief History of British Kings and Queens* (London: 1998). See also Clare Tomalin's absorbing *Mrs Jordan's Profession: The Actor and the Prince* (New York: Knopf, 1995).

[27] Hardie, *Political Influence*.

[28] The Parnell sisters, Anna and Fanny, were pioneers of an early form of feminist agitprop. See Elisabeth Kehoe, *Ireland's Misfortune: the Turbulent Life of Kitty O'Shea*. T. P. O'Connor wrote (*Memoirs of an Old Parliamentarian* (London: 1929) of Anna Parnell that she had an iron will but was 'absolutely reckless'. Fanny died suddenly in the 1870s, but Anna lived into the early 20th century, passing on the baton of protest to Maud Gonne.

[29] From Weintraub, *Victoria*. See also Kinealy, *Great Calamity*.

[30] See Longford, *Victoria*, and Kinealy, *Great Calamity*.

[31] Bowen, *Cardinal Cullen*. Later Archbishop MacHale complained of neglect of the famine cause (*Freeman's Journal*, 28 May 1849; cited in James H. Murphy, *Abject Loyalty: Nationalism and Monarchy in Ireland During the Reign of Queen Victoria* (Cork: 2001). In our time we also see the phenomenon of poorer countries refusing aid after a calamity, out of a sense of pride, as Burma initially did after floods in 2008.

[32] Bishop Samuel Wilberforce, the Bishop of Oxford was a celebrated Protestant preacher whose theme was 'papal error' (Wheeler, *Old Enemies*). His brothers, Henry and Robert, both subsequently became Roman Catholics and lived in or were associated with Connemara in Co Galway. See Tim Robinson, 'Connemara: The Last Pool of Darkness. The Irish lack of thrift and prudence in 'bringing their troubles on themselves.' (*The Times*, 5 September 1853).

[33] Entry for Russell in Colin Mathew and Brian Harrison (eds), *Oxford Dictionary of National Biography* (Oxford: OUP, 2004).

[34] J. J. Lee. *The Modernisation of Irish Society 1848-1912* (Dublin: 1973).

[35] Ibid.

[36] O'Connell loathed revolution and bloodshed, as his various biographers have underlined: he had experienced the French Revolution at first hand as a schoolboy in France, and never forgot the horrors of bloodshed and terrors of

mob disorder. The book that Daniel O'Connell dedicated to Queen Victoria was *A Memoir of Ireland Native and Saxon*, published in 1842. However, although dedicated to Her Majesty it was also, writes James Loughlin, 'intended for the enlightenment of the sovereign', being a litany of England's wrongs towards Ireland (Loughlin, *British Monarchy and Ireland*).

[37] By December 1880 *The Times*, normally a bastion of anti-Irish sentiment, would be lauding O'Connell (29 December 1880). In retrospect O'Connell became respectable, and seemed less of a threat than Parnell.

[38] Several biographies indicate that Sir John Conroy, an Irishman who was Victoria's mother's companion (and probable lover), had also urged the young queen to visit Ireland. As Victoria detested Conroy, the idea may have been contra-suggestive. He did have some influence with the Duchess of Kent (Victoria's mother), as she made a contribution to the building of Tuam cathedral (Loughlin, *British Monarchy and Ireland*).

[39] *Freeman's Journal*, 3 August.1849. Despite initial opposition to the visit, the newspaper was packed with excitement about the Queen's visit and provided a full list of the great throngs of persons attending levees and drawing-rooms at Dublin Castle: 'never had Queen such a Levee as that which our Queen had yesterday', the paper enthused on August 9. These included many Irish names – events were by no means confined to the Anglo-Irish gentry. There was also an increase in advertising – royal visits brought the press more revenue.

[40] RA VIC/Main/QVJ/1849: 3 August, *Victoria's Journal*.

[41] Ibid, 7 August 1849. Daniel Murray was not only silver-haired and distinguished looking – he was also 'loyal' and described as a 'Castle Catholic' by critics.

[42] Ibid.

[43] See R. B. McDowell's most entertaining description in *Historical Essays 1938–2001* (London, 2003).

[44] RA VIC/Main/QVJ/1849: 5 August, *Victoria's Journal*.

[45] Ibid, 6 August 1849.

[46] RA VIC/Main/QVJ/1849: 6 August 1849. During her tour of Dublin, a dove with an olive branch – extraordinarily – fell into her lap, which strangely pleased her: 'the dear little thing'. The weather was extremely hot and dusty.

[47] RA VIC/Main/QVJ/1849: 9 August 1849. They were to be dubbed 'Royal' in 1867, perhaps not coincidentally the same year the Fenians rebelled.

[48] RA VIC/Main/QVJ/1849: 10 August 1849.

[49] John Mitchel's thoughts on Victoria's welcome from *The Last Conquest of Ireland (Perhaps)*. He thought there was concealment of the poverty of Ireland – no doubt people put the best appearance on things, but Victoria's eye was sharp and she saw plenty of signs of poverty.

[50] William Smith O'Brien was a 'Young Irelander' involved in the unsuccessful rising in 1848. He was initially sentenced to death for his part in a skirmish in Ballingarry, Tipperary, but the sentence was commuted to life, and he too served five years in Tasmania. In 1856 he did finally receive an unconditional pardon and returned to Ireland and a quiet life.

[51] RA VIC/Main/QVJ/1849: 10 August, *Victoria's Journal*.

[52] 'I intend creating Bertie Earl of Dublin as a compliment to the town & country. He has no Irish title, though he is born with several Scotch ones, which he inherited from James I.' RA VIC/Main/QVJ/1849: 12 August, *Victoria's Journal*. It was reported that a newspaperman deliberately inserted the typographical error that 'Queen Victoria pissed over the bridge' (of the Liffey) in a newspaper report on Victoria in Dublin: this is cited in Loughlin (*British Monarchy and Ireland*), but it may be more apocryphal than factual.

[53] Stanley Weintraub, *Uncrowned King: The Life of Prince Albert* (New York: Free Press, 1997); and Walsh, *Religious Life*.

[54] R. F. Foster, *Modern Ireland: 1600–1972* (London: Penguin, 1990). In fairness, there was a commensurate increase in Anglican clergy in England over this period (Kehoe, *Kitty O'Shea*). It was a religious age.

[55] Over a period of 26 years, Cullen built 19 churches, 6 hospitals, 5 colleges, and 40 religious foundations (B.J. Canning, *Bishops of Ireland* (Donegal: 1987).

[56] RA VIC/Main/QVJ/1853: 29 August and RA VIC/Main/QVJ/1853: 1 September, *Victoria's Journal*. This was an unofficial visit and, technically, a private one, although Albert and Victoria were widely greeted.

[57] RA VIC/Main/QVJ/1853: 29 August.

[58] RA VIC/Main/QVJ/1853: 30 August 1853.

[59] See the entry on Dargan in Mathew & Harrison, *Dictionary of Biography*, and in Henry Boylan (ed), *A Dictionary of Irish Biography* (1998). For his donation to the National Gallery, see Kinealy in Swift & Kinealy, *Politics and Power*.

[60] RA VIC/Main/QVJ/1853: 30 August, *Victoria's Journal*.

[61] Ibid, 1 September.

[62] Ibid, 2 September 1853.

[63] Ibid, 3 September 1853. The figure of one million is given in Sir Sydney Lee's *Queen Victoria: A Biography*, 1st edn 1902 (Kila, Montana: 2nd edn Kessinger Publishing, 2006).

[64] RA VIC/Main/QVJ/1861: 23 August and 26 August, *Victoria's Journal*.

[65] Weintraub, *Victoria*.

[66] D. M. Potts and W. T. W. Potts, *Queen Victoria's Gene: Haemophilia and the Royal Family* (London: The History Press Ltd., 1999).

[67] Christopher Hibbert, *Edward VII: A Portrait* (London: 1976).

[68] RA VIC/Main/QVJ/1861: 28 August, *Victoria's Journal*

[69] Weintraub, *Uncrowned* King.

[70] Murphy, *Abject Loyalty*.

[71] Tom Garvin, *The Birth of Irish Democracy* (Dublin: 1996).

[72] The newspaper was *Reynolds' Weekly Newspaper*, cited in Weintraub, *Victoria*.

[73] See D. J. Hickey and J. E Doherty, *A New Dictionary of Irish History from 1800* (Dublin: 2005).

[74] Garvin, *Irish Democracy*.

[75] Murphy, *Abject Loyalty*.

[76] Ibid.

[77] Murphy, *Abject Loyalty*.

[78] Sir Frederick Ponsonby, *Recollections of Three Reigns* (London: 1951).

[79] See Murphy, *Abject Loyalty*, for the vote in Dublin Corporation. For Albert's disparaging remarks concerning Catholic Poland, see Loughlin, *British Monarchy and Ireland*.

[80] With thanks to the Office of Public Works in Dublin for arranging for me to see the statue and to Dr Jacqueline Moore for *Art in State Buildings*, 1922–1970.

[81] Longford, *Victoria*.

[82] Cited in T. P. O'Connor, *Memoirs*.

[83] F. S. L. Lyons, *Since the Famine*.

[84] Mary Kenny, *Goodbye to Catholic Ireland* (London: 1997).

[85] The peer who converted to Home Rule was Lord Spencer (Viceroy or Lord Lieutenant in Ireland 1868–74), an ancestor of Princess Diana. Victoria's comment cited in Weintraub, *Victoria*.

[86] Cited in Walsh, *Religious Life*.

[87] Longford, *Victoria*.

[88] Murphy in Peter Gray (ed), *Victoria's Ireland? Irishness and Britishness, 1837–1901* (Dublin: Four Courts Press, 2004).

[89] Murphy, *Abject Loyalty*.

[90] RA VIC/Main/D/32/79. Royal Archives, *Vols 11 & 12: Victoria* (Windsor). There is a very copious amount of worried political correspondence about the state of Ireland all through the 1880s. 'I cannot sufficiently express my horror …' (RA, *Victoria*, Doc. 23, no. 200, p. 78) the Queen wrote of the Phoenix Park murders to Gladstone. She went on, 'Many sad details of this horrible event had already reached [her] … all calculated to make one's blood run cold and to produce an indescribable thrill of horror.' 'Thrill' in the 19th century meant 'shiver', but perhaps there is a morbid interest in murder stories. Victoria was fascinated by the Maamtrasna murders, which had no political element.

[91] O'Connor, *Memoirs*. See also Shane Leslie, *The Irish Tangle for English Readers* (London: 1946): Sir Shane Leslie, a first cousin of Winston Churchill (their mothers being sisters) writes of how he joined G. K. Chesterton at the Phoenix Park 50 years later to pray for the souls of the deceased victims and perpetrators.

[92] Maurice Headlam, an ultra-Unionist, wrote with disgust in his memoirs that he had seen Catherine Cavendish lunch with John Redmond at the House of Commons: *Irish Reminiscences* (London: 1947).

[93] O'Connor, *Memoirs*.

[94] RA VIC/Main/D/29/200. There were other murders specifically condemned by the Queen: namely, the murder of Mr Boyd, Magistrate at New Ross, reported on 1 September 1880; the killing of a Mrs Smythe, shot dead in her carriage while out driving, reported on 9 April 1882; also a Mr Herbert on the same date. On 12 December 1880 Victoria wrote, with her customary underlining, 'The Queen is so *very* anxious about the present *very alarming* state of affairs that she cannot refrain from appealing to Lord Hartington in the *very strongest manner possible* to use *all his* influence with Mr Gladstone & his *Whig Colleagues* and to act *very strongly* & firmly at the present *very anxious moment* … The law is *openly defied, disobeyed* [in Ireland] & such an *example may* spread to England … It *must* be put down & nothing but boldness & firmness will succeed. … *Don't yield to*

satisfy Messrs Bright & Chamberlain; let them go; *declare* that you will not be parties to a *weak* & vacillating policy, which is ruining the country & bringing great discredit on the Government.'

[95] On Leitrim and other Irish landlords, see Mark Bence-Jones, *The Twilight of the Ascendancy* (London: 1987).

[96] Quoted in Robert Kee, *The Green Flag: A History of Irish Nationalism* (London: 1972).

[97] Quoted in Gray, *Victoria's Ireland?*

[98] For Elisabeth of Austria, see Murphy, *Abject Loyalty*. Also Andrew Sinclair, *Death by Fame: A Life of Elisabeth, Empress of Austria* (London: Constable, 1998).

[99] Gray, *Victoria's Ireland?*

[100] Ponsonby, *Recollections*.

[101] For progress in the Victorian age, see Roger Fulford, *Queen Victoria* (London: Collins, 1951).

[102] Weintraub, *Victoria*. A poor woman sent the fresh country eggs to London via a visiting cleric.

[103] Kehoe, *Kitty O'Shea*.

[104] For Ireland's reduction in crime see D. George Boyce, *Nineteenth Century Ireland: The Search for Stability*, rev edn (Dublin: Gill & Macmillan, 2005). Professor Boyce ascribes much of the reduction in crime to the establishment of the Royal Irish Constabulary, which reached its all-time maximum of 12,358 officers in 1850. Most RIC men were ordinary Irish Catholics.

[105] Kehoe, *Kitty O'Shea*.

[106] See Margaret Ward, *Maud Gonne: A Life* (London: 1990).

[107] See Maud Gonne MacBride, *A Servant of the Queen* (Dublin: 1938).

[108] *Freeman's Journal*, 23 June 1897.

[109] The enmity between Maud Gonne (abetted by W. B. Yeats) and Queen Victoria was the subject of a famous satire by the songwriter Percy French, which went, as if in the voice of Victoria: "'And that wan,' sez she / 'That Maud Gonne,' sez she / 'Dressin' in black,' sez she / 'To welcome me back,' sez she / ... 'And all that gammon,' sez she / 'About me bringing the famine,' sez she / 'Now Maud will write,' sez she / 'That I brought the blight,' sez she / 'For political raysons,' sez she / 'And I think there's a slate,' sez she / 'Off Willie Yeats,' sez she / 'He should be at home,' sez she / 'French-polishing a pome,' sez she.' (With thanks to Seamus Hosey for telling me about it, and to Professor John A. Murphy for sending me an extract.)

[110] R. F. Foster, *The Apprentice Mage: 1865–1914*, vol 1 of *W. B. Yeats: A Life*, 2 vols (Oxford, OUP, 2003).

[111] Figures cited in Gray, *Victoria's Ireland?*

[112] RA VIC/Main/QVJ/1900: 4 April, *Victoria's Journal*.

[113] RA VIC/Main/QVJ/1900: 7 April, Ponsonby, *Recollections*.

[114] RA, *Victoria's Journal*, 3 April 1900.

[115] RA VIC/Main/QVJ/1900: 5 April 1900.

[116] Ibid, 16 April 1900.

[117] Christine Kinealy notes in Swift & Kinealy (*Politics and Power*) that Victoria refused to make a donation on a Protestant-only basis.

[118] Ponsonby, *Recollections*.

[119] See Mathew & Harrison, *Dictionary of Biography*. After a fall from a horse his health declined and he died in modest circumstances. His widow was left impoverished.

[120] RA VIC/Main/QVJ/1900: 17 April. With special thanks to Sister Íde ní Riain, who has consulted the Mount Anville archives on my behalf. There were also spoken transmitted memories passed on to older nuns. Victoria visited Mount Anville on 17 April, and Loreto, Rathfarnham, on 20 April.

[121] Tennyson was the English poet most frequently praised in the *Irish Ecclesiastical Record* in the 1890s, as I observed when reading through this archive.

[122] RA VIC/Main/QVJ/1900: 26 April, *Victoria's Journal*.

[123] *Irish Independent*, 23 January 1901.

[124] Sebastian Barry's play, *The Steward of Christendom* (1995), was not only unforgettable theatre, it was a ground-breaking cultural event because it was the first time in the history of the Irish state when it was openly acknowledged that some Irishmen actually were dedicated to Queen Victoria.

CHAPTER 2

[1] RA VIC/Main/W/75/2. Royal Archives, *Edward VII* (Windsor), Doc. 12, 9 June 1906.

[2] *Irish Catholic*, 26 January 1901.

[3] T. P. O'Connor quoted in Sir Sydney Lee, *Edward VII: A Biography*, 2 vols, 1st edn 1926 (Kila, Montana: 2nd edn Kessinger Publishing, 2004).

[4] See Murphy, *Abject Loyalty*.

[5] In 1907 the *Freeman's Journal* wrote, 'The King brought an end to the Boer War' (11 July 1907). King Edward did not, of course, bring an end to the Boer War – British military power did that – but he did have an emollient effect on political attitudes. At his death, the Irish and Catholic newspapers hailed him as 'Edward the Peacemaker'.

[6] Lee, *Edward VII*. This was Viceroy Lord Cadogan (see Lee, *Edward VII*).

[7] See Hibbert, *Edward VII*, for his generosity to jockeys, and to groomsmen and stable-boys too. He would give the lad who looked after the horse a tip of £50, which could be a working man's annual salary in the 1900s.

[8] Various biographies of Edward VII mentioned this very cordial welcome at Maynooth. John Cafferky & Kevin Hannafin (*Scandal & Betrayal: Shackleton and the Irish Crown Jewels* (Cork: The Collins Press, 2002) report that it was Dr Mannix's idea to fly the racing colours rather than the Union Jack. For racing enthusiasts it is worth recording the details of Edward's Derby wins (for which I am indebted to Geoffrey Wheatcroft). On 3 June 1896 the Prince of Wales' Persimmon, by St Simon out of Perdita II, won at 5/1, trained by Marsh, ridden by Watts. On 30 May 1900 the Prince of Wales' Diamond Jubilee, by St Simon out of Perdita II, won at 6/4, trained by Marsh, ridden by Jones. On 26 May 1909 the King's Minoru, by Cyllene out of Mother Siegel, won at 7/2, trained by Marsh, ridden by Jones.

[9] See Philippe Jullian, *Edward and the Edwardians* (London: 1967) for Bertie's twelve changes of clothes.

[10] See Lee, *Edward VII*, for his support for the Duke of Devonshire.

[11] See the entry for the Duke of Devonshire in Mathew & Harrison, *Dictionary of National Biography*.

[12] For detail about landowners in Ireland see Bence-Jones, *Twilight*; Diarmaid Ferriter, *The Transformation of Ireland, 1900–2000* (London: 2005); and Christine Kinealy, *A New History of Ireland* (Stroud: Sutton Publishing, 2008).

[13] For Bertie and Gambetta, see Philip Magnus, *King Edward the Seventh* (London: 1964).

[14] See Sir Henry Robinson, *Memories: Wise and Otherwise* (London: 1923). The banner was devised by Father Glynn at Tully Cross (John Biggs-Davison & George Chowdharay-Best, *The Cross of St Patrick: The Catholic Unionist Tradition in Ireland* (Bourne End, Bucks: Kensal Press, 1984).

[15] *Irish Catholic*, 30 April 1910.

[16] For the banning of Catholic processions see Wheeler, *Old Enemies*.

[17] For Bertie's dislike of sectarianism, see Hibbert, *Edward VII*; and Magnus, *Edward Seventh*.

[18] See Sigmund Munz, *King Edward VII at Marienbad* (London: 1934). James H. Murphy (*Abject Loyalty*) writes that there were negative Unionist reactions to reports that the King had attended a Catholic Mass. One journal commented, 'This is what the Oxford Movement has done for England in the course of half a century, and for that portion of the British nation whose Christianity is veneered Paganism, Edward the Seventh is undoubtedly a fitting ruler.'

[19] For Mass at Spanish Place, 8 February 1908, see Hibbert, *Edward VII*.

[20] See Lee, *Edward VII*.

[21] For negotiations with Lord Salisbury, see Andrew Roberts, *Salisbury: Victorian Titan* (London: 1999).

[22] See Simon Heffer, *Power and Place: the Political Consequences of King Edward VII* (London: 1998).

[23] *Tablet* article reprinted in *The Irish Catholic*, 26 February 1901. Editorial in *The Irish Catholic* of same date.

[24] *Irish Catholic*, 16 February 1901. Chancery division of the High Court of Justice in Dublin: 4 Protestants, no Catholics. Queen's Bench Division of the High Court of Justice: 7 Protestants, 3 Catholics. Both chief law officers (Attorney-General and Solicitor-General) Protestants. First, second and third sergeants-at-court, Protestant: Recorders and county court judges: 14 Protestants, 7 Catholics. Resident magistrates: 48 Protestants, 19 Catholics. Employees in the Chief Secretary's Office: 31 Protestants, 5 Catholics. Employees in the Board of Works: 52 Protestants and 30 Catholics, but 'most in subordinate positions'. Employees in the Board of Trade: 24 salaried officials, all Protestant.

[25] *Irish Catholic*, 2 March 1901.

[26] For detail about civil servants trying to promote 'sound Unionists', see Eunan O'Halpin, *The Decline of the Union: British Government in Ireland, 1892-1920* (Dublin: 1987). Concern over not engaging enough 'sound Unionists' also emerges in Headlam, *Reminiscences*.

[27] See Hibbert, *Edward VII*. Also with thanks to Jane Ridley, who has researched the further career of Nellie Clifden for a forthcoming new biography of Edward VII.

[28] *Freeman's Journal*, May 9 1865.

[29] *Freeman's Journal*, 16 April and 20 April 1868.

[30] *Freeman's Journal*, 20 April 1868.

[31] See Cullen entry in Boylan, *Dictionary of Irish Biography* and Mathew & Harrison, *Dictionary of Biography*. The Irish hierarchy took St Paul's ordinance about respecting 'the rightful authority' very seriously, and Cullen was fiercely against rebellion partly for that reason. As the 'rightful authority' shifted from the Crown to the Free State in 1921–23, so, in general, did ecclesiastical support.

[32] Reported on 27 April 1896, as cited by Murphy, *Abject Loyalty*. See also Loughlin, *British Monarchy and Ireland*.

[33] See Murphy, *Abject Loyalty*. For the episode in Mallow, see Biggs-Davidson and Chowdharay-Best, *Cross of St Patrick*.

[34] See Lee, *Edward VII*.

[35] O'Connor, T.P., *Memoirs*.

[36] Wyndham, an ancestor of Lord Edward Fitzgerald, had many connections with the Irish gentry. He was related to the Earls of Mayo and Meath. His political mentor was Arthur Balfour, but he had a likeable maverick strain: he was a member of the aesthetic group 'The Souls'.

[37] Comment by John Redmond on Wyndham measures, See Denis Gwynn, *The Irish Free State 1922–1927* (London: 1928).

[38] The King had asked Sir Antony MacDonnell, Under-Secretary for Ireland (in effect head of the Irish civil service) if the Irish were 'disloyal'. Sir Antony said they were not, but they were discontented, for they wanted land and education. Bertie then replied: 'I shall come to Ireland with an education bill in one hand and a land bill in the other.' Richard Hough, *Edward and Alexandra: Their Private and Public Lives* (New York: St Martin's Press, 1993).

[39] John Biggs-Davison, *George Wyndham: A Study in Toryism* (London: 1951).

[40] *Freeman's Journal*, 21 July 1903.

[41] Biggs-Davison, *George Wyndham*.

[42] See Senia Paseta, 'Nationalist responses to two royal visits to Ireland, 1900 & 1903', *Irish Historical Studies*, vol 31, no 24 (November 1999).

[43] There were 16 bishops and archbishops gathered to meet the King. Cardinal Logue was in Rome for the Pope's funeral.

[44] See Kathleen Villiers-Tuthill, *The Connemara Railway* (Dublin, Connemara Girl Publications, 2003); and Henry Robinson, *Memories*.

[45] See Henry Robinson, *Memories*. It seems that Queen Alexandra did help to get this man a pardon and the episode is still remembered in Connemara: when I was attending the Clifden Community Arts Week in September 2008, a lady from Recess could still recall the way in which Alexandra's pardon had been treasured in local memory.

[46] Ibid.

[47] *Freeman's Journal*, 25 July 1903. RA PS/PSO/GV/PS/Main/4246/365. The whole visit is, of course, recaptured in James Plunkett's terrific novel, *Strumpet City*.

[48] See Foster, *Apprentice Mage*.

[49] The Earl of Aberdeen, as Lord Lieutenant of Ireland, wrote emolliently that 'one could understand' this attitude, and that it did not reflect personally on their Majesties in any way (RA, *Edward VII*, Doc. 74, p. 41a).

[50] See Maume, Patrick, *The Long Gestation: Irish Nationalist Life 1891–1918* (Dublin: 1999).

[51] See Biggs-Davison, *George Wyndham*. Also Lee, *Edward VII*.

[52] RA VIC/Main/W/75/12. Horace Plunkett to Lord Knollys, 30 November 1903.

[53] *Freeman's Journal*, 29 April 1904. It has already been noted that *Richard II* is sometimes called Shakespeare's 'Irish' play. The distinguished actor Timothy West (who played Edward VII in the noted BBC drama series) has researched this and comments, 'I've searched and can find no written evidence that *Richard II* was ever known as "The Irish Play", though of course it may well have been unofficially, among interested parties at significant moments in Irish-British political history. I do know that Act I, Scene IV, the scene in which it becomes clear that Richard intends raping the barons for funds for his Irish war, has often bothered directors, and in the 19th century it was quite common to leave it out. Interesting to know if they left it in for Edward VII.'

[54] Reported by *Freeman's Journal*, 28 April 1904.

[55] See entry for Dr Boylan in Boylan, *Dictionary of Irish Biography*.

[56] *The Times* of London (3 May 1904) reported that the 1904 visit was a great success, but commented, 'The Irish people are a puerile people. They have the credulity of the puerile and the suspiciousness of the half-civilised'. Thus, reasoned the newspaper (always inclined to see anything Irish in a negative light) they attached too much importance to the personal element in monarchy.

[57] *Oxford Dictionary of National Biography* (Oxford: OUP, 2004).

[58] See Lyons, *Since the Famine*.

[59] See Maume, *Long Gestation*.

[60] For Lady Aberdeen and her opponents, see Maureen Keane's biography, *Ishbel: Lady Aberdeen in Ireland* (Dublin: 1999).

[61] RA VIC/Main/W/75/2.

[62] RA VIC/Main/W/75/4, *Edward VII*, Doc. 14. See also Maume, *Long Gestation*, for a description of the further career of the Alderman.

[63] Ibid., *Edward VII*.

[64] RA VIC/Main/X/13/1-20 and RA VIC/Main/W/75-1–68. The crown jewels theft apparently took place on 10 June 1907: they were known to be missing from 11 June 1907. From 6 July 1907 all the Irish newspapers covered this story extensively.

[65] The 'Most Illustrious Order of Saint Patrick' was founded by George III in 1783 as an Irish counterpart to the English Order of the Garter and the Scottish Order of the Thistle. Its membership was originally limited to 15 knights, apart from the sovereign, but was increased to 22 in 1833. It was never awarded to those outside the peerage. The Lord Lieutenant (Viceroy) of the day was always ex officio Grand Master of the order, though not a member. After the foundation of the Irish Free State in 1922, only four new appointments were made, of which three were members of the British royal family. In 1927 the Attorney-General determined that, as a purely Irish Order, the matters relating to it were solely the concern of the government of Ireland and, while British govern-

ments did not agree with this ruling, moves to revive the Order came to nothing. The last surviving Knight, the Duke of Gloucester, died in 1974 (Micheál Ó Comain in Brian Laylor (ed), *The Encyclopaedia of Ireland* (Dublin: Gill & Macmillan, 2003).

[66] He was later given the Order of St Patrick by the Lord Lieutenant, Aberdeen.

[67] Bence-Jones, *Twilight*.

[68] For more on Sir Arthur Vicars' family background, see Susan Hood, *Royal Roots, Republican Heritage: The Survival of the Office of Arms* (Dublin: 2002).

[69] For more on the signatories to Sir Arthur's petition, see Hannafin & Cafferky, *Scandal and Betrayal*. Some of these peers, notably Lord Dunraven (a cousin of George Wyndham), were also supporting a move towards Irish devolution, whose object was to make the government of Ireland more in tune with Irish values.

[70] RA VIC/Main/X/13/7; RA VIC/Main/X/13/12; RA VIC/Main/X/13/15; RA VIC/Main/X/13/17. Letters between Knollys and Aberdeen and letters from Vicars.

[71] *Sunday Independent* (Ireland), 13 January 2008.

[72] Detective Chief Inspector John Kane of Scotland Yard was the officer in charge of the investigation (see Hannafin and Cafferky, *Scandal and Betrayal*).

[73] For background information on Shackleton and the other heralds, see Francis Bamford and Viola Bankes, *Vicious Circle: The Case of the Missing Irish Crown Jewels* (London: 1965); and Robert Perrin, *Jewels* (Lanham, MD: Rowman & Littlefield, 1979).

[74] For Shackleton's gay connections, see Hannafin & Cafferky, *Scandal and Betrayal*.

[75] Ibid.

[76] See Barbara Tuchman, *The Proud Tower: A Portrait of the World before the War, 1890–1914* (London: 1995), for the full story.

[77] The Eulenberg scandal was extensively covered in the London *Times*.

[78] Hannafin & Cafferkey, *Scandal and Betrayal*.

[79] See Bence-Jones, *Twilight*, for Sir Arthur's fate. See also Anthony Gaughan's *Listowel and its Vicinity* (Dublin: 2004). Father Gaughan says that the hapless Sir Arthur had merely been seen visiting the local British garrison, which would have been a normal action for a person with his background – although perhaps, in the circumstances, unwise. It was sufficient to label him a 'spy'.

[80] *Irish Independent*, 17 February 1908.

[81] RA VIC/Main/W/75/63 and 64, *Edward VII*, 19 February 1909. 'Cattle-driving', along with boycotting, was a tactic used by agrarian agitators to deter 'ranching' farmers from taking lands on short leases. Although the land acts had brought about many reforms, and given more tenants the right to buy, there still remained a substantial 'land hunger' among landless labourers and smallholders. See R.B. McDowell's *Crisis and Decline: The Fate of Southern Unionists* (Lilliput Press, Dublin: 1997).

[82] *Irish Catholic*, 30 April 1910.

[83] Norah Robertson, *Crowned Harp: Memories of the Last Years of the Crown in Ireland* (Dublin: Allen Figgis, 1960).

[84] From the *National and Leinster Times*, cited in Murphy, *Abject Loyalty*.

[85] *Irish Independent*, 7 May 1910.

[86] The Votive Mass was reported in the *Irish Independent*, 7 May 1910. Fenian republicans scrawled, 'Remember Terence Bellew MacManus' on the cathedral steps: see Léon Ó Broin, *The Chief Secretary: Augustine Birrell in Ireland* (London: Archon Books, 1969). Terence Bellew MacManus was a revolutionary Fenian who had died in 1860. He was sentenced to death for treason, but the sentence was commuted to transportation for life. He died in San Francisco (see MacManus entry in Boylan, *Dictionary of Irish Biography*).

[87] Foster, *Apprentice Mage*.

[88] *Irish Independent*, 6 May 1910.

[89] See Hibbert, *Edward VII*, for King Edward's visits to the theatre in Paris. Hibbert writes that the King, when in Paris, went to the theatre every evening: his favourites were the Theatre des Varieties, the Gymnase, the Vaudeville, the Odeon, the Palais-Royal, the Nouveautés, the Renaissance, the Porte St Martin, the Theatre Français, the Cabaret at the Lion d'Or, the Bouffes-Parisiens, the Moulin Rouge and the Café Anglais. These locations, mostly specialising in variety, music-hall and *spectacle*, do not suggest that the fare at the Abbey Theatre in Dublin would have been King Edward's cup of tea.

[90] I was charmed by a recital of Joyce's favourite Edwardian songs presented at Listowel Writers' Week in Co Kerry, May 2007, by Colm Stride O'Brien with the Teachers' Club Ensemble. When Joyce brought his father to London (with 12 guineas he had earned for an article on Ibsen) they spent nearly all their evenings at the music-hall. For 'The Man Who Broke the Bank at Monte Carlo', Eugene Sheehy had described Joyce 'with cane, hat and eyeglass, swaggering up and down the room' as he sang the song. Bertie, of course, makes his own walk-on appearance in *Ulysses*: 'Mr Deasy stared sternly for some moments over the mantelpiece at the shapely bulk of a man in tartan filibegs: Albert Edward, Prince of Wales.'

CHAPTER 3

[1] Quoted in Geoffrey Lewis, *Carson: The Man Who Divided Ireland* (London & New York: 2005).

[2] Quoted in F. A. Mackenzie, *King George in His Own Words* (London: Ernest Benn, 1929).

[3] See Harold Nicolson, *King George V: His Life and Reign* (London: 1952).

[4] Quoted in Piers Brendon and Phillip Whitehead, *The Windsors: A Dynasty Revealed, 1917-2000* (London: 2000).

[5] Tuchman, *Proud Tower*.

[6] Ó'Broin, *Chief Secretary*

[7] For George's view on homosexuals, see Brendon & Whitehead, *Windsors*.

[8] The ladies also had plans to burn down the Theatre Royal in Dublin, and actually made a start – fortunately, smoke was quickly detected (O'Broin, *Chief Secretary*).

[9] See Nicolson, *George V*.

[10] Brendon in Brendon & Whitehead, *Windsors*.

[11] John Gore tells of Alexandra teaching the young George his Bible in *King*

George V: A Personal Memoir (London: 1941). For further detail on George's childhood and upbringing see Kenneth Rose, *King George V* (London, 1983).

[12] Gore, *George V*.

[13] For George's early visits to Ireland, see Murphy, *Abject Loyalty*.

[14] For George's personal recollections of his time in Ireland, see Mackenzie, *King George*.

[15] For his offer to open the Dáil, see Nicolson, *George V*.

[16] Tuchman, *Proud Tower*.

[17] See Roy Jenkins, *Asquith* (London, 1964). Both Liberals and Unionists suggested, at one point or another, that the King might over-ride parliament, but this 'prerogative' had not been used since the reign of Queen Anne, and George V was far too correct a constitutional monarch to be pressed into it.

[18] See Lord Lansdowne's entry in Mathew & Harrison, *Dictionary of National Biography*. He was against awarding the old age pension in Ireland for fear it would discourage thrift. See also Ó Broin, *Chief Secretary*.

[19] This went down very well in Ireland among Catholics, and certain Irish Catholics wanted to present an expression of gratitude to the King. Lord Stamfordham, the King's Secretary, discouraged this idea. He wrote, 'No doubt the change in the Oath was an excellent one: but probably there are people in the North of Ireland who would like to present an address deploring the fact' (Royal Archives, *George V* (Windsor), PS 4246, Document 43, 13 June 1911). Stamfordham subsequently suggested that the 'majority of Protestants did not approve' (RA, *George V*, PS 4246, Doc. 76–7, 14 June 1911). This comment was written to Sir James Dougherty, the Under-Secretary for Ireland. Dougherty had previously been a Presbyterian Minister, a Liberal, and Professor of Philosophy at Magee College in Londonderry (O'Halpin, *Decline of the Union*).

[20] RA GV/PRIV/GVD/1911: 7 July, *George V's Diary*. Since there will never again be such a royal visit to Dublin, it is worth reproducing the programme of the Royal Progress into Dublin just for the record. 'The King and Queen were escorted from Holyhead to Kingstown by *HMS Cochrane* and *HMS Carnarvon* and by the Home Fleet [comprising]: the 1st Battle Squadron (8 ships and 2 attached cruisers); the 2nd Battle Squadron (8 ships and 1 attached cruiser); the 2nd Cruiser Squadron (5 ships); the 3rd Cruiser Squadron (3 ships). With the King and Queen: Prince of Wales; Princess Mary and Field-Marshal, the Duke of Connaught. Many other guests including: the Duchess of Devonshire, Mistress of the Robes; the Countess of Shaftesbury, Lady of the Bedchamber; Lady Bertha Dawkins, Woman of the Bedchamber; Earl of Shaftesbury, Lord Chamberlain to the Queen. Plus Crown Equerries, equerries in waiting, Master of the Household, Silver Stick in Waiting, aides-de-camp. Attending Their Majesties: the Lord Steward; the Acting Lord Chamberlain; the Master of the Horse; the Gold Stick in Waiting; the Vice-Admiral of the United Kingdom; the Aide-de-Camp General; the Crown Equerry; the Silver Stick in Waiting; the band, under the command of Lieut W. F. Sells, RN mounted at the Victoria Wharf (Kingstown). Address presented by the Urban District Council of Kingstown, read by the Town Clerk. His Majesty to reply. Miss Constance Vaughan to have

the honour of presenting a Bouquet to Princess Mary. Royal Carriage Route lined with men of the Royal Navy and Royal Marines. The Royal Procession consists of the following Royal Carriages: I. The King. The Queen. The Prince of Wales, Princess Mary; II. The Mistress of the Robes. The Lady in Waiting. The Lord Steward. The Chief Secretary; III. The Woman of the Bedchamber. The Acting Lord Chamberlain. The Lord in Waiting. The Vice-Admiral of the United Kingdom; IV. The Lord Chamberlain to the Queen. The Private Secretary. The First and Principal Naval ADC. The Groom in Waiting. Following on horseback: Field-Marshal, the Duke of Connaught; the Earl of Granard KP (Master of the Horse); Field-Marshal, Sir Evelyn Wood (Gold Stick); General, the Right Hon Sir Neville Lyttelton (Commander in Chief, the Forces in Ireland); Lieut-Gen Sir A. H. Paget KCB (Aide-de-Camp General); Capt, the Hon Charles Fitzwilliam, CVO (Crown Equerry); Col the Hon Sir Harry Legge, KCVO, Equerry in Waiting; and eight more military officers, including Clive Wigram and Captain C. Shawe, Aide de Camp to the Chief of the Forces in Ireland. Their Majesties to be attended by a Captain's Escort of the 5th Royal Irish Lancers. To Dublin Castle by Queen's Road, Longford Terrace East, George's Street, Cumberland Street, Longford Place, The Crescent, Monkstown Road, Temple Hill, Newtown Avenue, Blackrock, Williamstown, Booterstown, Merrion, Ballsbridge, Clyde Road, Wellington Place, Morehampton Road, Leeson Street Upper, Fitzwilliam Place, Fitzwilliam Square East, Fitzwilliam Street, Merrion Square East and North, Clare Street, Leinster Street, Naussau Street, Grafton Street (Lower), College Green, Dame Street and Cork Hill. At Ballsbridge: the Chief Commissioner of the Dublin Metropolitan Police, Sir John Ross; Cork Herald, Capt Lyonal Keith; Dublin Herald, Guillamore O'Grady Esq; Ulster King of Arms, Capt Nevile Wilkinson: plus Entourage. From Ballsbridge: the Dublin Mounted Metropolitan Police; Cork and Dublin Heralds in Tabards and Collars; two Troopers of the 1st Life Guards; Guard of Honour of 1st Battalion Irish Guards. Sword of State will be tendered to His Majesty by the Lord Lieutenant on arrival at Dublin Castle. Gentlemen of the Household and Officials taking part in the Ceremonial and Reception of Their Majesties will wear Levee Dress Uniform' (RA GV/PRIV/GVD/1911: 8 July; RA PS/PSO/GV/PS/Main/4246).

[21] Aberdeen, Marquis & Marchioness of Aberdeen & Temair, *More Cracks With 'We Twa'*, (London: Methuen, 1929).

[22] Royal College of Science, now the Taoiseach's office. The architects were Sir Aston Webb (who designed the Admiralty Arch in London) and Sir Thomas Manley Dean from Cork. The science college was incorporated into University College Dublin in 1926. In 1989 UCD vacated the building, and in 1991, after renovation by the Office of Public Works, it became the Taoiseach's department. With thanks to Kate O'Toole, Department of the Taoiseach.

[23] The children at the Iveagh Play Centre did 'Fancy Steps' and 'Step-Dancing'. They also performed the singing games called 'Mowing the Barley', and 'Oats & Beans & Barley' (RA PS/PSO/GS/PS/Main 4246/256). There were many and diverse invitations to the King and Queen, a large number of which they had to

turn down because of the pressure of the programme. One rather charming (but rejected) invitation came from Sir Charles Ball at the Dublin Zoo, suggesting that 'the King might like to see the tiger cubs, which he brought home from India and presented to us'. (RA PSO/GS/PS/Main/4246/160).

[24] Sunday, 9 July 1911. RA GV/PRIV/GVD/1911: 9 July The Archbishop of Armagh was John Crozier, considered to be a very fine preacher. His theme was 'Where there is no vision, the people perish.' With thanks to Dr Raymond Refaussé, librarian and archivist at the Church of Ireland archives in Dublin.

[25] See Kitchener entry, Mathew & Harrison, *Dictionary of National Biography*. Yet in spite of this clear bias Stamfordham, in planning the general programme, was most conscious of 'balancing' Catholic and Protestant interests in Dublin and Lord Aberdeen actually wrote specifically to say that if the King were to appear at Trinity College Dublin, there should be a 'balancing' visit to a Catholic institution (RA PS/PSO/GV/PS/Main/4246/373 and RA PS/PSO/GV/PS/Main/4246/306 and 306a). The King also disbursed contributions to certain charities with a keen eye for balance: indeed, the St Vincent de Paul Society received £200, while the Association for the Relief of Distressed Protestants only got £50.

[26] See entry for Murphy in Boylan, *Dictionary of Irish Biography*. In fact T. P. O'Connor called Murphy a 'great man' in 1929 (*Memoirs*).

[27] RA GV/PRIV/GVD/1911: 11 July 1911. There were 133 Loyal Addresses of welcome at the garden party, of which the King heard 111.

[28] RA PS/PSO/GV/PS/Main/4246/88B-C. Dublin ladies subscribed £311.2s.0d; Cork £125.10s.1d; and Belfast £114.14s.6d. Clare and Mayo, the most 'Catholic' counties in Ireland, subscribed £36.14s.5d and £40.8s.5d (and a halfpenny) respectively, outdoing the more Protestant county, Sligo (£26.7s.8d), and almost matching the wealthier Kildare (£53.12s.5d and a halfpenny), and Westmeath (£33.0s.6d.). The money raised was to be used for the education of nurses, and to be equally split between Protestant and Catholic training schools.

[29] *Irish Independent*, 18 July 1911. Helena Molony had been supporting Constance Markievicz in opposing the royal visit.

[30] RA GV/PRIV/GVD/1911: 12 July.

[31] RA GV/PRIV/GVD/1911: 12 July and RA PS/PSO/GV/PS/Main/4246/368. The success of this visit undoubtedly helped to sustain King George in his attempts to be fair to Ireland.

[32] *Church of Ireland Gazette*, 14 July 1911.

[33] *Irish Independent*, 5 July 1911.

[34] For the mounting Home Rule crisis, see Alvin Jackson, *Home Rule: An Irish History 1800–2000* (London: 2003).

[35] For background to Andrew Bonar Law and James Craig, see Mathew & Harrison, *Oxford Dictionary of National Biography*. For Carson, see Lewis, *Carson*.

[36] Jenkins, *Asquith*.

[37] *Church of Ireland Gazette*, 19 April 1912.

[38] At this time, when documents or newspapers referred to 'Ulster' they intended the full nine counties of the Irish province. Later, as a political partition loomed, 'Ulster' came to mean (in the British papers) the six counties of Northern

Ireland, shorn of Donegal, Cavan and Monaghan. These three counties also contained Unionists who signed Carson's Covenant, so 'Ulster' at this point is geographically exact.

[39] RA PS/PSO/GV/C/K/2553/1/16. This *cri de cœur* ('Never has a British Sovereign been placed in such a position …') occurs in King George's papers, at this period, at least half a dozen times. His complaint about his position is also in RA PS/PSO/GS/C/K/2553/5/98/B.

[40] Lewis, *Carson*. Carson was writing to his friend and mentor Lady Londonderry.

[41] Denis Gwynn, *The Life of John Redmond* (London: 1932). See also Hardie, *Political Influence*. Redmond was impressed by King George's concern and involvement, and it may have influenced him towards supporting the Crown at the outset of the Great War.

[42] Ó Broin, *Chief Secretary*. Also DNB.

[43] RA PS/PSO/G5/C/K/2553/3/53. Fitzmaurice was the son of the 5th Marquess of Lansdowne (*Who's Who*, 1911.) Other advice the king received was of similar sort, such as that coming from 'Anon. On Home Rule': 'The majority of the people are not at all favourable to Home Rule … I don't know that a more artificial political movement was ever saddled on a people than this one of Home Rule. During all the years which I have listened to it I have not heard one strong and convincing argument advanced as a ground for it (a necessity for it), not even in Parliament where it has now been debated on three historic occasions. … It is purely a sentimental question' from Ballincollig, Co Cork, a comment about Home Rule for 'Schemers and Dreamers … idiots who advocate revival of the Irish language which will be about the same commercial value as Choctaw Indian, or less' (RA/PS/4246/97).

[44] RA PS/PSO/GV/C/K/2553/4/66.

[45] RA PS/PSO/GV/C/K/2553/1/1. In 'Celtic Tiger' Ireland, the gombeen men would subsequently have been termed dynamic entrepreneurs, hailed as an example of prosperity, not ruination. However, this is unlikely to be the case now.

[46] RA PS/PSO/GV/C/K/2553/1/2: 27 September 1912. This is 'a note of observations made to HM by Mr Bonar Law'. Bonar Law erroneously believed the King could be pressed into using his prerogative to override Parliament.

[47] RA/PS/PSO/GV/C/K/2553/1/44. Long was a former Irish Secretary and an ultra-Unionist. He believed, effectively, in discrimination against Catholics in civil service jobs in Ireland. That is, he wanted only 'strong Unionists' in key positions serving the Crown – a recipe for alienation. Nevertheless, O'Halpin describes him as 'gullible' (O'Halpin, *Decline of the Union*).

[48] St Loe Strachey greatly admired Carson and campaigned for the Ulster cause in *The Spectator*. He was not unamusing – as with most journalists he liked to arouse controversy. His family seemed inclined to extremes. His son, John Strachey, was an ardent left-winger who famously predicted in the 1930s that the entire world would shortly be Communist – and a jolly good thing too.

[49] RA PS/PSO/GV/C/K/2553/1/22 and 23. Sir Robert Kennedy to the King.

[50] RA PS/PSO/GV/C/K/2553/1/17 and 18.

[51] The historians Professor John Murphy of Cork and Professor Alvin Jackson of Edinburgh have suggested that I am over-inflating the Ulster effect on Irish nationalists – both comment that the roots of Irish separatism lie much deeper. I accept their expertise is greater than mine, but I was so overwhelmed by the passionate sense of commitment and rebellion shown by the Ulster Loyalists when reading through these despatches that, had I been a young Irish nationalist in 1912, I would have immediately felt the contagion of this excitement. Imaginatively, I feel it must have been highly influential.

[52] Ruth Dudley Edwards, *Patrick Pearse: The Triumph of Failure*, 2nd edn (Dublin: Irish Academic Press, 2006).

[53] RA PS/PSO/GV/C/K/2553/2/20. Sir Robert Charles tells the King the North is ready to fight: 'The fight is *not* against their fellow-countrymen but against priestcraft that sows the seeds of dissension among as worthy a people as there is in the world. The mental strain on the people here is to the breaking point.'

[54] RA PS/PSO/GV/C/K/2553/2/20. Winston Churchill speaks with the King. Although Churchill has often been regarded critically by Irish historians, he was not hostile to Ireland and always believed in an Irish nation – in contradistinction to his father, Randolph. But he also believed that the Ulster Unionists could not, or should not, be coerced, which is what the majority of Irish people believe today, as is clear from referenda.

[55] RA PS/PSO/GV/C/K/2553/2/27. F. E. Smith sees the King. Smith, of course, was to become Lord Birkenhead.

[56] RA PS/PSO/GV/C/K/2553/2/85: 15 November 1913. This was reported by Lord Crichton, the eldest son of the Earl of Erne (who would have been the original object of 'boycotting' in Co Mayo, since Captain Boycott ran his estates). In her memoir, *Crowned Harp*, Nora Robertson recalls that King George V was considered by some Irish loyalists as not sufficiently 'loyal' to his own Crown. Truly, an illumination of the French phrase, *plus royaliste que le Roi*.

[57] RA/PS/PSO/GV/C/K/2553/4/37: 20 March 1914. Sir Francis Hopwood reporting to the King on rumours of the Curragh Mutiny.

[58] RA PS/PSO/GV/C/K/2553/4/39 and 49: 20 Mar 1914. To add insult to injury, the King was blamed by 'radical and socialist papers' for 'interference'.

[59] RA PS/PSO/GV/C/K/2553/5/9: 14 April 1914.

[60] See Hardie, *Political Influence*.

[61] Maurice Headlam describes Redmond as 'ugly' and 'squat' in his memoirs (*Reminiscences*).

[62] See Diarmuid Ferriter, *Transformation of Ireland*.

[63] RA PS/PSO/GV/C/K/2553/4/58: 7 April 1914. Yet another document (RA PS/PSO/GV/C/K/2553/5/28) indicates that Redmond was touched by King's invitation to the Buckingham Palace Conference.

[64] Murphy, *Abject Loyalty*. See Jackson, *Home Rule*, for the full political background to this episode and a political analysis of the Home Rule crisis of 1912–14.

[65] RA PS/PSO/GV/C/K/2553/6/104: September 1914. George V writes to Sir Francis Hopwood.

[66] Letter to the Prime Minister (RA, *George V*, PS 4246, Doc. 99, 17 Sept 1914).

[67] RA PS/PSO/GV/C/K/2553/6/103.

[68] See Hardie, *Political Influence*.

[69] 'What Redmond seems to have wanted [and was denied] was an Irish army corps, such as other "dominions" possessed,' Alvin Jackson writes. He was 'not denied all-Ireland regiments' (as some biographies claim). 'There were many historic Irish regiments in the British army – the Connaught Rangers, Royal Munster Fusiliers, Leinster Regiment, Royal Dublin Fusiliers – which ... recruited principally Catholic Irishmen.' Yet when John Redmond died, the King sent a representative to his funeral. With thanks to Prof John A. Murphy for this note.

[70] John Redmond was described as 'implacable' by the Archbishop of Canterbury, Andrew Bonar Law, in letters sent to the King (RA PS/PSO/GV/C/K/2553/4/5: 7 March 1914). Redmond had deprecated the exclusion of Ulster (RA PS/PSO/GV/C/K/2553/2/3/5: 30 Nov 1913), and Lord Morley, the Liberal parliamentarian, had warned that Redmond should be made aware that the bottom would be knocked out of Home Rule if there was bloodshed (RA PS/PSO/GV/C/K/2553/2/99).

[71] Lewis, *Carson*.

[72] Paul Bew, *Ireland: The Politics of Enmity, 1789–2006.* (Oxford: 2007).

[73] Jackson, *Home Rule*.

[74] Reported in J. J. Horgan's, *From Parnell to Pearse: Some Recollections and Reflections* (Dublin: Browne & Nolan, 1948). Professor Jackson (Ibid.) also notes that John Redmond's own son fought bravely in the Great War and was decorated with a DSO.

[75] It was a surprise to me, as a young reporter in London in 1966, that older journalists still spoke of the Easter Rising of 1916 as 'Ireland's stab in the back to England'. Philip Hope-Wallace, the very cordial opera critic of the *Guardian* and doyen of Fleet Street's El Vino, used this phrase about 1916 quite regularly.

[76] RA GV/PRIV/GVD/1916: 24–29 April and 3 May 1916. This quote and those which follow, taken from RA, *George's Diary*.

[77] Roy Foster, *Modern Ireland*.

[78] Jackson, *Home Rule*.

[79] Sir Alexander MacIntosh wrote in *Echoes of Big Ben: A Journalist's Parliamentary Diary, 1881–1940*, 2nd edn (London: Hutchinson, 1946), his memoir as a parliamentary correspondent, 'Irish nationalists were missed by old British colleagues. Life was seldom dull while they were in force at Westminster, with their vivacity and humour. Personally they were not unpopular.' Quoted by James McConnell in Gray, *Victoria's Ireland*. Alvin Jackson suggested in a memo to me that the Irish Parliamentary Party tradition was continued, to some degree, by T. M. Healy, Kevin O'Higgins and James Dillon. But these men were in Dublin – not Westminster – after 1916. See Maurice Manning, *James Dillon* (Dublin: 1999).

[80] Jackson, *Home Rule*.

[81] Nicolson, Harold, *George V*. The King writing to Stamfordham from a train near Sunderland: 'Very glad Govt are going to grant amnesty to Irish prisoners as it ought to help convention, I see it is to be announced in House today & I

have never been asked for my approval. Usual ways things are done in present day. I better join the King of Greece in exile.'

[82] For George's decision about the Tsar, see Rose, *George V*. The British Labour Party, in Harold Wilson's famous phrase, 'owed more to Methodism than to Marx'. Its roots were in Protestant Nonconformity rather than Marxism. Nevertheless, the Labour (and many elements of the Liberal) Party regarded the Tsar as a tyrant, and welcomed his downfall. In St Petersburg in 2008, I saw many icons of the 'Tsar-martyr' and his family in Russian churches, and a revival of veneration for the Romanovs.

[83] Pope Benedict XV preached many sermons on peace, and wisely suggested that when hostilities came to an end 'victors' justice' should be avoided. For his pains, he was labelled pro-German by the Allies. Only Turkey honoured him, erecting a statue to him in Istanbul as 'the great pope of the world tragedy ... the benefactor of all people, irrespective of nationality or religion': J. N. D. Kelly, *The Oxford Dictionary of Popes*, 6th edn (Oxford: OUP, 2006).

[84] *Messenger of the Sacred Heart* (circulation around 300,000 in 1920) was an example of one such magazine. Even Winston Churchill appreciated how important this movement was: he thought conscription for Ireland would be 'suicidal'.

[85] John A. Murphy, *Ireland in the 20th Century* (Dublin: 1975).

[86] See Gore, *George V*, and James Pope-Hennessy, *Queen Mary:1867–1953*, 1st edn (London: Allen & Unwin, 1959).

[87] Barbara Cartland, *We Danced All Night* (London: 1970). The author's account of society life in the London of the 1920s.

[88] By 1919 de Valera had good reason to object to the King's words: Brendan Sexton, *Ireland and the Crown, 1922–1936. The Governor-Generalship of the Irish Free State* (Dublin: 1989).

[89] For the King's disapproval of the Black and Tans, see Nicolson, *George V*.

[90] RA PS/PSO/GV/C/I/1514/17: 28 May 1921.

[91] Francis J. Costello writes in his biography of MacSwiney, *Enduring the Most* (Cork: 1995), that Stamfordham contacted J. C. Davison – a legal advisor to the Cabinet – about the King's concern over Terence MacSwiney, not just on compassionate grounds, but because his death would have very serious repercussions. (Moderate Irish Unionists from the south, such as Lord Dunraven and Horace Plunkett, also tried to plead on behalf of MacSwiney.) The Manchester *Guardian* reported that the King was prepared to exercise his prerogative of clemency, if constitutionally able to do so: this turned out not to be possible, since the King's pardon in these cases is usually, de facto, exercised by the Home Secretary. Queen Mary also added her voice, writing that while she could not express any political opinion '... in any political controversy human life should not be sacrificed on either side. Therefore as a woman she hopes the King's Ministers who have the power and are humane men may see their way to spare Ireland from additional sorrow' (quoted in Costello, *Most Enduring*). In the end, this dialogue was to no avail, as the British government did not wish to show 'leniency' (in a prequel to Margaret Thatcher with Bobby Sands in 1981). With thanks to Professor John

A. Murphy who recommended Costello's important book to me. Professor Murphy comments that the case of MacSwiney 'again raises the question about the possible use of the royal prerogative, illustrates royal unease about the repression/reprisals policy of the Government in regard to the Irish conflict, and shows an independent royal attitude at work on this subject.'

[92] Nicolson, *George V.*

[93] The king's visit to Belfast 1921: This file at Windsor is not yet fully catalogued, but most material pertaining to the correspondence is in RA PS/PSO/GV/Main/32977/A. There was copious correspondence about George V going to Belfast. Stamfordham told Craig that: 'The Editor of an important paper was here this morning and told me that he had yesterday interviewed an Irish Orangeman, who seriously doubted the advisability of the King's visit' (RA PS/PSO/GV/PS/Main/32977/A, 9 June 1821, marked 'secret'). Overall response to the news of the visit was mixed, to say the least. The Bishop of Chelmsford told Stamfordham that 'there is nothing but dismay at the visit of the King [to Belfast]. Not a single person that I have met approves and it would postpone any idea of settlement' (PS/PSO/GV/Main/32977/A) But there was a warm welcome awaiting from southern Irish Unionists, pleased the King should visit any part of Ireland: 'Your Majesty's Loyal Subjects in Southern Ireland, represented by the Irish Unionist Alliance, send you dutiful and cordial welcome on your visit to Ireland' (*The Times*).

[94] Both the drafts and the speech itself are printed in full in Nicolson, *George V.* On an interesting linguistic note, the King in his drafts for the Belfast speech referred to Northern Ireland as 'the Six Counties'.

[95] A. J. P. Taylor, *English History: 1914–1945* (Oxford: OUP, 2001), When George and Mary arrived back in London, they were greeted with public singing and chanting: 'For He's a Jolly Good Fellow'; 'Long Live Ireland – Long Live Their Majesties the King and Queen of Ireland' (for full report, see *The Times*, 21–24 June 1921).

[96] RA/PS/PSO/GV/PS/Main/32977K/702/3.

[97] For the opening of Belfast Parliament, see Harold Spender's piece in the *Daily Telegraph*, 23 June 1921. The press coverage for the King and Queen's Belfast trip was terrific, notably the way in which the popular press hailed the sovereigns' 'pluck'. *The Irish Catholic*, however, was more focused on Edward Carson's enigmatic absence: 'Lord Carson is a shrewd and hard-headed politician and it was not without good reason that he deliberately arranged months ago to refrain from identifying himself with the opening of the sham Legislature. Why did he do so? The answer is that he foresaw the failure of the freak parliament and made up his mind to wash his hands of the whole business' (25 June 1921). R. B. McDowell suggests that, to Carson, the separate government of Northern Ireland represented a sad failure of true Unionism, and that Carson felt part of a 'deserted garrison' (*Historical Essays*).

[98] On the same date *The Irish Catholic* also noted the 'all but total absence of Irish Catholics at the festivities. Only two figured on the official lists as being present.' It is not clear if Catholic officials stayed away on purpose. It was a period of bitter

sectarianism, and *The Irish Catholic* referred to the 'plotting for the extermination of Catholics in the Six Counties' (25 June 1921). In London, the Editor of the *Catholic Herald* (Charles Diamond, who edited the paper from 1888 to 1934), had written to the King asking him not to 'avoid driving through streets where the homes of large numbers of Catholics have been destroyed, simply because they are Catholic'. He also asked the King 'to express some opinions on the Irish massacres in the same way as was expressed through the Duke of Connaught with regard to the Amritzar Massacre' (some thirty Catholics had recently been killed in sectarian attacks). This letter was marked 'Rather disloyal in tone' by Stamfordham, and sent on to Sir James Craig (PS/PSO/GV/Main/32977/D/5). Stamfordham may, however, have been influenced by Diamond's reputation as a 'rebel'. When he died in 1934, *The Times* carried the following brief obituary on 20 February 1934: 'Mr Charles Diamond, editor of the *Catholic Herald*, died in London yesterday. He was born in Ireland in 1858, and founded many weekly newspapers in London and the provinces. From 1892–95 he sat as a Nationalist member for North Monaghan, and as a Labour candidate he later unsuccessfully contested Peckham, Rotherhithe, and Clapham. In March 1920, he was sentenced at the Central Criminal Court to six months' imprisonment in the second division in respect to an article, 'Killing No Murder', which appeared in the *Catholic Herald*. The defence was that the article was a philosophical and historical dissertation on an important political topic, and that the idea of inciting to outrage had never entered Mr Diamond's mind. A number of witnesses testified to his high character.' (With thanks to Luke Coppen, present Editor of the *Catholic Herald* for identifying Diamond as the editor in question and to Patrick West for providing *The Times* obituary.)

[99] For the letters from Mrs Pope-Hennessy and Mr J. F. Manning, see RA/PS/PSO/GV/Main/32977/D/16 and 24.

CHAPTER 4

[1] See Dáil debates at www.historical-debates.oireachtas.ie.

[2] Cartland, *We Danced*.

[3] The King had felt very pleased with the signing of the Treaty, and wrote in his diary, 'Tuesday December 6th. I got the joyful news the first thing this morning from the Prime Minister that at 2.30 this morning articles of agreement were signed between the British representatives & the Irish delegates involving complete acceptance of the British Govt's proposals, allegiance to the Throne & membership of the Empire. They sat from 11.00 till 2.30 before the agreement was arrived at. It is mostly due to the PM's patience & conciliatory spirit & it is a great feather in his cap & I trust now after seven centuries there may be peace in Ireland. Ulster has got the option of coming in within a year, if they wish, but they will not be coerced' (RA/GV/PRIV/GVD/1921: 6 December).

[4] See Dáil debates at www.historical-debates.oireachtas.ie. All subsequent quotations from this debate are from this excellent source.

[5] From the start, the Dáil (equivalent to the British House of Commons) decided not to emulate Westminster in nomenclature. Members were called 'deputies',

after the French fashion, in everyday parlance. 'Teachta Dáil' (TD) is the 'Member of Parliament' in Irish.

[6] Kathleen Clarke's memoir, *Revolutionary Woman: An Autobiography, 1878–1972* (Dublin: 1991), gives a vivid picture of those Irish nationalists who lived by the principle of 'Burn everything English but their coal'.

[7] Eoin MacNeill's speech was witty, but of course the monarchy had 'done' pageantry in what was, for Republicans, a dangerously seductive way. Mary MacSwiney's fears that young girls might be drawn into this pomp and ceremony (and she was not alone in this apprehension) may have been based on the ideas of the writer George Moore, whose novel, *A Drama in Muslin*, focuses on the obsession of society mothers with marriageable daughters on invitations from Dublin Castle. Moore had joined other advanced nationalists in objecting to the visit of Edward VII to Dublin. Lord Wimbourne, the Viceroy in 1916, had wanted MacNeill shot: but by that time Wimbourne had reacted to events by taking seriously to the brandy bottle (Ó Broin, *Chief Secretary*).

[8] See Foster, *Apprentice Mage*.

[9] See Denis Gwynn, *The Irish Free State, 1922–1927* (London: 1928); and Sexton, *Ireland and Crown*. In most Commonwealth countries, the Governor-General had previously been British. Professor Fanning notes that Beaverbrook, the influential press baron, backed Tim Healy. This is mentioned in volume 3 of Tom Jones' *Whitehall Diary*, 3 vols, ed. Keith Middlemas (Oxford: OUP, 1969).

[10] Peter Somerville-Large, *Irish Voices: an Informal History, 1916–1966* (London: 1999).

[11] Sexton, *Ireland and Crown*.

[12] See Gwynn, *Irish Free State*. There was a great deal of argument about emoluments for the Governor-General, for which see Sexton, *Ireland and Crown*.

[13] See Gwynn, *Irish Free State*.

[14] RA/PS/PSO/GV/C/0/1805/1: 30 August 1922. Lord Desart wrote (from Guildford in Surrey), 'Now that both Griffiths and Collins are dead I think the chances of the 'Free State' coming into existence are more precarious than they were. They were the only leaders left who were committed to the notorious agreement – and any one who tries to take their place will I think have to placate the extremists. … Griffiths [sic] was the only man who realised that there ought to be any consideration for minorities, or had a conception of Government & administration. I hope there will not be more gush about Collins – I have in my mind the deaths of British officers, British soldiers & Police where he was responsible. For them the Government apparently care nothing – or for the unfortunate Loyalists who did their duty, in the belief that England could not abandon them & leave them unprotected & helpless as it has done.' He then went on to say that 'the anarchy is complete – and men with revolvers go about saying openly that now there is no law they can do as they like and take what they want …' Stamfordham replied on September 2, saying the King had read his letter with much interest. He writes that 'to my mind the condition of things is deplorable and pathetic, and, as you say, many of the horrors perpetrated are never reported in our newspapers.' Later he adds, 'do not pray imagine that there

was any sympathy here with the … gush of the Press about Collins' (RA PS/PSO/GV/C/O/1805/2: 22 September 1922).

[15] Lord Castletown, *Ego* (London: 1923).

[16] 'Adult suffrage' meant including women in the vote, and it was widely feared that women would be more radical, and less responsible in their voting pattern: there was much fear of the 'flapper vote'. But if radical women gave that impression, in reality the mass of women voted more conservatively than men when they did get the vote.

[17] RA PS/PSO/GV/C/O/1805/2: 22 September 1922.

[18] See entry for Henry Wilson in Mathew & Harrison, *Oxford Dictionary of Biography*.

[19] Charles J. Haughey also considered reviving the Patrick in some form – mainly, some have suggested, to annoy the British. Since the death of the Duke of Gloucester in 1974, there is now only one member of the Order, Queen Elizabeth II. If Ireland were to revive the Order of St Patrick, it would be necessary to call it by a slightly different name: say, the Order of Merit of St Patrick, effectively to re-invent it. With thanks to Michael O'Sullivan for his expert knowledge in this field.

[20] See Terence de Vere White, *Kevin O'Higgins* (Dublin: 1997).

[21] For comment on divorce, censorship of films and the 'Irish soul' in 1920s Ireland, see Ronan Fanning, *Independent Ireland* (Dublin: 1983). The sea-green incorruptible Republicans regarded divorce as a form of English immorality (how little they knew King George V!). In the Treaty debates Constance Markievicz defined English ideals as: 'love of luxury, love of wealth, love of competition, trample on your neighbours to get to the top, immorality and divorce laws' (quoted in *Ireland and Crown*). There were also many exhortations from high-minded clergy about the purity of the simple life, eschewing jazz and modern materialism. High-minded Puritanism was also evident in Northern Ireland: values were shared even if politics were not.

[22] See Gwynn, *Irish Free State*.

[23] For the veteran in question, see Sir Christopher Lynch-Robinson's *The Last of the Irish RMs* (London: Cassell, 1951).

[24] Gwynn, *Irish Free State*.

[25] See R. F. Foster, *The Arch-Poet: 1915–1939*, vol 2 of *W. B. Yeats: A Life*, 2 vols (Oxford: OUP, 2003).

[26] See Sinead McCoole, *Hazel: A Life of Lady Lavery* (Dublin: 1996).

[27] Kevin O'Higgins' deathbed was an extraordinary illumination of the candour (and acceptance) with which death was approached in this period. '"Do you mind dying, Kevin?' his wife asked. A smile came over his face. 'Mind dying? Why should I? My hour has come. My job is done.'" The naturalness of male friendship is also graceful and uninhibited. O'Higgins' friend and colleague Patrick Hogan knelt beside him, and O'Higgins said, 'I loved you, Hogan' (from de Vere White, *O'Higgins*).

[28] National Archives of Ireland (Dublin), DT UCDA/P35B/115: 25 March 1931. George's fear that de Valera would be returned to power (since he was believed to be a radical revolutionary) was shared by southern Unionists in *The Church of*

Ireland Gazette at this time. When the King saw Dev's 'Document Number Two' in the run-up to the Treaty, in August 1921, he called it 'hopeless', something written by 'a dreamer & a visionary with nothing practical about it.' Yet just a month later, in September, the King telegrammed to the Prime Minister: 'Just received Mr de V's telegram of 17th. I cannot help thinking that it is intended to be conciliatory and to show his anxiety for immediate conference. Has he not made rather a good point that your previous conversations were unconditional and that hence he inferred you recognised him as what he considered himself "to be and to have been"?' (RA PS/PSO/GV/C/K/1702/A/9: Aug 1921 and RA/PS/PSO/GV/C/K/1702/A/52: Sept 21. In 1937 King George VI told John Dulanty that his father 'had always had a quiet but real admiration for Mr de Valera because [of] the news which reached his father from various sources … [and] the President's rare gift of natural good manners' (NAI, 2006/39, No. 17: 6.05.1957). Many who were alarmed by Éamon de Valera's radical republicanism at this time were charmed by his personal courtesy.

[29] For more detail on de Valera's intentions when forming his administration, see Frank Longford and Thomas P. O'Neill, *Éamon de Valera* (London: 1970).

[30] See de Vere White, *O'Higgins*; see also David Harkness, *The Restless Dominion: The Irish Free State and the British Commonwealth of Nations, 1921–31* (London: 1969).

[31] Land annuities were monies payable to the UK Exchequer by tenants on Irish estates who had purchased their holdings under the Land Acts that encouraged the former tenants to acquire their own land on something like a mortgage system.

[32] NAI DFA, Vol. IV.

[33] For Dulanty's brief on the oath, see Deirdre McMahon, *Republicans and Imperialists: Anglo-Irish Relations in the 1930s* (Yale & London: 1984).

[34] From his autobiography, *My Story* (London: 1937).

[35] King George on Jimmy Thomas (RA/PRIV/GVD/1933: 4 Sept 1933).

[36] Thomas, *My Story*.

[37] Ibid.

[38] On 13 April 1932 Sir Harry Batterbee of the Dominions Office wrote to the King's secretary: 'As a result of rapid but careful search of records, it does not appear that the question of the taking of an Oath by Ministers (apart from the Parliamentary Oath) was ever raised at the time of the Treaty Negotiations' (Quoted in Deirdre McMahon).

[39] RA, *George V*, PS 2484A.

[40] NAI, D.15.29.03/32: 5 April 1932 and RA/PS/C/L/2484/A/15 and A/23. With regard to his complaints against Britain 'extracting a financial tribute', he wrote that the 1921 Treaty involved 'no parity of sacrifice as between Gt Britain and Ireland. This agreement gave effect to what was the will of the British Government'. This was perhaps so, but his claim that the Treaty was 'on the other hand directly opposed to the will of the Irish people' ignores the fact that the majority of the Irish people endorsed it by vote.

[41] RA PS/PSO/GV/C/L/2484/E/20 and A23: 19 May 1932. Mr Dulanty put forward de Valera's theory that the Sinn Féin Republicans would not join in the

democratic process until the oath was removed. He was certain that de Valera did not want to leave the Commonwealth. Dev had stated that the oath 'is not a symbol of the connection of the Commonwealth. The Monarch is the connection. The Oath is a comparatively new thing. The Oath is a conscience test' (*Daily Express*, 2 May 1932). Perhaps he had in mind that, in the 19th century, Protestant members of certain official bodies in Ireland were not obliged to sign an Oath of Allegiance, whereas Catholic members were, hence the 'test of conscience'. He also told the King, via Wigram, that Erskine Childers' widow was 'the most dangerous and bitter woman in the Irish Free State'.

[42] See Sexton, *Ireland and Crown*, on abolishing the post of Governor-General.

[43] See McMahon, *Republicans and Imperialists*.

[44] RA PSO/GV/C/L/2484/A/15 and A/16, 29 Mar 1932.

[45] J. H. Thomas on Seán T. O'Kelly, *My Story*.

[46] *Irish Press*, 20 April 1932. On the same date, alongside the denunciations of the odiousness of the Oath of Allegiance, was the heading, 'Hindenberg Re-Elected but Hitler Gains Strength'.

[47] For the forthcoming Eucharistic Congress and Dev's clever way of avoiding a top hat, see RA PS/PSO/GV/C/L/2484/E/20. Later on, according to Tim Pat Coogan, he became rather fond of the topper: Coogan, Tim Pat, *Ireland in the 20th Century*, 2nd edn (London: Arrow Books, 2004).

[48] RA PS/PSO/GV/C/L/2484/E/20.

[49] For reports of the Congress, see *Irish Press*, 23–26 April 1932. Just prior to the Congress Mrs Margaret Pearse (mother of Patrick and Willie Pearse) had died. One hundred thousand people attended her State funeral, as well as the top political *gratin*. Mrs Pearse had suffered an irreparable loss (her second son, Willie, was executed simply because he was Patrick's brother) and her role as sacrificial mother was justly honoured, with a lying-in-state and flags at half-mast. Yet, like the bishops and the clergy, she was also (in a way) part of a new nobility of the Free State, and her very remarkable state funeral showed the need for ceremonials that touch and unite.

[50] Definition from *The Catholic Encyclopaedia*, 1930.

[51] *Irish Tatler*, July 1932. This edition is a particularly fascinating insight into the reconstruction of a social order. Arguably, the new elite class was composed of a more stimulating mixture than the Dublin Castle habitués of yore: a Trinity College gathering for 1932 features artists such as Mainie Jellet, diplomats, doctors (the distinguished Dr Solomons and his wife), Papal aristocracy (Countess van Cutsem, whose husband was Chamberlain of Cape and Sword to His Holiness Pope Pius), Oliver St John Gogarty, the Lady Mary Meade (daughter of the Countess of Clanwilliam), Professor Starkie, et cetera. Other celebrities shown in the magazine were the Countess of Fingall, Revd T. A. Finlay SJ, the Earl and Countess of Longford, Mr Shane Leslie ('the well-known Catholic author'), General and Mrs Cosgrave, the Earl of Granard, James Montgomery (who was the film censor), Miss Anne Gregory, and, of course, the Governor-General and his wife, Josephine. Incidentally, at TCD, the band played both 'The Soldier's Song' and 'God Save the King' on a parity-of-esteem basis.

[51] The hussars' costumes were certainly put together with love, as well as economy. Pauline Whelan wrote in *History Ireland* (vol. 16, no. 2, March/April 2008): 'At the time [of the Eucharistic Congress], the country was in severe financial trouble and could not afford new tack for the Blue Hussars. My father, a tailor by trade, was commissioned to make many of the blue saddle-covers for the horses.' This single tailor stitched the saddle-covers together unaided in his workshop.

[52] With thanks to Michael O'Sullivan for this information.

[53] His name was spelt thus in the Irish newspapers in 1932, but subsequently spelled 'Lorenzo' in history books.

[54] The *Irish Independent* featured a remarkable, if slightly startling, photograph of the Irish state planes flying in the form of a Christian cross (21 June 1932).

[55] The *Irish Press* on the Eucharistic Congress and the Irish diaspora (21 June 1932; visit reported in 21–29 June editions).

[56] *Irish Press*, 22 June 1932.

[57] David Lloyd George was now on the back benches of the House of Commons, but he had spoken critically about Ireland breaking with the Treaty conditions over the Oath of Allegiance.

[58] *Irish Press*, 22 June 1932.

[59] The drip-drip humiliation of James McNeill is described in detail in Sexton, *Ireland and Crown*.

[60] The comments that follow are all from the *Irish Tatler*, July 1932.

[61] *Irish Press*, 26 June 1932.

[62] Finola Kennedy commented on Æ's actions and words during this period in *What If There Had Been No Eucharistic Congress?* Presented by D. Ferriter on RTÉ Radio 1, 3 June 2007.

[63] For the King's attitudes and comments on divorce, see Brendon & Whitehead, *Windsors*, and Robert Sencourt, *The Reign of Edward VIII* (London: 1962).

[64] C.V. Balsan, *The Glitter and the Gold* (London: 1952).

[65] For Fitzgerald's description of the conversation between the Prince of Wales and McGilligan, see NAI.536. DT.S2485A and UCDA, Document P80/1411.

[66] Comments from the public on the Prince of Wales' visit (E VIII PWH/Main/2496): November 1932.

[67] Ibid. Drafts for the Prince of Wales' speech at the formal opening of Stormont, 16 November 1932. For a more detailed commentary on the political aspect of Edward, Prince of Wales's opening of Stormont, see Chapter 14 of Loughlin, *The British Monarchy and Ireland*.

[68] Ibid. Ward Price's comments.

[69] This is mentioned in several texts, including Manning, *Dillon*, and Fanning, *Independent Ireland*.

[70] Rose, Kenneth, *King George V.*

[71] *Irish Press*, 22 June 1932. There was a strong emphasis on 'Ireland's unbroken *allegiance*' and the 'eternal *loyalty*' of the Irish people to the Holy See, not coincidentally drawing on words and phrases often associated with the Crown. It both mirrored what Ulster Unionists said about the Crown, and enflamed – and confirmed – their prejudices.

[72] Nicolson, *George V*. In 1930, George V told Ramsay MacDonald, 'What fools we were not to have accepted Gladstone's Home Rule Bill. The Empire would not have had the Irish Free State giving us so much trouble and pulling us to pieces.' See also Rose, *George V*.

[73] Dev to J.H. Thomas on Jubilee. NAI No. 222. UCDA P 150/2298, 16 May 1934. Quoted in Crowe, Ronan et al., Vol IV of DIFP (Documents on Irish Foreign Policy).

[74] Saorstát Éireann was deliberately absent from the official Jubilee celebrations. There were sectarian riots in Belfast at this time, which made it particularly sensitive: difficult to judge whether Éire's abstention inflamed the Orangemen more or served to placate the Ulster nationalists. However, Joseph Walshe, Mr de Valera's adviser, did relent somewhat in agreeing that the Irish High Commission should conform to general attitudes taken by other diplomats in London: Catriona Crowe et al (eds), *Documents on Irish Foreign Policy, Volume IV: 1932–1936* (Dublin: Royal Irish Academy, 2004), NAI 34/117A, Doc. 256, 9 March 1935).

[75] McMahon, *Republicans and Imperialists*.

[76] The semi-comical saga of Domhnall O'Buachalla's period as Governor-General is excellently reported in a number of sources. Sexton, *Ireland and Crown* is most detailed. See also Patrick Murray, *Oracles of God: The Roman Catholic Church and Irish Politics, 1922–37* (Dublin: UCD Press, 2000).

[77] Murray, *Oracles*.

[78] Joseph Walshe told Sir Edward Harding, Permanent Under-Secretary at the Dominions Office, that it was difficult for an Englishman to appreciate how intense the feeling for the Irish language was. As my brother Carlos was being thrashed severely at his school for the offence of speaking English out of school hours just around this time, Mr Walshe spoke more meaningfully than he knew (for the King's refusal to sign Irish documents, see Crowe et al, *Documents, Vol IV*, NAI, TNA 35/398/1, Doc. 144, 29 Oct 1932).

[79] Dominions Secretary, Jimmy Thomas, strongly supported the partial ban on Irish imports – he felt that the Irish had too often treated the King shabbily.

[80] Sencourt, *Edward VIII*.

[81] Rose, *George V*.

[82] For instructions on how the King's death was to be treated by the Irish Free State, see Crowe et al, *Documents, Vol IV*, NAI DT S8524, Doc. 316. It was also noted that while the accession of Edward VIII was proclaimed in London, 'no action' would be taken in Dublin (NAI, DT S8520, Doc. 314).

[83] RA, *George V*, PS 018/003, March 1936.

[84] Clive Wigram noted that there had also been headaches over replies to letters sent during George V's Jubilee. He wrote that 'I saw the High Commissioner on 22nd February and expressed myself strongly on this matter, but to no effect' (RA PS/PSO/GVI/C/018/002 and C/018/004). Letters of condolence came from many bodies in the Free State, many of them with 'Southern Unionist' connections, such as Royal Irish Yacht Club, the College of St Columba, the Protestant Orphans Society, the Royal Zoological Society, the Royal Dublin Fusiliers Old Comrades Association, The Royal Hibernian Academy of Arts, the

Boy Scouts Association, the Parishioners of Glenageary, and many more, including sections of the British Legion in the Free State. It is noted that 'thousands of Free State Loyalists' posted letters from Holyhead in Wales, indicating a lack of trust in the Irish administration. On 18 February 1936 there is correspondence between Joseph Walshe and John Dulanty, marked 'Secret and Confidential', on the question of these letters of condolence. Walshe instructs Dulanty to communicate the following: 'Replies originating in the Palace are altogether unnecessary. They would rather tend to lessen the atmosphere of appeasement and good will, which has been created by the Government's attitude on the King's death. Lord Wigram's replies from the Palace would be regarded by the ordinary Irishman as irritating propaganda and they might have – in some cases certainly would have – the effect of rousing anti-monarchist passions.' Joseph Walshe clearly did not quite understand the psychology of the Royal Irish Yacht Club or the Protestant Orphans Society (Crowe et al, *Documents, Vol IV*, Doc. 317).

[85] See Tim Pat Coogan, *De Valera: Long Fellow, Long Shadow* (London: 1995).

[86] NAI, 2006/39/8, Doc. 16.

[87] See Sencourt, *Edward VIII*. Clement Attlee was a very unsentimental man, and he always supported the monarchy and the constitutional position.

[88] Crowe et al, *Documents, Vol IV*, 19.11.36, NAI 2003/17/181, Doc. 382.

[89] For de Valera's romantic attitude to King Edward's relationship with Mrs Simpson, see Longford & O'Neill, *De Valera*; and for his thoughts in the text that follows, see Crowe et al, *Documents, Vol IV*, TNA:PRO CAB 127/156, Doc. 383. De Valera also thought that divorce was fine for English Protestants, but not Irish Catholics. He mentions that it is looked on quite differently in the two cultures. But that was not quite so. As the evidence in the Mrs Simpson case shows, the English Protestant Establishment abhorred it.

[90] For the opinion of governments in the Dominions on the King's affair, see Sencourt, *Edward VIII*.

[91] *Irish Catholic*, 10 Dec 1936. The *Church of Ireland Gazette* expressed the concern of Irish Anglicans and other Protestants that the monarchy might be harmed by this scandal (18 Dec 1936). Ed Kelly, presently teaching in Budapest, mentions a Father Doyle in Naas, who was very exercised about the King marrying a divorced woman: politically, he felt that Prime Minister Baldwin should be supported. Kelly adds, 'He was the priest who received Michael Collins' body at the North Wall when it was returned from Cork in 1922.'

[92] Eileen Clare and other individuals mentioned here very kindly wrote to me about their recollections, after I sought such memories through *The Irish Times*, *Irish Independent*, and *Examiner*. With gratitude to those who wrote to me. So many correspondents made the point that there was great personal and family interest in the events leading up to the Abdication, and people kept boxes of mementoes about it for years afterwards.

[93] Yeats' support for Edward is mentioned in Bill McCormack's *Blood Kindred: The Politics of Yeats and his Death* (London: Pimlico Books, 2005).

[94] Professor O'Sullivan was particularly critical of the haste with which this leg-

islation was put through (see www.oireachtas.ie for the transcript of his comments). *The Church of Ireland Gazette* was also coruscating. However, it is clear that Republicans (in Fianna Fáil and in Sinn Féin) were pleased to get the King out of the Irish constitution.

[95] David Twiston-Davies, writing in the *Daily Telegraph*, 21 January 1992. He quotes the constitutional lawyer, Rex Mackey, then a senior member of the Irish Bar who claims that Ireland is still, theoretically, a monarchy because the Abdication Act was not correctly carried through in Dublin. Mackey's book, *Windward of the Law*, rev 2nd edn (Dublin: Round Hall Press, 1991), presses home this point. It is a rather playful constitutional nicety but it is still remembered, and mentioned by constitutional buffs when the subject comes up.

CHAPTER 5

[1] Cited in Garvin, *Irish Democracy*.

[2] 'Must you leave the family?' A slightly different version of this question is given in Sarah Bradford's *King George VI* (London: 1989). The version used here is the one seen by Daithí Ó Ceallaigh, Irish Ambassador to London (2002–7), in diplomatic papers (reported to me by Mr O Ceallaigh).

[3] Cited in the Duke of Windsor's autobiography, *A King's Story* (London: 1951).

[4] See Ferriter, *Transformation of Ireland*. It will be recalled that this description was given to Parnell and, before Parnell, to O'Connell.

[5] See Harkness, *Restless Dominion*.

[6] See Bradford, *George VI*. For his various detractors, see: Andrew Roberts, *Eminent Churchillians* (London: 1995); Hugo Vickers, *Elizabeth, The Queen Mother* (London: 2005); and Brendon & Whitehead, *Windsors*.

[7] Queen Elizabeth's obstetrical history marked a small landmark in the annals of birth control: the Church of England was not wholly approving of contraception in the 1930s, sharing, with the Catholic church, the view that 'marriage was instituted, first, for the procreation of children', as spelled out in *The Book of Common Prayer*. However, it did accept that fertility control was acceptable in cases such as Queen Elizabeth's: for health reasons, and not merely for pleasure. For the Queen Mother's Caesarian, see Ben Pimlott, *The Queen: A Biography of Elizabeth the Second* (Glasgow: HarperCollins, 1997); for the acceptance of contraception by the Church of England, see Audrey Leathard, *The Fight for Family Planning* (London: Palgrave Macmillan, 1980). The Church of England only fully accepted birth control in 1958: and then, of course, only for married couples.

[8] See NAI, 2006/39 29.6.03.37. This was a riveting conversation in which the King unburdened himself at some length to the High Commissioner (see also Chapter 4, note 28).

[9] *Irish Press*, 12 May 1937.

[10] *Irish Press*, 13 May 1937.

[11] See Fanning, *Independent Ireland*.

[12] For O'Buachalla's reason for taking on the Governor-Generalship, see Murray, *Oracles*.

[13] For James Dillon's attendance, see Manning, *Dillon*. Pamela O'Mahony wrote to the *Irish Press* in September 1979 (significantly, after the death of Lord Mountbatten) remembering her father's courage in also attending, and at his own expense.

[14] For de Valera's instruction to official 'detachment', see NAI, 2006/39/12, Doc. 14; Mr Dulanty's comments to the King are included in the same document.

[15] 'Éire' is used here purely descriptively and as a word of its time. It is not now used to denote the 26 counties (although it is, naturally, used in the Irish language for 'Ireland'), however in the late 1930s and 1940s it was used in official documents to denote the political area of the Free State.

[16] NAI 2006/39, 29.6.03.37. Talking about raising children.

[17] Keen to attend the Coronation himself, as ever Mr Dulanty was meticulously diplomatic in urging Dublin to be co-operative over this question (Joseph Walshe kept the British waiting until the last moment with his answer of Yea or Nay – it was Nay, although documents make it clear that the British establishment, especially Sir Harry Batterbee, were keen to have Dev at the ceremony). NAI 2003/17/181. No 50. 30 April 1937.

[18] NAI, 2006/39/12, Doc. 14. Malcolm MacDonald had succeeded Jimmy Thomas at the Dominions Office. Thomas had – rather honourably – resigned after accidentally leaking information about a forthcoming budget. The progressively educated MacDonald was less of an ardent monarchist than the working-class Jimmy Thomas.

[19] NAI 2006/39, No 23, 19 February 1937; NAI 2003/17/181, No 39, 23 March 1937. John Dulanty also had correspondence with Sir Harry Batterbee on the heraldic aspect of the coronation, claiming that such offices as the High Constable of Ireland, the High Steward of Ireland, the Ulster King of Arms and the Dublin herald were now 'anachronisms'. He added that Mr de Valera would not, however, object to the Protestant Archbishop of Dublin participating in the coronation (Crowe et al, *Documents, Vol IV*, NAI 2006/39/12, Doc. 23).

[20] See Brendon & Whitehead, *Windsors*, for the descriptions of the procession cavalcade.

[21] Discussed by Bradford, *George VI*.

[22] *Irish Independent*, 12 & 13 May 1937.

[23] NAI, 2006/39/12, Doc. 17.

[24] *Church of Ireland Gazette*, 22 Jan 1937.

[25] Cited in Somerville-Large, *Irish Voices*.

[26] See Dermot Keogh and Andrew McCarthy, *The Making of the Irish Constitution, 1937* (Cork: 2007). That the constitution was 'not Catholic enough' was a point made in correspondence in *The Irish Catholic* at the time.

[27] The prohibition on divorce was finally deleted after a hard-fought referendum (the second) in 1995.

[28] UCDA P150/2410, No 43, 22 April 1937, Quoted in Crowe, Fanning et al: DIFP, Vol V 1937-39. Joseph Walshe went specially to Rome to speak to the Cardinal Secretary of State, Eugenio Pacelli, who would become Pius XII. Mr Walshe pronounced himself 'very disappointed' at the papal withholding of

approval. The English text of the Latin was given as 'I do not approve, neither do I not disapprove, we shall maintain silence'. The double negative puzzled Walshe, but the sense was the same.

[29] Longford & O'Neill, *De Valera*.

[30] See Nadia Clare Smith's *Dorothy Macardle: A Life* (Dublin: 2007); also Diarmuid Ferriter, *Judging Dev* (Dublin: 2007).

[31] Máire de Blacam wrote to the *Irish Independent* on 24 June 1937 to explain why she was not complaining, as a woman, about the constitution: 'Sir – I received an invitation to attend the meeting of women graduates convened to protest against the Constitution as detrimental to the status and just claims of women. For two reasons I ignored the circular. First, because I cannot find anything in reference to women in the Constitution that is worthy of condemnation. Every responsible woman who has at heart the interests of a Christian society and sees the dangers to the proper equilibrium of the family must rejoice that the Constitution seeks to protect the father of the family as breadwinner, and the mother as home-maker. My second reason for abstaining from participation in that meeting was that I knew the two university Professors who took such a prominent part in the organising and holding of it to have been consistently opposed to the whole national movement and one of them even to have opposed Women's Suffrage. Thus the meeting seemed to appeal only to the agitating and anti-national elements among the women voters.'

[32] Conor Cruise O'Brien has suggested that privately the great Gaelgoir was probably a Unionist – see *States of Ireland* (London: 1972).

[33] See Coogan, *De Valera*, for de Valera and Hyde at tea with the papal nuncio, 4 May 1938.

[34] See RA PS PSO/GVI/PS/COR/1000/75/A/68 and 75/D/20, for the reports on visitors from the Irish Free State; also Gray, *Ireland This Century*, for Dubliners travelling up to Belfast.

[35] RA PS/PSO/GVI/018/004 and RA PS PSO/GVI/PS/COR/0100/75/A: 3 August 1938. Despite his reassurances, Ulster Unionists were rattled that as much British media attention was on the threat (and reality) of IRA violence as on the King and Queen. See Chapter 14 of Loughlin, *The British Monarchy and Ireland*.

[36] RA, *George VI*, 018/003.

[37] RA, *George VI*, 018/007: 23 May 1938.

[38] Sometimes these 'small matters' were *particularly* small. For example Irishmen wearing uniforms of the British forces on holiday in Ireland were reported by the Dublin administration to the British authorities, as there was an agreement that uniforms of the Crown forces would not be worn in the Irish Free State. Sometimes these were just local lads (possibly trying to impress their girls.) On one occasion, the offenders were teenage matelots who were only cabin boys on board ship (John Breen and Evan Furlong of Wexford), but they were duly reported to the Admiralty by Joseph Walshe for the offence of stepping ashore in their Royal Navy togs (NAI, 2006/39/12, Doc. 22, March 1937).

[39] See Maurice Manning, *James Dillon* (Dublin: 1999).

[40] J.J. Lee, *Modernisation of Irish Society*.

[41] Andrew Roberts, *Eminent Churchillians* suggests that George VI could (and perhaps should) have intervened, but that he was too trusting of Chamberlain to do so.

[42] When I was researching a biography on William Joyce, *Germany Calling: A Personal Biography of William Joyce, 'Lord Haw-Haw'* (Dublin: New Island, 2004), I was astonished to come across so many groups in Britain in the late 1930s who were initially against war.

[43] For Dev, Munich, Chamberlain, and George VI, see Roberts, *Eminent Churchillians.*

[44] For de Valera's congratulations on the repossession of Czechoslovakia, see Coogan, *De Valera.*

[45] See Coogan, *De Valera.*

[46] It has been claimed that de Valera appealed to the King for a pardon, but this never occurred. With thanks to David O'Donoghue, who has researched this for his forthcoming book on the Coventry bombings. The King was inclined to be merciful to Barnes and McCormick and grant them a reprieve, but he was overruled by the government, James Loughlin, *The British Monarchy and Ireland.*

[47] Paul Bew and Henry Patterson, *Seán Lemass and the Making of Modern Ireland* (London: 1982).

[48] See Brendon & Whitehead, *Windsors.*

[49] Ibid. for Queen Mary in wartime.

[50] For comment on Elizabeth, the Queen Mother, in wartime, see Vickers, *Queen Mother.*

[51] For Roosevelt's view of Ireland in the Second World War, see Brian Girvin, *The Emergency: Neutral Ireland, 1939–45* (London: 2006).

[52] An unnamed source (identified only as 'X') sent a memo to the Irish government in August 1942 reporting a conversation with Winston Churchill in which Churchill said, 'I would do anything to get a united Ireland but I would not coerce the Six County Government.' He was asked what he meant by coercion. He replied, 'By coercion I mean having troops there and using physical force to compel these people to take a course against their will. But I am willing to use pressure and have indeed done so. I have also used persuasion and am ready to do these things again, but I must have something from Mr de Valera on which I can build … some gesture of friendship towards both the Six County Government and Great Britain.' The source said, 'Churchill friendly to Ireland in 1908 and on other occasions, but a violent reversal of that process since about 1932.' The source then added that 'WC's attitude to Ireland was far more liberal than I had given him credit for. For WC, once a battle is over, it's over' (NAI, 2007/39/16, Doc. 22, 12 August 1942).

[53] NAI, 2007/39/16 IA, Doc. 9.

[54] See Brendan Anderson, *Joe Cahill: A Life in the IRA* (Dublin: O'Brien Press, 2003). According to information provided to the Irish government, Cardinal Hinsley of Westminster wrote to Churchill, Herbert Morrison, and Sir John Anderson pleading for clemency and was supported in this by the Archbishop of Canterbury. George Bernard Shaw wrote a letter to *The Times* on 28 August 1942. However it was noted that Clement Attlee was 'cold and detached on the subject',

whereas Anthony Eden was 'sympathetic'. The Irish in Britain were pro-Labour and would vote for Attlee, but he was a man devoid of sentimentality, and would make decisions on principles not 'sympathy' (NAI, 2007/39/16, Doc. 25 & 26).

[55] These 'social and personal' reports are taken at random from the *Irish Independent* in 1939. The *Irish Independent* readership was mainly Catholic, often agricultural, and moderately nationalist.

[56] Sister Marie wrote to me with her recollections.

[57] See Gorham, *Forty Years*.

[58] See Peter Vansittart, *In The Fifties* (London: 1995).

[59] Girvin (*Emergency*) points out that he did not visit the American Embassy after Roosevelt's death.

[60] For the complete text of Churchill's speech, see Winston Churchill, *The War Speeches of Winston Churchill* (London: 1952). See also Longford and O'Neill, *de Valera*.

[61] Longford & O'Neill, *De Valera*.

[62] Listowel Writers' Week, 29 May 2008.

[63] Randolph Churchill, Winston's son, had a long conversation with John Dulanty later in 1945, in which he indicated an apology by proxy for his father's May-time outburst against Éire and de Valera. Randolph said that 'his father's reference to Ireland and the Taoiseach was a piece of folly. His father was the first to accept it.' Randolph commented that the Taoiseach's reply to Winston was 'a master-piece'. He also added that, in his own opinion, 'partition was finished. Everybody in England who thought about the question at all realised that it was a histori-cal injustice which must be remedied … generally speaking, people were sick of the Belfast Unionists peddling their prejudices about Westminster and there was a very general feeling that the partition of Ireland was wrong as a matter of principle' (NAI, 2006/39/18, Doc. 17a, 27 October 1945).

[64] Spain and Portugal, neutral in the war and still in the grip of Franco and Salazar, were the exceptions. *Dublin Opinion*, the gently satirical monthly magazine which was widely read in the 1940s and 1950s, alluded only half-ironically to Spain's achievement as the only country yet which had defeated a Communist takeover.

[65] See MacBride's entry in Boylan, *Dictionary of Irish Biography*.

[66] Every modern Irish history has dealt extensively with this question, but it is worth giving a brief resumé here. The coalition government involving Clann na Poblachta proposed a health scheme to support mother and child care. The Catholic church (and the medical profession) objected: the Church because it regarded the proposal as an interference with private morality and a form of creeping communism, the doctors because the scheme assumed more power and control over the medical profession. Seán MacBride sided with the Church against his own colleagues, notably the radical Noel Browne, who was made to re-iterate his fidelity to the Catholic Church. The scheme was dropped (the bill itself was also said not to have been well-drafted) and Browne was forced to resign. Later a subsequent government introduced a modified version. The con-troversy is regarded as a classical case of 'church v state' in which the Catholic Church had little compunction in exercising its authority, and in forcing politi-

cians to defer. Later on in the century, the Church had to pay the price, many times over, for this exercise in perceived arrogance. As with many issues, the 'mother-and-child' controversy is more nuanced on close examination than appears when citing this simple adversarial version of the story.

[67] See Ronan Fanning, 'The Response of the London & Belfast Governments to the Declaration of the Republic of Ireland, 1948–49', in *International Affairs*, vol. 58, no. 1, 1981–2.

[68] Tony Benn recollected Mountbatten's comment about the servants voting Tory in his diaries *The Benn Diaries: 1940–1990* (London: Arrow Books, 1998). See Roberts, *Eminent Churchillians*, for Mountbatten's last night in India with Dev and Frank Aiken.

[69] See Noel Browne, *Against the Tide* (Dublin: 1986).

[70] See R. F. Foster, *Lord Randolph Churchill: A Political Life.* (Oxford: 1981).

[71] For the events at Ottawa, see Browne, *Against the Tide*. See also Anthony J. Jordan's *John A. Costello: Compromise Taoiseach, 1891–1976* (Dublin: Westport Books, 2007).

[72] See Ian McCabe, *A Diplomatic History of Ireland*.

[73] For Earl Alexander of Tunis, see Mathew & Harrison, *Dictionary of National Biography*. With thanks to Tom McGurk for telling me about Caledon.

[74] See Bradford, *George VI*, for the dialogue at this party.

[75] For Dulanty's conversation with King, see NAI, 2006/39/21, Doc. 16, 30 Oct 1948.

[76] Ibid. Queen Elizabeth did not think the Irish government was 'given to forgetting'.

[77] Attlee's government responded to the declaration of the Irish Republic by giving a guarantee to Northern Ireland that its status would never be altered by Britain without the consent of the Northern Ireland Parliament. This had the effect of 'cementing' partition.

[78] RA PS/PSO/GVI/C/312/23 and 312/24: 11 April 1949.

[79] RA PS/PSO/GVI/C/312/33: 17 April 1949.

[80] RA PS/PSO/GVI/C/312/37: 18 April 1949.

[81] RA PS/PSO/GVI/C/312/46: 18 April 1949.

[82] RA PS/PSO/GVI/C/312/55: 18 April 1949.

[83] RA PS/PSO/GVI/C/312/66: 5 May 1949.

CHAPTER 6

[1] *Irish Press*, 7 Feb 1952.

[2] In the nationalist newspapers at this time 'The Archbishop' meant the Catholic archbishop: in British and Unionist newspapers an archbishop would be automatically Anglican, unless specifically denoted as 'Roman Catholic'. In my 1950s childhood I was taught that 'the only Roman Catholics who exist are Catholics who live in Rome', and the term 'RC' was regarded as somewhat disdainful. In Britain, Catholics were referred to in slang as 'Arsees', designed to be jokingly disparaging: English Catholics were miffed by the appellation, since they con-

sidered themselves as holding to an older English faith than the one established by law.

[3] To be fair to Seán T. O'Kelly, the 'whipping John Bull' speech was in the middle of an election, when politicians tend to make hot-headed claims.

[4] *Irish Press*, 7 Feb 1952.

[5] *Irish Press*, 15 Feb 1953.

[6] The *Irish Press* reported the questions in the Dáil (21 Feb 1953), but the newspaper's display of the story was significant, since it was 'down-page' and on the inside of the paper. Had it carried de Valera's approval, it would have been centre-page and on the front.

[7] Elizabeth II was crowned as 'Queen of the United Kingdom of Great Britain and Northern Ireland'. In the few political allusions she has made over a reign of more than 50 years, she has indicated that the union of her Kingdom, as defined by her coronation vow, has been meaningful to her. See Sarah Bradford's, *Elizabeth II* (London: 1996).

[8] Cahir Healy and Michael O'Neill were interesting characters, in that (unlike many other, or subsequent, politicians) they had led full lives before entering parliament: they had both published poetry and plays, had been involved in commerce and a wider community life, and they had a 'hinterland' of culture. Cahir Healy was a persistent campaigner to bring back the remains of Roger Casement to Ireland (a goal finally achieved under the Labour Home Secretary, Roy Jenkins, in 1968), but he was basically old Liberal in values (*Who's Who*, 1954).

[9] Conor Cruise O'Brien, who directed propaganda for the Irish government in the Irish News Agency, has written of this 'sore thumb' approach in *States of Ireland*, and other writings. Partition was to be raised to vex and embarrass the British as widely as possible.

[10] NAI, 2006/39/21, Doc. 7. Writing in *The Irish Times* on 5 June 1997, Tom Farrell reported that in July 1946 the Dáil had urged the de Valera government to apply for United Nations membership. 'Our application was supported by six nations, but opposed by Andrei Gromyko of the Soviet Union on the grounds of alleged sympathy with the Axis powers during 1939–45.'

[11] Churchill approached his old friend John Dulanty at the Cenotaph on 4 November 1948 and told him: 'I said a few words in Parliament the other day about your country because I still hope for a united Ireland. You *must* get those fellows from the North in, though you can't do it by force. There is not, and never was, any bitterness in my heart towards your country' (NAI, 2006/39/21).

[12] These landladies' notices are mentioned frequently in accounts of the time: Bob Geldof refers to them even in his experience as a student worker in England in the 1960s: see his autobiography *Is That It?* (London: Penguin, 1986). Yet Dónall MacAmhlaigh's account of his life as an Irish navvy in England describes, on the whole, a rather friendly reception to Irish workers: *An Irish Navvy: The Diary of an Exile*, trs Valentin Iremonger, 2nd edn. (Cork: Collins Press, 2003).

[13] The Archbishop of Dublin, John Charles McQuaid, was able to close the planned production of *The Ginger Man* in Dublin in 1959, though he had no statutory authority to do so. Such pressure also succeeded because managements (and newspaper editors) too weakly ceded to pressure.

[14] In Anthony Cronin's hilarious memoir of life with Brendan Behan, the homo-sexual world of Dublin bohemia in the 1940s and 1950s is unaffectedly described: *Dead As Doornails: A Memoir*, 2nd edn. (Dublin: Lilliput Press, 2000).

[15] See Nancy Mitford, *A Talent to Annoy: Essays, Articles and Reviews, 1929–68* (London: Hamish Hamilton, 1986). Mitford had family connections in Ireland: her sister Diana was married to Sir Oswald Mosley and they lived for some time in Ireland in the 1950s. Her nephew was Desmond Guinness of the Irish Georgian Society. Miss Mitford's other sister, Deborah, was (and is) the Duchess of Devonshire, chatelaine of the beautiful Lismore Castle in Co Waterford.

[16] MacAmhlaigh, *Irish Navvy*.

[17] An unnamed Irish labourer, quoted in Ronan Fanning's *Independent Ireland*. After Ireland left the Commonwealth in 1948–49, there was speculation that Irish people in Britain would be treated in the same way as other aliens. Lord Rugby wrote to the Taoiseach on 7 October 1948: 'The probable effect of the repeal of the External Relations Act is being urgently considered in London. If the legal effect of the repeal of the Act is held to be, as may well be the case, that Éire becomes a foreign country in relation to the other countries of the Commonwealth, there would flow from that relationship important consequences, particularly in the field of preferences and nationality' (NAI, 2006/39/21, Doc. 14, Jan–Dec 1948). Sir Stafford Cripps also gave John Dulanty 'a lecture' about Ireland wanting it every which way (Ibid, Doc. 25). In the end, Ireland did have it both ways: out of the Commonwealth, but still treated as a friendly neighbour, which shows you can sometimes get what you want by pushing the envelope.

[18] For the Festival of Britain, see Vansittart, *Fifties*; and Jonathan Bastable (ed), *Yesterday's Britain* (London: Reader's Digest, 1998).

[19] *An Tostal* ran from 5–26 April.

[20] Tony Gray has called it 'a dismal failure' (*Ireland This Century*). However it did spark off a new interest in heraldry in Ireland (*Irish Press*, 9 March 1953). Programmes for *An Tostal* were announced from early March of 1953. It was noted later in the month that Queen Mary had died on the same day that the festival began, and the *Irish Press* recalled that John Dulanty had had many inter-esting talks with her about antiques (26 March 1953). Antiques were her passion and he was a social genius at relating to people through their interests: he had many cordial conversations with Queen Mary over the course of their acquain-tance. During a delicate moment in 1936, Dulanty's admirable social tact was noted in the archives. There was a cordial lunch with Queen Mary who 'recalled a time in Ireland, on the Shannon, when it rained and rained.' The Queen and another guest spoke about 'the kindness of the Irish people and the simple good manners of the peasant folk' (UCDA, P35B/115,). Though couched in what we would now regard as patronising language, it was intended to be emollient at a time when Anglo-Irish relations were scratchy.

[21] Queen Elizabeth visited Northern Ireland from 1–3 July 1953. David Maxwell Fyfe was a pillar of the establishment, and a strong upholder of law and order, but he had written an affectionate biography of T. P. O'Connor, the Irish parlia-mentarian.

[22] *Irish Press*, 2 July 1953.

[23] Ibid.

[24] *Irish Press*, 3 July 1953

[25] Ibid.

[26] The Queen was pictured with two great Lambeg Drums in *The Irish Times*, 3 July 1953.

[27] The Harris report was reprinted in the *Irish Press* on 8 July 1953.

[28] The *Irish Press* (3 July 1953) reported both the attack on the Great Northern Line, and the way in which the Anti-Partition Association picketed members of the British Legion and ex-servicemen travelling to Belfast.

[29] For reports on the procession at Knock and a 'rosary crusade' in Galway, see the *Irish Independent*, 10 May 1954. '700 at Mass in Factory' was reported by the *Irish Independent* on 11 May 1954. Coincidentally (or not) this last report was accompanied by a display advert from *The Illustrated London News* for a special edition about Queen Elizabeth's tours, with an especially radiant picture of the young queen in white ermine fur and diamond crown.

[30] For reports of the Corpus Christi processions in Dublin ('Dublin Marks Marian Year with Solemn Processions'), see the *Irish Independent*, 14 & 17 May 1954.

[31] John Dulanty received a fine obituary in *The Times* of London on 12 February 1955, reprinted in *The Times, Great Irish Lives, An Era in Obituaries,* Charles Lysaght (London: HarperCollins, 2008).

[32] See Boylan, *Dictionary of Irish Biography.*

[33] Boland's report appears in a file at the National Archives of Ireland for the 1950s, with the date of 26 October, but it was not categorised at the time I noted it. The Ambassador's despatches were usually political and austere, so this narrative about Princess Margaret was not really his style. By 27 October 1955, the *Irish Independent* was reporting the story openly. The *Irish Press* had picked up a comment from the left-wing *Tribune* in July 1953, to the effect that the 'British Cabinet prevented Princess Margaret from marrying a divorced man' (*Irish Press*, 8 July 1953).

[34] That Margaret might inherit the throne seemed within the realms of possibility at the time. She was then fourth in line, after Charles and Anne, and as they were young children, Margaret would have qualified as Regent in the event of the Queen's death.

[35] Dr Leslie Weatherhead quoted in the *Irish Independent* (28 Oct 1956).

[36] Cited in Tim Heald, *Princess Margaret: A Life Unravelled* (London: 2007).

[37] The church Margaret attended was All Saints, in Margaret Street, W1. Lord Snowdon told me that Princess Margaret was 'episodically' religious.

[38] NAI, 9 Nov 1956.

[39] Union Jack torn down at dance. Reported in the *Irish Independent* (27 Oct 1955). Student says: 'Nowhere in the world where Britain was in occupation would students tolerate a display of the Union Jack in such circumstances'.

[40] Martina Devlin in the *Irish Independent* (22 Nov 2007).

[41] With thanks to Elizabeth McCluskey, who wrote to me with these recollections.

[42] Altrincham's remarks here, and in the text that follows, cited in Bradford, *Elizabeth II.*

[43] See Jordan, *Costello.*

[44] F. S. L. Lyons, *Ireland Since the Famine*.

[45] 'The Patriot Game' was written by Dominic Behan, and has been recorded by many fine groups, including The Dubliners and The Clancy Brothers. The latter group omitted a verse blaming Éamon de Valera for the situation in the North, much to the annoyance of Dominic Behan. It went thus: 'This Ireland of mine has for long been half free / Six counties are under John Bull's tyranny. / And still de Valera is greatly to blame / For shirking his part in the patriot game.' This certainly is not a fair assessment of de Valera, who focused on the 'national question' to the detriment of so many other pressing issues.

[46] *Irish Independent* (11 June 1961). In 1978 I interviewed Princess Grace in London and it was clear she was very attached to her Irish roots in Co Mayo.

[47] Cited in Heald, *Princess Margaret*.

[48] See Anne de Courcy, *Snowdon: The Biography* (London: Weidenfeld & Nicolson, 2008).

[49] Lord Snowdon's personal recollections of Ireland are all courtesy of the interview he gave me on 3 March 2006.

[50] This story about Brendan Behan also came out in the course of my interview with Lord Snowdon. Brendan Behan's association with the Coventry bombings of 1939 will be documented in David O'Donoghue's forthcoming book, *The Devil's Deal: The IRA, Nazi Germany and the Double Life of Jim O'Donovan*.

[51] *Irish Times*, 2 Jan 1965.

[52] See *Irish Times*, 6 Jan 1965 and subsequently, for letters about the Snowdons' visit.

[53] With regard to the new celebrity of the rock and pop world, a telling incident is related by Bence-Jones in *Twilight of the Ascendancy* (London: 1987), when he describes the handover of Kilkenny Castle to the state by Lord Ormonde on 12 August 1967: suddenly it seems that the public is much more interested in the arrival of the Rolling Stones. 'To the media, they were far more interesting than Lord Ormonde, the 6th Marquess, the 24th Earl, the 30th Hereditary Chief Butler of Ireland ...'

[54] See Bew, *Politics of Enmity*.

[55] Gormley, *Irish Times*, 4 April 1967.

[56] John Horgan, *The Irish Times* religious correspondent, had written that Irish Catholics, particularly in the West, were most keen to embrace their Protestant neighbours during this period of 'ecumenism': their main anxiety was that there would not be enough Protestants to go around (see Kenny, *Goodbye to Catholic Ireland*).

[57] Fanning, *Independent Ireland*.

[58] 'Dublin in the Rare Aul' Times'.

[59] The circumstances of Trimble's death were recalled in the *Irish Independent*, 22 August 1979. See also Christine Casey's *Dublin: The City Within the Grand and Royal Canals and the Circular Road, with Phoenix Park* (Yale: University Press, 2006).

[60] See Somerville-Large, *Irish Voices*; and Cruise O'Brien, *States*.

[61] For memories of 1916, see Mary Daly and Margaret O'Callaghan (eds), *1916*

in 1966: Commemorating the Easter Rising (Dublin: 2007). A most poignant and affecting memoir of the men of 1916 was published in 1971, with Piaras F. Mac Lochlainn's *Last Words: Letters and Statements of the Leaders Executed after the Rising at Easter 1916* (Dublin: Stationery Office: 1971).

[62] Stanley Baldwin once opened a letter from de Valera, saw it was about Roger Casement, and immediately closed it again (NAI, 2006/39/8, Doc. 10, 21 February 1936). Requests from Dublin had continued over the years: time and persistence eventually delivered the remains.

[63] The *Irish Independent* reported the incident in its 'Irish News' section, 5 July 1966. *The Sunday Times* in London was at this point beginning to campaign for civil rights in Northern Ireland, with such editorials as 'John Bull's Political Slum'.

[64] *Irish Times*, 7 July 1966.

[65] See Peter Taylor's *Brits: The War Against the IRA* (London: 2001). Taylor, regarded by many as the most authoritative reporter on the Bloody Sunday episode, concluded after much research that 'it was a dreadful mistake and should never have happened': but ultimately that it was not part of a political plan to shoot down Irish nationalists.

[66] With thanks to Noel Dorr for this insight – and for several others.

[67] *Irish Independent*, 6 August 1977.

[68] The *Irish Times* reporting John Hume's comments, 9 Aug 1977.

[69] Cited in Bradford, *Elizabeth II*.

[70] *Irish Independent* editorial, 9 August 1977.

[71] *Irish Times*, 9 August 1977.

[72] The Official IRA had by this point withdrawn from armed struggle. As most people know, the Irish Republican Army and its political body, Sinn Féin, split into 'Official' and 'Provisional' wings in a stormy party conference in January 1970. The 'Official' wing was Marxist and the 'Provisional' wing more nationalist. The nationalist wing prevailed. Tribal nationalism nearly always prevails, in the final analysis, over theories of international brotherhood and socialist notions about the distribution of wealth, since it does seem that Darwin's theories are more relevant to human nature than those of Marx. For a short but clear and comprehensive account of the evolution and changes within the IRA, see Hickey & Doherty, *New Dictionary of Irish History*.

[73] Benn, *Diaries: 1940–1990*.

[74] The comments and reports in the following text have been taken from both the Irish and English press immediately after the assassination, from 28 August to 4 September 1979. See especially: the *Irish Press*; *The Irish Times*; the *Irish Independent*; and the London *Times*.

[75] *Irish Press*, 28 August 1979

[76] *Irish Independent*, September 1979.

[77] *Irish Press*, 6 September 1979.

[78] *Irish Press*, 4 September 1979.

[79] *Irish Press*, 4 September 1979.

[80] For Paul Maxwell's reaction to Thomas McMahon;s release, see *Sligo Weekender*, 24 August 2004.

[81] The Pope did turn down the opportunity to go to Northern Ireland, possibly because of the Mountbatten death. Máire Mac an tSaoi said it was deplorable that he would not visit Armagh, which had such close associations with St Patrick (*Irish Independent*, 16 August 1979).

[82] For a report on the Phoenix Park Mass, see *Irish Independent*, 30 September 1979. See also Mary Kenny, *3 Days in September: When the Pope Came to Ireland* (Dublin: Liberties Press, 2004).

[83] See Penelope Mortimer's *Queen Elizabeth: A Life of the Queen Mother* (London: 1986).

[84] Sarah Bradford, *Diana* (London: 2006).

[85] Roy Foster analyses the extent to which Irish diplomacy contributed to peace and reconciliation in *Luck and the Irish* (London: 2007).

[86] Michael O'Sullivan, *Mary Robinson: Portrait of an Irish Liberal* (Dublin: 1992).

[87] Senator John Robb in *The Irish Times*, 22 May 1993. Mrs Jennifer Lyons in *The Irish Times*, May 1993. *The Irish Times* also wrote of 'satisfaction' at President's historic visit, 28 May 1993. For a full account of the visit see O'Sullivan, *Mary Robinson*; and Olivia O'Leary and Helen Burke, *Mary Robinson: The Authorised Biography* (London: 1998).

[88] *The Irish Times*, 22 May 1993

[89] Ibid.

[90] Miriam Lord was writing in the *Irish Independent* on 1 June 1995. For a full report on Charles' visit, see the *Irish Independent* on 29 & 31 May 1995.

[91] For the Dublin mammies greeting the Prince, see *The Irish Times*, 2 June 1995. Ironically, the *Irish Press*, the most anti-monarchist of the Dublin newspapers, was just closing down in June 1995 as the Prince of Wales was visiting. John Bruton, then Taoiseach, was reported as saying it was 'the proudest moment of my life' (when meeting Charles). On this trip, Charles also visited Newgrange, Ireland's Stonehenge. Subsequently, the Prince of Wales with the Duchess of Cornwall have paid private visits to Ireland, notably to Lismore in Co Waterford, where they have stayed with the Devonshire family – and have been made welcome by everyone in the locality, I am told.

[92] *Irish Times*, 5 May 1995.

[93] The Prince of Wales was welcomed to Glencree on 26 February 2002 by Professor Colum Kenny, whom I am very pleased to say is my cousin.

[94] www.glencree.ie.

[95] *The Irish Times*, 4–7 June 1996.

[96] *The Irish Times*. When Princess Anne was married on 14 November 1973, Maeve Binchy filed a very amusing report in *The Irish Times*. It was also irreverent, and Maeve received one of the biggest postbags – of protest – she has had during her journalistic career. 'Most were from ordinary Irish people – and particularly women and mothers,' she says. 'The correspondents were not scions of the old Anglo-Irish ascendancy. Readers felt I had been too mocking of a Christian ceremony and my attitude had lacked respect. Several suggested I should be named "Maeve Bitchy".' Maeve didn't intend to be mean-spirited – it is not in her nature – but she thought a little raillery in an entertaining report was part of journalistic tradition. But it showed her that there was still, at that time, also a feeling of respect for the British royals, and 'memories of affection

for "the Little Princesses" who had stayed in London during the Blitz.' Conversation with MB.

[97] President McAleese spoke to me about her hope that Queen Elizabeth might visit Ireland, in answer to a question that I put to her on 23 November 2007, when she was speaking at the Longford Trust, London.

[98] The ambassadors in conversation with author.

[99] Stewart Eldon, writing in *The Irish Times* on 9 August 2006.

[100] John Waters writing in *The Irish Times* on 23 June 2007.

[101] For a report on the address, see *The Irish Times* and the *Irish Independent*, 16 May 2007.

[102] David Cooney in conversation with the author.

Epilogue

[1] Irish state papers released in 2009 indicated that President Hillery did consider a State visit to Britain in 1979 – which would have opened the door to a return visit from Queen Elizabeth – but was dissuaded from pursuing this initiative, being told that Queen Elizabeth 'didn't like the Irish'. As Elizabeth is a cautious and constitutional monarch who has never expressed feelings about any national group, it seems to me this is more likely to have been an official's excuse – in the midst of the Troubles in Northern Ireland – rather than a royal opinion. Although, coming after the death of Mountbatten, and the highly uncomfortable experiences in Belfast in 1977, such a royal opinion cannot be ruled out. But President McAleese has certainly claimed that by the end of the century, the monarch was more than willing.

[2] Murphy, *Abject Loyalty*.

[3] A. T. Q. Stewart.

BIBLIOGRAPHY

Aberdeen, Marquis & Marchioness of, *More Cracks With 'We Twa'* (London: Methuen, 1929).

Andrews, C. S., *Man of No Property* (Cork: 1982).

Arnold, Bruce, *Haughey: His Life and Unlucky Deeds* (London: 1993).

Aronson, Theo, *Princess Margaret* (London: 1997).

Ashley, Mike, *A Brief History of British Kings and Queens* (London: 1998).

Bamford, Francis, & Bankes, Viola, *Vicious Circle: The Case of the Missing Irish Crown Jewels* (London: 1965).

Bardon, Jonathan, *A History of Ulster* (Belfast: 1992).

Barker, Brian, *When the Queen was Crowned* (London: 1976).

Barry, Sebastian, *The Steward of Christendom* (London: 1995).

Bastable, Jonathan (ed), *Yesterday's Britain* (London: Reader's Digest, 1998).

Bence-Jones, Mark, *Twilight of the Ascendancy* (London: 1987).

Benn, A., *The Benn Diaries: 1940–1990* (London: Arrow Books, 1998).

Bennett, Richard, *The Black and Tans* (London: 1976).

Bentley, Michael, *Politics Without Democracy* (London: 1984).

Bew, Paul, *Ireland: The Politics of Enmity, 1789–2006* (Oxford: 2007).

Bew, Paul, & Patterson, Henry, *Seán Lemass and the Making of Modern Ireland* (London: 1982).

Biggs-Davison, John, *George Wyndham: A Study in Toryism* (London: 1951).

Biggs-Davison, John, & Chowdharay-Best, George, *The Cross of St Patrick: The Catholic Unionist Tradition in Ireland* (Bourne End, Bucks: Kensal Press, 1984).

Blake, Robert, *Disraeli* (London: 1967).

Bogdanor, Vernon, *Devolution in the United Kingdom* (Oxford: 1999).

Bourke, Richard, *Peace in Ireland* (London: 2003).

Bowen, Desmond, *Paul, Cardinal Cullen, and the Shaping of Modern Irish Catholicism* (Dublin: 1983).

Bowman, John, *De Valera & the Ulster Question, 1917–1973* (Oxford: 1982).

Boyce, George, D., *Nineteenth Century Ireland: The Search for Stability* (Dublin: 2005).

Boylan, Henry (ed), *A Dictionary of Irish Biography* (Dublin: 1998).

Bradford, Sarah, *King George VI* (London: 1989).

Bradford, Sarah, *Elizabeth II* (London: 1996).

Bradford, Sarah, *Diana* (London: 2006).

Brandreth, Gyles, *Philip & Elizabeth: Portrait of a Marriage* (London: 2004).

Brendon, Piers, & Whitehead, Phillip, *The Windsors: A Dynasty Revealed, 1917–2000* (London: 2000).

Browne, Noel, *Against the Tide* (Dublin: 1986).

Burke, Helen & O'Leary, Olivia, *Mary Robinson: The Authorised Biography* (London: 1998).

Burleigh, Michael, *Blood and Rage: A Cultural History of Terrorism* (London: 2008).

Cafferky, John, & Hannafin, Kevin, *Scandal & Betrayal: Shackleton & the Irish Crown Jewels* (Cork: The Collins Press, 2002).

Canning, B. J., *Bishops of Ireland* (Donegal: 1987).

Carbery, Mary, *Lady Carbery's West Cork Journal*, ed Jeremy Sandford (Dublin, 1998).

Cartland, Barbara, *We Danced All Night* (London: 1998).

Casey, Christine, *Dublin: The City Within the Grand and Royal Canals and the Circular Road, with Phoenix Park* (Yale: University Press, 2006).

Castletown, Lord, *Ego* (London: 1923).

Catholic Encyclopaedia, The (NY: 1967).

Cecil, Algernon, *Queen Victoria and her Prime Ministers* (London: 1953).

Cecil, David, *Lord Melbourne* (London: 1954).

Chambers, Anne, *At Arm's Length: Aristocrats in the Republic of Ireland* (Dublin: 2004).

Churchill, Sir Winston, *The War Speeches of Winston Churchill* (London: 1952).

Clarke, Kathleen, *Revolutionary Woman: An Autobiography, 1878–1972* (Dublin: 1991).

Coogan, Tim Pat, *De Valera: Long Fellow, Long Shadow* (London: 1995).

Coogan, Tim Pat, *Ireland in the 20th Century*, 2nd edn (London: Arrow Books, 2004).

Cooney, John, *John Charles McQuaid: Ruler of Catholic Ireland* (Dublin: 1999).

Corry, Finbarr, *The Automobile Treasury of Ireland* (London: 1979).

Costello, Francis, J., *Enduring the Most* (Cork: 1995).

Crowe, C., Fanning, R., Kennedy, M., & Keogh, D. (eds), *Documents on Irish Foreign Policy, Volume IV: 1932–1936* (Dublin: Royal Irish Academy, 2004).

Crowe, C., et al (eds), *Documents on Irish Foreign Policy, Volume V: 1937–1939* (Dublin: Royal Irish Academy, 2006).

Crowe, C., et al (eds), *Documents on Irish Foreign Policy, Volume VI: 1939–1941* (Dublin: Royal Irish Academy, 2008).

Cruise O'Brien, Conor, *States of Ireland* (London: 1972).

Daly, Mary, E., & O'Callaghan, Margaret (eds), *1916 in 1966: Commemorating the Easter Rising* (Dublin: 2007).

D'Arcy McGee, T., *Art MacMurrogh* (Dublin: 1847).

De Vere White, Terence, *Kevin O'Higgins* (Dublin: 1997).

Doherty, J. E. & Hickey, D.J., *A Chronology of Irish History since 1500* (Dublin: 1989).

Doherty, J. E. & Hickey, D.J., *A New Dictionary of Irish History from 1800* (Dublin: 2005).

Dudley Edwards, Ruth, *Patrick Pearse: The Triumph of Failure*, 2nd edn (Dublin: Irish Academic Press, 2006).

English, Richard, *Irish Freedom: The History of Nationalism in Ireland* (London: 2006).

Fanning, Ronan, *Independent Ireland* (Dublin: 1983).

Fanning, Ronan, 'The Response of the London & Belfast Governments to the Declaration of the Republic of Ireland, 1948–49', in *International Affairs*, vol 58, no. 1, 1981–2.

Fennell, Thomas, *The Royal Irish Constabulary* (Dublin: 2003)

Ferriter, Diarmaid, *The Transformation of Ireland, 1900–2000* (London: 2005).

Ferriter, Diarmaid, *Judging Dev* (Dublin: 2007).

Fitzgerald, Garret, *Ireland in the World: Further Reflections* (Dublin: 2005).

Fitzpatrick, David, *The Two Irelands, 1912–1939* (Oxford: 1998).

Foster, R. F., *Lord Randolph Churchill: A Political Life* (Oxford: 1981).

Foster, R. F., *Modern Ireland: 1600–1972* (London: Penguin, 1990).

Foster, R. F., *The Apprentice Mage: 1865–1914*, vol 1 of *W. B. Yeats: A Life*, 2 vols (Oxford: OUP, 1998).

Foster, R. F., *The Arch-Poet: 1915–1939*, vol 2 of *W. B. Yeats: A Life*, 2 vols (Oxford: OUP, 2003).

Foster, R. F., *Luck and the Irish* (London: 2007).

Fraser, Antonia (ed), *The House of Hanover and Saxe-Coburg-Gotha* (London: 2000).

Fulford, Roger, *Queen Victoria* (London: Collins, 1951).

Garvin, Tom, *1922: The Birth of Irish Democracy* (Dublin: 1996).

Gaughan, J., Anthony, *Listowel and its Vicinity* (Dublin: 2004).

Girvin, Brian, *The Emergency: Neutral Ireland, 1939–45* (London: 2006).

Girvin, Brian & Murphy, Gary, *The Lemass Era: Politics and Society in the Ireland of Seán Lemass* (Dublin: 2005).

Gonne MacBride, Maud, *A Servant of the Queen* (Dublin: 1938).

Gore, John, *King George V: A Personal Memoir* (London: 1941).

Gorham, Maurice, *Forty Years of Irish Broadcasting* (Dublin: 1967).

Gray, Peter (ed), *Victoria's Ireland? Irishness and Britishness, 1837–1901* (Dublin: Four Courts Press, 2004).

Gray, Tony, *Ireland This Century* (London: 1994).

Griffith, Arthur, *The Resurrection of Hungary* (Dublin: 1904).

Gwynn, Denis, *The Irish Free State, 1922–1927* (London: 1928).

Gwynn, Denis, *The Life of John Redmond* (London: 1932).

Hardie, Frank, *The Political Influence of the British Monarchy, 1868–1952* (London: 1970).

Hardman, Robert, *Monarchy: The Royal Family at Work* (London: 2007).

Harkness, D.W., *The Restless Dominion: The Irish Free State and the British Commonwealth of Nations, 1921–31* (London: 1969).

Harrison, B. & Mathew, H. C. G. (eds), *Oxford Dictionary of National Biography* (Oxford: OUP, 2004).

Headlam, Maurice, *Irish Reminiscences* (London: 1947).

Heald, Tim, *Princess Margaret: A Life Unravelled* (London: 2007).

Heffer, Simon, *Power and Place: the Political Consequences of King Edward VII* (London: 1998).

Hibbert, Christopher, *Edward VII: A Portrait* (London: 1976).

Hood, Susan, *Royal Roots, Republican Heritage: The Survival of the Office of Arms* (Dublin: 2002).

Horgan, J. J., *From Parnell to Pearse: Some Recollections and Reflections* (Dublin: Browne & Nolan, 1948).

Hough, Richard, A., *Edward and Alexandra: Their Private and Public Lives* (New York: St Martin's Press, 1993).

Jackson, Alvin, *Home Rule: An Irish History, 1800–2000* (London: 2003).

James, Robert Rhodes, *Winston Churchill: A Study in Failure, 1900–1939* (London: 1970).

Jenkins, Roy, *Asquith* (London: 1964).

Jones, T. J., *Whitehall Diary*, 3 vols, ed Keith Middlemas (Oxford: OUP, 1969).

Jordan, Anthony, J., *John A. Costello: Compromise Taoiseach, 1891–1976* (Dublin: Westport Books, 2007).

Joyce, James, *Ulysses* (Oxford: OUP, 1993).

Jullian, Philippe, *Edward and the Edwardians* (London: 1967).

Keane, Maureen, *Ishbel: Lady Aberdeen in Ireland* (Dublin: 1999).

Kee, Robert, *The Green Flag: A History of Irish Nationalism* (London: 2000).

Kehoe, Elisabeth, *Ireland's Misfortune: The Turbulent Life of Kitty O'Shea* (Dublin: Atlantic Books, 2008).

Kelly, J. N. D., *The Oxford Dictionary of Popes*, 6th edn (Oxford: OUP, 2006).

Kenny, Colum, *Moments that Changed Us* (Dublin: 2006).

Kenny, Kevin (ed), *Ireland and the British Empire* (Oxford: 2004).

Kenny, Mary, *Goodbye to Catholic Ireland* (London: Sinclair Stevenson, 1997).

Kenny, Mary, *Germany Calling* (Dublin: 2004).

Kenny, Mary, *3 Days in September: When the Pope Came to Ireland* (Dublin: Liberties Press, 2004).

Keogh, Dermot, & McCarthy, Andrew, *The Making of the Irish Constitution, 1937* (Cork: 2007).

Kiberd, Declan, *Anglo-Irish Attitudes* (Derry: 1984).

Kiberd, Declan, *Inventing Ireland: The Literature of Modern Ireland* (London: 1996).

Kinealy, Christine, *This Great Calamity: The Irish Famine, 1845–52* (Boulder, Colorado: Roberts Rinehart Publishing, 1995).

Kinealy, Christine, *A New History of Ireland* (Stroud: Sutton Publishing, 2008).

Lalor, Brian (ed), *The Encyclopaedia of Ireland* (Dublin: Gill & Macmillan, 2003).

Leathard, Audrey, *The Fight for Family Planning* (London: Palgrave Macmillan, 1980).

Lee, J. J., *The Modernisation of Irish Society* (Dublin: 1973).

Lee, J.J., *Ireland 1912–1985: Politics and Society* (Cambridge: 1989).

Lee, Sir Sydney, *Edward VII: A Biography*, 2 vols, 1st edn 1926 (Kila, Montana: 2nd edn Kessinger Publishing, 2004).

Lee, Sir Sydney, *Queen Victoria: A Biography*, 1st edn 1902 (Kila, Montana: 2nd edn Kessinger Publishing, 2006).

Leslie, Shane, *The Irish Tangle for English Readers* (London: 1946).

Lewis, Geoffrey, *Carson: The Man Who Divided Ireland* (London & New York: 2005).

Lloyd, Alan, *King John* (London: 1973).

Lloyd, T.O., *Empire to Welfare State: English History, 1906–1967* (Oxford: 1970).

Longford, Elizabeth, *Queen Victoria* (London: 1964).

Longford, Frank, *Peace by Ordeal* (London: 1935).

Longford, Frank, & O'Neill, Thomas, P., *Éamon de Valera* (London: 1970).

Loughlin, James, *British Monarchy and Ireland: 1800 to the Present*, (Cambridge: 2007).

Lynch-Robinson, C., *The Last of the Irish RMs* (London: Cassell, 1951).

Lyons, F. S. L., *The Irish Parliamentary Party* (London: 1951).

Lyons, F. S. L., *Ireland Since the Famine* (Dublin: 1971).

Lysaght, Charles (ed), *The Times, Great Irish Lives: An Era in Obituaries* (London: HarperCollins, 2008).

MacAmhlaigh, Dónall, *An Irish Navvy: The Diary of an Exile*, trs Valentin Iremonger, 2nd edn (Cork: Collins Press, 2003).

MacDonagh, Oliver, *The Hereditary Bondsman: Daniel O'Connell, 1775–1829* (London: 1988).

MacIntosh, Sir Alexander, *Echoes of Big Ben: A Journalist's Parliamentary Diary, 1881–1940,* 2nd edn (London: Hutchinson, 1946).

Mackey, R., *Windward of the Law*, rev 2nd edn (Dublin: Round Hall Press, 1991).

Mackenzie, F. A., *King George in His Own Words* (London: Ernest Benn, 1929).

Mac Lochlainn, Piaras, F., *Last Words: Letters and Statements of the Leaders Executed after the Rising at Easter 1916* (Dublin: Stationery Office, 1971).

McCabe, Ian, *A Diplomatic History of Ireland, 1948–49* (Dublin: 1991).

McCoole, Sinéad, *Hazel: A Life of Lady Lavery* (Dublin: 1996).

McCormack, W. J., *Blood Kindred: The Politics of Yeats and his Death* (London: Pimlico Books, 2005).

McDowell, R. B., *Land and Learning: Two Irish Clubs* (Dublin: 1993).

McDowell, R. B., *Historical Essays 1938–2001* (London: 2003).

McKinstry, Leo, *Rosebery: Statesman in Turmoil* (London: 2005).

McMahon, Deirdre, *Republicans and Imperialists: Anglo-Irish Relations in the 1930s* (Yale & London: 1984).

Magnus, Philip, *Gladstone: a Biography* (London: 1954).

Magnus, Philip, *King Edward the Seventh* (London: 1964).

Manning, Maurice, *James Dillon* (Dublin: 1999).

Manning, Maurice, *The Blueshirts* (Dublin: 2005).

Mathew, H. C. G. & Harrison, B. (eds), *Oxford Dictionary of National Biography* (Oxford: OUP, 2004).

Maume, Patrick, *The Long Gestation: Irish Nationalist Life, 1891–1918* (Dublin: 1999).

Maye, Brian, *Arthur Griffith* (Dublin: 1997).

Middlemas, Keith, *The Life and Times of Edward VII* (London: 1972).

Mitchel, John, *The Last Conquest of Ireland (Perhaps)* (Dublin: 2005).

Monahan, Maud, *Life and Letters of Janet Erskine Stuart, Superior-General of the Sacred Heart, 1857 to 1914* (London: 1923).

Mortimer, Penelope, *Queen Elizabeth: A Life of the Queen Mother* (London: 1986).

Munz, Sigmund, *King Edward VII at Marienbad* (London: 1934).

Murphy, James H., *Abject Loyalty: Nationalism and Monarchy in Ireland during the Reign of Queen Victoria* (Cork: 2001).

Murphy, John A., *Ireland in the 20th Century* (Dublin: 1975).

Murray, Patrick, *Oracles of God: The Roman Catholic Church and Irish Politics, 1922–37* (Dublin: UCD Press, 2000).

Nicolson, Harold, *King George V: His Life and Reign* (London: 1952).

Norman, Diana, *Terrible Beauty: A Life of Constance Markievicz* (London: 1987).

Ó Broin, Léon, *The Chief Secretary: Augustine Birrell in Ireland* (London: Archon Books, 1969).

O'Connell, Maurice R. (ed), *Daniel O'Connell: The Man and His Politics* (Dublin: 1990).

O'Connor, T. P., *Memoirs of an Old Parliamentarian* (London: 1929).

O'Halpin, Eunan, *The Decline of the Union: British Government in Ireland, 1892–1920* (Dublin: 1987).

O'Halpin, Eunan, *Spying on Ireland* (Oxford: 2008).

O'Rourke, John (Canon), *The Centenary Life of O'Connell* (Dublin: 1875).

O'Sullivan, Michael, *Mary Robinson: Portrait of an Irish Liberal* (Dublin: 1992).

Paseta, Senia, 'Nationalist responses to two royal visits to Ireland, 1900 & 1903', *Irish Historical Studies*, vol 31, no 24 (November 1999).

Paxman, Jeremy, *On Royalty* (London: 2006).

Perrin, Robert, *Jewels* (Lanham, MD: Rowman & Littlefield, 1979).

Pimlott, Ben, *The Queen: A Biography of Elizabeth the Second* (Glasgow: HarperCollins, 1997).

Plunkett, James, *Strumpet City* (London: 1969).

Ponsonby, Sir Frederick, *Recollections of Three Reigns* (London: 1951).

Pope-Hennessy, James, *Queen Mary: 1867–1953*, 1st edn (London: Allen & Unwin, 1959).

Potts, D. M., & Potts, W. T. W., *Queen Victoria's Gene: Haemophilia and the Royal Family* (London: The History Press Ltd., 1999).

Powell, Jonathan, *Great Hatred, Little Room: Making Peace in Northern Ireland* (London: 2008).

Ring, Jim, *Erskine Childers* (London: 1996).

Roberts, Andrew, *Eminent Churchillians* (London: 1995).

Roberts, Andrew, *Salisbury: Victorian Titan* (London: 1999).

Robertson, Nora, *Crowned Harp: Memories of the Last Years of the Crown in Ireland* (Dublin: Allen Figgis, 1960).

Robins, Joseph, *Champagne and Silver Buckles: The Viceregal Court at Dublin Castle, 1700–1922*.

Robinson, Sir Henry, *Memories: Wise and Otherwise* (London: 1923).

Rose, Kenneth, *King George V* (London: 1983).

Rosenbaum, S. (ed), *Against Home Rule* (London: 1912).

Rowley, George, *A Memoir: Original Writing* (Dublin: 2007).

Sencourt, Robert, *The Reign of Edward VIII* (London: 1962).

Sewell, Dennis, *Catholics* (London: 2001).

Sexton, Brendan, *Ireland and the Crown, 1922–1936: The Governor-Generalship of the Irish Free State* (Dublin: 1989).

Sinclair, Andrew, *Death by Fame: A Life of Elisabeth, Empress of Austria* (London: Constable, 1998)

Smith, Nadia Clare, *Dorothy Macardle: A Life* (Dublin: 2007).

Somerville-Large, Peter, *Irish Voices: an Informal History, 1916–1966* (London: 1999).

Stansky, Peter, *Gladstone: A Progress in Politics* (Boston: 1979).

St Aubyn, Giles, *Queen Victoria: A Portrait* (London: 1991).

Stewart, A. T. Q., *The Ulster Crisis* (London: 1967).

Swift, Roger & Kinealy, Christine, *Politics and Power in Victorian Ireland* (Dublin: Four Courts, 2006).

Taylor, Peter, *Brits: The War Against the IRA* (London: 2001).

Thomas, J. H., *My Story* (London: 1937).

Tuchman, Barbara, *The Proud Tower: A Portrait of the World before the War, 1890–1914* (London: 1995).

Vansittart, Peter, *In The Fifties* (London: 1995).

Vickers, Hugo, *Elizabeth, The Queen Mother* (London: 2005).

Villiers-Tuthill, Kathleen, *The Connemara Railway* (Dublin: Connemara Girl Publications, 2003).

Walsh, Walter, *The Religious Life and Influence of Queen Victoria* (London: 1902).

Ward, Margaret, *Maud Gonne: A Life* (London: 1990).

Weintraub, Stanley, *Victoria: Biography of a Queen* (London: 1987).

Weintraub, Stanley, *Uncrowned King: The Life of Prince Albert* (New York: Free Press, 1997).

Weight, Richard, *Patriots* (London: 2002).

Wells, Warre B., *John Redmond: A Biography* (London: 1919).

Wheeler, Michael, *The Old Enemies: Catholic and Protestant in Nineteenth-Century English Culture* (Cambridge: CUP, 2006).

Wills, Clair, *That Neutral Island* (London: 2007).

Wilson, A. N., *The Victorians* (London: 2002).

Wilson, A. N., *After the Victorians: The World our Parents Knew* (London: 2006).

Windsor, Edward, Duke of, *A King's Story* (London: 1951).

Woodham-Smith, Cecil, *The Great Hunger: Ireland 1845–9* (London: 1962).

Ziegler, Philip, *Melbourne* (London: 1976)

Ziegler, Philip, *Mountbatten* (London: 1985).

Index

INDEX

INDEX

INDEX

Index